The Community Mental Health Center

THE COMMUNITY MENTAL HEALTH CENTER

STRATEGIES AND PROGRAMS

EDITED BY

ALLAN BEIGEL

AND

ALAN I. LEVENSON

BASIC BOOKS, INC., PUBLISHERS

NEW YORK   LONDON

Library of Congress Catalog Card Number: 72–76918
SBN 465–01316–3
Manufactured in the United States of America
DESIGNED BY THE INKWELL STUDIO

THE AUTHORS

SISTER MARY AMELIA is Director of the Mid-Houston Community Mental Health Center associated with the St. Joseph's Hospital of Houston, Texas. As director of one of the first community mental health centers, she has testified on several occasions before Congress on matters relating to community mental health.

T. M. ATKINSON, JR. is a member of the staff of the Mountain Mental Health Services in Prestonsberg, Kentucky.

HAROUTUN M. BABIGIAN is Associate Professor of Psychiatry at the University of Rochester School of Medicine and Dentistry, and Director of the Division of Preventive and Social Psychiatry.

CHARLES F. BALTIMORE is Associate Director of the Western Psychiatric Institute Community Mental Health and Mental Retardation Center, and Assistant Professor of Psychiatry in the Department of Psychiatry at the University of Pittsburgh School of Medicine.

ROBERT H. BARNES is Professor of Psychiatry at the University of Texas Medical School in San Antonio and, formerly, Director of the Greater Kansas City Mental Health Foundation.

ALLAN BEIGEL is Assistant Professor of Psychiatry at the University of Arizona College of Medicine, Director of the Southern Arizona Mental Health Center, and Coordinator of the Combined Mental Health Care Program of Pima County, Tucson, Arizona. He currently serves as a member of the Mental Health Services Committee of the Group for the Advancement of Psychiatry, and as a Special Consultant to the National Institute of Mental Health Regional Office in Dallas, Texas, and the National Institute of Alcoholism and Alcohol Abuse. He was formerly associated with the National Institute of Mental Health as a Staff Psychiatrist in the Division of Mental Health Service Programs which is responsible for the administration of the National Community Mental Health Center Program.

CLIFFORD J. BODARKY is Professor and Executive Professor of the Department of Mental Health Sciences at the Hahnemann Medical College and Hospital.

VERNON C. BOHR is in the private practice of psychiatry in Glendora, California, and, formerly, associated with the Ingleside Community Mental Health Center in Rosemead, California.

WILLIAM M. BOLMAN is Professor of Psychiatry in the Department of Psychiatry of the University of Hawaii Medical School in Honolulu, and is now Director of the Psychiatric Services of the Leho Hospital in Honolulu. Formerly, he was Director of the Westside Community Mental Health Center in San Francisco, California.

ROBERT E. BUXBAUM is in private practice as a social worker in San Antonio, Texas. He was formerly coordinator-supervisor of the Mental Health Assistants Training Program at the Northwest San Antonio Community Mental Health Center.

RAFAEL CANTON is Director of the Ventura County Mental Health Department, and is associated with the Ventura Community Mental Health Center in Ventura, California.

DENNIS P. CANTWELL is currently in training at the Maudsley Hospital Institute of Psychiatry in London, England. He was formerly a Resident Fellow, in child psychiatry, at the Department of Psychiatry of the University of California Medical School at Los Angeles.

JOHN CARVER is currently Chairman of the Board of Directors of the National Council of Community Mental Health Centers, and Executive Director of the American Foundation for Human Development in Mental Health. He was formerly Director of the Multi-County Community Mental Health Center in Tullahoma, Tennessee, and is now in the private practice of psychology in Nashville, Tennessee.

STEPHEN C. CAULFIELD is currently Assistant Dean in charge of Allied Health Manpower at the Albert Einstein College of Medicine in New York City. He was formerly with the Soundview-Throgs Neck Community Mental Health Center in the Bronx.

SAM D. CLEMENTS is Associate Professor of Psychiatry at the University of Arkansas School of Medicine, and Executive Director of the Child Study Center at the Greater Little Rock Community Mental Health Center.

DONALD R. DAGGETT is Director of Professional Services of the Metropolitan Medical Center Community Mental Health Program. He is also Chief of Psychiatry at the Minneapolis Clinic of Psychiatry and Neurology, and a Clinical Associate Professor of Psychiatry at the University of Minnesota School of Medicine.

RAYMOND J. DEMBINSKI is Administrative Director of the Developmental Disability Program in Indianapolis, Indiana. He is also associated with the Riley Hospital in Indianapolis.

IRMGARD S. DOBROW is in the private practice of psychiatry and child psychiatry, and was formerly Director of the Jefferson County Community Mental Health Center in Lakewood, Colorado.

ROY J. ELLISON, JR. is Director of the Community Mental Health Center at the Marshall I. Pickens Hospital in Greenville, South Carolina.

EDWIN E. FAIR is Psychiatrist-Director of the Bi-State Mental Health Foundation in Ponca City, Oklahoma.

MORTON L. FLAX is Director of School Services for the Arapahoe Community Mental Health Center in Englewood, Colorado.

THOMAS L. FOSTER is in the private practice of psychiatry in Ponca City, Oklahoma. He was formerly Director of the Inpatient Service at the Bi-State Community Mental Health Center, and is currently a consultant to that Center.

ALFRED M. FREEDMAN is Professor and Chairman of the Department of Psychiatry of the New York College of Medicine in New York City. With Harold I. Kaplan, he edited the *Comprehensive Textbook of Psychiatry*.

HENRY FREY is Director of the Adams County Mental Health Center in Commerce City, Colorado. He is a member of the Board of Directors of the National Council of Comprehensive Community Mental Health Centers.

THE AUTHORS

WILLIAM F. GANDY is Director of Pastoral Services at the Bi-State Mental Health Foundation in Ponca City, Oklahoma.

THOMAS T. GLASSCOCK is in the private practice of adult and child psychiatry in Englewood, Colorado, and was formerly Director of the Arapahoe Mental Health Center in that same community.

WILLIAM GOLDMAN is Director of the Westside Community Mental Health Center in San Francisco, California. He is also Vice-Chairman of the National Council of Community Mental Health Centers, and Assistant Chief of Psychiatry at Mt. Zion Hospital in San Francisco.

CHESTER W. GROCHOLA is Director of the Nassau County Medical Center and Meadowbrook Comprehensive Community Mental Health Center in East Meadow, Long Island, New York.

JOHN GUERRANT is Program Chief for the Marin County Community Mental Health Services Program, and Director of the Marin County Community Mental Health Center in San Rafael, California. He is an Associate Clinical Professor of Psychiatry at the University of California Medical Center in San Francisco, California.

VAN BUREN O. HAMMETT is Professor and Chairman of the Department of Mental Health Sciences at the Hahnemann Medical College and Hospital in Philadelphia, Pennsylvania.

HIAWATHA HARRIS is the Director of the Central City Community Mental Health Center in Los Angeles, California, and is Chairman of Mental Retardation Services of Los Angeles County. She is also Vice-Chairman of the Citizen Advisory Board of the State of California.

LOUISA HOWE is Assistant Professor of Sociology in the Department of Psychiatry at Harvard Medical School in Boston, Massachusetts.

MARY JONES has a Master's Degree in Nursing and is associated with the Clinical Program of the Metropolitan Medical Center Community Mental Health Center in Minneapolis, Minnesota.

MITCHELL JONES is in the private practice of child psychiatry, and is associated with the Kilgore Child Psychiatric Center and Hospital in Amarillo, Texas. He was formerly Director of the Prairie View Mental Health Center in Newton, Kansas.

SYDNEY KORET is Director of the Convalescent Hospital for Children in Rochester, New York, the only community mental health center specifically designed for children and their families in the nation. He is a Clinical Associate Professor at the University of Rochester Graduate School, Department of Psychology, and is associated with the University of Rochester School of Medicine and Dentistry, Department of Psychiatry. He is also President-Elect of the American Association of Children's Residential Centers.

ELMER R. KRAMER is Director of the Regional Mental Health Center in Boise, Idaho, and is associated with the Community Institute for Human Resources of the Ada County Mental Health Center.

GEORGE KREGER is actively involved in providing residential treatment services to recovering alcoholics. He was formerly House Manager of the Halfway House associated with the Alcoholism Program of the Bi-State Mental Health Foundation in Ponca City, Oklahoma.

BERNARD M. KUHR is Director of the Palo Verde Hospital in Tucson, Arizona.

He was formerly Director of the Good Samaritan Hospital Community Mental Health Center in Dayton, Ohio.

H. RICHARD LAMB is the Chief of Rehabilitation Services for the County of San Mateo in California. He is Senior Editor of the *Handbook of Community Mental Health Practice*, and also serves as a consultant to the San Mateo Police Department. He is a Clinical Instructor in the Department of Psychiatry at Stanford University School of Medicine in Palo Alto, California.

ROBERT L. LEOPOLD is Director of the West Philadelphia Community Mental Health Consortium in Philadelphia, Pennsylvania.

ALAN I. LEVENSON is Professor and Head of the Department of Psychiatry of the University of Arizona College of Medicine, and Medical Director of the Palo Verde Foundation for Mental Health in Tucson, Arizona. He is currently a member of the Mental Health Services Committee of the Group for the Advancement of Psychiatry, a Fellow of the American College of Psychiatrists, the American Psychiatric Association, and the American Public Health Association. He was formerly Director of the Division of Mental Health Service Programs at the National Institute of Mental Health from 1967–1969.

JEROME LEVY is Associate Professor in Psychiatry, and Director of Continuing Education in the Department of Psychiatry of the University of New Mexico School of Medicine in Albuquerque, New Mexico.

DANIEL LIEBERMAN is Professor and Associate Chairman of the Department of Psychiatry at the Jefferson Medical College in Philadelphia, Pennsylvania.

GEORGE A. LOPES is Executive Director of the Carroll County Mental Health Services in North Conway, New Hampshire. He was formerly Administrator of the North Central Mental Health-Mental Retardation Center in Minot, North Dakota.

ROLLEE LOWENSTEIN is a lawyer, and Chief of the Legislature Services Branch of the National Institute of Mental Health in Rockville, Maryland.

THURMAN MCGINNIS is the Community Relations Officer of the San Mateo Police Department in San Mateo, California.

GEORGE G. MEYER is Professor of Psychiatry in the Department of Psychiatry of the University of Texas Medical School at San Antonio, and Director of the Northwest San Antonio Mental Health Center. He also serves as a Board Member of the Economic Development Corporation for the Mexican-American community in San Antonio.

DONALD J. MORRISON is Director of the Northern Wyoming Mental Health Center in Sheridan, Wyoming.

DAVID J. MULLER is Assistant Director for Clinical Services at the Adams County Mental Health Center in Commerce City, Colorado.

BARCUS B. NUNLEY, JR. is a Social Worker, and Director of Partial Hospitalization Programs at the Travis County Mental Health-Mental Retardation Center in Austin, Texas. He was formerly associated with the Rio Grande Community Mental Health Center in Harlingen, Texas.

WILLIAM T. PAYNTER is Deputy Commissioner of Mental Health in the Indiana Department of Mental Health in Indianapolis, Indiana. He was formerly Medical Director of the Marion County General Hospital Community Mental Health Center in Indianapolis.

viii

THE AUTHORS

STEPHEN R. PERLS is Assistant Professor of Psychiatry at the University of New Mexico School of Medicine in Albuquerque, New Mexico, and Director of the New Careers Training Program.

JOHN E. PETERS is Professor and Head of the Division of Child and Adolescent Psychiatry at the University of Arkansas School of Medicine in Little Rock, Arkansas. He is also Director of the Child Study Center of the Greater Little Rock Community Mental Health Center.

LORAN E. PILLING is Clinical Program Director of the Metropolitan Medical Center Community Mental Health Center, and Clinical Assistant Professor of Psychiatry at the University of Minnesota School of Medicine.

RHETT F. POTTER is Director of the Weber County Mental Health Center in Ogden, Utah.

SHIRLEY R. REFF is in the Office of the Director of the Division of Mental Health Service Programs in the National Institute of Mental Health in Rockville, Maryland.

C. ALLEN ROEHL is Administrative Director of the Panhandle Mental Health Center in Scotts Bluff, Nebraska.

AARON SATLOFF is Clinical Assistant Professor of Psychiatry at the University of Rochester School of Medicine and Dentistry in Rochester, New York. He is also in the private practice of psychiatry in Pittsford, New York.

JAMES H. SATTERFIELD is Director of Research at the Gateways Hospital Community Mental Health Center in Los Angeles, California.

NORMAN SEGAL is a Staff Social Worker at the Minneapolis Clinic of Psychiatry and Neurology, and is associated with the Metropolitan Medical Center Community Mental Health Center in Minneapolis, Minnesota.

ROBERT A. SENESCU is on sabbatical, and is with the Psychiatry Training Branch of the National Institute of Mental Health in Rockville, Maryland. He is also Chairman of the Department of Psychiatry at the University of New Mexico School of Medicine in Albuquerque, New Mexico.

MARGARET SPEICHER is Chief Social Worker at the Northwest San Antonio Mental Health Center in San Antonio, Texas.

RICHARD STAI is Executive Director of the Mountain Mental Health Services in Prestonsberg, Kentucky.

MARGARET M. TAYLOR is Mental Health Nurse Coordinator of the Escambia County Community Mental Health Center in Pensacola, Florida.

STEVE WALTERS is Administrator of the Northwest Texas Hospital, a Community Mental Health Center affiliate, in Amarillo, Texas.

HENRY WEIHOFEN is Professor of Law at the University of New Mexico Law School at Albuquerque, New Mexico. He is also the author of *Legal Services and Community Mental Health Centers*.

DONALD WESTON is Assistant Dean of the Department of Psychiatry at the Michigan State University School of Medicine, and is a consultant to the Department of Human Medicine in that same institution. He is the former Director of the Community Mental Health Center in Lansing, Michigan.

REGINALD P. WHITE is the Director of the East Mississippi State Hospital in Meridian, Mississippi.

JACK F. WILDER is Acting Director and Acting Chairman of the Department of Psychiatry of the Bronx Municipal Hospital Center in New York City, a Division of the Albert Einstein College of Medicine. He is the former Director of the Soundview-Throgs Neck Community Mental Health Center in the Bronx.

DONALD P. WILSON is Director of Community Mental Health Services in Napa County, California, and was formerly Director of the Marin County Community Mental Health Center also in California.

JACK WOLFORD is the Director of the Western Psychiatric Institute Community Mental Health and Mental Retardation Center in Pittsburgh, Pennsylvania. He is also Secretary for the Group for the Advancement of Psychiatry, and Chairman of the Council on Internal Affairs of the American Psychiatric Association.

JACK ZUSMAN is Professor and Director of the Division of Community Psychiatry in the Department of Psychiatry at the State University of New York Medical School at Buffalo.

FOREWORD

For those of us in the National Institute of Mental Health and elsewhere who have been involved in the evolution of the comprehensive community mental health center program since its inception, this book is a challenge relived.

Reading it, I found myself reminiscing—about our efforts to translate the concept of community-based treatment of mental illness and emotional disturbance into federal legislation; about our discussions of necessary regulations under which federal support of the program could be administered, once the legislation had been adopted by Congress; about the conflicts resolved and the compromises renegotiated as the states and local communities worked to establish their eligibility for federal support; and about our determination that the quality of care for the patient or client would not be sacrificed to ease administrative and funding dilemmas.

Then came the days when the first applicants to receive federal grants opened those first community mental health centers and the concept began its development as an operational reality. Those were heady and exciting times for members of the NIMH staff involved in this program. A twenty-four-hour day was much too short, because there was so much to be done in this bold, new approach to the treatment and prevention of mental illness.

No one who has ranged across the United States and back defending the "catchment area" principle, explaining the rationale of the "five essential services," and participating in the "medical model" debate will ever forget those pioneering efforts to provide support for community-based delivery of mental health services. The initial and subsequent developments which have shaped the organization and operation of the community mental health centers program—since the passage of the Comprehensive Community Mental Health Centers Act in 1963—have all occurred in less than one decade. However, that decade has been crowded with social events affecting and relating to *all* human services throughout the United States. It is, therefore, of great importance that the editors and authors of this book have assembled information about the mechanisms through which the community mental health centers— in their infinite variety—have recognized their needs, faced their problems, and confronted the ideological, social, and political issues in terms of the practical techniques of administration, operation, treatment, consultation, and education.

This volume is focused on the practical strategies which are currently being used by many community mental health centers to implement the services they have the responsibility to provide. Further, it is an attempt to move away from theoretical concepts into a consideration of some of the practical problems and issues which confront the community mental health professional in his attempts to carry out the intent and mandates of the Community Mental Health Centers Act. Consequently, the material selected by the editors for inclusion in this volume concerns itself primarily with problems related to community mental health center planning, organization, and programming. Its content serves as a record of achievement; but perhaps even more importantly, it may serve as an impetus for future development of community mental health services within the far broader context of human services required and—increasingly—demanded by the population.

Thus far, community mental health centers have demonstrated their role in providing new mechanisms for giving service and a new way of thinking about the mentally ill. There continues to be criticism of medical professionals for their alleged over-emphasis on pathology. Some of this criticism is valid; but my personal and professional belief, as a physician, is that the primary responsibility of the community mental health center staff is to treat those men, women, and children who are sick. This belief in no way denegates the responsibility to improve the social quality of life for individuals within the mental health centers' jurisdiction. It has become evident during the 1960s, in communities where mental health centers are in operation, that various segments of the population request and expect mental health centers to provide an ever-widening range of services designed to improve the environment and mitigate the social pressures of modern society.

It will be essential throughout the 1970s to fuse these expectations within the operational programs of mental health centers. But it is also essential to differentiate these forces in providing comprehensive human service programs. Both the treatment and the social reform components of the community mental health centers program are designed to effect change. Certainly, the two major thrusts of such programs will overlap, but the overlapping areas of the program cannot be confused by an effort of community mental health centers to assume responsibility for the total reform of society.

Each community mental health center will define the style in which its staff attempts to satisfy its own and its community expectations, in preventing mental illness by seeking to solve the contributory social problems. All mental health professionals should remember that they were given not only the opportunity, but the responsibility to develop the means for the prevention of mental illness, as stated in the regulations under which the Centers Act is administered.

By requiring establishment of consultation and education as service components within each mental health center, the federal government, for the first time, made preventive services a mandatory part of federally-supported community mental health programs. For everyone concerned, therefore, now that the pioneering experience has provided a base for future development, the preventive aspects of the delivery of mental health services will be the area of adventure throughout the 1970s, of which social reform will be a free, exploratory component.

The future developments of these explorations will be effected by the fiscal and political events that have occurred simultaneously with the practical, operational evolution of techniques within community mental health centers. In the past few years, fiscal constraints, at all levels of government, have severely limited the funds necessary for the expansion of the community mental health centers program. In 1971, however, both the executive branch of the federal government and Congress indicated a desire to support the further development of community mental health centers.

This significant change in attitude, however, places the delivery of mental health care in a truly comprehensive setting. In response to the growing public demand for comprehensive health care as a human right, the total health community has become involved in a controversy over the best means of providing and financing a national health care program. In this search, the federal government, through the Department of Health, Education, and Welfare, is developing a plan to fund comprehensive health programs through support of what are termed Health Maintenance Organizations. By grouping all components of health care, it is hoped that the health professions will, in actuality, be able to provide preventive health services as well as treatment for illness.

Of necessity, Health Maintenance Organizations, in order to meet this goal, will be concerned with the provision of mental health services. The resolution of administrative and operational techniques to achieve this goal poses a current practical challenge for comprehensive community mental health centers. Certainly, planning for HMOs is based to an extent on the experience of the community-based mental health service program. Discussions on the funding of health services through third-party prepayment insurance plans is likewise based to an extent on the work done by mental health professionals in their efforts to expand the mental health benefits provided through existing insurance plans. At the present time, all of these discussions are being held on the threshhold of a new arena, which governments, health professionals, and insurance administrators must enter if a national health policy and a national health program are to be established.

For the mental health community—whose leaders initiated the practice of community-based care in its modern form—the concern lies in the manner in which their efforts can be joined with the overriding need for comprehensive human services, without becoming overwhelmed or submerged in the current evolution of physical medicine.

It seems to me that no matter how the political and administrative factors of this transition are evolved, the mental health movement has one unique responsibility: to serve as a humanizing force in making certain that any national health care system is designed to serve the needs of individuals rather than the needs of any system. We have deep responsibilities in this area to provide moral leadership and to participate with all groups in coping with social problems. On balance, the community mental health program has never lost sight of this fundamental responsibility. This volume, by setting forth the practical experiences of organization and development, should be of help to those involved in equating health with mental health, in its broadest sense, and in providing care for the transcendent health needs of the American people.

Bertram S. Brown, M.D.
Director
National Institute of Mental Health

PREFACE

With the passage of the Community Mental Health Centers Act in 1963 and the appropriation of federal funds for construction and staffing, the nation's mental health care givers were provided with a directive and a plan for the provision of comprehensive services, including evaluation, treatment, and rehabilitation, for the mentally ill. By June 1971, over 400 community mental health centers had received funds for construction, staffing, or both, and more than 200 were in operation.

Between the stage of conceptualization and legislation on the one hand and the effective delivery of mental health services on the other, there is need for a period of organization and planning. Ideological issues must be recognized and discussed; concepts must be clarified; and practical problems must be identified and solved.

The purpose of this book is the dissemination of information about the ways in which various community mental health centers have dealt with issues in their development. Areas to be covered include the assessment of the mental health needs of the catchment area; the variety of administrative structures which have been employed by community mental health centers; the concept of continuity of care and methods for its implementation; the planning of the essential services (inpatient, partial hospitalization, outpatient, emergency, consultation and education); the initiation of children's services; the patterns of meeting manpower needs; and the description of methods for funding the operation of the center.

Authors have been selected whose knowledge and experience about the community mental health center programs have been derived from direct contact with their planning and development. By clarifying concepts and describing their practical consequences and results, it is hoped that the reader, whatever his background or orientation, will derive a greater understanding of what a community mental health center is and can be.

The large number of community mental health centers and the variety of programs make it impossible for the authors to present a complete picture of all developments in community mental health centers during the past eight years. The selection of material for this book has been determined on the principle that a representative sampling of programs in different socioeconomic, geographical, and cultural settings will provide the readers with a basic fund of information about the community mental health center concept. Each chapter includes a bibliography which will further elucidate many of the issues which are presented in this book and present other aspects of community mental health center programs.

It is hoped that this text on community mental health centers will serve not only as a source of added information for those involved in existing community mental health center programs, but also as an impetus for other mental health professionals and nonprofessionals to develop community mental health center programs in the catchment areas which are not being served at the present time.

A. B.
A. L.

CONTENTS

I

The Community Mental Health Center: Origin and Concepts

ALLAN BEIGEL, M.D., AND ALAN I. LEVENSON, M.D.   3

II

Community Mental Health Center Planning

EDITORS' INTRODUCTION   19

1 The Catchment Area Concept   20
   JACK ZUSMAN, M.D.

2 The Role of Epidemiology and Mental Health Care
   Statistics in the Planning of Mental Health Centers   32
   HAROUTUN M. BABIGIAN, M.D.

3 Planning Community Mental Health Services in an
   Urban Ghetto   48
   HIAWATHA HARRIS, M.D.

4 Community Involvement in the Planning of a Rural
   Mental Health Center   54
   MITCHELL JONES, M.D.

5 The Community Mental Health Center Team   59
   RAFAEL CANTON, M.D.

III

Organization and Administration

EDITORS' INTRODUCTION   71

6 The San Francisco Westside Community Mental
   Health Center, Inc.: Development of a Mental Health
   Consortium of Private Agencies   72
   WILLIAM M. BOLMAN, M.D., AND
   WILLIAM GOLDMAN, M.D.

7 The Community Mental Health Center and the
General Hospital   89
    CHESTER W. GROCHOLA, M.A.

8 The Community Mental Health Center and
Academic Psychiatry   94
    CLIFFORD J. BODARKY, ED.D., AND VAN BUREN O.
    HAMMETT, M.D.

9 The Development of the Model Cities—Community
Health Center Health Care Delivery System   99
    WILLIAM T. PAYNTER, M.D., AND RAYMOND J.
    DEMBINSKI, ED.D.

10 An Experiment in Cooperative Puzzle-Solving: The
Philadelphia Forum of Mental Health/Mental
Retardation Centers   103
    ROBERT L. LEOPOLD, M.D.

IV

Providing Continuity of Care

EDITORS' INTRODUCTION   115
11 Affiliation Contracts—The Tie That Binds   116
    ROLLEE LOWENSTEIN, J.D.
12 Confidentiality   124
    HENRY WEIHOFEN, J.D.
13 A Community Mental Health Center and a State
Mental Hospital in Partnership   135
    DANIEL LIEBERMAN, M.D.
14 An Information System for a Comprehensive
Community Mental Health Center   142
    ROBERT H. BARNES, M.D.

V

Inpatient Services

EDITORS' INTRODUCTION   149
15 Organizing Inpatient/Partial Care Services   150
    DONALD P. WILSON, M.D., AND JOHN GUERRANT, M.D.
16 Community Mental Health Center and State Hospital

Collaboration through Busing of Twenty-Four Patients 155
HENRY FREY, M.D., AND DAVID J. MULLER, M.D.

17 Reducing the Need for a State Hospital Backup to a
Community Mental Health Center Inpatient Service 163
RHETT F. POTTER

18 A Community Mental Health Center Program to
Provide Emergency Inpatient Services in a
Rural Area 169
BARCUS B. NUNLEY, JR., M.S.S.W., A.C.S.W.

VI

Partial Hospitalization Services

EDITORS' INTRODUCTION 177

19 Partial Hospitalization and the General Hospital 179
BERNARD M. KUHR, M.D.

20 Partial Hospitalization Programs in Rural Mental
Health Centers 190
DONALD J. MORRISON, M.D.

21 Rehabilitation Workshops in a Partial Hospital
Program 194
JACK F. WILDER, M.D., AND STEPHEN C.
CAULFIELD, M.S.W.

22 A Community Mental Health Center Alcoholism
Program with a Focus on Partial Hospitalization 202
EDWIN E. FAIR, M.D., CHAPLAIN WILLIAM F. GANDY,
THOMAS L. FOSTER, M.D., AND GEORGE KREGER

VII

Delivery Systems for Outpatient Services

EDITORS' INTRODUCTION 209

23 Decentralized Outpatient Services in an Urban Setting 210
SISTER MARY AMELIA

24 Decentralized Outpatient Services in a Rural Setting 216
RICHARD STAI, M.S.W., AND T. M. ATKINSON,
JR., M.S.W.

VIII

New Approaches to Emergency Care

EDITORS' INTRODUCTION   223

25 Development of a Psychiatric Emergency Service
    under the Direction of a Nurse   224
    DONALD WESTON, M.D.

26 Development of an Emergency Listening Post
    Manned by Ministers   231
    REGINALD P. WHITE, M.D.

27 The Use of Volunteers in the Amarillo Crisis
    Intervention Center   234
    STEVE WALTERS

28 The Use of Boarding or Holding Beds in the
    Emergency Service   240
    AARON SATLOFF, M.D.

IX

Consultation and Education Services

EDITORS' INTRODUCTION   245

29 Programs for Consultation to Schools   247
    THOMAS T. GLASSCOCK, M.D., AND MORTON L.
    FLAX, ED.D.

30 Consultation to the Police   251
    H. RICHARD LAMB, M.D., AND THURMAN MCGINNIS

31 Behavior Modification in the Consultation-Education
    Element of Service   263
    JOHN CARVER, PH.D.

X

Specialized Services for Children

EDITORS' INTRODUCTION   273

32 A Community Mental Health Center for Children:
    Issues and Problems   274
    SYDNEY KORET, PH.D.

CONTENTS

33 A Children's Re-Ed Center as Part of a Community
    Mental Health Center   283
        ROY J. ELLISON, JR., M.D.

34 A School Program for Emotionally Disturbed
    Children   287
        IRMGARD S. DOBROW, M.D.

35 Development of an Evaluation and Treatment
    Outpatient Clinic for Hyperactive Children   290
        JAMES H. SATTERFIELD, M.D., AND DENNIS P.
        CANTWELL, M.D.

36 The Therapeutic Day School: A Service Strategy
    of Partial Hospitalization for Children with Learning
    and Behavioral Disabilities   299
        SAM D. CLEMENTS, PH.D., AND JOHN E. PETERS, M.D.

XI

Innovative Approaches to the Manpower Problem

EDITORS' INTRODUCTION   305

37 Private Psychiatrists as Staff Team Leaders   307
        DONALD R. DAGGETT, M.D., LORAN E. PILLING, M.D.,
        MARY JONES, R.N., M.S., AND NORMAN SEGAL, M.S.W.

38 The Volunteer vs. the Professional in a
    Resocialization Approach   316
        ELMER R. KRAMER

39 Development and Delivery of Mental Health Services
    to Seven Rural Counties in North Dakota   320
        GEORGE A. LOPES

40 The Use of Students as Employees in a Community
    Mental Health Center   332
        VERNON C. BOHR, M.D.

41 The Indigenous American Indian Mental Health
    Worker: Evolution of a Job and a Concept   337
        C. ALLEN ROEHL, PH.D.

XII

Providing for Staff Development

EDITORS' INTRODUCTION 347

42 A New Professionals' Career Program 349
STEPHEN R. PERLS, ED.D., JEROME LEVY, PH.D., AND
ROBERT A. SENESCU, M.D.

43 Training the Mental Health Assistant 356
GEORGE G. MEYER, M.D., MARGARET SPEICHER,
M.S.W., AND ROBERT E. BUXBAUM, S.T.M., M.S.W.

44 The Training of Nurses: The General Hospital and
the Community Mental Health Center 363
MARGARET M. TAYLOR, R.N.

XIII

Critical Issues for Community Mental Health Centers

EDITORS' INTRODUCTION 373

45 The Concept of Community 374
LOUISA HOWE, PH.D.

46 The Role of the Administrator 388
ALFRED M. FREEDMAN, M.D.

47 The Nondegree Community Mental Health Worker
and the Community 397
CHARLES F. BALTIMORE, M.D., AND JACK A.
WOLFORD, M.D.

48 Income Sources for Community Mental Health
Centers 407
SHIRLEY R. REFF, PH.D.

INDEX 417

The Community
Mental Health Center

I
The Community Mental Health Center: Origin and Concepts

ALLAN BEIGEL, M.D., and
ALAN I. LEVENSON, M.D.

Federal support for the delivery of mental health services is still a rather new phenomenon. The Community Mental Health Centers Act of 1963 was, in fact, the first piece of federal legislation aimed at large-scale funding of treatment programs for the mentally ill. Prior to the passage of the Act, the costs of public mental health programs were carried primarily by state governments, and prior to the middle of the nineteenth century the responsibility had rested almost exclusively with local governments.

Public care for the mentally ill was practically nonexistent in the United States of the early nineteenth century. For the most part, jails were used to confine those members of the community who were mentally ill, or alternatively, the potential patients were simply sent out of the community entirely and left to fend for themselves. It was largely in response to this fact that Dorothea Dix worked to have treatment facili-

3

ties established by each of the several states. In connection with her efforts in this regard, she also sought to have the Congress enact federal legislation that would have provided assistance in the development of the state and territorial facilities. The legislative mechanism she proposed was a program similar to the federal land grant program for public colleges. Under the terms of her proposal, large tracts of federally owned land would have been turned over to the individual states and territories to be used as the sites for mental hospitals. For several years during the 1840's, Miss Dix lobbied intensively for the passage of this bill. In 1847 a bill was finally adopted by both Houses of the Congress, but it was then vetoed by President Franklin Pierce.

Pierce's veto message stated a philosophy of public policy that was upheld for over a century, namely that the federal government had no role in regard to mental health services except with respect to certain special population groups. These groups have traditionally included military personnel and dependents, merchant seamen, reservation dwelling Indians, and the residents of the District of Columbia. (It should be noted that, just as Dorothea Dix was successful in her efforts to have state and territorial legislatures establish mental hospitals, she was also successful in her efforts to have the Congress establish a mental hospital for the District of Columbia. St. Elizabeth's Hospital was established by Congress in the mid-nineteenth century, and it has continued throughout the years to serve as the District of Columbia's mental hospital.)

As the years passed, the federal government also assumed some responsibility in regard to specialized problem areas relevant to mental health. Thus, two federal narcotic hospitals were established during the 1930's and in 1946 the National Mental Health Act was passed. This act authorized the creation of the National Institute of Mental Health, and the NIMH began operation in 1948. As originally authorized, the work of the NIMH was primarily in the area of research and education. The Institute was seen as a federal mechanism for the support and promotion of mental health research. The Institute was also authorized to make grants for the training of mental health personnel. The support of mental health service programs, however, was not seen initially as a major role of the NIMH. Indeed, its early service-oriented activities were limited to the support of pilot and demonstration projects that were technically considered applied research ventures.

CHANGE IN PUBLIC ATTITUDE

In general, policies of the federal government can be thought of as reflecting the typical or modal attitude of the nation's citizens regarding a particular area of public interest. Accordingly, the role of the federal government in regard to the care of the mentally ill was not to be modified until there was a change in the overall public attitude toward mental illness in general and mental patients in particular. This necessary change in public attitude did not come until the close of World War II, and it is therefore not surprising that federal mental health service programs were initiated so recently.

After the close of World War II, there developed a new level of national interest and concern about the plight of the mentally ill. Suddenly the problem of mental illness became a matter of national significance, and indeed it was in this context that the National Mental Health Act was passed in 1946. Certainly a social change of this magnitude was the product of many complex forces, but it is possible to trace its origin in part to phenomena that were observed during the war itself. One of these was the large number of men who were rejected for military service as the result of a neuropsychiatric problem. Americans had typically thought of themselves as a healthy people, but Selective Service records indicated that five million men were rejected from the draft because of their failure to meet medical standards, and of this total, some 40 percent were excluded from service because of a neuropsychiatric defect. Moreover, similar statistics were collected for those men who actually were inducted and later discharged for medical reasons. Neuropsychiatric disabilities provided the most frequent cause for medical discharge.

Given this indication of the extent of mental illness in the military, it became increasingly difficult to ignore the extent of mental illness among the civilian population. Probably for the first time, the public became generally aware of the large numbers of patients who were hospitalized in state mental institutions. When World War II ended, our state hospitals housed some 450,000 patients. By the mid-1940's, many of these patients had already been hospitalized for long periods of time, and it soon became patently but tragically clear that these patients and many others were destined to remain in these institutions for many years to come. Indeed, the state hospital patient population continued to rise on

5

an annual basis, and by 1955 there were 550,000 such patients throughout the nation.

Of course, major changes in public attitude do not occur spontaneously. Some kind of action must be taken to focus public attention on the problem, and in the immediate post-World War II period, attention was focused on the problems of mental illness by a number of books and articles appearing in newspapers and periodicals. Examples include works by Albert Deutsch and Mike Gorman. These men and others emphasized not only the extent to which mental illness constituted a major national health problem, but also the extremely limited availability of resources for dealing with the problem. The resources being utilized were quantitatively inadequate and, what is more, they were being applied in a manner which was not really effective.

There was an obvious need for a new method of dealing with mental illness. In the mid-nineteenth century, Dorothea Dix had brought about the establishment of large state-sponsored institutions, but by the middle of the twentieth century it was clear that these institutions were not adequate to the task at hand.

As in so many other areas of national life, the experiences of World War II had brought about not only the recognition of a social problem but also the potential for solution. In regard to care for the nation's mentally ill, the potential solution lay in the methods of care that had been developed and utilized by military psychiatrists during the war. Prior to the war, civilian practice had emphasized chronic illness and long-term care. During the war, however, military psychiatrists dealt with mental disorders as acute problems and they sought to utilize short-term treatment methods. What is more, they made every effort to treat the acutely mentally ill serviceman in a hospital which was located as close as possible to the site of battle. Civilian methods of care had been characterized by the removal of patients from their premorbid surroundings, but the military psychiatrists treated their patients in the very setting in which the illness had developed. Thus, rather than mentally ill servicemen being returned to the continental United States for hospitalization, they were treated instead in hospitals very close to the front. Understandably, when these psychiatrists themselves returned home after the war, they were eager to find and develop civilian applications for their new techniques.

THE FEDERAL GOVERNMENT'S RESPONSE

There were thus several different forces pressing for change in our mental health services delivery system. In response to these forces, the Congress took a step which was unprecedented, at least in regard to the problem of mental health and mental illness. The Congress acted to establish a body that was charged with the responsibility for studying the nation's mental health status. Specifically, in adopting the Mental Health Study Act of 1955, authorization was given for the establishment of the Joint Commission on Mental Illness and Mental Health. Although created by the Congress, the Joint Commission was so structured that its members included representatives of a wide variety of professional and citizen organizations.

A series of exhaustive studies was conducted under the auspices of the Joint Commission. Indeed, the work represented what was undoubtedly, the first full-scale analysis and assessment of the nation's mental health requirements and capabilities. The final report of the Commission was published in 1960 with the title *Action for Mental Health*. That document made a number of sweeping recommendations with regard to the care of the mentally ill. Of particular significance in that volume was a call for the development of services on a local basis. The Commission recommended that local mental health clinics and general hospitals replace the large state institutions as the primary focal point for the delivery of mental health services. As a parallel recommendation, the Commission proposed that existing large state hospitals be gradually reduced in size. Implicit in the recommendation was the concept that each community must assume responsibility for the care of its own residents.

The Federal Community Mental Health Centers Program was developed in response to the recommendations of the Joint Commissions on Mental Illness and Mental Health. It took several years for the recommendations to be implemented and the new program to be established. Indeed, it was not until February 1963 that President Kennedy sent to the Congress the first presidential message on mental health. In it he asked for a federal program that would provide a "bold new approach" to the problems of mental illness. When the Community Mental Health Centers Act of 1963 was passed, the basic elements of this new approach became eminently clear.

In essence, the primary goal of the act was to stimulate local communities to assume responsibility for the care of their own mentally ill citizens. The emphasis was on local program development and operation, but the local communities were not being asked to meet their own needs independently. Rather, the act called for a partnership in the development of needed services. Federal, state, and local governments were all to be involved, public agencies and voluntary organizations were both to be involved, and financial resources were to be derived from both public and private sources.

BASIC CONCEPTS AND THEIR IMPLEMENTATION

Emphasis on local involvement in the development and operation of a mental health service program added a new dimension in terms of the program's organization and administration. In addition, this same local orientation is critical in making the services maximally effective. Mental health services must be readily available when and where they are needed by the patient. This constitutes one of the basic lessons learned about the provision of mental health services during World War II. The patient must be able to obtain needed services easily, and he must be able to obtain them without isolating himself from the people and surroundings that are familiar to him.

A second fundamental concept of the new federally sponsored approach to mental health services was that the services themselves should be comprehensive in scope. Each patient needs different types of services at different stages of his illness, and different patients require a variety of services that are consistent with their age and background as well as with the nature of their illness. In the past it was typical for mental health agencies to offer, or at least emphasize, only one type of service. Thus, state hospitals were concerned primarily with inpatient programs, while mental health clinics were typically established to provide outpatient care. When the Community Mental Health Centers Act was passed, however, its goal was the establishment of multiserivce programs that could meet many different needs.

Closely related to the matter of comprehensiveness was a third basic concept, namely, continuity of care. The availability of multiple services is clearly of little value if an individual patient cannot move easily from one service to another whenever his clinical needs change. Moreover, when he does move from one service to another, it is essential that the treatment programs be thoroughly coordinated.

Still another basic concept of the new federal program was one related to the need for efforts to prevent mental illness as well as to treat it. Mental health service programs had traditionally focused on the need for diagnosis and treatment. Little attention had been paid to the need, or indeed to the potential, for prevention. When the Community Mental Health Centers Act was passed, however, prevention was brought to the forefront of concern. It was recognized that some methods were already available and that others could be developed to achieve effective prevention of many forms of mental disorder.

In summary, then, the basic concepts embodied in the Community Mental Health Centers Act of 1963 were these: community oriented programs with accessibility of care; comprehensive services; continuity of care; and an emphasis on prevention as well as treatment. Each of these had to be operationally defined for purposes of the act and the federal program authorized by it. Each of the basic concepts offered several alternative approaches for implementation, and a specific approach therefore had to be identified and defined.

The concept of local service and community orientation was implemented through the introduction of the idea of the catchment area. The emphasis on local services required that there be a means of identifying the community to be served, and, effectively, the catchment area is this focal community. As defined in terms of the federal program, a catchment area is a designated geographic area having no fewer than 75,000 people and no more than 200,000 people. These upper and lower limits were chosen because they appeared to provide a basis for effective programming. When the federal program was established, it appeared that a population of fewer than 75,000 people would be too small to support the comprehensive services required of a community mental health center. On the other hand, the upper limit of 200,000 people was selected because it appeared that a center serving more than this number would not be able to develop the needed program ties with other human service agencies in the area. Accordingly, although the federal regulations allowed for exceptions to these population requirements, the catchment area of 75,000–200,000 became the basic community unit for the new approach to mental health services delivery.

The second concept, comprehensiveness of services, was implemented through the definition of a group of services which each center was required to provide. In addition, the federal regulation also identified a second group of services which were recommended but not required. The required services have come to be thought of as the basic and essential ingredients of a community mental health program. These are inpatient care, outpatient care, emergency care, partial hospitalization services, and community consultation and education programs. The group of recommended (but not required) services includes specialized diagnostic services, rehabilitation, preadmission and postdischarge services for state hospital patients, research and evaluation programs, and training and education activities.

It should be noted, of course, that the concept of comprehensiveness of care was also defined in terms of the patient population to be served. Mental illness occurs in a variety of forms and it affects people of all ages. Accordingly, each community mental health center was required to provide services to patients regardless of their diagnosis and regardless of their age. Under the terms of the regulations, a center could not turn away a patient who might be an alcoholic in favor of treating one who might be neurotic, and, in like manner, the center could not turn away a child or adolescent in favor of providing services for an adult.

The third basic concept, continuity of care, was again defined in rather specific terms. In this case the definition was presented in terms of those program elements most likely to provide linkages between or among the various services of a center. Essentially, the linkages were seen in terms of people and information. People, both staff and patients, had to be able to move from one service to another, and in like manner it had to be possible for information to be moved from one service to another. Accordingly, the federal regulations placed several specific requirements on each center. It was necessary that the center make provisions for the free transfer of clinical records from one service to another. It was also required that the center establish procedures whereby staff members who provided care for a patient through one clinical service (for example, inpatient) had to be able to participate also in the care provided for that patient through any other service of the center. Finally, it was required that persons who were deemed to be eligible for one type of care also had to be considered eligible for all the other types of service being provided by the community mental health center.

The last of the basic concepts, a commitment to prevention, represented a major difference between the new idea of the community mental health center and traditional forms of mental health services. In the past, mental health programs had focused almost exclusively on problems of diagnosis and treatment. Now, however, prevention was to be one of their functions. In standard public health terminology, there are in effect three types of prevention. *Primary prevention* refers to the elimination of those factors which cause or contribute to the development of disease. For the community mental health center, this type of prevention was to be implemented through the provision of mental health consultation and education programs for professionals engaged in providing a variety of human services. Included among the consultees were to be teachers, clergymen, welfare workers, probation officers, and a host of others. The members of the various "care giver" groups were clearly involved in providing services to people during times of stress and crisis, and accordingly it seemed clear that consultation from mental health center staff members would make it possible for these professionals to help their clients to handle their crises effectively and without the development of a mental disorder. *Secondary prevention* has been traditionally defined as the early detection of disease and the earliest possible initiation of treatment. The community mental health center was to be involved in secondary prevention because of its emphasis on providing readily accessible care for acute illness, often on an emergency basis. *Tertiary prevention* has been defined as the elimination or reduction of residual disability following illness. In this regard, each community mental health center was expected to play a role not only because of its specific rehabilitation programs but also because of its commitment to providing definitive and comprehensive treatment services.

FEDERAL SUPPORT FOR CONSTRUCTION

As first proposed by the Kennedy administration, the community mental health center legislation was to include provisions for two kinds of federal support. Grants were to be made both to assist in the construction of mental health center facilities, and grants were also to be made to assist in meeting the costs of staffing these facilities. When the Congress adopted the Community Mental Health Centers Act of 1963 (Public Law 88–164), however, it chose to include only the provisions for construction support. The construction legislation fared well in the Congress in part because there was already a substantial history of federal grant support for the construction of other types of health facilities, especially general hospitals. The Hill-Burton program, as originally enacted in the mid-1940's, provided grants for the construction of new general hospital facilities, and the amended Hill-Harris program extended the availability of this support to remodeling and renovation projects as well.

In actual fact, the Community Mental Health Centers Act of 1963 authorized a program that was in many respects very similar to the Hill-Harris program. The basic approach called for the availability of federal

11

funds on a grant-in-aid basis. This meant that each state was to have available to it a predetermined portion of the funds appropriated for the program in a given year. Thus, the several center applicants within a single state were to compete with each other for the available funds rather than competing with all other center applicants across the country.

The allocation of funds to each state was to be determined on the basis of a formula which took into account the total population size of the state and its socioeconomic status. These same factors were also used in the determination of what has come to be called the "federal share" for each state. This share is actually the percentage of eligible construction costs that can be covered by a federal grant. Under the terms of the 1963 legislation, the federal share ranged from a low of 33⅓ percent in the larger and more well-to-do states to a high of 66⅔ percent in the smaller and poorer states. Once established by the federal government for a given state in a year, the federal share or percentage was the same for all construction grants made to community mental health centers in that state.

Although each state had available to it a specified and predetermined amount of federal money, it must be noted that the federal legislation of 1963 did provide a mechanism whereby funds could be transferred from one state to another. These so-called interstate transfers made it possible for a center in one state to utilize funds that otherwise would have gone unused in a second state. Thus, if there were not enough fundable projects in one state in a given year to use that state's entire allocation, then the governor of that state was authorized to make the money available for a specific project (or projects) in one or more other states. At the time that the Community Mental Health Centers Act of 1963 was adopted, the several states showed varying degrees of readiness to begin the construction of new community mental health centers. Because of this differential readiness, the interstate transfer mechanism proved to be invaluable in promoting the development of multiple centers in some of the more highly populated states.

Another provision of the original legislation and, indeed, a provision of the preexisting general construction program as well, was the requirement that a plan for the construction of community mental health centers be developed for each state during each fiscal year. The governor of the state was authorized to designate one state agency as having responsibility for the preparation of the state plan, and this plan was to indicate the relative needs for community mental health centers in the different areas of the state. This priority of need was to be determined

on the basis of such factors as the number of mentally ill persons residing in that area, the existence of mental health service facilities, such
indices of social stress as crime rate and juvenile delinquency statistics,
and socioeconomic criteria such as the average income level and the
rate of unemployment.

It must be noted that the state agency responsible for the development of the state plan was also to be responsible for conducting a review of each construction grant application developed in the state. More
specifically, each state was required to establish a review panel at the
state level, and an individual application could be considered by the
federal reviewers only after it had received the approval of the state review panel and the designated state authority.

The community mental health centers' construction program was administered according to the terms of the 1963 legislation until 1970. In
that year the Congress adopted a series of amendments, which are
known simply as the Community Mental Health Center Amendments of
1970 (Public Law 91-211). The major change introduced by this new
legislation related to the concept of the federal share. As noted above,
construction grant applicants were originally eligible for federal support
ranging from one-third to two-thirds of the total cost of construction.
Moreover, under the terms of the original legislation, all center grantees
in a single state received the same percentage level of federal construction support. With the passage of the 1970 Amendments, however, both
these provisions were changed. The new law made it possible for centers serving poverty areas to receive construction support amounting to
as much as ninety percent of the total costs of construction. Eligibility for
this increased level of funding depended only on designation of the center's catchment areas as a poverty area by the federal government. Once
this designation was made, the center was eligible for ninety percent
construction support regardless of the level at which the federal share
had been previously set for that state.

FEDERAL SUPPORT FOR STAFFING

It was not until 1965 that the Congress adopted legislation authorizing
federal support for the costs of staffing a community mental health center. The amendment adopted in that year (Public Law 89-105) added
the authority that had been defeated in 1963. In actual fact, however,
the 1965 legislation broadened the concept of staffing support. As originally proposed in 1963, staffing support was to be available only to

those community mental health centers that had already received a construction grant. In effect, the staffing grants were to be used to help centers implement services in facilities that had been constructed with the help of federal funds. As enacted in 1965, however, staffing support was to be available to all community mental health centers, regardless of whether or not they had previously received any construction assistance.

In many basic respects, the staffing grant program as enacted in 1965 was identical to the construction program which had been authorized two years earlier. Eligibility requirements for staffing and construction grants were the same in all respects. In order to be eligible for either a construction or a staffing grant, a community mental health center had to offer at least the five essential services, it had to provide services for a catchment area of 75,000 to 200,000 people, and it had to assure continuity of care. At the same time, however, the 1965 legislation made the staffing program very different in regard to its operational format. Thus, whereas the construction program was a grant-in-aid or formula program, staffing support was to be administered as a project grant program. This meant that all applications were to compete on a nationwide basis, and it also meant that all centers throughout the country were to be eligible for the same level of percentage of federal support.

Under the terms of the 1965 legislation, staffing support was to be provided at a level of 75 percent of eligible costs during the first fifteen months of the life of the staffing grant. During the next twelve months, the federal government was to provide 60 percent of eligible costs. During the next two twelve month periods, the federal government was to provide staffing support at a level of 45 percent and 30 percent of eligible costs respectively. Under this formula, federal staffing support was available to the center for a total period of fifty-one months.

In 1970, when the new legislation increased the maximum federal share for construction grants, the level of federal staffing support was also increased. All centers became eligible for support over a total period of ninety-six months (eight years) rather than the fifty-one months that had originally been authorized. The levels of federal support were revised so that 75 percent of eligible costs was to be covered by the federal grant during the first two years of support. For the third year, the level of federal support was set at 60 percent; for the fourth year, it was set at 45 percent; and for the final four years of the grant, it was set at 30 percent.

In addition, just as the 1970 amendments provided preferential construction support for centers serving poverty areas, so too the 1970 amendments authorized preferential staffing support for the centers serving these same designated areas. Poverty area centers were to be eligible for support over a period of ninety-six months (eight years), just as in the case of centers not serving poverty areas. Unlike the latter centers, however, the poverty area center became eligible for support at a level of 90 percent of eligible costs during the first two years, 80 percent during the third year of the grant, 75 percent during the fourth and fifth year, and 70 percent during the final three years of the grant.

Another important element of the staffing legislation related to the definition of eligible costs. The 1965 legislation authorized federal support only for those professional and technical personnel who were charged with responsibility for direct patient care. Federal funds could thus not be obtained to help pay the salaries of staff members whose responsibilities lay in administrative, clerical, maintenance and housekeeping, or kitchen activities. With the passage of the 1970 amendments, however, a much broader range of personnel became eligible for federal support. The legislative history of the amendments made it clear that support was now to be extended to almost all personnel of the center. The only exclusion maintained was that staffing grant money could not be used to pay salaries of maintenance, housekeeping and minor clerical personnel.

It can be seen that the 1970 amendments to the original Community Mental Health Centers Act made a number of substantial changes in regard to the basic staffing and construction support program. In addition, this recent legislation also expanded the availability of federal support to community mental health centers in several significant respects. One important addition to the federal program was the authorization of specifically earmarked funds for the support of staffing costs related to services for alcoholic patients, drug-abuse patients, and children and adolescents. In addition, the same legislation (Public Law 91-211) authorized the awarding of grants to support the process of organizing and establishing a new community mental health center. These "initiation and development" grants were made available to centers which serve poverty areas and also to those centers which are developing specialized services for children and adolescents, alcoholic patients, and/or drug-abuse patients. These grants can be made for a term of one year and they can provide the center with up to $50,000 of support.

It should be noted that one major provision of the original staffing legislation has not been modified by subsequent amendments. This is the requirement that staffing grants be made only to assist in meeting the costs of new services. The Congress has defined the role of the federal government as providing assistance to centers in regard to services that have not previously been available.

For operational purposes, the federal regulations provide that a service is "new" if it meets one or more of several criteria. One criterion, obviously, is that the service not have been previously offered by the agency developing the community mental health center or any of its affiliates. Alternatively, a community mental health center is eligible to receive support for a service which is to be provided through the use of a delivery method or treatment approach which has not been previously available. Also, a service can be defined as "new" if it has been in operation on a trial or pilot basis for a period of not more than nine months prior to the time that the community mental health center files its application.

ADMINISTRATION

Responsibility for the operation and the administration of the federal Community Mental Health Centers Program has been vested in the National Institute of Mental Health. The NIMH has had responsibility both for the grants management aspects of the program and also for the policy development aspects. Originally, review and approval of grant applications were the responsibility of the NIMH central office (Washington area) staff, and the regional office staff was responsible for providing consultation to potential and actual applicants in regard to the preparation of their applications. Now, however, the situation is somewhat different. The central office staff has retained responsibility for policy development and program analysis functions, but the regional office staff has assumed responsibility for grant review and approval in addition to continuing the consultation function. It should also be noted that at this time the regional offices have also assumed responsibility for much of the fiscal management of the program.

When the Community Mental Health Centers Act of 1963 was adopted, the goal was the establishment of 2,000 community mental health centers. These were to serve the population of the entire nation, the average catchment area having a population of 100,000 people. By mid-1971, a total of 400 centers had been funded by the federal government, and of these well over 200 were already in operation.

In many respects, the goal of 2,000 centers is still far off, but it is clear that the federal Community Mental Health Centers Program has had an enormous impact on the delivery of mental health services throughout the United States. Community mental health has become the major thrust of our mental health services, and the community mental health centers have come to serve as the primary vehicle for the implementation of community mental health concepts and programs. In this sense, the centers are indeed the vehicle of a "bold new approach" to the care of the mentally ill, and they have demonstrated this approach to be both creative and effective.

REFERENCES

Brown, B. S., and Cain, H. P. "The Many Meanings of Comprehensive." *American Journal of Orthopsychiatry* 34(1964): 834–839.

Deutsch, A. *The Shame of the States.* New York: Harcourt Brace, 1948.

Federal Register. *Community Mental Health Centers Act of 1963, Public Law 88–164,* May 6, 1964.

Federal Register. *Mental Retardation Facilities and Community Mental Health Centers Construction Act Amendments of 1965, Public Law 89–105,* March 1, 1966.

Ginzberg, E. "Army Hospitalization, Retrospect and Prospect." *Bulletin U.S. Army Medical Department* 8(1948): 38–47.

Glass, A. J. "Combat Psychiatry and Civilian Medical Practice." *Transactions of the College of Physicians* 23(1955): 14–23.

Glasscote, R. M., and Kanno, C. M. *General Hospital Psychiatric Units.* Washington, D.C.: Joint Information Service, 1965.

Gorman, M. *Every Other Bed.* Cleveland: World Publishing Company, 1956.

Grinker, R., and Spiegel, J. P. *Men Under Stress.* Philadelphia: Blakiston, 1945.

Joint Commission on Mental Illness and Health. *Action for Mental Health.* New York: Basic Books, 1961.

GENERAL REFERENCES

Bolman, W. M. "Theoretical and Empirical Bases of Community Mental Health." *American Journal of Psychiatry* 124(1967): Supplement 8–13.

Freedman, A. M. "Decussational Psychiatry: The First Phase in Community Mental Health Center Development." *Proceedings of the American Psychopathology Association* 57(1968): 128–141.

Levenson, A. I., and Brown, B. S. "Social Implications of the Community Mental Health Center Concept." *Proceedings of the American Psychopathology Association* 57(1968): 117–127.

McInnes, R. S., Dickover, R., Palmer, J. T., and Goldfarb, A. "Community Psychiatric Care as a Substitute for State Hospitals." Presented at the annual meeting of the American Public Health Association, Kansas City, 1963.

Osterweil, J. "Mental Health Planning: Prelude to Comprehensive Health Planning." *Bulletin of the New York Academy of Medicine* 44(1968): 194–198.

Ozarin, L. D. "The Community Mental Health Center: Concept and Commitment." *Mental Hygiene* 52(1968): 76–80.

Jones, C. L. *Architecture for the Community Mental Health Center*. New York: Mental Health Materials Center, Inc., 1967.

Kaufman, M. R., ed. *The Psychiatric Unit in a General Hospital*. New York: International Universities Press, 1964.

Kennedy, J. F. *Message from the President of the United States Relative to Mental Illness and Mental Retardation*. Washington, D.C., February 5, 1963, 88th Congress, 1st session, Document Number 58.

Menninger, W. C. *Psychiatry in a Troubled World*. New York: Macmillan, 1948.

U.S. Department of Health, Education, and Welfare, Public Health Service. *Patients in Mental Institutions—Part II, State and County Mental Health Hospitals*. Washington, D.C.: U.S. Government Printing Office. 1957.

II
Community
Mental Health
Center Planning

EDITORS' INTRODUCTION

Planning for a community mental health center resembles planning for many other types of activities, particularly those related to the delivery of human services. Planning efforts are now under way in regard to the urban environment, economic development, general ecology, and comprehensive health services. The process of planning for a community mental health center is similar to these and other planning efforts in regard to basic mechanisms and approaches. Thus, the community mental health center planner must identify goals, set objectives, recognize the available resources, and determine the means by which the available resources will be used to achieve the specific goals and objectives.

Because of a recent emphasis on planning activities in all areas, many people in every community are involved. Many of these planning authorities are working in fields outside the traditional mental health arena and, in a single community, their numbers may include housing planners, community development planners, and economic or business planners. The developers of a community mental health center should recognize the existence and availability of these planning experts in other fields and request their assistance.

Although the mental health planner and other planning experts are essential to the process of developing a community mental health center, they alone are not enough. In addition, the planning process should emphasize the involvement of local residents who are to be served by the center. The local residents can play several vital roles. Not only can they participate in the actual planning of services and the organization of the center, but they can also serve as agents for the dissemination of information about the center and can perform the critical function of mobilizing local community support for the center and its efforts.

It is unfortunate that the importance of planning has often been neglected by many mental health centers during their developmental phases. This apparently has often occurred because of the urgent need to develop services rapidly to meet local needs. The crucial importance of this early planning has now been given a new emphasis by the most recent amendments to the Community Mental Health Centers Act. Adopted in 1970, they provide for the awarding of federal grants of up to $50,000 to support the "Initiation and Development" of community mental health centers during a one-year period.

The passage of these amendments, in part, reflects the history of a number of operating community mental health centers, which, in effect, have demonstrated through their experience, the serious disadvantages of beginning services with limited advance planning. It is probably true that for many centers the only element of advance planning was the preparation of the community mental health center grant application. At the same time, in addition to recognizing the lack of early planning, the staff of these centers have now come to realize the significance of planning as an ongoing process. Planning is not simply a matter of devising a scheme or schedule prior to the opening of the center. Rather, planning in a community mental health center must be continued beyond the time the center opens and becomes a regular part of the center's operation.

---

1   *Jack Zusman*, M.D.

The Catchment Area Concept

Catchment area is a new term in psychiatry which has been given wide currency by its association with regulations for federal funding of comprehensive community mental health centers. The catchment area may be defined as the geographic area containing the population which a community mental health center serves.

The term has also been extended to apply to situations where geography is not a consideration. A "functional catchment area" described a well defined population entitled to service whose members are distinguished by some characteristic other than residence. For example, members of a union or enrollees in a prepaid medical plan may be served by a mental health agency. This agency would relate to its service-eligible population in the same way as a mental health center would to a catchment area.

The essential element of the catchment area concept is that it refers to a clearly defined population which is eligible for service. The agency's concern is for the population from which its patients will come rather than for the patients alone. Clinical research, evaluation studies, planning of services—all should involve the group "at risk" of becoming ill, not just those on whom a diagnosis has been made.

This is in contrast to earlier conceptions of patient and community relationships in which patients alone would be considered and studied and the characteristics of the population group from which the patients came would be neglected. Indeed, when a service organization defines its admission requirements through patient characteristics (for instance, schizophrenics over age sixteen), the organization usually cannot determine from which populations its patients come. Because of this deficiency, the service organization will have great difficulty in relating to any particular community group and usually cannot function as a comprehensive community mental health center.

The catchment area is important to two groups of professionals working in community mental health services—the central planners who must design catchment areas and local service administrators who must serve catchment areas. Each of these groups has a different task and is influenced by different considerations. This discussion will be from the point of view of the local administrator who is given a catchment over whose boundaries he has no control and who is told to develop services for the area.

Although the term catchment area has only recently been used to refer to the service district of a (local) community mental health agency, the service district concept has long been recognized and is applied world-wide. In a sense, all national and local governments have service districts in that governments serve and relate to populations of a geographically defined area. The "catchment area" of a national government may contain a population of millions; that of a village government may contain a few thousand. Nevertheless, the concept is the same.

In the United States, "Special Districts" are governmental units commonly organized to provide special public services in addition to the ones routinely provided by local government. Services provided in this way include, for example, schools, sewers, water, highways, and mosquito control. Other services such as mail delivery, police, public health, and building code enforcement are also usually districted.

The community mental health service catchment area, however, differs from both these kinds of districts in a number of ways. Special Districts often have their own taxing power and their own elected officials (for example, school boards). This insures a relatively direct relationship between the population served and those providing the service. It also produces community interest in and a means of control over the service organization's policy, efficiency, and administration.

For service agencies which do not have Special Districts, such as police or public health, there usually is still a fairly close link between the agency and elected officials. There is also usually an annual budgeting process which includes legislative review. These relationships tend to strengthen community ties and interest between the community and the agency.

At their present level of development, mental health catchment areas do not yet have the traditional advantages of other kinds of districts. Community mental health centers serving catchment areas usually have neither the connection to the political system nor the budgetary review to assist in maintaining community relationships and consonance with community desires. Another important distinction is that for most other kinds of agencies, the existence of a district guarantees a service and encourages uniformity of service from one district to another. For example, where an urban area is divided into police precincts, the police department usually is responsible for providing service to all precincts and the type and amount of patrolling will be fairly similar from one precinct to another.

With the present development of community mental health services, the existence of catchment areas in no way guarantees the provision of mental health services. The division of a political unit into catchment areas resembles assignment of business franchises more than it does usual governmental districting. The catchment area provides an exclusive right to serve a territory and a likelihood of some financial support in establishing a service. However, no service will be provided until some entrepreneur comes forward to take up the opportunity.

Jack Zusman

When a governmental agency such as a state mental health authority subdivides its territory into catchment areas, it does not commit itself to provide service. It usually leaves it to local groups to organize to provide the service. It is already clear that this approach will have a profound effect on the manner in which local community mental health services develop. In most states, general hospital services have developed in a similar way and the result has been many unfortunate situations, both financial and organizational, as well as some advantages.

Most areas which have been divided into catchment areas or "catchmented" have been broken into areas containing between 75,000 and 200,000 population. This has been done in order to meet federal regulations for financial support of community mental health center construction and staffing. It is interesting to note that this has happened despite the fact that federal monies cannot possibly pay for more than a small fraction of the services which will be developed in each state and, in many cases, the federal limitations are not particularly suited for local conditions.

Very little has been written to explain how the federal regulations were arrived at. It is apparent, however, that by holding the upper limit of catchment size at a relatively low level, it has been made impossible for state hospitals and other large psychiatric units, such as those in large county hospitals, to become community mental health centers and take advantage of the federal funds without first undergoing major reorganization.

The catchment area requirement has indeed encouraged a major reorganization of mental health services in most of the United States. This simple regulation with the bait of a relatively small amount of federal funds attached to it has been remarkably effective in producing change. Had the federal administrators set out to produce the change through education and persuasion, it is doubtful they could have had a fraction of the effect despite an expenditure of many times the amount of funds.

The changes brought about by the catchment area requirement are a mixed group—some are clearly good and others clearly bad. Others may result in either improvement or deterioration of service depending upon local circumstances.

Some of the major desirable changes associated with the federal regulations will be discussed first. Catchment areas lead to general improvement in the distribution and some aspects of quality of service. The catchment area regulation makes it certain that mental health services will be located closer to patients' homes than they had been previously. Even though in some states the entire population may comprise no more than three or four catchment areas, each one spread over many miles, this is still an improvement over service at a single state hospital still further removed from most of the patients' homes.

Catchment areas make it easier for patients to obtain service, both because services must be located closer to home and because it is difficult for a service agency to institute admission requirements beyond those that an individual be mentally ill and live within the catchment area. Whereas agencies were free previously to set all kinds of admission standards without regard to the public interest or the welfare of prospective patients, agencies can no longer do this, at least officially. Even where the primary mental health agency is not equipped to provide a particular needed service, it must see to it that the service is nevertheless made available to its patients. By making it easier to obtain care regardless of a patient's personal attractiveness, ability to pay, or type of illness, the catchment area regulation encourages equality of service for all patients. The catchment area encourages continuity of care in that a patient will return repeatedly to the same agency for treatment despite changes in his diagnosis, severity of illness, age, or other factors which have traditionally led to transfer.

The tie between a community mental health center or another mental health agency and a defined community encourages a number of developments. It becomes simple and very much in the interest of the service organization to engage in preventive activities in a community and to get out into the community to develop citizen support and interagency liaison. Previously most local agencies had no particular community to relate to and, in any case, had no necessary interest in preventing mental illness since they were free to restrict admissions regardless of the number of cases attempting to get service. Agencies undertaking prevention could actually be penalized since they were diverting manpower from direct treatment services and the benefit of effective prevention would not clearly accrue to the agency.

Agency accountability to the community is encouraged by catchment areas since the agency relates to a specific community and the community has a natural interest in seeing that its service is functioning effectively. Epidemiologic studies are made possible since service is being provided for a defined community and all cases presumably will be known to a single agency. Evaluation of preventive efforts also becomes possible since these efforts are focused on a defined population and it becomes possible to determine any reduction in the number of cases coming from a particular population.

Gaps in the range of services also become obvious because it is not possible for an agency to dismiss patients for whom it has no facilities. Unless adequate services are available within an agency or available upon referral, the agency service system will soon back up with patients for whom no treatment is available and yet for whom the agency has responsibility.

Planning of new or additional services is simplified in that the necessary epidemiologic and evaluation studies can be done and the projected service needs of a particular population can be estimated.

Finally, the catchment area regulation has served to encourage the development of relatively small community mental health service units. Just by virtue of smallness, these are likely to be more therapeutic than large state hospitals. In a small unit it is possible for patients and staff to get to know each other well and the dehumanizing mass processing which often takes place under the auspices of a large highly organized bureaucracy is far less likely to occur.

The disadvantages of catchmenting include the discouragement of specialization which occurs when every community mental health center must be prepared to serve a full range of patients coming from its area. Agencies with a previous tradition of service to a particular patient group must now develop expertise in other areas, quite possibly at the cost of their traditional strength in one area. Training of specialized staff as well as recruitment of outstanding specialists can be considerably hampered by the generalist approach to be found in most community mental health centers.

The proliferation of many small service units where previously there were just a few large ones inevitably results in an increase in administrative and housekeeping costs and a resultant decrease in efficiency, at least from a financial point of view. Where previously there was a need for only one agency director's salary, one central purchasing office, one laundry, and one power plant, there will now be a need for one for each catchment area.

Reorganization of existing agencies or new ones can result in the disruption of long established and traditional service patterns and administrative relationships. Patients who are accustomed to going to a particular hospital, for example, and who have great confidence in the staff of that hospital are now directed to go elsewhere. Physicians who have long served on the voluntary staff of a hospital may be told that their private patients will no longer be given priority or that their services are required in an agency closer to home.

A county hospital with legal responsibility for serving an entire county may be told that in order to receive federal funds, it must separate a portion of its countywide psychiatry service in order to focus on the population of one catchment area. This can result in two classes of service for residents of a single county—diagnosis and brief treatment or state hospital transfer for most applicants, and complete service for those in the selected catchment area. Yet, patients from both parts of the county are paying the same tax rate and would seem to be entitled to the same service except that some of them have the misfortune to reside outside the catchment area.

The establishment of a number of community mental health centers which may themselves then further subdivide into satellite units results in the scattering of scarce professional staff and expensive equipment. Professionals are then faced with a choice between considerably reducing their interaction with colleagues or spending a significant amount of time traveling to some central meeting place. Patients, too, may have to spend a great deal of time traveling from one facility to another when, for example, some much needed rehabilitation equipment is not centrally located but is placed in a satellite.

Finally, the development of catchment areas and community mental health centers considerably increases the difficulty of central program planning and control. In many cases, state and county agencies have a legislative mandate to carry on such activities; yet they are able to do so only through a group of mental health centers which are all relatively independent financially and programmatically. The central agency may therefore have the responsibility but not the authority to carry out a program. Where previously it might have been able to act by giving an order to a state hospital director or persuading a relatively small group of voluntary agency directors, it is now faced with a much larger group of independent individuals who must be persuaded.

The effects of some aspects of catchment area reorganization depend upon the local situation. For example, division into catchment areas may result in reinstitution of racially or socioeconomically segregated service facilities where major efforts have been made in the past to eliminate this segregation. Catchment area boundaries may be deliberately or unintentionally drawn so that they produce this result. In some cases, because of the size of a minority group in a community, it may be necessary to design a catchment area which will be composed completely or almost completely of minority group members. When this happens, it then becomes easier for pressures from various groups to lead to unfair or uneven allocation of resources. Where previously, for example, mental health services were budgeted on a statewide basis, and all state residents had available the same service, the state mental hospital, it now becomes easier to provide one kind of service for middle class persons in one catchment area and another kind of service for lower class persons in a neighboring area.

Catchment area boundaries may also divide natural communities and lead to fragmentation of a community rather than unification. This fragmentation may make it difficult for the community mental health center to provide a good service and may also sever ties of political support and professional accountability which had developed between a mental health agency and locally elected representatives. In many cases, catchment area boundaries have been drawn without consideration for the boundaries of political districts. The mental health center must then relate to a number of legislators and each legislator must relate to more than one mental health center. This becomes an unnecessarily complicated process.

AGENCY—CATCHMENT AREA RELATIONSHIPS

The institution of a catchment area tends to bring about a major change in the relationship between an agency and its community as has been previously discussed. Very clearly, one of the important changes is an increase in accountability of the agency to the population which it is attempting to serve. Federal regulations encourage the development of local boards to assist in governing of service agencies and, at the least, to act as advisors to agency administration. Although the intent of this has been to improve service, it has actually been a mixed blessing. Formal accountability can have no useful effect on the quality of service unless those to whom the agency is accountable are competent to judge the agency's work. When the community advisory board is composed of a group who have very little knowledge of the problems and processes of mental health services, it will be difficult for the board to function effectively regardless of good intentions. Rather, board members may be reduced to engaging in rhetorical battles over issues which are peripheral to the agency or over which the agency has no control. They may also see themselves as political representatives of particular groups in the catchment area and force the agency into accommodations to meet the demands of these conflicting groups. One of the first responsibilities of an agency, therefore, is to educate its community board and then to involve the board increasingly in the major decisions facing the agency administration. Only when the board understands agency problems and is qualified to evaluate the agency's work, can accountability occur in a valid and useful way.

Educating and informing the board can become a job of major proportions. It seems likely that over the next few years, a new profession or at least a subspecialty is going to develop in community mental health services (and probably in other human service agencies as well), that of agency-community liaison worker. This will happen because liaison is such a complicated, important, and time consuming task. It will be the responsibility of this worker to act as executive secretary to the community board and to coordinate the education and communication activities which agency professionals carry out with the board. The liaison worker will represent the board and the community to the agency and carry out other kinds of tasks involving communication between the community and the agency.

The agency has a number of other responsibilities to the catchment area. One of the foremost is its responsibility to give priority to admissions from the catchment area. The question of catchment area admissions has been a much misunderstood one since it is often assumed that federal regulations require that a community mental health center admit only those patients who come from the catchment area. Rather, the requirement is that priority be given to catchment area patients. Once the needs of the catchment area are taken care of, it is quite possible to admit patients from outside of the area.

Where agencies have a tradition of wide geographic responsibility, this priority question sometimes has created problems. For example, although the agency may agree it will give priority to catchment area patients, what happens when all beds are filled, some of them with noncatchment area patients, and an applicant from the catchment area arrives? Does his priority entitle him to force out a noncatchment patient even though the latter is not ready for discharge? Generally the answer to this in practice seems to be "no." By general agreement, it seems that catchment area patients have relative priority over noncatchment area patients but not absolutely so.

Another responsibility of the agency to its community is to know the community and its people. This requires constant efforts at communication, perhaps a special staff person, as described above, as well as participation in community activities by professionals far beyond what the professionals are accustomed to. In some cases, agencies have prepared formal courses for their staffs regarding history and culture of their communities. Other agencies have provided foreign language courses for the staffs where this has been an important consideration. Agency staff members must be encouraged to become active in local organizations, make informal contacts in the neighborhood, when possible become local residents, and spend a good deal of their extracurricular time participating in local recreational activities.

When the agency comes to know its community, it then must tailor its services to the needs and the desires of the community. In some cases, this is relatively simple. In other cases, there may be conflict between the priorities of the community and those of the professionals. For example, professionals may feel an important investment of their time would be in a major consultation activity with the schools in the hope of preventing mental illness. Local residents may prefer more of an investment in direct services for those who have already become overtly mentally ill. It seems that the professionals have a responsibility to make their views known and to attempt to explain to community representatives the bases of their opinions. However, once the community representatives understand the professionals' reasoning, if they still continue to have different priorities, the professionals would be best advised to go along with the community or to seek work elsewhere. In most cases, this impasse will never be reached provided the professionals make an effort to educate the community. Most community groups seem only too happy to listen to the professionals if they have the feeling the professionals are making an attempt to educate them.

The agency also has a responsibility to involve the community in planning agency programs and in the governance of the agency. This is usually carried out through a community advisory group. Selection of the group is a task of primary importance and one which often is not well carried out. The difficulty is that community individuals with whom the professionals tend to feel most comfortable and who are closest to the professionals' point of view often are not in good contact with the community. When appointed to advisory boards, they act as rubber stamps for the professionals but are unable to make commitments which the community will back up. Such persons are easy to find and appoint to boards because they tend to make themselves known to the professionals and indicate their interest in working with the professionals.

On the other hand, many of the individuals who can speak for the community and who are in close contact with community desires are not particularly interested in mental health issues and, particularly in poverty areas, have little in common with the professionals. If appointed to advisory boards, they may become involved in major conflicts with the professionals and make demands which the professionals feel are quite unreasonable. Moreover, since such individuals are difficult to find, even when it is decided that it is desirable to appoint them to the board, finding such individuals and convincing them to become involved requires a good knowledge of the local community.

In some cases, attempts have been made to hold elections to choose community board members. A serious difficulty with this approach is that community interest in the election is usually low. Even in general elections for political office which involve major expenditures of funds to excite community interest, the electoral turnout at the polls is likely to be disappointing. An election for a community board, when little or nothing can be spent to educate or interest the voters usually has a far poorer turnout and those elected are therefore not truly representative of the community.

There is no final answer to the problem of assembling a satisfactory advisory board. Perhaps the best way is a compromise to include a number of key community leaders with a number of community residents who are particularly interested in mental health.

A final important responsibility which the agency has to the community is to guard community resources. Specifically, this involves spending money and professional manpower very carefully. Professionals, particularly those who do not have administrative responsibility, are traditionally inclined to make treatment plans with little consideration for the limits of agency resources or practical realities of the budget. Under these circumstances, what happens is that a relatively small number of patients who are chosen either by professional preference or by chance, receive the lion's share of the service. Those who are accepted for service but are not part of the chosen few get second class service and many other prospective patients get no service at all. A more responsible approach to providing service would be to make an estimate of the total resources available in a year and an estimate of the number of patients likely to apply to use these resources. It then becomes possible to arrive at a realistic estimate of the amount of service which can be made available to each patient. Planning a treatment program for each individual patient can be done with the total picture in mind.

The catchment area has reciprocal responsibilities to its mental health agency. This is one aspect of catchment area-agency relationships which is often overlooked. Yet, professionals are human beings with needs just like community residents. The community has a responsibility to see that its professionals work under satisfactory conditions and are given the tools to do their jobs. Even above average pay rates cannot make up for poor working situations. Thus, the community's responsibility is to find out from the agency what it needs to meet the mental health service needs of the community and then to help provide these resources, both through financial contributions and through political influence with legislators. This is particularly so when the community feels that an agency is doing a good job or that staff have extended themselves beyond the call of duty. It has been unfortunate that at times communities have been quick to criticize agencies but very slow to recognize improvement or exceptional service. Even when these are recognized, it is often in terms of contributions by individual staff members rather than the work of a staff as a whole.

The community has a responsibility to pay attention to its agency. Some members of a community, usually those on the advisory board, should be in a position to know how much and what quality work the agency is turning out and how well it is meeting the mandate which the public has given it. These facts should be given public attention. The community has a responsibility to call attention to deficits in the agency program, to criticize the agency where it is not living up to expectations, and to praise it where it is doing well.

The community has a responsibility to understand the agency. In the past, criticism has often been heaped on agencies by community members who have little understanding of the conditions under which agencies were operating or the limits of budget and manpower which were imposed. Often agencies were called upon to undertake tasks for which agency staff was not trained or to accept goals which were impossible to attain. For example, in the rush of enthusiasm generated by the renaissance of the community mental health movement, it has been sometimes felt that with proper applications of community mental health techniques all of the unpleasant and perhaps insoluble problems of the American cities could be eliminated. Indeed, some mental health professionals have encouraged this mirage. Yet, it seems very obvious that the problems of the cities are problems of economics, politics, intergroup conflict, and improper distributions of populations. Conflicts which exist between groups often result from real conflicts of interest rather than misperceptions or poor communication. These can never be solved by mental health principles or practice.

The community has a responsibility to assist the agency in recruitment of professionals. The community should participate both in the selection and in the encouragement of professionals to come work in the agency. Community representatives can play a very important part in this in that they can sell prospective employees on the advantages of living and working in the community. The community cannot expect the agency alone to carry out this selling job. The community also should assist agency professionals in choosing employees. The community representatives' expertise in this can be in the selection of prospective employees who are able to communicate well and who make a good impression with community residents.

CONCLUSION

Assignment of catchment areas to community mental health services provides a unique opportunity both for communities and their mental health service agencies to work together and get to know each other. Although service agencies in other disciplines have long had local districts, community mental health professionals are faced with this challenge for the first time. This gives them an opportunity to learn from the mistakes of others and to take advantage of the excitement generated by a new situation. Catchment area ties present an advantage and provide a springboard for new achievements in comprehensive community mental health services.

---

2   *Haroutun M. Babigian,* M.D.

The Role of Epidemiology and Mental Health Care Statistics in the Planning of Mental Health Centers

Planners and administrators let their idiosyncratic experiences and preferences guide the plans they devise. All too often health facilities are planned using impressionistic ideas rather than documented sets of data. The significance of recent innovations in the provision of psychiatric care in the United States goes beyond considerations of the organization of services and the delivery of comprehensive care to specified communities. Perhaps the most significant new approach is the emphasis on planning and on the evaluation of community mental health centers.

The use of epidemiologic and other mental health care statistics in the planning of centers is the subject of this paper. Our experience in the development of two new mental health centers in Monroe County, New York, will serve to illustrate the issues discussed.

The definition of planning in Webster's dictionary is "devising a scheme for doing, making or arranging." It is important to consider this definition in two separate segments; one "devising a scheme" and the other "for doing, making or arranging." Devising a scheme may or may not result in execution of that scheme. Execution depends on the approaches and attitudes of the different components of a community working towards the achievement of a goal. By different components of a community we mean: planners, administrators, staff, and consumers. The development of a scheme is dependent on the needs of particular communities, their resources, and the availability of data.

Epidemiologic and health care statistics can provide an estimate of need for different services; isolate areas of need for care to subpopulations in a community; determine the load on already existing services; determine the effectiveness of these facilities in the delivery of care; explore the degree of communication or lack of communication between facilities; study the proper and improper utilization of different existing facilities due to lack of other services or lack of proper utilization of different services and facilities; and determine the impact of lack of adequate services on the functioning of families, communities or a whole catchment area. Of course not every community has similar sets of data available for planners; planners must utilize all available data and collect other needed data for adequate and comprehensive planning. Many communities may not have mental health statistical data or epidemiologic studies. These communities then have to assess their needs and develop their plans based on other studies in comparable communities and on data they are able to collect from their own community at the time of planning.

General guidelines for the planning and development of community mental health centers have been defined and clarified by Levenson[1], Beigel[2], and Osterweil.[3] The tremendous potential of statistical and epidemiologic data in the planning and evaluation of centers has been demonstrated by Kramer[4], Bahn[5], Gardner[6], and Sata.[7] Yet, thus far the demonstration of the important role of statistical data has been promulgated by epidemiologists, mental health statisticians, and other behavioral scientists with little interest on the part of implementors and administrators.

Regardless of differences, strengths, or weaknesses of a community, we recognize three different approaches to the use of statistical epidemiologic data in the planning process: (1) to estimate the need for services in a community; (2) to develop a rational plan for implementation of a program tailored to the resources and potentials of that community to meet that need; and, (3) to go beyond planning to assess the impact which different plans will have on health care, that is, extrapolating from present data to show what the outcome will most likely be for each plan. The three approaches are dependent on the working relationships between planners, administrators, and the community.

1. The use of data to indicate need for services is the most frequent request from planners. Frazier [8] points out "that it is easier, and in the short run more effective, to use data in the advocacy role than in the rational planning role." Stated another way, it is usually more effective, in the short run, to use data to "point with alarm" than it is to use it to justify a step-by-step development of a program plan. If this is the expressed wish of administrators, then very little communication is expected between planners, administrators, and the community. Planners make their recommendations to the administrators who then have to make decisions in implementation. Woloshin and Pomp in discussing the gulf between planning and implementation state: "We contend that the widening separation between the implementors and the planners will have grave consequences. In fact, we hypothesize that the greater the separation, the greater will be the degree of error in assessing needs and producing services to meet those needs. . . . Many a program has failed not because its ideas or hypotheses were invalid, but because they were transferred from a different sphere of activity without sufficient planning." [9] In many instances communities are forced into a position where they have to develop a plan prior to their knowing who will be the administrators of a program. In such instances the administrators are faced with a *fait accompli* which may be totally impractical and impossible to achieve.

2. The development of rational planning requires close cooperation between planners, administrators, and community. The emphasis is not solely on the demonstration of need; it goes beyond that to devising methods and services to meet the needs realistically within the limits of the available resources and potentials of the community. In this instance, planners usually consider their job terminated following the completion of the planning phase and they do not go any further.

3. Planners can use the statistical material they prepare to simulate the operation of the program. Together with the administrators they assume that the center is fully operational at a point in time (short or long-term—two to five years later), and rearrange the set of data used in the schematics in different ways to decide the impact of the center with different alternative sets of data. This implies that prior to the implementation of a program, the responsible administrators have a baseline and sets of alternative data that would suggest the full or partial success

of their programs. Such a process would enable the responsible administrators and implementors to think about evaluation early, and about the consequences of the evaluation to bring about changes in programs on an ongoing basis. This concept is further elaborated elsewhere.[10] In addition planners can help administrators set up different data collection mechanisms that would enhance the evaluation and monitoring processes which in turn would guide implementors in the directions they take.

THE MONROE COUNTY PSYCHIATRIC CASE REGISTER

The remainder of this paper will be devoted to the demonstration of the use of data in Monroe County, New York, for planning of mental health services. I will not attempt to describe the total process of planning of the two community mental health centers in this community but will illustrate how epidemiologic and statistical data were used in planning some of the key areas in community mental health center development.

Monroe County had a population of approximately 700,000 in 1970. It is an urban industrial community with approximately 40 percent of the population living in the city (Rochester) and the remainder of the population residing in suburban and rural areas. Prior to the passage of the Community Mental Health Centers Act (Public Law 88-164 in 1964; and Public Law 89-105 in 1965 and 1966) the county had developed a comprehensive network of psychiatric services. The Monroe County Psychiatric Case Register was begun on January 1, 1960, and continues to the present time. A detailed description of the Register has been reported by Gardner, el al.[11] The Register records the psychiatric experiences of Monroe County residents who come in contact with any of the major providers of psychiatric services in the county. It is the source of data for epidemiologic studies and also provides a unique kind of mental health data in that each patient is a unit with a longitudinal history accounting for all the services and facilities used by him over a period of time. The reporting facilities comprise a university hospital with inpatient, outpatient, and emergency services; an acute inpatient observation unit; a state hospital with its inpatient, outpatient, alcoholism and home care services; a veterans administration hospital; a children's treatment center with inpatient, outpatient, and day care facilities; two child guidance clinics; a court clinic that serves the court system; an alcoholism clinic; and approximately 95 percent of the private psychiatrists in Monroe County.

Planning for two new community mental health centers began in Monroe County in 1965. On January 1, 1967, the Rochester Mental Health Center opened its doors with inpatient, outpatient, day care, emergency, and consultation services, to both adults and children. The alcoholism clinic and one child guidance clinic were incorporated in this center. On July 1, 1968, the University Mental Health Center began operation as a division of the Department of Psychiatry of the University of Rochester. The Convalescent Hospital for Children became a community mental health center for children serving the same catchment area as the University Mental Health Center. Two additional mental health centers for the community are currently being planned.

This part of the paper will demonstrate the usefulness of Register data in the design of the two new community mental health centers in Monroe County mentioned above. Since it would take too much space to discuss all aspects of planning we will focus on the following areas: (1) the catchment area concept; how many catchment areas were needed in Monroe County and how decisions were made; (2) prediction of the load on the two community mental health centers from baseline data available in the Register for the previous seven years; (3) the issue of hospitalization and numbers of beds; (4) planning for outpatient and emergency services.

Catchment Areas   The guidelines for the development of community mental health centers specify that catchment areas should encompass a geographic area with no less than 75,000 and no more than 200,000 inhabitants. Monroe County had a population of over 600,000 in 1965 thus ideally requiring four community mental health centers for total coverage of the community. Figure 2-1 is the Monroe County map, including the city of Rochester, with boundaries for four catchment areas, A, B, C, and D. Since only two community mental health centers were going to be operational by 1968, the planners included the majority of lowest socioeconomic levels in the city in the two operational community mental health centers. Each community mental health center was planned at the location of a general hospital: the University of Rochester Mental Health Center at the University of Rochester's Medical Center as a division of the Department of Psychiatry and the Convalescent Hospital for Children for services to children; the Rochester Mental Health Center at the Rochester General Hospital. The population of catchment areas C and D are now served by the general University Department of Psychiatry and the Observation Unit of the Monroe Community Hospital. Planning for these two community mental health centers (for catchment areas C and D) is in progress.

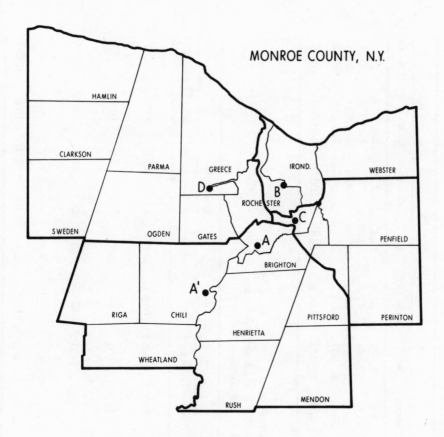

FIGURE 2–1

Monroe County (N. Y.) Comprehensive
Community Mental Health Centers
Catchment Areas within the City
of Rochester and Monroe County

1970 Projected Populations

A University of Rochester Community Mental Health Center and the Convalescent Hospital for Children (A′)
    Existing (1968) City Population—78,444
    Suburban and rural population—86,330

B Rochester Mental Health Center, Rochester General Hospital
    Existing (1967) City Population—82,250
    Suburban and rural population—92,316

C Genesee Hospital (projected)
    City Population—60,889
    Suburban and rural population—81,449

D Park Ridge Hospital (projected)
    City Population—64,870
    Suburban and rural population—136,455

TABLE 2–1

Distribution of the Four Catchment Area Populations (by Socioeconomic Areas—Monroe County, 1968)

	I		II		III		IV		V		TOTAL	
	NO.	PERCENT	NO.	PERCENT	NO.	PERCENT	NO.	PERCENT	NO.	PERCENT	NO.	PERCENT
A	27,209	31.9	51,005	22.8	62,539	23.4	15,768	21.8	8,253	24.2	164,774	24.1
B	30,347	35.5	54,586	24.4	44,902	16.8	9,294	12.8	3,209	9.4	142,338	20.8
C	27,804	32.6	44,417	19.8	57,009	21.3	24,607	33.9	20,729	60.7	174,566	25.6
D	0	0	73,777	33.0	102,789	38.5	22,807	31.5	1,952	5.7	201,325	29.5
Total	85,360	100.0	223,785	100.0	267,239	100.0	72,476	100.0	34,143	100.0	683,003	100.0

TABLE 2–2

Number of Individuals Served by Psychiatric Facilities in Monroe County in 1966 (by Catchment Area and Type of Contact)

	A		B		C		D		UNKNOWN		TOTAL	
	NO.	PERCENT	NO.	PERCENT	NO.	PERCENT	NO.	PERCENT	NO.	PERCENT	NO.	PERCENT
First Lifetime Contact with Psychiatric Facilities	1258	35.5	1109	35.0	866	29.2	1062	33.8	43	33.1	4338	33.5
First Register Contact but not First Lifetime Contact	310	8.8	211	6.6	285	9.6	255	8.1	9	6.9	1070	8.3
Other Than First Contact with Register	667	18.9	630	19.9	641	21.6	608	19.3	29	22.3	2575	19.9
Care Continued into 1966 from Previous Year (1965)	1297	36.8	1223	38.5	1178	39.6	1215	38.8	49	37.7	4962	38.3
Total	3532	100.0	3173	100.0	2970	100.0	3140	100.0	130	100.0	12945	100.0

Table 2–1 presents the distribution of the Monroe County population by community mental health center and socioeconomic areas (using the 1968 projected population). Each census tract in Monroe County has been classified into one of five groups from I (highest) to V (lowest) using a composite index combining median value of owned homes, median rental value, percentage of skilled, semiskilled and unskilled workers, median years of education, and percentage sound dwelling units, determined by the 1960 census. Fifty-six percent of the total area IV population and 85 percent of the area V population are within the catchment areas of the two operational community mental health centers (A and B). It is obvious that an effort was made to include most of the lower socioeconomic areas in the catchment areas of operational centers while preserving a reasonable combination of all socioeconomic levels in each catchment area, close to the distribution of the total county population.

Using the 1960 census the University of Rochester Mental Health Center's catchment area contained a total population of 137,294—23.4 percent of the Monroe County population. Ninety-one percent of the total population of the catchment area was white. There was a Negro population of 12,078 which was 8.2 percent of the total catchment area population and 49.9 percent of the county's Negro residents. There were 345 individuals of other races in this catchment area, comprising only 0.3 percent of the total catchment area population and 39.1 percent of the 883 persons of other races in the county. Design of the catchment area utilized data on median age, marital status, school years completed, school enrollment, median family income, labor force, means of transportation, housing and mobility. (Material available on request.)

This demonstrates how the long range planning for total coverage of a community was undertaken prior to the specific and individual planning of centers. The implementation of this overall plan will undoubtedly take many years.

DETERMINATION OF EXPECTED PATIENT LOAD ON COMMUNITY MENTAL HEALTH CENTERS

The Register can provide data to answer specific questions on patient load and utilization of facilities. The early diagnosed and treated prevalence and incidence figures are provided in Table 2–2 by catchment area for the calendar year 1966. Similar data are available yearly since 1960.

Twelve thousand nine hundred and forty-five county residents, or approximately 2 percent of the total county population, was cared for by the psychiatric network of services with each catchment area accounting for a quarter of the total load. One-third of the patients cared for entered psychiatric services for the first time in their lifetime, 8.3 percent had their first Register contact but this did not represent a first lifetime contact, 20 percent were already in the Register but returned for care in 1966 and 38.3 percent continued in care from the previous year. Assuming that a new community mental health center opening its doors on January 1, 1970, would attempt to provide care for its catchment area, they should at least count on serving 80 percent of both the new contacts and the group that re-enters care from the new catchment area (the other 20 percent is cared for by private practice). For catchment area B (Rochester Mental Health Center) which started operation on January 1, 1967, this would mean serving a minimum of 1,560 individuals. The average yearly increase since 1960 has been 6 percent, so the expected number of patients to be served would be 1,654. This figure is an estimate of the minimum number of individuals who would require service. It does not account for new case detection methods or new types of services to populations that have not been adequately cared for in the past.

To estimate the expected load on different inpatient and ambulatory services, Tables 2–3 and 2–4 present the number of contacts in 1966 with different facilities for the fifteen year and older population of Monroe County by catchment area. Since one individual could contact and utilize more than one facility he is counted several times in these tables. Similar figures are available for children. Forty percent of all inpatient contacts are at the State Hospital and the Veterans Administration Hospital, 35 percent at the acute observation unit and 25 percent at the University Hospital. Hospitalization will be discussed further in a later section.

Of the total ambulatory contacts 35 percent were at the emergency division of the University, 19 percent private practice, 15 percent at the University Outpatient Clinic and the remaining 31 percent at the Court Clinic, Alcoholism Clinic, Veterans Administration and State Hospital clinics. The Rochester Mental Health Center should expect a minimum of 2,122 ambulatory contacts for the fifteen and over population of its catchment area.

TABLE 2-3

Distribution of Inpatient Contacts in 1966
(by Catchment Area and Hospital for Persons Fifteen Years of Age and Over °)

	RSH		MCH		SMH		VA		TOTAL	
	NO.	PERCENT	NO.	PERCENT	NO.	PERCENT	NO.	PERCENT	NO.	PERCENT
A	488	38.5	452	35.6	291	22.9	39	3.0	1270	100.0
B	469	41.3	374	33.0	262	23.1	30	2.6	1135	100.0
C	493	39.2	476	37.8	261	20.7	28	2.3	1258	100.0
D	439	39.0	397	35.3	256	22.8	33	2.9	1125	100.0
Unknown	38	45.8	43	51.8	0	0	2	2.4	83	100.0
Total	1927	39.6	1742	35.7	1070	22.0	132	2.7	4871	100.0

RSH—Rochester State Hospital
MCH—Monroe Community Hospital
SMH—Strong Memorial Hospital
VA—Veterans Administration Hospital

° Totals do not represent total number of individuals since one individual could have been hospitalized in several different facilities or more than once in the same facility.

TABLE 2-4

Distribution of Ambulatory Contacts in 1966

(by Catchment Area and Facility for Persons Fifteen Years of Age and Over °)

	ED		OPD		ALCOHOLISM CLINIC		RSH		PVT		VA		COURT		OTHER		TOTAL
	NO.	PERCENT	NO.	PERCENT	NO.	PERCENT	NO.	PERCENT	NO.	PERCENT	NO.	PERCENT	NO.	PERCENT	NO.	PERCENT	NO.
A	831	34.2	388	16.0	116	6.8	103	4.2	412	16.9	40	1.6	207	8.5	336	13.8	2433
B	784	37.0	316	14.8	108	5.1	120	5.7	353	16.6	51	2.4	234	11.0	156	7.3	2122
C	679	34.0	298	14.9	98	4.9	115	5.8	454	22.7	31	1.6	184	9.2	138	6.9	1997
D	761	36.6	328	15.8	80	3.8	105	5.1	413	19.8	49	2.4	169	8.1	174	8.4	2079
Unknown	9	23.1	4	10.2	8	20.5	0	0	2	5.1	0	0	15	38.5	1	2.6	39
Total	3064	35.3	1334	15.4	410	4.7	443	5.1	1634	18.9	171	2.0	809	9.3	805	9.3	8670

ED—University Hospital Emergency Service
OPD—University Hospital Outpatient Clinic
Alcoholism Clinic—incorporated in the Rochester Mental Health Center
RSH—Rochester State Hospital Aftercare Clinic
PVT—Private Practice
VA—Veterans Administration Clinic
Court—Monroe County Psychiatric Clinic for Courts and Probation

° Totals do not represent total number of individuals since one individual could have received care in several facilities during the year.

HOSPITALIZATION

The incidence rate of hospitalization in Monroe County (first lifetime hospitalization) is 2.42 per thousand, 25 percent of this rate (0.60 per thousand) is accounted for by persons diagnosed as schizophrenic. Monroe County had the following number of beds in 1966: University Hospital (acute) with eighty-seven beds; Rochester State Hospital with 3,200 beds (serving several other counties, approximately one half of the beds occupied by Monroe County residents); Veterans Administration Hospital with many beds, few used for county residents; Convalescent Hospital (for children) with twenty-four beds. The Monroe Community Hospital (acute observation unit) with thirty-five beds.

In 1966, 408 individuals from catchment area B experienced their first lifetime hospitalization. Table 2–5 classifies this group by age, sex, and facility of hospitalization. Twenty-four percent of this population went to the State Hospital for their first lifetime hospitalization, 40 percent to the Community Hospital, and 34 percent to the University Hospital. A new community mental health center should attempt to serve all of this population in its facilities especially considering the fact that length of stay at the State Hospital for first admissions is 3–4 times more than that of the University Hospital (twenty-five days). The length of stay at the Community Hospital is six days. Fifty-four of the 408 patients (13 percent) were rehospitalized during the same year mostly at the State Hospital and the Community Hospital. In addition to the 408 new admissions in 1966, there were 1,043 individuals who experienced readmissions and continued hospital care in the different hospitals with 70 percent of them at the State Hospital. An effective community mental health center would be expected to reverse these figures and decrease the incidence rate of hospitalization, the rate of rehospitalization and the length of stay. This, of course, will also depend on the effectiveness of the ambulatory care and partial hospitalization services.

To determine the number of beds needed for catchment area B let us assume that they hospitalize all 408 first admissions and the fifty-four readmissions for that year and plan a fifteen day average length of stay. Then this community mental health center will require 6930 patient bed days which at a 100 percent occupancy rate would account for a nineteen bed unit. At a 90 percent occupany rate twenty-one beds would be needed. Of course this does not account for other readmissions and for avoidance of hospitalization by use of partial hospitalization services

TABLE 2-5

First Lifetime Hospitalization of Catchment Area B Patients in 1966
(by Age, Sex, and Facility)

MALE

FACILITY	00–14 NO.	00–14 PERCENT	15–24 NO.	15–24 PERCENT	25–44 NO.	25–44 PERCENT	45–64 NO.	45–64 PERCENT	65+ NO.	65+ PERCENT	TOTAL NO.	TOTAL PERCENT
RSH	4	80.0	9	24.3	19	23.3	14	23.4	10	25.6	56	25.1
MCH	0	0	16	43.3	40	48.7	20	33.3	24	61.5	100	44.8
SMH	1	20.0	12	32.4	18	22.0	24	40.0	4	10.3	59	26.5
CVA	0	0	0	0	5	6.0	2	3.3	1	2.6	8	3.6
Other												
Total	5	100.0	37	100.0	82	100.0	60	100.0	39	100.0	223	100.0

FEMALE

FACILITY	00–14 NO.	00–14 PERCENT	15–24 NO.	15–24 PERCENT	25–44 NO.	25–44 PERCENT	45–64 NO.	45–64 PERCENT	65+ NO.	65+ PERCENT	TOTAL NO.	TOTAL PERCENT
RSH	0	0	8	25.0	18	29.5	2	4.5	14	31.1	42	22.7
MCH	0	0	7	21.9	18	29.5	19	42.2	19	42.2	63	34.1
SMH	2	100.0	17	53.1	25	41.0	24	53.3	11	24.5	79	42.7
CVA												
Other									1	2.2	1	.5
Total	2	100.0	32	100.0	61	100.0	45	100.0	45	100.0	185	100.0

RSH—Rochester State Hospital
MCH—Monroe Community Hospital (Acute Observation Unit)
SMH—Department of Psychiatry, University of Rochester
CVA—Canandaigua Veterans Administration Hospital

and continuity of care. But it would be safe to assume that the catchment area B center should have an inpatient unit of twenty to thirty beds and make arrangements for continuity of care with the State Hospital. The Rochester Mental Health Center actually has a thirty bed inpatient unit which should serve the community adequately.

PLANNING FOR OUTPATIENT AND EMERGENCY SERVICES

Before the establishment of community mental health centers, the University Department of Psychiatry provided the only emergency psychiatric services for Monroe County and the surrounding counties and the only outpatient psychiatric clinic available for county residents. In addition to providing service, both the emergency and outpatient clinic carry the responsibility for the training and education of residents, medical students, and other mental health professionals. During the planning of centers three different sets of data from various studies were utilized.

1. The Register provided the data presented here on the expected load. In addition to that, a longitudinal study [12] indicated that although the lower socioeconomic areas were represented in the Register at higher rates than other areas, their outpatient care consisted more of diagnostic contacts rather than treatment. Patients from the lower socioeconomic areas utilized the emergency services more than other groups but did not go on from there into outpatient treatment. These studies suggest a breakdown in continuity of care between emergency and outpatient clinics especially for patients with limited financial resources. A demonstration project for the provision of continuity of care and coordination of an agency's efforts was undertaken following these studies.[13]

2. The second set of data was provided by a five month study of the operation of the outpatient clinic in 1966.[14] All telephone calls for appointments were recorded and followed up to determine dropout rates and reasons for patients dropping out of the clinic at various stages. In a period of five months, 591 calls came in for appointments and of these 365 patients were seen for screening interviews. Of the 163 persons who dropped out in the interval between the initial telephone contact and screening seventy failed to call back for an appointment (they were asked to call back in a week because no appointment times were available) and eighty-four failed to appear for scheduled appointments. Of

the 365 patients screened 175 (48 percent) continued in diagnostic interviews. Patients screened were predominantly white, Christian, single and married persons, twenty to thirty-nine years of age, residing in middle class urban areas. On followup, most of the individuals who dropped out in the different stages were judged to have emotional problems of a moderate to significant extent needing care.

Three major factors were involved in the dropout process: (1) the individual's social class—higher dropout rates for lower classes; (2) the number of steps one had to take before receiving a screening appointment, and (3) whether or not they had received psychiatric care within the past five years. Those who had received care dropped out at a higher rate than those who had no prior care in five years (20 percent versus 47 percent for those who had received care in the past five years).

It becomes obvious that in planning ambulatory services, the centers had to eliminate obstacles for patients to enter service. Early case detection has been encouraged by many, yet, before engaging in it, one had to assure service for all those who identify themselves as in need of care but are turned away for various reasons. The Rochester Mental Health Center instituted a walk-in policy and adopted group therapy as the primary modality for outpatient care while the University Center provided appointments quickly with a team approach to care. Both centers developed outreach services with neighborhood health centers to provide comprehensive care to lower socioeconomic groups.

3. Studies of the rate of psychiatric disorders in the practices of general practitioners, internists and industrial clinics [15] provide yet another way of utilizing data in planning. These studies in Monroe County indicated that 17 percent of the white, fifteen years and older, patient population cared for by internists and general practitioners suffered from psychiatric problems. Sixty percent of these patients were judged to have moderate to severe impairment because of psychiatric problems. It was estimated that if all these patients with moderate to severe impairment were referred to the psychiatric network of services, the actual psychiatric caseload of Monroe County would double.

Community Mental Health Centers should consider internists and general practitioners as major providers of mental health care and relate to them accordingly with consultation and education and other related programs.

CONCLUSIONS

The Monroe County Psychiatric Case Register provided most of the data used in the planning of mental health services of the county. Through Register data, an attempt was made to provide answers to questions from planners and administrators. Mental health statistics are helpful in initiating the planning process which has to progress from data to organization and determination of priorities and goals. Undoubtedly the ultimate success of planning is dependent on implementation. It is essential to keep in mind early in the planning process that the same data used in planning should also guide the evaluation programs of mental health centers.

NOTES

NOTE: The author wishes to thank Dr. Harold C. Miles, Director, Monroe County Mental Health Services, for the catchment area data and his helpful suggestions.

1. A. I. Levenson, "Organizational Patterns of Community Mental Health Centers," in L. Bellak, and H. Barten, eds., *Progress in Community Mental Health*, (New York: Grune and Strattan, 1969).

2. A. Beigel, "Planning for the Development of a Community Mental Health Center," *Community Mental Health Journal*, 10(1970): 267–275.

3. J. Osterweil, "Application of Epidemiological Findings to Community Mental Health Planning," in *Psychiatric Research Reports of the American Psychiatric Association*, 22(1967): 249–258.

4. M. Kramer, "Epidemiology, Biostatistics, and Mental Health Planning," *Psychiatric Research Reports of the American Psychiatric Association*, 22(1970): 553–562; M. Kramer, "Problems in Psychiatric Epidemiology, *Proceedings of the Royal Society of Medicine*, 63(1970): 553–562.

5. A. Bahn, "Research Tools for Planning and Evaluation," in R. H. Williams, and L. Ozarin, eds., *Community Mental Health*, (San Francisco: Jossey Bass Publishers, 1968).

6. E. A. Gardner, "The Use of a Psychiatric Case Register in the Planning and Evaluation of a Mental Health Program," *Psychiatric Research Reports of the American Psychiatric Association*, 22(1967): 259–281.

7. L. S. Sata, "Epidemiology: Prerequisite for Planning," L. Bellak, and H. Barten, eds., *Progress in Community Mental Health*, (New York: Grune and Strattan, 1969).

8. T. Frazier, "The Questionable Role of Statistics in Comprehensive Health Planning," *American Journal of Public Health*, 60(1970): 1701–1705.

9. A. A. Woloshin, and H. C. Pomp, "The Gulf between Planning and Implementing Mental Health Programs," *Hospital and Community Psychiatry*, 19(1968): 58–61.

10. D. Harper, and H. M. Babigian, "Evaluation Research: The Consequences of Program Evaluation," *Mental Hygiene*, 45(1971): 151–156.

11. E. A. Gardner, H. C. Miles, H. P. Iker, and J. Romano, "A Cumulative Register of Psychiatric Services in a Community," *American Journal of Public Health*, 53(1963): 1269–1277.

12. E. A. Gardner, and H. M. Babigian, "A Longitudinal Comparison of Psychiatric Service," *American Journal of Orthopsychiatry*, 36(1966): 818–828.

13. R. J. Reichler, H. M. Babigian, and E. A. Gardner, "The Mental Health Team," *American Journal of Orthopsychiatry*, 36(1966): 434–443.

14. L. Maltin, H. M. Babigian, and D. B. Schuster, "The University Psychiatric Outpatient Clinic," submitted for publication.

15. B. Locke, D. Finucane, and F. Hassler, "Emotionally Disturbed Patients under Care of Private Non-Psychiatric Physicians," *Psychiatric Research Reports of the American Psychiatric Association*, 22(1967): 235–248; B. Locke, and E. A. Gardner, "Psychiatric Disorders among the Patients of General Practitioners and Internists," *Public Health Reports*, 84(1969): 167–173; B. M. Rosen, B. Z. Locke, I. D. Goldberg, and H. M. Babigian, "Identifying Emotional Disturbance in Persons Seen in Industrial Dispensaries," *Mental Hygiene*, 54(1970): 271–279.

---

3   *Hiawatha Harris*, M.D.

Planning Community Mental Health Services in an Urban Ghetto

From the dawn of recorded history, the poor, uneducated masses have never been involved in the process of planning for their own destiny. They have depended upon the benevolence of the people who supply them with their needs on a charitable basis. Charity became a part of religions, institutions and cultures. Rarely were the people, toward whom the charity was directed, involved in the planning for themselves. The givers thought that what they perceived as good would also be cherished and relished by those that did not have riches and education. They traditionally went around and observed the conditions of the people in need, the poor, and from their observations made conclusions and plans.

The Labor Movement in this country brought about the first real involvement of poor people in planning for themselves. This only resulted after a long, hard struggle that was frequently punctuated by violence and loss of lives. This involvement phenomenon occurred because people had a commonality that was represented by their employment.

Later, organizations for involvement within the Inner City developed as a political strategy designed primarily to maintain a particular party or person in office. The politician used charisma, promises, or patronage to persuade the Inner City resident to organize to keep him in office. Deeds and services were increased prior to elections and then were dropped off precipitously after the election.

The Inner City has always been victimized by the lack of health care services. As black people became the majority population of the Inner City, services related to health diminished. The streets were not cleaned; the garbage pick-up service was reduced; the general external environment was allowed to deteriorate because of the lack of any control over the owners or the people who were responsible for restoring and preserving the environmental appearance.

With the deterioration of these services, the need for health facilities and health services increased. At the same time, residents of the Inner City, lacking effective leadership pertaining to health service needs, are unable to demand or exercise their rights to good health care and facilities.

It soon becomes the duty of public agencies to provide health care. However, public agencies are usually restricted by budgets and conscious or unconscious racism. The administrators of health programs are rarely members of the resident population. If they are, they have often adopted the majority philosophy of charity. With insensitive administrators, these public facilities will never be able to provide the needed health care for the people of the Inner City. Furthermore, organized medicine and other special interests groups (universities, teaching institutions, research groups) often form a coalition to deny the needed services. Their rationale is that they are in partnership to improve the delivery of services, to fight inroads into the private practice of medicine, and prevent the development of so-called "socialized medicine." The "sanctity of the private practice of medicine" becomes a euphemism—those who have money or insurance will get the needed medical service and those who do not will have to go to the charity clinic for services. As it was the tradition of the benevolent courts, kings, and successful merchants to provide charity, it became the tradition of benevolent universities and multicredentialed health professionals to provide charity health care for Inner City inhabitants. This care was given in charity or county hospitals and public health clinics.

With this backdrop, it is not strange to those of us involved in trying to bring mental health services to the urban Inner City to find ourselves dealing with people who have never been asked before to help plan facilities for themselves; and who view with suspicion anyone coming from the outside bringing them details of good mental health services.

This distrust is compounded by the experiences of the Inner City residents with government people who have been bringing programs—mostly poverty—to them for a long period of time; programs that promised a great deal, but delivered very little; programs that are given the "Madison Avenue" treatment, but like the wares of Madison Avenue are found to be packaged in disposable cartons; programs that are disposed of as soon as some economy-minded politician makes a ripple.

Mental health and psychiatry are viewed as only available in the far reaches of the county or state at the State Hospital. Clinics, psychologists, and psychiatrists are often words of a foreign language since most Inner City residents have never seen one of their own people in that profession or come in contact with one who was sincerely interested in them. They view these services as either out of their reach or for those who are "really crazy."

In the Inner City, the traditional providers of mental health services have been the church and the general practitioner who cannot find anything physically wrong with the patient and who tells him it is his "nerves" and prescribes pills of the most recent tranquilizer that a retail man has given him.

Therefore, we find ourselves trying to seduce a community into becoming involved in the planning of a Community Mental Health Center that would take care of problems that most of the community were not aware existed. To get the community involved at all, planners will have to educate the population to the types of problems in their community that can be solved through a Community Mental Health Center and will have to deal with the psychological or group effects which will occur when the community is told that it is "sick" and needs certain kinds of mental health services. Those people who have been previously exposed to mental health or psychiatric services have often received them in a punitive manner after they have gone from clinic to clinic within the local charity hospitals. Those who are familiar with psychiatry probably have the fantasy of psychoanalysis and the couch.

These issues must be "worked through" both by those who come with gifts of mental health and those who receive the gifts. Perhaps the three wise men who came to Bethlehem to honor the birth of Christ would be a perfect analogy for developers of urban Community Mental Health Centers. Acceptance as sages was not enough. The fact that each of them was from a different racial group insured their entree into the community.

The process of community involvement in planning for an urban

Community Mental Health Center poses a few more problems than the "Maximum Feasible Participation" that is supported by the OEO for poverty programs. Local participation in poverty programs was probably more vigorous and intense because people were able to see the immediate results of the programs and, consequently, gain some hope that, by participating, they would be able to alleviate some of the more immediate economic issues that faced them. A poverty program meant training and a chance to step on the escalator out of the ghetto. A Community Mental Health Center, to some extent, means the same thing, but the meaning is not as obvious and the program has to be sold to the people involved.

The most ideal situation in planning for a Community Mental Health Center in an urban area is to have the planners and the implementors of the program living in the community to be served. This will preempt many of the problems that arise in getting an uninformed citizenry involved in the planning process. Having resident professionals from the area will still pose some problems if they have not been involved in the struggle for the rights of the people of the Inner City. I am assuming that most of the Inner City residents are predominantly black, or another racial minority group, and poor. The suspicion that greets the white professional will not be nearly as great as the suspicion and hostility that a black professional will meet. Most black (or Chicano) professionals have had to lose their identity in order to become professionals. If the planners of a Community Mental Health Center can find a black professional who will be involved in the implementation and planning of the Community Mental Health Center and who has also been involved in the civil rights and/or local militant struggle for rights of the people, then the obtaining of community support and sanction is easier.

If an effective black or resident professional identified with the neighborhood is not available, my first choice for a liaison person would probably be a playground director of a facility that is heavily visited by the youth of the community. I feel that this person will be more attuned to the pulse of the community and have the respect of the residents of the community, both the youth and the adults—the youth because they deal with him every day and the adults because he probably is the one most active in keeping their children out of trouble with law enforcement officers. In an area serving approximately one hundred and twenty thousand people, there will be probably only one or two playgrounds where children congregate. In many ways, a recreation person is preferable to a health professional primarily because of his overall community orientation and involvement.

This liaison person, whether he is a health professional or a recreation worker should not be too controversial, but at the same time should be well known to most of the people in the community, both the so-called militants and the nonmilitant but involved groups. He should set up a series of meetings with agencies and groups within the community and from these meetings should evolve the next step in process—setting up a Community Advisory Board to help and be involved in the actual planning and implementation of the Community Mental Health Center.

The Community Advisory Board should be all-inclusive but not too cumbersome. It should involve representatives of the community on all age levels who are willing to work for the organization of a Community Mental Health Center. Expenses for attendance at meetings should be included in early budgets. Money for babysitters is a must if you want involved and interested parents.

Early meetings should be held by the Board involving small groups of people discussing the community's needs without specifically focusing on mental health needs. If these groups are already organized in the form of a social club, a block club, senior citizens club or a political club, this will be important for future support.

Later meetings can be used to acquaint the particular community group with the people who will be involved in the planning of the program, that is, the community liaison person introducing the major planner, the professional, who will write the grant, and other professionals, if possible, who will be involved in the Community Mental Health Center after it is funded. The exogenous staff should use this time to become acquainted with the community and with each other. They will eventually have to develop their own liaison with the community because the community liaison person is primarily an introductory person and a convener. He should not be put in the position of defending the long years of neglect by the establishment. The planning group must be very careful not to take away the legitimacy and the long years of confidence-building that the community liaison man has built up in his community. It must be sincere in its efforts and not a group of do-gooders who are out to make a name for themselves in the professional ranks. In addition, the exogenous professional personnel will have to expect and handle a great deal of hostility from the indigenous population who will look at them and see many years of neglect and poor services, in addition to the possibility of being studied, tested, examined, and again denied services.

Conversations in community meetings will allow the professionals to determine the greatest needs of the people. Because of training and expertise, they *assist* the resident in establishing basic problems and priorities. One should not be concerned with the rules about carrying out the five basic services or the four basic services initially. These services can and will come with modification by a sensitive and innovative staff.

In planning services for the Inner City, I use the broadest definition of the function of a Community Mental Health Center. The function of a Community Mental Health Center is to serve the needs, mental health or otherwise, of the community while carrying out the mandate of their staffing and construction grants. If the community is in need of some type of organization to bring a basic service into the area, then the Community Mental Health Center should serve that function. It should find out if there are such organizations in the community to do the job or, if not, help the community to organize to bring this about themselves. An example in our area was the need for a red light on a busy street near a school. For a long time citizens were unable to get the Division of Traffic to put a light on the corner. Collectively, the Center brought parents together and drew up a petition and circulated the petition to most of the parents of the neighborhood, and then a group led by the Community Service Director of the Center went down to the City Councilman's office and from there to the Division of Traffic. Within a few days the traffic light was placed on the corner. After that, however, the traffic light favored the busy traffic over the slow cross street which meant that children would get in the middle of the street and become confused because the traffic sign flashed "don't walk." Again, the parents appealed to the Traffic Department and the time mechanism on the light was changed to allow the children ample time to cross the street during the peak hours of traffic. After the Center became involved in this particular episode, mothers began to refer their children and also themselves to the Clinic for needed help in the mental health areas.

Community involvement in a Community Mental Health Center can be a revolutionary process for people who have never been involved in planning for themselves. The revolutionary aspects of this are more in the form of bringing people together and showing them that with meaningful planning and making the right type of organizing moves, institutions can be established within their community that are responsive to their needs and their needs alone. It can also be a process by which the young and the disenchanted can be shown how the system can work for them and how they can acquire the tools that are necessary to help and improve their community. The involvement of the community in the planning and implementation process will allow some members of the community to increase their awareness of the entire health establishment and the interdigitation of the health establishment with the political establishment. It can also be used as a means of decreasing the apathetic and hopeless feelings that many of the residents of the Inner City have.

Even in those urban areas where community involvement has led to what might appear as a disastrous end, the process itself nevertheless has been very meaningful and helpful. It demonstrates to the people of the community that they have some control over their destiny, whereas before they did not.

The urban Community Mental Health Center must see itself as an instrument for change not only in the delivery of mental health service, but in the entire community. Good health begins in an environment that is physically adequate—homes, streets, parks—and mentally nourishing —jobs, schools, churches, and justice. The Community Mental Health Center must be the leader or the catalyst in bringing about these changes.

---

4 *Mitchell Jones,* M.D.

Community Involvement in the Planning
of a Rural Mental Health Center

Community mental health centers in areas where county populations range from ten to fifty thousand have certain inbuilt advantages for stimulating real community participation in planning and operation. Many rural communities still present a relatively unstratified, unspecialized social system where work, play, service, and social organizations include the same fairly wide sampling of community members and where community identity as a circumscribed entity exists to a considerable extent. The community mental health center staff member is often indeed "indigenous" and his interest, contribution and commitment to the community outside his work may be the most important factor in gaining effective, sustained participation by the community in the center program.

A total center program could be planned before operation begins, but most grow from a limited base and evolve to their final shape so that planning and operation are intertwined and mutually dependent processes. Realistic planning for a center allows for moveable walls in the buildings and flexible boundaries in the programs.

Prairie View is a mental health center located in a town of fifteen thousand and in a three-county catchment area of sixty thousand. We began with a small, closely knit staff group primarily involved with providing traditional private inpatient and outpatient clinical services. We established our initial base by meeting clearly definable community needs, demonstrating our own special area of professional competency, and developing natural ties with the medical community and other agencies.

As a result of joint planning with the community, our program then evolved from this base to a fully comprehensive mental health center with a relatively large diversely trained staff. The development of this comprehensive program in a short time represented the culmination and surfacing of processes started much earlier. The staff members had been community members for some time, active in outside boards, civic groups and social organizations. We knew the social help agencies, individuals in the medical community, the businessmen and the governmental officials. Our children were in the schools and recreational programs, and our own identities were with the community. When planning for development of new programs began, we knew who in the community was interested, who was indifferent, and where support and power lay. We also felt we knew many of the needs of the community from our first-hand experience.

When the community, led by persons with whom we already had working and social relationships (probate judge, pediatrician, college sociology professor, for example), developed the interest and drive to provide community financed clinical services, *we* joined *them* to plan for this. Since we had a going clinical operation from a private non-profit base, the decision to use our services on a contractual basis was a natural one. A subsidiary corporation, with board members made up from community members nominated by the community and affirmed by the Prairie View Board, was set up to serve as negotiating agent between professional mental health services and the governmental unit (county commissioners), to represent community interests, to ferret out community needs to inform the community, to plan programs and to set priorities for use of resources. The Community Mental Health Center Board represented a blend of people with varied occupations, interests, and personal philosophies; hopefully truly representative of the community and hopefully without deeply vested private interests. Board members were

55

selected for their special interests and competencies and ties with community needs and resources.

The organization of the Center was a confederation of self-operative systems not too interdependent on each other so that the success or failure of any one did not vitally affect any other. These separate projects, following the lead of the Community Mental Health Center Board itself, were planned and carried out by small groups, combining mental health center staff and interested or specially skilled community members. They followed life courses, some long lived and stable, others flaring briefly and dying, still others (like the Loch Ness Monster) appearing and disappearing periodically according to need, interest and the varying winds of fortune. The following are examples of these separate programs.

Church and Human Relations Committee A group of center staff, board members and specially interested community members who met and planned as a relatively autonomous group and carried out such projects as providing training scholarships for area ministers, conducting training programs in human relations for church lay leaders, and sponsoring workshops and conferences in the area of the church's contribution to better community and personal relationships.

Industrial Relations Committee This group consisted of center staff and personnel managers of local industry who met periodically to discuss and deal with problems of mental health in industry.

Work Incentive Project This project was developed by a committee of center staff in coordination with welfare and labor department, and set up and operated a program for preparing welfare recipients for return to work.

Community Leadership Project This long term project was planned and operated by community leaders with the support and participation of center staff (and later separately incorporated), to provide communication and stimulation for joint action to community leaders. The project's organizational framework cut across a broad spectrum of community leadership and made use of some laboratory training techniques.

These projects and programs began as only vague concepts and ideas and came into being during exploratory meetings between interested persons. Free wheeling, wide ranging discussion was followed by trial runs and then by more focused discussion which gradually led to a working program. We tapped the community as a pool of potential planning talent even as our own staff members were used similarly by other organizations. We invited special interest groups to come to meet with us, to become acquainted and to explore possibilities for mutual help. The results obtained from the cultivation, sustaining of interest, and use of potential community help in our Prairie View experience suggest the following principles and observations about community mental health center planning, particularly in a rural area:

1. In planning programs, listen carefully to what the community sees as the existing need and work from that point back to your own conception (if it differs). If a college wants individual students seen, begin there and work to broader consultation as the relationship develops.

2. Couch your observations about need and program in language and terms compatible with the community's language and view of problems.

3. Be patient when ideas or programs are slow to be accepted. Be willing to let new ideas "soak" for a time before pushing them.

4. Watch your own prejudice. Don't use a project (its success or failure) to "clobber" the community, or portions of it.

5. Be sure that community participants get credit for their part of the effort. It is better for you to get results without credit than to go down heroically.

6. If the community shares your program, has helped plan it, and is identified with it, then it will also defend the program when needed. A community member who has good feelings about any small portion of the total program is apt to stick up for any other portion which becomes threatened. Often controversial programs such as Family Life Education (sex education) can be sustained against pressure if there has been solid community participation in planning. Support, like morning glories, is best found early in the day.

7. Integrate what you do with other agency efforts. Try not to duplicate programming and do not be patronizing toward other agencies.

8. Use creative administrators to lead in the planning, structuring, operation and integration of programs. A capable administrator with "running room" is at least as valuable as a capable clinician, and the twain don't often meet in the same person. The complicated organizational and operational structure of Prairie View, as well as the conception of many new programs, came from a very capable and creative administrator.

9. Encourage and allow staff to develop their own ideas, plan projects and select community members to help in them. Nothing bad ever happened at Prairie View because staff was given room to experiment with their own pet ideas.

10. Use outside consultant help freely and let others in the community benefit from your consultant by having presentations or open meetings

where the community or especially interested segments of the community are invited to participate. Joint sponsorship of a consultant with other groups is very effective. We once jointly sponsored a two-day consultation on intracultural adjustment problems with an association of small colleges and a denominational missionary board. The primary consultant made an evening presentation, open to the public, on his personal Peace Corps experience in addition to participating in more formal working sessions with professional groups during the day.

11. Keep the community informed about activities. The employment of a professional writer to prepare material for local papers will result in more accurate reflections of activity than if it is left to the routine reporting of newspapers or if it is done randomly by less experienced center staff.

12. Share involvement in information activities with the community. A series of radio programs which took the form of panel discussions with a community moderator, one or two center staff members and one or two other community members was such a project. We covered topics such as drugs, signs of mental illness, problems in school, problems of old age, police function and problems, and problems in industry. The information provided to the public by these programs may have been helpful, but the acquaintance with community members involved in making the programs possible and our education of each other as we prepared for them were probably the greatest benefits of the project.

13. The use of volunteer help in all levels of the program provides similar benefits. There is not only the direct help given by the volunteer but also the education of the volunteer by the center and the education of the center by the volunteer.

14. Study or reading groups in which center staff and community members share are also opportunities for two-way communication. Prairie View had three ongoing biweekly groups in which leadership was shared between center staff and community members and a wide range of books and ideas were discussed. The membership changed gradually so that a large number of community members participated.

15. Be nonthreatening in the planning and operation of projects and programs. An agency or individual will let you do any amount of work, including what he could or should be doing, as long as you don't either threaten his security or imply criticism of him. Results in service are more important than demonstrating someone else's weakness.

16. Be sure you are familiar with available statewide and national services so that you can convey to the community your program's position in a wider interconnected system. The community will appreciate

recognition from higher levels as well as respond to usable available resources.

17. Build in self-assessment and measuring devices as parts of all programs and projects so that you have at least a rough idea of results and can intelligently convey these to the community and use them in continued planning.

18. Take projects and programs to the community. In a rural area, several widely scattered small towns may exist in the catchment area. It is important, to the extent possible, to take parts of the program to these towns. We set up educational programs in small towns, participated in their community planning, held aftercare groups, and set up a satellite clinic in one. The same advantages of developing town identity with the program and of getting feedback about town needs occur here as in the larger towns of the rural area. Home visitation by nurses, and occasionally other staff members, over a wide area was extremely effective in reaching persons who would never otherwise have been seen. Your demonstrated willingness to meet others on their home ground either through house calls to individuals, or by going to the clinics of physicians or offices of agencies, paves the way for their cooperation in future endeavors of the center. At Prairie View, "house calls" with police did more to foster common understanding and cooperation than any other contact with law enforcement groups.

19. Lastly, trust the community to plan intelligently and lead capably. Drive, energy and creative activity will not occur where responsibility and authority are not freely shared and where mutual respect does not exist.

---

5   *Rafael Canton*, M.D.

The Community Mental Health Center Team

"Man is the measure of all things." This ancient Greek insight is basic to the community mental health movement. We wanted it to be the architectural message of our new community mental health center building. This chapter will describe the highlights in the process that led to a successful solution.

PREPARATORY STAGES

In 1965, the Ventura County Mental Health Services consisted of two professionals and two secretaries. When the new director was hired, he became aware that the community wanted a more ambitious program to replace the rudimentary psychiatric detention unit of the County General Hospital and this required a new building.

This was reinforced by the expectations of the National Institute of Mental Health through the Community Mental Health Center Act. Accordingly, the program was planned to have inpatient, day treatment, outpatient services, and the administrative services for developing decentralized services in other areas of the county. To determine the smallest center that would be appropriate, the following method was used:

The existing inpatient unit admitted seventy patients a month. The new director estimated that an average length of stay of twelve days would require 10,008 patient days a year, and that this could be provided by thirty-two beds at 90 percent capacity. Admittedly, this left little margin, but it would create pressure to use alternatives to hospitalization.

It was estimated that the day treatment unit would have an average length of stay of one month and that it would admit about a third as many patients as the inpatient unit. Therefore, we settled for a capacity of twenty patients at any one time, and a maximum admission rate of thirty-five patients a month.

The County owned a rectangular lot, 200 feet by 460 feet, adjacent to the County Hospital, the Welfare Department, the Health Department and Juvenile Hall, in the fastest growing sector of the county seat. It was unanimously agreed that this was the logical place.

The motivation to use a consultative approach came from two main sources. One was the Department's established practice of using this style of management. The other was the architect's wishes, brought about by their reading of *Planning, Programming, and Design of the Community Mental Health Center*.[1] This book pointed out that there had been very little input from the mental health staff in the elaboration of architectural plans and that there had been no published material on the evaluation of centers constructed.

First, the mental health staff and the architects easily agreed on the following basic guidelines:

1. Emphasize "open" appearance to reassure people of our investment in voluntary treatment.

2. Make it esthetically pleasing.

3. Keep dimensions to human proportions to express our wish to strengthen the individual's self-esteem and his ability to function in small groups.

4. Take advantage of Ventura's Mediterranean climate.

5. Avoid long halls which distort the human figure in the distance.

6. Keep it within the budgeted amount.

7. Abide by the timetable and other requirements of the grant.

Daily meetings between the architects (one, two, or all three of them) and several of the mental health staff (for the Ventura catchment area) took place. A "modified brainstorming" approach was used. The director would ask questions like what was the next aspect to consider; what additional data should be obtained and who would obtain it; who else should be consulted or informed; what were the alternative solutions; what were their advantages and disadvantages. He was assisted in this role by the chief psychiatric social worker. The resultant discussion led to consensus at almost every step. The architects modified the schematic drawings a number of times during that period. In addition they drew many free-hand sketches. The final schematic drawings looked substantially like the way the center was eventually built, which was quite different from the first schematic drawings.

TEAMWORK AND ARCHITECTS

By the end of this period, many decisions had been reached. The following were permanently retained:

1. to use simple lines imaginatively to avoid "the boxy look";

2. to give the Center a Southern California architectural flavor;

3. to do without air-conditioning;

4. to plan the rehabilitation therapy areas and the dining-meeting area so they could be used by both inpatients, partial hospitalization patients and outpatients, providing an opportunity for common experiences and obtaining maximum use of the facilities;

5. to separate the buildings, to reinforce the patients' sense of orientation;

6. to add a small, centrally located Admissions Building;

7. to place the buildings at an angle to the street and to each other, so as to look attractive from the outside and to create two rectangular "activity courts" within;

8. to connect the buildings by covered esplanades for traffic flow;

9. to use deep roof overhangs, to give shelter from the elements and a feeling of protection;

10. to locate the partial hospitalization service on the first floor of Building C, around an inner court;

11. to add open traffic lanes to this court, rather than have a hall;

12. to build an "occupational therapy kitchen" in the partial hospitalization unit;

13. to build the outpatient and administrative offices on the second floor of Building C on the premise that these services are used by persons who can climb stairs;

14. to connect the offices on the second floor of Building C by a partially protected peripheral balcony;

15. to use movable partitions, in the second floor of Building C, so as to afford future flexibility;

16. to arrange the inpatient beds in "modules" of four beds, two of which would form a "cluster" of eight beds, thus facilitating the formation of family-type and neighborhood-type groups;

17. to use Murphy-type beds, so that sleeping quarters could be easily converted to daytime use;

18. to make our inpatient building a square, totally roofed over;

19. to locate our inpatient unit as near as possible to the emergency room of the General Hospital;

20. to elevate the center roof of our inpatient unit and to use a clerestory around that part so as to bring in an adequate amount of natural light;

21. to place all bedrooms and social activity areas facing landscaped open courts;

22. to design a separate multipurpose building for dining, recreation, meetings and movies;

23. to see the Center as essentially complete, except for the possibility of 10–15 percent future additions. The foundations would not be adequate for an additional floor. Future growth would be decentralized to other catchment areas in the county;

24. to add to the general feeling of warmth and human comfort by extensive use of residential lighting, wood textures, carpeting, and soft, appealing colors.

Our application, submitted on July 29, 1966, described a total cost of $1,598,434 for a fully equipped 35,722 square foot building (at $32 a square foot, as determined by other facility research). The federal and state shares were $498,618 each. The county share was $601,198. It included $102,581 of non-participation expenditures, such as 90 percent of a new boiler for the County Hospital, to handle the increased load, and for other reasons.

THE NEXT FIVE MONTHS

This period extended from July 29, 1966 to December 20, 1966, and was characterized by uncertainty as to whether or not, or how soon, local funds would be available. As a result, consultation with the architects practically ceased. However, the architects continued to read up on the matter.[2]

The original plan called for obtaining the county share through a bond issue. Two other propositions were on the ballot—a girls' home for probationers, and a new jail. The three Department heads met with community leaders who wanted to support the bond issue. All three propositions got over half the votes. The Mental Health Center got 59 percent of the votes, which was the highest percentage but below the needed two-thirds. On October 6, 1966, the grant had been awarded, for a total of $1,441,000, and a state-federal share of $444,743 each. This led the Board of Supervisors to re-allocate the local share from a building fund it had been accumulating for a new county center. This was done on November 29, 1966. Although consultation ceased during this period, additional research and meditation continued.

Reading *Parkinson's Law* was somewhat disquieting. It contained phrases like: "It is now known that a perfection of planned layouts is achieved only by institutions on the point of collapse . . . perfection of planning is a symptom of decay. During a period of exciting discovery or progress there is no time to plan the perfect headquarters. The time for that comes later, when all the important work has been done. Perfection, we know, is finality; and finality is death."

Another dilemma that was brought to our attention was the thesis that the new Community Mental Health Center would inevitably be middle class in appearance, and that this might keep away some of the very people most in need of our services. Jokingly, we toyed with the idea of "constructing an old building." Seriously, the antidote we saw was to inform the public of our desire to give priority to the most urgent needs of people, irrespective of their social class.

PRELIMINARY AND WORKING DRAWINGS

This period extended from December 20, 1966, to March 8, 1967. It began when the local funds were made available and the architects were appointed. These two decisions enabled us to comply with the timetable required by the grant. However, because of inflation, there was considerable concern about the risk that we might exceed our budgeted amount.

In this phase, consultation took place approximately twice a week. Considerable use was made of staff from related county departments, such as the food services manager of the County Hospital and the county director of communications. One consultative session was held between the mental health staff and the executive secretary of the Taxpayers' Association. Here again, the architects made many free hand sketches and several versions of the preliminary drawings adding to the clarity of the discussions. A three-dimensional model was built, to determine whether the sun would shine, in the winter, on a pool planned for the inner court in Building C. The architects consulted a structural engineer regarding weight-bearing points and other matters.

As was necessary throughout the entire process, decisions, such as the following, had to be made to reduce expense:

1. Decrease the area by approximately 3500 square feet (mostly in the Multipurpose Building and in the administration-outpatient area).

2. Eliminate the therapeutic swimming pool.

3. Lower most of the ceiling lights to a residential height and reduce the overhang from eight feet to six feet.

4. Eliminate a fountain and simplify all exterior work wherever possible.

5. Reduce covered and uncovered walks to a minimum.

6. Omit a stage in the Multipurpose Building.

7. Omit several counters and cabinets.

8. Change some floor and wall coverings to less expensive materials.

9. Simplify the windows in the inpatient and partial hospitalization areas.

The following decisions were also made to implement changing concepts:

1. Move the living-room to the center of the Inpatient Building. We obtained approval from Washington to use overhead sprinklers, instead of surrounding the living room with fireproof walls. The result has been a huge success.

2. Move the inpatient nursing office to the area adjacent to the emergency entrance.

3. Design the buildings so there would be a minimum of weight-bearing walls, thus facilitating future flexibility in the use of space.

4. Use slumpstone blocks instead of reinforced concrete. Slumpstone is more esthetic and less expensive to build and maintain.

5. Eliminate the sauna in partial hospitalization. This was based on the wish to reduce expense and the belief that it would require more medical and nursing supervision than we could expect to supply.

6. The fireplace in partial hospitalization was changed to a location in the wall. Originally, it was planned in the middle of the room, so as to utilize "the primitive urge to gather around the fire." However, it was changed because it would have been more expensive, it would limit the use of the room and might, perhaps, let smoke into the room.

7. Have a resilient floor for a dance therapy room. This added about $2,000 to the cost, but it was considered important, especially by the occupational therapist.

8. Omit the courtroom in the Multipurpose Building. This was based on the theory that, in years to come, court cases in mental health would become fewer, and that they could be handled in the community room, in the Admissions Building.

The architects' interest in what they described as "control" caused a temporary rift in the relationship. The mental health staff thought they were referring to physically limiting the patients' movements. When it became clear that all they wanted was to make it easier to see what went on, harmony was restored.

BIDS AND CONSTRUCTION

The bids were opened on December 6, 1967. Several contractors submitted bids. They were surprisingly low, the lowest one for $797,000. This was due to the prevailing construction slump; to the cost-decreasing changes we made; and to some program-related decisions, such as open traffic lanes and balcony, instead of conventional halls. Special coordination was required including the National Institute of Mental Health, the California State Departments of Mental Hygiene and Public Works, the County Mental Health Department, the County Hospital, and the County Department of Public Works, as well as the contractors, subcontractors, and suppliers. As a result, actual construction started on March 8, 1968. The terms of the contract made it expensive for the contractor to be late in finishing construction and for us to introduce changes. The termination date originally agreed to was March 15, 1969.

During this stage, consultation was done in a number of ways. The in-patient team had a copy of the drawings, which was used to consult the evening and night shifts. The drawings were put on the bulletin board and the patients were asked to make suggestions. The County Public Works Department had an inspector to assure compliance with the contract. The architect visited the construction site often. We hired an administrative aide to coordinate the ordering and receiving of movable equipment. These three persons made us aware of problems and opportunities. The mental health team discussed the matter, consulted with whoever had appropriate knowledge or authority, and made a decision.

Most problems were minor. The following, however, were not:

1. The contractor was using trees, bushes and grass as part of the fill. Fortunately, he was forced to replace it by acceptable material.

2. The slumpstone blocks were scuffed while in transit, requiring retreatment to again make them uniform in color.

3. A strike in another part of the country delayed receipt of the movable partitions.

4. The parking lot was not covered by the grant, because it could not be included in the same contract, as it would be built later, as part of another project.

5. The utilities were classified as "non-participating" for a similar reason.

6. There was a storm that was classified as of the one-in-a-hundred-years type.

It was hard to convince the staff that the time for changes was coming to an end. New staff members and new experience, especially in the incipient partial hospitalization unit, led to pressure for changes. The last change initiated by our staff was incorporated two months before completion of the building. There were a total of twenty-five "bulletins" and nineteen "change orders." Some changes resulted from unforeseen problems in the construction itself. Most changes were very small. With the Board of Supervisors' approval, some of the features which had been omitted to save costs were reinstated. These were carpeting, seamless flooring, and vinyl wall covering.

THE INTERIOR DESIGNER

In one brainstorming session, a mental health nurse suggested hiring a professional interior designer. No other government building was known where this had been done. The county purchasing agent was asked and liked the idea. The initial message received was that one or more members of the staff should do it. One thought was that the "multidisciplinary team" idea was applicable to avoid an amateurish job on a million-dollar building. Three candidates were interviewed. Two were manufacturers of hospital supplies, who would provide an interior designer for a fee, or with the purchase of all or part of the movable equipment. The third was a small interior design firm from Los Angeles (Ecological Design Associates) who impressed the staff with their concern for the psychosocial implications of the environment. We computed the number of hours that it would take our staff to design the interior, the average hourly cost, and concluded that it was cheaper (and wiser) to hire this firm, for $6,000. The Board of Supervisors agreed.

The interior designer, Mr. Robert D'Amico, attended two general staff meetings and one or two meetings with the team that was going to occupy each building or part of a building. He brought catalogs, color pictures, slides, models, and samples of materials, and two types of chairs. He combined individual staff preferences and an overall harmonious plan. He also met about a dozen times with the architects and communicated with them by letter and by telephone. Some misunderstanding and differences of opinion came up which seemed to be colored by professional rivalry. However, they were satisfactorily solved.

One contribution of the interior designer was his knowledge of the construction of furniture. For example, he told us that all rockers were poorly built. We wanted some anyway, and two of them broke with remarkably little use. Another contribution was his concept of saving in some things so we could afford a few luxuries, as would a family.

THE LANDSCAPE ARCHITECT

Again, the initial expectation was that landscaping would have to be "improvised." However, perhaps because of our previous success with the multidisciplinary team, the Board of Supervisors agreed to hire the only professionally trained landscape architect in the county (Robert Fleckenstein). His fee was $1,500.

The landscape architect met once with the general staff and twice with each team. The total time spent with our staff was definitely less than the time spent by the interior designer, perhaps because the number of our patients had increased, and time was required to order and receive equipment. The landscape architect spent almost as much time with the architect as the interior designer did.

Some contributions of the landscape architect were:

1. to introduce the concept of carefully planning and furnishing the "outdoor living room" area;

2. to surround the site with greenery for sound attenuation and for beauty;

3. to use plants to further emphasize spatial orientation by differentiation of the various parts of the Community Mental Health Center.

SUMMARY

The process of consultation included approximately 300 hours from the architects, about fifty hours from the interior designers and about thirty hours from the landscape architect. The architects drew several hundred sketches, about one-fourth of which were discussed with our staff. They also did several dozen architectural drawings, at various stages. Dozens of people were involved, from our staff and from other departments and agencies. Altogether, the time spent in consultation amounted to several hundred (possibly a thousand) man-hours. The result was a community mental health center that was tailored to our program, built at a cost approximately one-third below the budgeted amount.

NOTES

1. "Planning, Programming, and Design of the Community Mental Health Center," National Institute of Mental Health, Bethesda (Spring 1966) Project Officer, NIMH: Clyde Dorsett, Architect. Conducted by The Western Institute for Research in Mental Health, San Francisco.

2. "Community Health Center for Marin County, at San Rafael, California" (Kaplan and McLaughlin, Architects), *Architectural Design, Data and Cost; Architecture for the Community Mental Health Center* (Fall 1966) Project Officer, NIMH: Clyde H. Dorsett, Architect. Rice Design Fete III, conducted by the School of Architecture, Rice University, Houston, Texas.

III
Organization
and
Administration

EDITORS' INTRODUCTION

The development of a community mental health center calls for a new form of organizing mental health services which can be expressed through a variety of different organizational forms. As a result, a community is not generally able to use existing organizational structures for the development of a new center, but, at the same time, does not need to adhere to a rigid or prescribed format. Each community must create a community mental health center structure which is consistent with both the needs of the community and the resources available to meet these needs.

This organizational structure may involve the participation of only one or two agencies and, indeed, there are some community mental health centers which have been formed simply by the reorganization of a previously existing single agency. Typically, however, many different organizations are involved in the operation of a community mental health center with several different agencies providing the identifiable center services and other agencies contributing related or supporting programs.

As more and more communities have developed community mental health centers, a number of common organizational models have emerged. These have been found to be effective in bringing together the range of services and supports that are necessary for a comprehensive mental health program. The emerging models of mental health center organization are sufficiently varied and flexible that it seems possible for them to be adapted to the needs of many different communities.

At the same time, however, it should be noted that all of these different models of mental health center organization share several common things. One of these is the involvement of multiple agencies in the center's development. Even when one agency is responsible for the provision of the basic center services, a truly comprehensive program can be developed only if outside agencies and outside services are also involved. Another common theme in the organization of community mental health centers is a combination of public and private resources in the operation of center programs. Many centers combine services of publicly supported agencies with those of privately supported agencies to create a program which is comprehensive in scope and relevant to community needs.

Most organizational and administrative issues focus on the individual center and its program. However, there are also organizational issues which must be considered at an intercenter or multicenter level. A national organization of community mental health centers has now been established for the purpose of providing a common meeting ground for the discussion and resolution of problems facing all centers. Efforts are also now underway to develop organizations of the several centers which serve a single metropolitan area. The citywide association of centers is another important device for the resolution of common concerns.

6
William M. Bolman, M.D., *and*
William Goldman, M.D.

The San Francisco Westside Community Mental Health Center, Inc.: Development of a Mental Health Consortium of Private Agencies

There has been a growing trend nationwide for hospitals, social agencies, and heterogeneous programs to band together in new partnerships in order to provide comprehensive mental health services. As of January 1970, 85 percent of all federally funded community mental health centers were organized by two or more affiliating agencies. The legislation authorizing these centers mandated five essential services: inpatient, outpatient, partial hospitalization, twenty-four-hour emergency, consultation and education. Since few service providers have all of these components, this legislation provided fiscal incentives for collaboration among different mental health services. In some places the resulting partnership or association has been called a consortium. There are several possible types of consortium, including those between public services, between university-linked services, between private services or various admixtures of these. The purpose of this paper is to describe the early history of one consortium in the private sector.

BACKGROUND

The City and County of San Francisco contains five mental health catchment districts, each containing approximately 110,000 to 200,000 persons. The Westside district, which is typical of many central cities, contains an extraordinary combination of multiple agencies and multiple human problems. Within this geographic area reside most of the private hospitals with psychiatric programs and the social service agencies. It also has within it almost all of the halfway houses, free-standing psychiatric clinics, and many of the drug treatment programs in San Francisco. It encompasses diverse neighborhoods including Anglo-American, Japanese-American, black-American and hippie (the Haight/Ashbury) communities.

From the outset it was clear that the construction of a single, free-standing, public-operated community health center would not be appropriate in the Westside area. Such a facility would only further compound the duplication of existing services, widen the separation between public and private health sectors, and impair the tradition of community service by voluntary agencies. By late 1966, this was recognized by a number of key people in San Francisco in both the private agencies and city and state government. Consequently, these individuals were willing to subscribe to a private, voluntary, nonprofit consortium concept for provision of public services. However, their willingness alone would not have resulted in the development of a public-supported mental health consortium composed of private, nonprofit members.

The creation of a viable consortium also required the combination of financial support available through a federal community mental health center staffing grant; the preexistence of public mental health contracts for services by the city with private agencies in San Francisco through a state program providing 75 percent reimbursement by the state to the local community * (this formula was changed to 90 percent state reimbursement in 1969 †); the availability of Medicaid funds (Medi-Cal in California); the prevailing trend toward regional health planning; and the prolonged effective leadership provided by one of the Westside hospitals.

The initial phase was described as follows:

In reviewing the first year of development of the Westside Center, we saw a rather complex series of processes occurring simultaneously at various levels. It must be borne in mind that they varied considerably both with the individuals and the agencies involved. Regarding participation in the Westside Center, these processes included, in rough chronological order: (1) education; (2) reassurance as to aims and objectives; (3) wide involvement of key people holding responsible positions in the mental health agencies and programs; (4) the forming of the individuals involved into a group with the setting of preliminary goals and working through of long-standing doubts; (5) the gradual transformation of suspicion into trust, of unfamiliarity and ignorance into awareness and acceptance; (6) the clarification of potential gratifications in continued or further involvement and participation in the Center; (7) the growth of cooperative planning and sharing of program aspirations; (8) a shift from agency to Center considerations, and finally, (9) the beginning of identification with the concepts and objectives of the center.[1]

After these processes were under way, a number of concrete and often delicate questions were raised and negotiated. For example, was there a need for an independent corporate structure to receive all funds and administer the Center? Should all direct services be provided by subcontract with component agencies? Which services would be provided where? What new staff would be required to deliver such services? How would record-keeping systems be established for payment and bio-statistical reporting? What mechanisms would be needed for cooperation and integration of existing services and new program development? Would the small agencies be dominated by or even amalgamated by the larger ones? What would be the extent of community involvement? Who would have the power to design service priorities and to hire and fire personnel? If priority for service were given to Westside residents, how would this affect the identity and financial support of the sectarian

* Short-Doyle Act
† Lanterman-Petris-Short Act

74

agencies? Some of these issues are generic to the consortium model of service delivery and will be discussed below.

Without minimizing the importance of the service components or the many challenging and fascinating clinical problems that have emerged, it cannot be stated too strongly that *the clinical advantages of a consortium are entirely dependent upon policy, administration, and funding*. Although the interrelationship between clinical functioning, policy, administration and funding should be obvious, health professionals have usually tended to ignore or underestimate their importance. In the case of the Westside Center, it has been very clear that the consortium partnership would have deteriorated rapidly without constant attention to these variables. Therefore, this presentation will stress these three elements rather than the programmatic aspects of the Center.

POLICY

The Westside Center accepted the premises that health care was a right and not a privilege. This inevitably led to a new view of community participation in planning and programming for health care delivery. Today, community participation in this process is often discussed in terms of consumer participation. Although there have always been consumers in positions of power on boards of hospitals and health care agencies, the term consumer, as used today is a euphemism for the poor and/or the powerless. From the beginning of the Westside Project, the multiple agency and heterogeneous population characteristics of the Westside catchment area posed a serious and complicated challenge to any conventional decision-making structure. If the Center's policy was dominated by the professionals or the institutions, it was clear that the programmatic adaptions necessary to involve and effectively reach the black, Japanese, poor white, and hippie communities would not occur. On the other hand, it was impossible to conceive of a completely community-dominated program in an area with so many voluntary agencies with such a long history of institutional autonomy. Instead, a mechanism was required that would provide the community and the agencies broad representation while maintaining stable policy-making structures capable of flexibility and as free as possible from frozen bureaucratic hindrances. These considerations led to the creation of a double board structure.

The Center's Board of Directors is the fiscal agent and has the traditional policy-making role. It is composed of 30 people, one half representing each of the 15 constituent agencies, while the other half is elected by the Community Advisory Board. The Community Advisory Board, in turn, is elected by an annual community forum. The agency representatives consist of lay members of the Boards of Trustees of the agencies and the professional heads of their mental health services. However, such a structure does not guarantee effective representative policy-making. The creation of a working board requires recognition of several realities.

First, professional board members must take time out from pressing responsibilities to attend meetings or hide behind those responsibilities and delegate important board functions to lower level staff. Nonprofessional working people cannot take time off from work. Therefore, the time and place of important board or committee meetings is of great significance, literally and symbolically, if trust and cooperation is to develop. Agency lay board representatives are not accustomed to spending large amounts of time in a variety of agency board tasks. Nonagency community people are often more familiar with this.

Second, the policy issues themselves are extraordinarily knotty. They involve issues around which there are often divergent points of view. For example, what mixture of prevention, treatment, and rehabiliation programs is required to serve the needs of the psychiatric casualties in the community? Mental health professionals themselves differ over whether preventive programs are possible, whether hospitalization has a significant role, and what the goals of rehabilitation should be. The differences are even greater when one gets into the potential roles of the mental health center in job training, in social action, and in taking stands on political issues. It takes a great deal of staff time and support to enable the diverse board groups to maintain their commitment and work together to create a stable policy-making structure. There are unavoidable genuine stresses and conflicts inherent within such a structure. The critical point is that such conflicts are *necessary* if true cooperative relationships are to evolve. The agency representatives must be able to confront the community representatives genuinely and not avoid the natural disagreements that will and must arise. The new alliance's viability depends on working through real differences not in avoiding them.

For instance, it is possible to discuss and argue with urban consumer representatives, that is poor people, especially from minority groups, whether programs to reduce state hospitalization should have a higher priority than mental health career development (jobs) for poor people.

But it is more difficult to accept that this heretofore professional decision based on professional values might be overruled by the policy-making body within this new structure.

Some polarization between goals is therefore inevitable. On the one hand, there is the social action goal, interpreted by some as being implied by the word community. On the other hand, there is the goal of avoiding unnecessary state hospitalization and treating "mentally ill" persons close to home which is interpreted by many as the primary intent of the sponsoring legislation. The difficult task is melding the two in a program that can be committed to both ends, one that can affect the quality of life in the community to eventually prevent psychosocial dysfunction as well as to care for the casualties of the society. Whether this dual role can in fact be achieved by community mental health centers with present funding remains questionable.

Returning to our double board structure, the charge to the second board, the Community Advisory Board, was to assist in the identification of unmet needs, to serve as the conscience of the community, and to provide the mechanism for the formal input of community control to balance the control of the established institutions.

It is not easy to settle who speaks for the community. In the Westside, it was resolved pragmatically. After a year-long process of discussions with over eighty-five diverse community groups from tenant unions and neighborhood councils to long-entrenched agencies, a widely publicized Westwide Community Health Forum was held. Representatives of all of the known community groups were invited to join in the task of determining the future of the Westside Center through the process of electing the Community Advisory Board. This Board self-consciously represented the interests of four minority groups: the blacks, the Japanese, the hippies, and youth. Minority groups lacking explicit representation on the Community Advisory Board are the rich white and poor nonhippie white. The aged were involved at first through an elected representative who did not continue to participate, probably because of lack of staff time to work with this group.

The representatives of the Community Advisory Board, when mixed with the agency representatives to form the permanent Board of Directors, have provided a natural cross-section of the total population of the Westside. To date our experience with this type of community representation has gone beyond our expectation in helping to bring together for the first time the diverse groups within our catchment area. This has created an ongoing forum to allow the agency and community "antago-

77

nists" to learn that their differences are not simply those of power but also those of cross-cultural differences in the perception of mental health services.

The impression so far has been that the community people know perfectly well that they do not have the technical knowledge to tell the professionals how to do their job. Instead, they will press for the inclusion of minority professionals whom they feel they can trust and who will represent their interests in the institutions. The significance of these minority professionals in positions of power in the new programs cannot be underestimated in terms of its meaning to the minority communities. The fact that community representatives have neither the time nor the inclination to interfere in technical matters is as true as their intense wish to feel secure that their interests will be protected and that programs and therapeutic practices will not unwittingly violate their cultural values.

It would be naïve to ignore the additional fact that any new service program with a budget of over a million dollars a year also elicits a great deal of individual and group concern that as much of that money as possible remain in that community in the form of salaries and expenditures for supportive services. To put it more concisely, they want a piece of the action. This community mental health center program has become economically integrated into its community. As many services as possible are purchased directly from indigenous businesses.

It also behooves all mental health professionals to be knowledgeable about the ideas, values, attitudes, traditions, and behaviors that have emerged from minority communities. In the case of the Westside, this has meant knowing about the black experience particularly, but also includes knowing about the hippie and the Japanese subgroups.

Community control can be a powerful ally for mental health services. The urban disenfranchised are committed to *change*, which is the salient force needed today in our encrusted health care nonsystem. Haynes has recently written:

Professionals have been concerned that if the consumer is allowed to share in such decisions, he may not know where to draw the lines. In cases where the community has had a chance to participate, these fears have seldom been justified. When consumers are given an opportunity to share in making decisions, they will often find a new solution or accept old ones with greater grace.[2]

Even more cogently, he states:

Professionals have sometimes felt that consumers, especially poor consumers, could hardly be expected to communicate with health experts. Experience indicates that most of the inability is on the side of the professionals.

The following report by the Chairman of the Board of Directors to the third annual Westside Community Mental Health Forum was delivered in June 1970, and illustrates how active and effective this structure has been:

The Westside Center was the first community mental health center in the United States to have its Board of Directors composed of 50 percent elected community representatives before beginning services. The direction that the Board has taken in the past eighteen months has been clearly dominated by the needs expressed by these community representatives.

The following represent just a partial list of some of the actions taken by the Board in this period:

1. the inclusion of youth at the Board of Directors level;
2. the need for a comprehensive day care program for children of working mothers;
3. the need for a comprehensive drug treatment program as the first priority of the Westside community;
4. the involvement of community representatives at professional conferences;
5. the admission of seven new agencies to bring the consortium to a total of fifteen agencies;
6. the submission of an extensive grant for the comprehensive drug treatment program and support for community drug programs in the interim period, including securing funds from the United Bay Area Crusade and private foundations;
7. the development of a new student mental health service at San Francisco City College, and help with obtaining foundation grants as well as federal funds for that program;
8. the development of a grant for alternatives to hospitalization;
9. support for a variety of community needs, including the moratorium on testing of minority students in the San Francisco school district; support for transferring dependent and neglected children from the Juvenile Probation Department to the Department of Social Services; a call for a reordering of national priorities to increase support of health, education and welfare in response to the Cambodian crisis; and support of a separate San Francisco Department of Community Mental Health Services;
10. the development of new personnel practices for Westside funded positions by the Personnel Committee of the Board in order to collaborate with the agencies in hiring for these positions;
11. the development of a program committee to review and develop new programmatic ideas for the Westside Center;
12. the development of an ongoing internal fiscal auditing process for the Westside program for the Finance Committee.[3]

The *necessity* of community participation will undoubtedly be a central issue in health care delivery throughout the coming decade. Our reading of the trend in health services in urban areas is that the issue is not one of permissive community participation but rather one of planned community-consumer control. Unless the gap between needs and services diminishes, the continuing white suburban migration and shift in national priorities can only lead to ever more intense charges by urban Americans, minority or otherwise, of irrelevancy at best and racism at worst.

ADMINISTRATION

There appear to be at least six essential administrative activities necessary for the maintenance of a community mental health center. These are executive, fiscal and bookkeeping, secretarial and clerical, communications and liaison, research and evaluation, and program development. In the Westside consortium the number and complexity of linkages, alliances and interfaces between fifteen agencies, multiple communities, a variety of clinical services in existence or planned, and city, state, and federal mental health authorities have presented a continuing and ever-shifting array of opportunities and problems. Other centers planning to use consortium arrangements should anticipate a very broad range of administrative needs if they wish to avoid the pitfalls of inadequate staffing and inappropriate role demands, particularly with the centralization of many complex fiscal relationships and multiple interagency contracts. It is dangerous to underestimate the critical need for a strong and competent administrative team.

This organization must focus on the ability to raise and supervise money, to recruit and utilize new personnel, and to acquire and transmit needed information. These tasks are difficult in a traditional organizational structure, especially when the goals are as diffuse as in community mental health. When one adds to this a consortium of autonomous member organizations, each with its own structure, traditions and objectives, the task of coherent administration becomes even more trying. Should the management of money, personnel or information in any part of the system be neglected, the power to maintain the cohesion of the organization rapidly diminishes.

The problem does not end here. The commitment to develop and maintain stable links to the total community does not mean that one can simply adopt a stance of "acceptance" and "liberalism." Community ties depend upon knowledge, respect, joint effort, and a host of similar qualities that require new activities, dislocations of routines, conflict and prolonged divergences in points of view. These efforts can be very rewarding programmatically, both in terms of community support for funding and in increased utilization of relevant services, but they can have even more far-reaching effects. This new alliance of consumer and provider can *greatly* influence the movement of the center's entire mental health system toward new linkages with training programs, jobs, day care, housing, physical health services, delinquency prevention, policy-community relations and many similar related areas. Appreciation of this fact leads to the need for prolonged and skillful efforts to strengthen and unify these new alliances. Strong links between administration and community can validate the term "community" in community mental health centers and make the term "mental health" more than a euphemism. It must be stressed again, however, that the task requires time, openness, strength, patience, flexibility, imagination, and conviction regarding its worth. In this context, specific staffing and role assignments are crucial, especially in highly visible center positions and the points of maximal community-clinical contact. The history of community programs documents that this has become today's high-risk interface in health care delivery.

In this pluralistic system with a heterogeneity of agencies, disciplines, fiscal arrangements, schools of thought and operational styles, another vital administrative task was the creation of new intrasystem alliances among the mental health professionals. A major effort was expended to break down the barrier to treatment that had traditionally existed through each agency's idiosyncratic eligibility procedures. The Westside community had never offered twenty-four-hour emergency service, a day treatment center, organized consultation and education services, or inpatient services for public patients. There did exist extensive outpatient services throughout the consortium, and three small private inpatient units at Mt. Zion, Pacific-Presbyterian, and St. Mary's Hospitals. These institutions made a major commitment to the Westside by allocating over 50 percent of their inpatient beds to the new community program. Because of its central location, it was agreed that the most logical place to house the new twenty-four-hour walk-in psychiatric emergency service was at Mt. Zion Hospital which could best staff this kind of program. The major breakthrough came when all three inpatient units agreed that all patients to be admitted would be funneled first through this single emergency and crisis intervention service, or at least cleared through it with no duplicate evaluation process for hospitalization. This radical change in admission procedures was also extended to the new Day Treatment Center at Pacific-Presbyterian Hospital. Each patient referred from one of the consortium agencies would have to be accepted in the program. A commitment was also made by the consortium agencies to shift their priorities for services in their preexisting programs so that Westside residents received first priority for care regardless of whether there was a new contract for a new service. In addition, in 1969, under the aegis of the three member family service agencies, a new Westside Social Services Agency was incorporated to develop new aftercare and other family and community programs.

Much of this was achieved by significant shifts in philosophy in the consortium agencies toward reduction in length of hospital stay, emphasis on alternatives to hospitalization, crisis intervention, home visiting and aftercare. Perhaps more importantly, however, this was coupled with new views of relevance which meant the suspension of parochial professional inclinations in favor of the needs of the community as seen by the community.

Before concluding this section on administrative issues in a private sector consortium, it is important to mention the relationships with public funding and regulatory authorities. For most areas this will involve agencies of the local, state, and federal governments. For some it may include regional planning or regulatory groups. Some of these issues will be discussed in the section on funding, but some will be mentioned here as they require rather continuous administrative response if the community mental health center (consortium or otherwise) is to flourish.

First, a good deal of attention must be paid to the requirements that any publicly funded organization must follow. These requirements are written into the applicable local, state, and federal laws or contracts. The ability to keep abreast of existing and forthcoming legislation and regulations is essential. Most funding sources require prodigious applications for public support. Hence, knowledge of mental health grant support sources and skill at grant writing is extremely valuable. Today, many local, state, and federal agencies offer experienced consultation in these fields.

Secondly, attention should be paid to the sphere of communication between the private and public agencies to avoid competitiveness which can impair effective relationships. In many areas, this involves the long-standing antagonism between the private and public sectors. The private sector boasts "quality services" (for the few), and the public sector boasts "quantitative services" (for the many). Left to itself, this conflict can effectively polarize these groups which should function in a working alliance and obscure their major areas of common purpose and opportunity for complementary effort.

It gradually became recognized that effective administrative linkages would require creating a more elaborate central administrative organization.

As new central office positions were created, it became apparent that this organizational structure may have a proclivity for creating a new third force, beyond the professionals and the community, composed of the central administrative and research staff. This group, having few prior links with the agencies and not being designated in any formal way as representatives of the community, tends to develop its own semi-autonomous identity and new alliances. Ideally, these relate to the consortium as a system. The central office staff should serve the many intermediate and system-maintaining roles that exist in such a complex organization. On the other hand, the inevitable uncertainty, ambiguity, and multiple goals of urban mental health can also lead to inappropriate alliances with individual agencies, service elements or community groups which further complicate the creation of policy and its implementation through the formal board structure. This is a new and as yet undescribed aspect of the functions of a consortium that will require ongoing evaluation in order to avoid stifling the important contributions of this group without allowing them precedence in the system.

To summarize this section briefly, we wish to stress the need in planning a consortium model in the private sector to balance the operational advantages against the added administrative complexity. The advantages include the maximum use of multiple existing facilities, freedom from civil service bureaucracy, opportunity for flexibility, and rapid response in program development. The problems relate to the absence of prior experience with this kind of partnership, its potential for fragmentation and the absence of reserve capital. In an excellent text on administration, Drucker observes, "The larger the organization, the more time will be needed just to keep the organization together and running rather than to make it function and produce." [4] Though it was intended at the outset that the Westside consortium be a "center without walls" and not another new superagency, we find that some new hybrid seems inevitable.

FUNDING

The third basic aspect of the support and maintenance of clinical mental health services is funding. It is of equal, if not overriding, importance to policy and administration. If the center's development is all of a piece, it is closely linked to both. In other words, the sources and distribution of funds are inseparable from policy-making (money is power) and the accounting for program income and expenditures is equally inseparable from administration (program follows money).

We believe that a center that develops from a base of community organization with local financial support is on the soundest footing. Clearly it will survive longer and stronger given the current vicissitudes of government support. This in no way minimizes the fact that only the Federal Government has sufficient funds to adequately underwrite new programs.

In the case of Westside, both policy and funding developed together initially. On the policy side, there were extensive discussions among service providers about who would provide what services at the same time that active community involvement was being developed. On the administrative side, the National Institute of Mental Health staffing grant was being prepared at the same time that negotiations with city and state mental health authorities were being advanced. Once the NIMH staffing grant and the city and state funds were obtained, the full Board of Directors functioning, and operations begun on January 1, 1969, this parallel development of funding, policy and administration was severely stressed. We had underestimated how large and complex the operations would become and how rapidly demand would materialize and services expand.

We felt that it was essential that a new public program be financed by public dollars as a public commitment and that the whole area of mental health and of community care was a public responsibility. However, in urban areas generally the costs of the delivery of health services are higher, and San Francisco is probably the third most expensive place to live in the United States. Hence, the idea that the public dollar could completely cover such a new program would have been naïve and unlikely. Therefore, the development of all potential sources of income became critical. This was related not only to the endurance of the essential elements of the program, but also to the expansion necessary to meet unfilled needs and to maintain the momentum required to fulfill the multiple mandates to the community mental health center mentioned earlier.

The use of multiple sources proved to be both a strength and a problem. The problem was the need for sophisticated knowledge and skill in obtaining and managing so many different kinds of money. For example, at present we need a full-time accountant and full-time bookkeeper to maintain five different sets of books, each requiring somewhat different management.

One mechanism that helps to assure the fullest possible use of available funds has been included in the contracts with every agency. This is the requirement that all other sources be billed prior to billing Westside. Our billing forms show the total costs for services rendered, minus deductions for the amounts collected from patient fees, private insurance, Medicaid, Medicare, and NIMH staffing grant support. The net cost is then paid from our annual city-state (Short-Doyle) appropriation.

This type of fiscal accounting appears to work well for our consortium structure, but we continue to encounter problems of internal monitoring of the system. For example, we have no systematic way of knowing how efficiently the consortium members are collecting patient fees, Medicaid, and so forth. We have had indications that, in some instances, agencies billed Westside for services rendered rather than pursue the other sources requiring more clerical effort.

When we look at the kind of fiscal supports needed to really make the center viable and able to expand clinical services, the areas of Medicaid and insurance coverage emerge as central. We were in a very advantageous position because this center was developed in the private sector. Our ties with private hospitals as established vendors already recognized by the Medicaid program was crucial for our inpatient, emergency, and day care programs. This probably has allowed us our greatest area of expansion.

Another potential source of funds that needs special attention is philanthropic and foundation support. This can be especially useful in providing seed money or partial support for developing innovative and experimental programs. The 1969 tax reforms may further the availability of these funds. Of perhaps greater importance is the increasing criticism in many cities over the distribution of funds raised by drives such as the Red Feather (United Fund, United Crusade, and so forth). Because these philanthropic efforts emerged in response to the needs of social agencies at a previous time, they are now generally out of touch with present urban problems and emergent community needs. In some cities the criticism from poor and minority communities has led to a slight shift in policy toward the newer needs. For instance, in the Westside catchment area, one of the most acute was the rapid rise of heroin addiction. Although Westside member agencies (Reality House West and Walden House) possessed special interest and expertise in drug problems, they could not meet the overwhelming clinical demands. Neither had enough community stature or longevity to have qualified for any stable public or private support. Fortunately, the fact that these new groups were included with established helping agencies in a recognized administrative unit has made it possible to attract support from the United Bay Area Crusade as well as obtain a small federal contract under the Narcotic Addict Rehabilitation Act.

Another very important fiscal area is that of patient payments, a tradition with sound roots in clinical practice. We believe it is significant for a patient to pay for the service he gets, whether the bill is fifty cents or fifty dollars. There is still some difficulty in breaking through the old traditions of agencies who do not really expect patients to pay—a paternalistic viewpoint which sees patients as just being taken care of rather than being engaged as individuals in their own care via payment.

Finally, although it is not a direct source of funds, we should mention that one of the underlying motives of this private sector consortium was to demonstrate that a center could develop the maximum use of existing programs and in fact would have long-range economies because there were ready-made facilities. We did not need construction. We also hoped to show that ready-made administrative structures precluded the need for a new superagency and might avoid the inefficiencies of bureaucratization.

We find that the most critical aspect of the relationship between funding and administration involves the development of working systems for clinical and fiscal accountability as applied to a consortium of private hospitals and agencies. We agreed that the component institutions should be paid at cost for services rendered. Funding sources should have assurance that their dollars are being well spent and properly monitored. Patients should experience the benefit of coordinated mental health services in this setting. It became necessary therefore to centralize a great deal of information regarding billing and biostatistics in the Westside central administrative office.

In setting up the billing procedures we had to establish mechanisms able to account for multiple sources of income. After establishing such a complex system, however, it turned out to be a full-time job for several people. The fiscal offices of the agencies did not gear up or get sufficient administrative direction to meet the billing and bookkeeping demands that the new and rapidly expanding services placed on them. Despite repeated meetings on procedures, participating members either heard different things or did not understand their immediate relevance. It became clear that the clerical and accounting personnel did not identify with these new programs, which they did not see as integrated parts of their agency. It was only when withholding funds was threatened that sufficient attention began to be paid to shared fiscal problems. Constant policing of this system was necessary until the remaining problems were worked out. The final step that we have not yet completed is that of the formal periodic review of the system to endure that methods do not take precedence over goals. Reducing state hospitalization is not an end in itself, either clinically or fiscally. It should not be confused with the goal of appropriate community care for the total population.

Although closely tied to the billing process, the collection of biostatistical service data is partly separate and requires a great deal of attention. The problem involved with this is generic to any consortium delivery system, especially with public contracts, and there are various possible solutions. One central problem is that each component member of the center counts patients as admissions and discharges, whereas the center counts them as transfers whenever a patient moves within the system from agency to agency for additional care. For example, a patient can be admitted as a Westside Community Mental Health Center patient simply by coming once to the twenty-four-hour walk-in crisis clinic located at Mt. Zion Hospital. Should he be admitted to inpatient care, he goes to whatever hospital has a bed available, for instance at St. Mary's Hospital. Following inpatient care the person may need a halfway house situation, Conard House for instance, and concomitant visits to the Day Treatment Center at Pacific-Presbyterian Medical Center. Following this the patient is discharged. Of the four admissions and four discharges, only the entrance and exit ones should be reported regarding the patient's relationship to the center. The others are to be treated as transfers from one service component to the other. To date we have worked out only the simple mechanics of this process. We are now attempting to see to what degree transfer from one component to another carries with it both the substantive and administrative information that is relevant to the programmatic concepts implied in the terms comprehensive services, continuity of care, and coordinated services.

This step requires an entirely different set of reports than those transmitting billing and epidemiological data. Rather than focusing on admissions and discharges, it looks at the operational reality of the transfer and referral system. Clearly, if a consortium of separate service providers is to prove functional, quantitative information is needed about the outcome of each referral or transfer, the number of patients in multiple treatment arrangements, the number of chronic repeating emergencies, and the frequency of need for referral outside the network.

This monitoring and evaluation of the efficiency and quality of our system was regarded as of such central importance that during the planning phase a specific evaluation research component was included. From this planning, a computer based transactional reporting system has emerged and we are presently concluding a pilot study to "de-bug" the system.

Both out of sensitivity to the concerns of the minority community that it cease being the object of external research projects, and out of concern with demonstrating that a consortium partnership can be a useful model of mental health care delivery, we have focused on the delivery system rather than its clients in our research efforts. One of the difficulties in operationalizing this crucial aspect of the program has been the shortage of well trained professionals skilled in program evaluation research. This fact, coupled with the wariness and lack of commitment to this aspect of the program on the part of clinicians, agencies, and the community, has retarded this process considerably.

CONCLUSION

It is still too soon to draw any conclusions from the Westside Community Mental Health Center's one and a half years development. It should be remembered that the entire history of federally funded community mental health centers is only of five years duration, and only modest conclusions are possible. We would stress that this Center was structured at the outset to achieve the best possible fit with the service and population characteristics of an arbitrary geographic sector. We would also emphasize that the resulting fifteen member, two board, multiple-funded consortium is a very complex system (reflecting the complex nature of community mental health generally), and that the Center will continue to evolve as it attempts to become a valued and lasting community institution.

NOTES

1. W. Goldman, Personal Communication, 1969.
2. M. A. Haynes, "Professionals and the Community Confront Change," *American Journal of Public Health*, 60(March 1970): 519–523.
3. C. J. Matthew, mimeo., 1970.
4. P. Drucker, *The Effective Executive*, New York: Harper and Row, 1967.

7

Chester W. Grochola, M.A.

The Community Mental Health Center
and the General Hospital

Meadowbrook Hospital is the county hospital for the approximately two million residents of Nassau County (New York). Prior to and since the opening of the community mental health center, the hospital has had an active Department of Psychiatry which has operated in the mainstream of hospital psychiatry utilizing classical psychiatric techniques and procedures for implementing patient care.

In 1967, at the request and with the encouragement of the Director of the Nassau County Mental Health Board, the hospital prepared an application for a National Institute of Mental Health staffing grant to begin a community health center in a catchment area with just under 200,000 residents.

Because of the urgent need for increased mental health services, the center was opened (after the approval of the application) while planning was still in progress. This led to early problems stemming from the absence of clear definitions pertaining to the administrative relationships between the community mental health center and the general hospital. Several examples will illustrate the nature of these difficulties and suggest certain important steps which should be undertaken to insure the successful operation of a community mental health center which is administratively tied to a general hospital.

STAFFING

All staff appointments to the community mental health center required the approval of the Nassau County Civil Service Commission. Consequently, enormous paper work resulted and several crucial appointments were delayed for many months. For example, the Director was not officially approved until four months after his initial appointment. If this project had not had a high priority because of its use of federal funds, the amount of time necessary to organize the staff might have been longer.

Whenever possible, to circumvent this problem, staff for the center was obtained from the existing staff of the general hospital. Personnel were sought from the Departments of Psychiatry, Psychology, Social Work, Nursing, Occupational Therapy, and Recreation. Some assignments to the community mental health center's staff were made arbitrarily to avoid further delay which might have resulted in the loss of a portion of the available federal funds. As a result, some potential staff members felt that the community mental health center was a dumping ground for "bad" staff.

ADMINISTRATION

To counteract any image of the community mental health center as a stepchild of the Department of Psychiatry, the center was organized as an independent operation with its Director responsible, like the Department Chairman, to the Hospital Superintendent. In addition to increasing the center's status, this step enabled it to develop a nontraditional and innovative approach to the delivery of mental health services. By encouraging the testing of new approaches for the solutions of old problems, negative feelings, present in those staff members assigned to the center, practically disappeared. These developments have placed the community mental health center in a favorable position with regard to staff recruitment.

The solution of one problem can lead, however, to other problems. Although the community mental health center Director has only one immediate superior, the Hospital Superintendent, other members of the center staff such as social workers, nurses, psychologists, and occupational therapists, have two superiors: the center Director and the Director of their respective hospital departments. If effective cooperative arrangements with each of these departments are not developed and maintained by the center, conflicts can occur which will undermine communication. Recognizing in advance the possibility of this problem arising enabled us to deal with it by having regular meetings between the community mental health center Director and each of the department chiefs in addition to those staff meetings which each department holds for its own staff. These meetings have been used for the purpose of exchanging information about the center program and providing feedback concerning staff reactions to it.

PURCHASING PROCEDURES

Another example of an early administrative difficulty, resulting from deficient planning, was in the area of purchasing procedures. We discovered very early that, according to hospital policy, equipment needed for center activities could only be ordered at certain times of the year. For example, during the first spring of the center's operation, a plan of the day hospital patients to build a garden as a part of their milieu treatment was almost dropped when it was discovered that the necessary equipment could only be ordered in January. This resulted in a considerable delay in the initiation of an important therapeutic activity and is a good example of the type of issue which can be easily overlooked during the development of administrative arrangements between the center and the general hospital.

THE USE OF SPACE

When a community mental health center is established in a general hospital setting, the allocation of space can also be a critical issue. The decision to begin a community mental health center did include a request for funds to construct new facilities. However, none of the existing facilities had been designed for use by a community mental health center and did not foster the mental health center concept. Inpatient wards were locked and provided little space for recreational activities while outpatient areas were small. Consequently, some patient rooms were eliminated to obtain space for a day room and the second floor of an old employee dormitory was converted to an outpatient department. This lack of adequate facilities was a negative factor in our attempt to improve staff morale and cohesiveness.

ADVANTAGES

Each of these examples illustrates a specific and important aspect of the difficulties which can arise during the development of a community mental health center program in a general hospital. Nevertheless, there are several advantages to this administrative arrangement in comparison to the independently operating community mental health center.

Personnel records of center employees are kept by the various parent departments. Burdensome administrative activities such as computing sick leave and vacation time are performed for the center enabling center personnel to direct more attention toward the delivery of mental health care to the catchment area.

Furthermore, all routine support services (such as purchasing, housekeeping, building maintenance, and dietary services) are provided by the hospital. Although accurate cost accounting figures are not available, the provision of these services by the general hospital should reduce the center's operating budget and help to avoid the duplication of many personnel and purchasing procedures. Consequently, a greater percentage of expenditures is available for direct patient services.

The administrative link between the community health center and the general hospital can also facilitate the movement of patients who need help into the mental health delivery system. Even in the 1970's, there are many who are reluctant to seek help for emotional problems in a clearly identified independent mental health facility. Coming to a general hospital, in our opinion, can be a less stigmatizing or traumatic experience from the patient's view than seeking help at an independent mental health center.

This close association between the two organizations also allows easy access to the many medically related facilities in the general hospital. Specialized services such as electrocardiography, electroencephalography, and roentgenology are readily available and the presence of consultants from all medical specialties will strengthen the center's ability to care for the total patient. Furthermore, with the growing use of psychotropic drugs, the importance of having a general laboratory available to the community mental health center cannot be minimized. All of these services help to reassure both staff and patient and provide comprehensive care.

When an accident occurs, as can easily happen in a day hospital equipped with tools and machinery for use in occupational therapy and prevocational training programs, it can be immediately handled in the emergency room of the general hospital. Or, if a psychiatric inpatient develops a physical illness, treatment can often be provided in the psychiatric setting and a transfer to a general hospital, which could be an additional emotional stress for the patient, is not necessary.

Consequently, the close relationship between the general hospital and the center offers many advantages which overcome those disadvantages resulting from enlarging the bureaucracy within which the community mental health center must operate.

Two other important aspects of this administration relationship should be noted. Some of our nonmedical house staff and those psychiatrists whose education and training has been heavily weighted on the side of their specialty feel that our close medical affiliation does not contribute significantly to the community mental health center program. Nevertheless, they have often been relieved and reassured during an acute medical crisis to find the general hospital and its facilities so readily available.

The community mental health center has also had an important effect on the general hospital's Department of Psychiatry. Since the inception of the community mental health center program, the department has become less traditional in its treatment orientation and has, for example, started its own day hospital to serve residents from other parts of the county.

In summary, the association of the community mental health center with a general hospital offers numerous advantages which can be maximized if certain important basic principles, derived from our experience, are kept in mind both before and after the initiation of center services.

1. To function adequately within a general hospital, the community mental health center must be an independent organization clearly identified as separate from the general hospital's Department of Psychiatry. Without this status, it will be difficult for the community mental health center to achieve visability to the residents of the catchment area and difficulties in staff recruitment and the provision of appropriate facilities and services will persist.

2. When a community mental health center is located within a general hospital, it must often depend on other departments for personnel services. Therefore, it is extremely critical that careful agreements are formulated between the center and these departments. They should be in writing to minimize later disagreements and breakdown in communication.

3. Establishing communication between the heads of these departments and the center director is crucial. An executive committee should be organized composed of the chiefs from all of the professional and administrative disciplines concerned with the center's operation. At the Meadowbrook Community Mental Health Center, this executive committee meets weekly to discuss programmatic concepts and the center's business. Detailed information concerning the performance of each division as related to the community mental health center's activities is

shared. Feedback of feelings and attitudes regarding the center is also obtained.

4. A community mental health center associated with a general hospital Department of Psychiatry should develop new facilities which will distinguish the center from other facilities which have been tied to more traditional concepts of mental health care delivery. This can be accomplished without jeopardizing the administrative relationship with the general hospital.

This discussion emphasizes the need for the most careful planning prior to the inception of a community mental health center program within a general hospital. Unfortunately, knowledge of the complexities of this situation is not as great when the program is begun as it is later. Any party interested in developing a community mental health center within a general hospital should give careful attention to these organizational problems early if the center's program is to grow.

8
Clifford J. Bodarky, ED.D., *and*
Van Buren O. Hammett, M.D.

The Community Mental Health Center
and Academic Psychiatry

The authors of this paper have labored to develop a somewhat unique mental health center administrative system by insisting on its integration, from the start, with a traditional department of psychiatry. Recognizing that the department of psychiatry represented a system with a focus on training and research, the opportunity to add an impressive dimension of psychiatric community service was welcome.

This paper will describe certain features of the process of developing a program of community mental health intimately related to an academic department of psychiatry. There are many questions about the relationship of community psychiatry to academic psychiatry, most of which are as yet unsettled and have inspired a good deal of writing and far greater amount of discussion. How close should the relationship be between the academic department and the community health center and its activities? The community program emphasizes service; how acceptable is this to the department with its traditional emphasis upon education and research? Can the department provide service in greatly augmented quantity without compromising its standards of quality? If the community program emphasizes decentralization—movement away from the complex medical center out into the medically naïve community; will the department and its parent institution look with favor upon this? The community program proposes to develop new categories of personnel which are for the most part, less extensively educated and trained; should an academic department countenance such "dilution?" These are some of the questions and psychiatrists are by no means in agreement as to the answers. This communication is intended as a specific contribution to this dialectic.

The prevailing attitude within academic psychiatry appears to be characterized by a wariness towards community mental health center programs. This is reflected in the literature, but is more clearly evident in vocal communications, whether in discussions at meetings or in informal conversation. For various reasons, academicians clearly regard community psychiatry with caution and some measure of distrust which can be summed up as a fear that it will dilute and downgrade psychiatry's hard won position in medicine. This attitude is summarized in the statement of a colleague: "To preserve the integrity of academic psychiatry it is necessary that it be divorced from community mental health." (Reflecting this attitude is the fact that at the present time fewer than 25 percent of academic departments of psychiatry are operating community mental health programs in any state of relatedness, intimate or aloof.)

Presumably in consequence of this prevailing attitude, among those department-related programs which do exist, the typical model is characterized by a tendency to separate the academic departmental structure and the community mental health program. The latter is regarded as a service function more or less unrelated to the teaching and research goals of the department, with different personnel, different facilities, different schedules and, indeed, very little in common.

An alternative model is possible, however, which has the objective of bringing the academic department and the community program into the closest possible relationship. In this model the community program is not regarded as a necessary service function separate from the department; it is looked upon as an essential part of the basic structure.

The traditional concept of the university as an institution concerned only with the pursuit of knowledge (research) and its transmission (education) has become anachronistic. The modern university cannot in good conscience remain aloof from the everyday concerns of society and

95

its needs for service, nor can the medical school's department of psychiatry. The effective rendering of sophisticated services is as much a knowledgeable thing as many other university pursuits.

The basic theoretical principles of community psychiatry are essential components of the teaching program if the department is to train medical students and residents to provide the most effective management for their future patients. Continuity of care, the provision of complete care within the home community, and the amelioration of stigmatization and rejection by the family and neighborhood are cardinal principles of community psychiatry; they are also the most effective deterrents of institutional neurosis, chronicity, and the social breakdown syndrome. Furthermore, considerations of ego development and function support the validity of community psychiatry principles as essential components of good psychiatric management.[1]

The introduction of a vigorous program of community psychiatry to an academic department oriented to traditional concepts is not an easy process.[2] The amount of resulting friction and conflict is directly proportional to the degree of ambivalence in the minds of the departmental chairman and the director of the community program; the former must really be convinced about community psychiatry and the latter needs conviction about the importance of training and research. Both must feel and be able to transmit to the staff the commitment to a Gestalt triad of service, training and research, as a sum which is indeed different and richer than any of its component parts. O'Connor has pointed out that the attitude of the leadership largely determines whether the new enterprise is seen as the intrusion of a foreign body into the system or the painful but natural growth of a dynamic department.[3]

In the summer of 1966, the Department of Psychiatry of the Hahnemann Medical College and Hospital submitted its application to the federal and state mental health authorities for the funds to develop a community mental health center. In the development of the project application certain professional policies were promulgated and two have become the practical underpinnings of this effort.

The first was, and continues to be, the emphasis on building sufficient clinical capacity to treat the psychiatric casualties of the catchment area.

The second was, and continues to be, the insistence on integrating the services of the community mental health center with the customary training and research functions of a department of psychiatry.

The first functional premise, to treat the psychiatric casualty, was responsive to the belief that the community mental health center had a public charge to treat the historically unattended, socioeconomically deprived victims of mental illness. The relationship of poverty, slums, and social injustice to personal disorganization is well documented. Indeed, the Hahnemann catchment area is characterized by the highest priority of need for mental health services throughout the State of Pennsylvania, based on indices which purport to represent social and familial breakdown. The victims of these complex social and personally destructive forces may be compared to the wounded and fallen battlefield casualties; a startling analogy when one remembers that in the summer of 1964, soldiers, tanks, and street fighting in the catchment area created more than an illusion of war.

It may be safely assumed that maximum timely help is not being offered by taking a public address system to a battlefield and encouraging the wounded to write to their congressmen. If one has the training and skill to bind the wounds, that should be first. Those thousands of residents who have received prompt and high quality treatment since the inception of this program would have been without attention if this clinical capacity were absent. Most of them were in no shape to challenge the power structure or argue for their rights.

The central concern of this mental health program has been the development of high quality and quantity services. One supposition was that a better job could be done by starting with familiar skills and experience. Therefore, many of the Center's treatment modalities are considered traditional. "Traditional" has become an embarrassing word and "innovative" is the latest shibboleth. The authors are troubled by the credulity with which any proclaimed innovation seems likely to be met. There are mediocre and asinine efforts at innovation just as there are tired and nonsensical traditions.

The availability of immediate and high quality psychiatric attention to the residents of a large and impoverished geographic area is a tradition worth establishing and is effectively innovative. During the period July 1968 through June 1969, almost 4,000 new patients were admitted to all services, with 1,729 continuing in treatment of one type or another on June 30, 1969; representing a 77 percent increase in the quantity of patient care over the previous twelve months.

The attainment of the second goal has been established: expanded training and research programs based on the community mental health center's services.

In June 1967, six psychiatric residents were enrolled in the National Institute of Mental Health accredited three-year basic psychiatry training program, and four psychiatric residents were in the accredited two-year child psychiatry training. In June 1969, there were seventeen psychiatry residents in basic psychiatry, and eight in child psychiatry, an increase from ten to twenty-five psychiatric residents in two years.

In June 1967, eight senior medical students took electives in psychiatry; in June 1969, there were thirteen. During the summer of 1967, eight students were enrolled in the summer fellowship program; in June 1969, there were twenty-three with more than half directly assigned and located in the community.

There are additional and comparable increases in education and training for mental health personnel. By June 1969, there were 118 nonpsychiatric physicians enrolled in thirteen postgraduate courses. Nine art therapy students had been graduated and twenty new students were entering the training program. Eleven ministers were being trained in pastoral counseling while thirteen students who were candidates for the Associate Degree in Mental Health Work at the Community College of Philadelphia had their practicum supervised by departmental faculty and staff.

In June 1967, there were fourteen research programs underway in the department; in June 1969, there were fifty. There were forty-five publications by eighteen personnel of the department for the year ending June 1967, and seventy-two by twenty-four researchers for the year ending June 1969. The encouragement of the research orientation is pervasive with the employment of researchers a matter of prime interest.

This paper has described the theoretical bases and the realistic experience of the development of a community mental health center as an integrated system of service, training and research, within a department of psychiatry. This system has emphasized the development of an impressive array of clinical services, based on the conviction that it was, and is, important to treat the mentally disabled. The authors are the Chairman and the Executive Director of the Department of Psychiatry of the Hahnemann Medical College and Hospital, and they fulfill similar responsibilities in the Hahnemann Community Mental Health Center. This is really only one job for each, as the concerns and functions are inseparable in one mental health system.

NOTES

1. A. R. Foley, and D. S. Sanders, "Theoretical Considerations for the Development of the Community Mental Health Center Concept," *American Journal of Psychiatry*, 122(March 1966): 985–990.

2. M. Rosenbaum, and I. Zwerling, "Impact of Social Psychiatry," *Archives of General Psychiatry,* 11(1964): 31–39.

3. J. F. O'Connor, quoted in *The Medical School and the Community Mental Health Center,* Public Health Service Publication No. 1858, 30(1967).

---

9   *William T. Paynter,* M.D., *and*
                           Raymond J. Dembinski, ED.D.

The Development of the Model Cities—Community
Health Center Health Care Delivery System

THE DEVELOPMENT OF THE COMPREHENSIVE
MENTAL HEALTH CENTER

The Community Mental Health Center at Marion County General Hospital is an integrated part of a 960 bed public hospital, located in the inner city area of Indianapolis. The hospital serves a population of approximately 850,000 people. The hospital administration decided in 1963 to develop a community mental health center in conjunction with an overall program of hospital expansion. A new psychiatric section was planned to provide ninety-four inpatient beds and an outpatient clinic. The Community Mental Health Center was designed to function in a five-story facility which is physically attached to the hospital. A federal construction grant was received in 1966 and the building program was completed in May of 1969. Prior to receipt of the construction award, a staffing grant proposal was submitted and approved. It was thus possible to set the starting date for the center's operation as February 1, 1969.

The decision was made to operate the entire ninety-four bed unit as if it were all a comprehensive community mental health center. This strategy satisfied the need to provide services external to the federal catchment area as well as fulfilling commitments to the catchment area. The designated catchment area had a population of 230,000 people, most of whom were disadvantaged persons living in the inner city. The hospital, however, had traditionally supplied limited psychiatric services for indigent persons throughout the entire county. Accordingly, it was decided to operate the program through four staff teams, each of which would be responsible both for patients in the catchment area and for others outside it as well. The territory was divided in such a way that each team served a quadrant of the county.

The physical plant of the center provided four separate wards of approximately twenty-three beds each. The staff, divided into four teams, provided each section with a full-time staff psychiatrist, approximately four psychiatric nurses, four psychiatric social workers, and supporting psychiatric technicians. (The administrative, educational, research, and psychological staff provided centralized supportive services for all four teams.) Requests for service were assigned to the appropriate team on the basis of identification by census tract. This plan provided continuity of care through all areas of the center's services and it made it possible for continuity to be maintained should additional service be requested at a future date.

It should be noted that this arrangement placed the center's physical, administrative, and fiscal operations directly related to the parent public hospital. The public hospital also provided services in the areas of medicine, surgery, pathology and the like.

DEVELOPMENT OF THE MODEL CITIES
HEALTH PROGRAM

Initial development of a proposal for a Model Cities planning grant was undertaken during 1968. The planning grant was implemented in March of 1969, one month after the opening of the Mental Health Center. During the planning year, the General Hospital and its parent corporation, the Health and Hospital Corporation of Marion County, provided the Model Cities program organizers with resource people, planners, and technical advisors. One of the particular problems during the planning year arose from reluctance on the part of the Model Cities area residents to accept the Health and Hospital Corporation and General Hospital as the prime contractor for health services. There was historically a general feeling of dissatisfaction with the public hospital's health care delivery system on the part of the neighborhood residents.

During the planning year, the Community Mental Health Center staff was not directly involved with the Model Cities group. The negotiations with the Model Cities organization were conducted by the General Hospital and its parent Health and Hospital Corporation. The center staff, meanwhile, directed its energies toward inservice training programs. The center experimented with a variety of methods to enhance efficiency in managing the large numbers of patients already enrolled in its programs and entering its new facility. Much of the center's patient population was from the Model Cities demonstration area. The contact with this population permitted the center staff to learn more about the nature of the problems prevalent in the target area. Pilot projects were designed and implemented both to provide service in this area as well as to serve as a laboratory for future plans and programs.

In April of 1970, the Model Cities plan was finalized and submitted for review and approval. At this same time also, the original temporary Model Cities staff was replaced in its entirety. The new Model Cities staff arrived in the city early in June of 1970. They performed a rapid survey of the city's resources and the progress in planning that had been accomplished up to that time.

It was at this stage that the Community Mental Health Center became directly involved with the Model Cities program. The center staff was contacted by the new Model Cities staff and informed that there were critical deadlines, approximately one month away, necessitating an entire revision of the planning grant. The Model Cities staff had many specific questions about the center and its programs. The major focus of these inquiries was on current and planned programs in the areas of drug abuse and child and adolescent services. The Community Mental Health Center staff was asked to indicate officially a willingness to collaborate in providing psychosocial services in the model neighborhood and, at the same time, it was invited to participate in planning the psychiatric aspects of a total health care plan. With the help of the Mental Health Center staff, the Model Cities staff completed a revised application which met the critical deadline and was approved.

Once the grant had been approved, there began a long series of meetings at the General Hospital. These meetings, which were held during July, August, and September of 1970, were designed to bring together officials of the Health and Hospital Corporation, staff of the hospital, representatives of the public health section of the Corporation, Model Cities staff members, a representative from the City Demonstration Agency (CDA) board, and professionals representing organizations which had previously been involved in operating clinical services in the Model Cities neighborhood. The sole purpose of these meetings was to develop a plan for the delivery of health services in the Model Cities area and to execute such a plan. The General Hospital added to its staff an experienced administrator who was charged with responsibility for developing community health services within the Model Cities neighborhood. This new administrator gradually assumed the role of the coordinator of these meetings, and the Medical Director of the Community Mental Health Center also met with the group from the very first. The product of the many meetings was a play for the provision of services which seemed to fit the needs in the Model Cities area and seemed capable of implementation in a matter of a few months.

The intention of the Community Mental Health Center staff involved in the planning process was to bring about a plan that provided for the incorporation of the Mental Health Center's services into the total health delivery system in the Model Cities area. As much as was possible, common elements in the health delivery were to be centralized and shared (for instance, the record keeping system, pharmaceutical services, rehabilitative and social services, basic laboratory services, and education and training activities). In addition, a transportation service proposed for the target area would be equally shared and thus be available to all types of patients.

In October of 1970 the Health and Hospital Corporation was formally designated as the prime contractor for the delivery of health services to the Model Cities program. Concurrently, a new Model Cities Health Task Force was appointed. This Task Force included neighborhood representatives from the five regions in the Model Cities demonstration area, the medical and technical people who served as resource persons for the initial year and a half of planning, the General Hospital's coordinator of community health services, and the medical director of the Community Health Center.

In summary, the Community Mental Health Center has attempted to affiliate with the Model Cities program as a participant in a system of total health services designed to serve the Model Cities area. The Community Mental Health Center has attempted to influence the total system in such a manner as to facilitate the integration of its services in a total approach with a minimum of duplication of services, a maximum of sharing of professional staff, and the efficient use of available funds.

An Experiment in Cooperative Puzzle-Solving:
The Philadelphia Forum of
Mental Health / Mental Retardation Centers

INTRODUCTION

The jigsaw puzzle image, always so tempting in discussing community
mental health centers, becomes virtually irresistible in introducing the
Philadelphia Forum of Community Mental Health/Mental Retardation
Centers. Here, at least, one assures oneself, a little variation is possible!
Imagine a house. In separate rooms, people (let's call them A-groups)
are trying to put together a jigsaw puzzle. Each A-group's puzzle bears
the same title: "Keeping a Community Mental Health Center Alive and
Well." In a special meeting room, a group we may designate as "B,"
composed of representatives of the A-groups and other concerned persons, are examining the many parts of the puzzle that are presenting
problems common to the A-groups, and seeking ways of working them
out. These approaches may or may not be implemented cooperatively in
action taken by group B, depending on the expressed wishes of the A-
groups. In short, group B is trying to help each A-group put the puzzle
together, but at no sacrifice of its individuality, autonomy, or right to independent puzzle-solving.

Having yielded to the irresistible, one may still avoid dwelling fondly
on obvious analogies, and proceed quickly to a definition in broad operational terms. The forum is a working association, undertaken voluntarily, of the Community Mental Health Centers in Philadelphia (that is,
the city and the conterminous county). Its general purposes are to exchange views, search for common solutions to common problems, and, in
association with the Mental Health Association of Southeastern Pennsylvania, provide a central source of information about the community
mental health centers and pertinent issues, and a nucleus for concerted
measures to arouse interest, concern, and action favorable to the community mental health centers and to those issues.

CONCEPTION AND BIRTH

One spring day in 1966, the directors of the three mental health centers in Philadelphia then either in operation or approaching it, sat down to an informal meeting convened by the director of one of them. Although planned only as an ad hoc measure for discussion of common problems and an exchange of views, the meeting actually might be called the conception of the forum. By the fall of 1966, these three directors believed firmly that, since their centers and others then still in the planning phase had mutual problems, all could derive mutual benefit from a sharing of thinking and experience in regular and more formal meetings. The same idea had simultaneously been developing in the minds of other concerned persons, including, in fact, key state personnel who had been helping to meet Pennsylvania's responsibility for developing the community mental health centers in the Philadelphia area. Thus there was little difficulty in arranging a formal meeting in October 1966, to which the directors of all community mental health centers then in operation or in the planning phase were invited. At this meeting, the forum was offically born, for the directors, daily growing more aware of the puzzle's complexities, were readily convinced of the need for cooperation.

Since at that time no one had much idea of how cooperation should proceed, the forum's early meetings were mainly exploratory of resources and possible approaches. They also helped the directors to get to know each other, as well as many other interested and concerned people who had also been invited to participate as representatives of a wide range of pertinent caretaking agencies. These included, for example, the Philadelphia State Hospital; the Mental Health Association of Southeastern Pennsylvania; the Philadelphia Association for Retarded Children; various groups committed to such special interests as juvenile delinquency, criminal psychopathology, and narcotics and alcohol addiction; the Health and Welfare Council of Philadelphia; and the Philadelphia school system.

The search for a cooperative structure soon demonstrated that although the directors shared broad concerns with the noncommunity mental health center agencies, they also faced immediate and urgent problems, more specific to their jobs, which would require their concentrated attention outside the large open meetings. Accordingly, in early 1967, an executive committee, consisting of all current directors and one other staff member from each community mental health center, was formed. As new community mental health centers have been approved for federal funding, their directors (and a staff associate in each case, when this became possible) have joined the committee.° There are now also two nonvoting members who are not associated with any community mental health center: (1) the executive director of the Mental Health Association of Southeastern Pennsylvania, which is the forum's official sponsor, and contractor with the National Institute of Mental Health for some special tasks related to the forum; (2) and the executive director of the Philadelphia Association for Retarded Children, which has worked closely with some of the community mental health centers to develop mental retardation services.

COMPONENT PARTS

The Executive Committee has become primarily responsible for implementing the forum's purposes. If a brief return to the initial image may be forgiven, group B, in effect, has divided into two major subgroups: B-1 (the Executive Committee) focuses much more directly and immediately on the task of helping the A-groups (the community mental health centers) to put the pieces of the puzzle together than B-2, to which Webster's third definition of "forum" may now be conveniently applied: an assembly.

Let us deal with second things first. There is no intent here to derogate the assembly's importance to the forum's overall purposes. Rather, its efforts are so long-range and so difficult to measure that in the context of a puzzle called "Keeping a Community Mental Health Center Alive and Well," practicality suggests explaining the assembly briefly, and then moving on to matters bearing more urgently on the community mental health center's day-to-day survival. Open meetings are held about once a month. The attendance includes not only representation from the centers, but from many of the same agencies that participated in the early forum meetings (before the Executive Committee was formed) and from the caretaking community in general. Although action may subsequently be taken by concerned individuals and agencies as a *result* of the meetings, their *immediate* purpose is communication and expression of views pertaining to mental health and retardation, and related issues; and, more specifically, to what the centers are doing about

---

° Nine are funded at this writing (see Appendix A).

these issues, might be doing, or should be doing. Programs for the meetings were previously planned by the Executive Committee; now a special subcommittee arranges for appropriate speakers, panels, and the like. Meetings are developed around specific topics (for example, the state hospital and the community mental health centers; the state public welfare program and the state mental health and mental retardation program; and the mentally ill offender).

Now back to first things: the more direct puzzle-solving efforts to which the balance of this paper is primarily devoted. From now on, purely for convenience, "the forum" will designate the Executive Committee, and by extension, the other working bodies it has developed to carry out its responsibilities; the designation does *not* include the assembly. In brief summary, these other bodies now consist of five standing committees corresponding with the basic service areas of each community mental health center. The committees are as follows: (1) administrative practices and procedures; (2) clinical services for adults; (3) clinical services for children; ° (4) consultation and education; (5) research and evaluation; a variety of ad hoc subcommittees and task forces sponsored by the standing committees; and a paid staff at the forum's headquarters office. These offices, situated independently of any single center, and the paid staff were made possible in June 1970, when the contract referred to earlier between the Mental Health Association of Southeastern Pennsylvania, the forum's sponsor, and the National Institute of Mental Health became effective. The staff comprises an executive director and a program coordinator (both professional social workers), who are responsible for implementing the Executive Committee's decisions, and two secretaries.

The standing committee membership is representative of all the participating centers. The ad hoc committee and task force membership is determined by specific need; in addition to community mental health center staff, it may include representation from other agencies, if this is deemed useful by the appropriate sponsoring committee, or by the chairman of the forum. The forum at this writing is developing its bylaws; the committee structure outlined here is therefore tentative pend-

---

° No separate committees for mental retardation services or for adolescent services were set up. The forum feels strongly that mental retardation should not be considered a discrete service category, but that services for mentally retarded persons should be included in all services, whether for children or adults. The forum is less certain about a service category for adolescents. At least for the present, the continuum between adolescent and adult problems makes a single service category for both seem more reasonable.

ing their adoption.° Regardless of organizational details, however, the forum is not, and will not be, either a hierarchy or an authoritarian organization. It is an association of colleagues cooperating toward a common goal, and its members are determined to retain that model. Indeed, the Mental Health Association of Southeastern Pennsylvania was asked to sponsor the forum because, among other reasons, it is a nonprofessional, voluntary, citizens' organization with no vested interest in any single community mental health center. Rather, its sole interest is in helping *all* the centers to seek certain goals consonant with the association's own goal of promoting mental health care, including prevention of mental illness, for the entire community. Its control of funding makes possible a check on any conceivable tendency within the forum to develop a power structure.

SPECIFICS

Obviously, the time has come to describe the forum's specific tasks. Only some samples can be presented here because forum activities are so numerous, and they must be presented rather at random, since forum activities do not lend themselves to tidy classification. Three descriptions are expanded into brief case studies for richer illustration.

FORUM ACTIVITIES

1. The forum assisted in formulation of the regulations pertaining to Pennsylvania's Mental Health and Mental Retardation Act of 1966; subsequently it studied and interpreted them, and was instrumental in effecting changes in instances where compliance was a practical impossibility for the community mental health centers. It also helped the state and local governmental agencies responsible for implementing the 1966 act in setting up an overall Philadelphia city/county program, and continues, on request, to provide them with consultation.

2. Working with various citizens' groups, primarily the Mental Health Association of Southeastern Pennsylvania, the forum maintains close touch with legislative and executive proceedings in the state capital and

° The size and complexity of the forum suggest that another committee may be necessary: a steering committee to carry out the business of the organization between regular meetings.

speaks as the collective voice of the Philadelphia centers in efforts to effect action consonant with their purposes and goals. At the national level, the forum is considering a discrete membership in the National Council of Community Mental Health Centers. Meanwhile, it keeps abreast of pertinent developments through direct, almost daily, staff contacts with the Council.

3. When inevitable sudden crises arise in delivering mental health care, the forum unites the centers in concerted action to deal with them. For example, the juvenile court in Philadelphia recently announced that it would release a number of acutely disturbed children to the responsibility of the centers following the closing of a state facility that would normally serve them, at least temporarily. In a city notoriously deficient in children's resources, none of the centers has had time to develop services adequate to handle the influx. The forum's negotiations with the court have modified its attitude. Consequently, temporary arrangements with other agencies have given the centers breathing time before they assume total responsibility for these children.

4. To promote coordination and cooperation between the centers and other local mental health and retardation programs in place of duplication and cross-purpose efforts, the forum has established a working relationship with the Philadelphia City-Wide Alliance of Mental Health and Mental Retardation Agencies.

5. Owing to certain anomalies in the 1966 Mental Health/Mental Retardation Act, commitment provisions present some grave problems for the centers, as they do for other pertinent agencies and individuals. The forum speaks for the centers on these issues through its representative on a state-appointed Task Force on Commitment Provisions, which is charged both with interpreting the law as it now stands and with devising corrective legislative amendments for the future.

6. The forum has involved the centers in an ongoing approach to the problems of the mentally ill offender, chiefly through working relationships with the Crime Commission of Philadelphia, and the District Attorney's office.

Case Study: Salary Scales and the State   An early impediment to acquisition of manpower in Pennsylvania's community mental health centers was the state's insistence that their salary scales must conform to those established for what it considered comparable positions in state hospitals. The comparison was rarely realistic. For example, the center psychiatrist is almost always required to serve in clinical, administrative, consultative, and educative roles—a mix demanding unusual personal and professional qualifications. A center social worker with an MSW may head a complicated innovative unit (perhaps an aftercare and rehabilitation program), requiring, in addition to clinical and supervisory skills, unique ability to mobilize an extraordinary range of community resources. Similarly, the mental health assistant, who usually holds only a high school diploma (if that), is expected nevertheless to learn a new career requiring a wide range of therapeutic and ancillary skills, a range not yet even completely charted. On the old state salary scale, the compensation levels for these personnel were equated respectively to that for a state hospital staff psychiatrist, chief social worker, and psychiatric orderly, each of whose duties are far more circumscribed and conventional.

A subcommittee studied the problem for months. Detailed salary schedules and job descriptions were prepared, showing that the centers were paying essentially the same rates for equivalent jobs within their systems. But when the center jobs were described in terms of actual duties performed, performance almost always outweighed the state's description. Moreover, center personnel do not enjoy the job security or fringe benefits comparable to those accorded state employees. Reports submitted to the state set forth these facts, reassured the state that there was no intent to "pirate" state employees, and critically important, demonstrated that the centers are concerned with what people are achieving rather than with their academic credentials. Finally, the subcommittee and the forum's chairman met with appropriate state personnel for open discussion. Eventually the forum was at least partially instrumental in effecting new state job classifications applying to community mental health center personnel, and increasing the state's participation in their salaries. Despite this reform, the salary scale problem is still far from solved. Particularly troubling is the salary scale for paraprofessional workers (frequently minority group members) who bitterly resent the emphasis on formal credentials that so severely limits their earnings; but the centers, by speaking up in a collective voice, have taken a step toward curing "credentialitis," as well as other salary scale ills.

Case Study: The State Hospital and the CMHC—Aftercare and Rehabilitation In January 1968, the centers in Philadelphia learned that during the ensuing year, as part of a broad administrative and therapeutic reorganization, some 1,000 patients in the Philadelphia State Hospital would be released and made the responsibility of the centers, and that discharges would continue thereafter at only slightly diminished rates. Although the centers had aftercare and rehabilitation programs in various stages of development, none was really prepared for so large and sudden an influx. Worse yet, the state then set up an independent care system: a "Community Socialization Unit" manned by social workers whose sole job was to work with the dischargees, most of whom were also being seen by center staff. There was no provision made for coordination of communication between the two groups and, moreover, this duplication came at a time when the centers were pleading for state funds for adequate staffing! A forum subcommittee on state hospitals studied this and other aspects of the relations between the centers and the state hospitals, and planned corrective approaches. Subsequently, center representatives met with the superintendent of the Philadelphia State Hospital, the regional director of the Community Socialization Unit, and other concerned persons, and formulated plans whereby the unit workers established liaison with the center workers. This enabled the centers to reassign their own staff to other vital tasks.

Another aspect of this case demonstrates the worth of shared experience and thinking. When the subcommittee was appointed, one of the oldest centers was using some beds in the Philadelphia State Hospital as one unit of its inpatient service. Within this unit, it was developing aftercare and rehabilitation functions for the patients served there. The subcommittee, which, incidentally, was chaired by a senior staff member of the community mental health center in question, examined the model and reviewed its experience, and concluded that it was proving less effective than expected. Consequently, the subcommittee recommended preferred consideration for other models under discussion, because they would eliminate some grave flaws in the first and could be adapted to the individual center use at less cost. As a result, the forum made it possible for individual centers to conserve resources by avoiding experimentation with a model that had not been totally satisfactory.

One general comment should be added. The discussions, negotiations, and consultations with State Hospital personnel necessitated by these issues have helped to build a generally smoother working relationship between the centers and the State Hospital. This seems to spill over into a variety of situations not reviewed here, but of equally critical importance to each center. Working together on one section of the puzzle frequently does yield extra dividends in other sections.

Case Study: Research and Evaluation Although well-developed research and evaluation functions are central to community mental health center philosophy and goals, they have been severely limited in all the Philadelphia centers by low priorities in funding, by the community's misunderstanding of these functions, and even by the reluctance of some center staff outside the research and evaluation department to cooperate in nonclinical activities. Recognizing these mutual limitations, the forum has established its research and evaluation committee. Its members are representatives of most of the operating centers in the city working in consultation with representatives of the city/county agency that implements the Mental Health and Retardation Act of 1966. The committee makes it possible for the research and evaluation units of the member centers to share current thoughts and experiences in regard to research. Also, it is strongly oriented toward development of certain joint efforts, which, by serving the needs of multiple centers, can conserve resources and reduce both intrusions into the community's privacy and conflicts in staff obligations and goals. Currently, for example, the group is attempting to initiate a multicatchment area evaluation project concerning patient and staff perceptions of patient problems and treatment effectiveness.

CURRENT PROJECTS

In addition to the projects described above, the forum currently has a number of activities in the planning stage. These include exploration of ways to tie mental health services into regional health planning, efforts to devise collaborative and coordinated programs of in-service training and continuing education for center staff and other caretaker agency staff, the development of public education programs, and the compilation of information on potential approaches to center financing.

Clearly, however, a major forum responsibility continues to be the communication of information among the forum members; indeed, this function is implicit in all the projects and activities described thus far. Accordingly, the forum is continuously studying the question of how best to provide communication in a continuous way and on a formal basis without relying exclusively on the committee structure. (In fact, the NIMH-MHASP contract stipulates that the forum shall explore the role and function of a local and regional voluntary organization in stimulating and coordinating information exchange and program development among all centers in Philadelphia.) The professional staff at forum headquarters now telephones all directors to report critical developments, for example, a confrontation between one center and the local community, the outcome of which may well affect the total pattern of community-center relations in Philadelphia. The staff is also investigating the feasibility of a frequent newsletter or similar communication to all directors.

The Philadelphia Forum of Mental Health/Mental Retardation Centers tries to extend each member CMHC's resources for dealing with problems common to all members, but it accords each center the right to pursue an independent course when it so chooses. This concept of cooperation coupled with autonomy is implemented in processes that one might label, by way of summary, "communication of vital information," "concerted measures to effect favorable action," "developing collaborative programs," and so on. But the labels require less emphasis than the focus of the processes, which is the general good of the community. The forum's sponsorship by a community-wide citizens' organization, the Mental Health Association of Southeastern Pennsylvania, facilitates maintaining that focus in the face of the centers' undeniable potential for competition rather than cooperation.

The forum has brought many of the centers' problems into focus and it is apparently helping the centers to solve these problems. Moreover, it is developing some useful working patterns for a cooperative problem-solving effort. The forum is frankly innovative, largely experimental, and almost entirely empirical. Only beginnings have been reported here; only time will determine their effectiveness.

APPENDIX A
PHILADELPHIA FORUM OF MENTAL HEALTH/MENTAL RETARDATION CENTERS

Albert Einstein Community Mental Health/Mental Retardation Center, Bernard Borislow, Ph.D., Director.

Hahnemann Community Mental Health/Mental Retardation Center, Clifford J. Bodarky, Ed.D., Director.

Jefferson Community Mental Health/Mental Retardation Center, Daniel Lieberman, M.D., Director.

Northeast Community Mental Health Center, Walter H. Mikulich, Ed.D., Director.

Northwest Center for Community Mental Health/Mental Retardation Programs, Robert C. Panaccio, M.S.S., Codirector; Bijan Etemad, M.C., Codirector.

Pennsylvania Hospital Community Mental Health/Mental Retardation Center, Alfred S. Roberts, Jr., M.D., Director.

Community Mental Health Center of Philadelphia Psychiatric Center, Robert C. Taber, A.C.S.W., Acting Director.

Robert L. Leopold

Temple University Community Mental Health Center, R. Bruce
Sloane, M.D., Acting Director.
West Philadelphia Community Mental Health Consortium, Robert L.
Leopold, M.D., Director.

REFERENCES

Bartlett, F. L. "Present-Day Requirements for State Hospitals Joining the Community." *New England Journal Medicine* 276(Jan. 12, 1967): 90–94.
Bartlett, F. L. "Involving Hospital Superintendents in Developing Community Mental Health Centers." *Hospital Community Psychiatry* 20(July 1969): 213–215.
Boyles, P. D., Waldrop, G. S. "Development of a Community-Oriented Program in a Large State Hospital of Limited Resources." *American Journal Psychiatry* 124(Oct. 1967): Supplement 29–31.
Cochran, W. "A Community Mental Health Center Built Around a Private Practice." *American Journal Psychiatry* 126(July 1969): 70–76.
Fishman, R. "A Conglomerate Model for Community Mental Health." *Hospital Community Psychiatry* 21(April 1970): 127–128.
Halpert, H. P., Silverman, C. "Approaches to Interagency Cooperation." *Hospital Community Psychiatry* 18(March 1967): 84–87.
Leopold, R. L. "The West Philadelphia Mental Health Consortium: Administrative Planning in a Multihospital Catchment Area." *American Journal Psychiatry* 124(October 1967): Supplement 69–76.
Tarail, M. "A General Hospital Program for Serving Community Mental Health Needs." *Hospitals* 42(February 1, 1968): 47–51.
Turner, W. E., Smith, D. C., Medley, P. "Integration of Mental Health into Public Health Programs—Advantages and Disadvantages." *American Journal of Public Health* 57(August 1967): 1322–1326.

IV
Providing
Continuity of
Care

EDITORS' INTRODUCTION

Essential to the community mental health center approach is the concept of continuity of care. As pointed out in the previous chapters, multiple agencies are usually involved in the operation of a single community mental health center. Therefore, provisions to assure continuity of care for each patient must involve mechanisms that relate different agencies and different services to each other.

Implementing these crucial relationships requires a careful consideration of interagency responsibilities to the development of the total community mental health center program. Although these concepts were enunciated early in the development of the community mental health center program, it has been only more recently that the crucial importance of clearly written and well-defined agreements has been noted. These agreements are essential to effective interagency cooperation and development of continuity of care as related to the delivery of services.

These agreements must spell out how the community mental health center will meet the requirements for continuity of care which are included in the regulations of the Federal Community Mental Health Center Program. These regulations provide that all cooperating agencies will assure that the transfer of records, patients, and staff will be readily facilitated. In implementing them, the community mental health center must pay careful attention to the collection of necessary data in a variety of forms. Furthermore, since these data are often transferred from one agency to another or from one element of service to another, appropriate guarantees must be included that will maintain the right of confidentiality for each patient.

The concept of continuity of care is not only important within the community mental health center, but is also crucial between one type of mental health delivery system and another. Most relevant to this issue is the relationship between the community mental health center and the state hospital system. To some advocates of the community mental health center, a goal has been the elimination of the state hospital system. A more realistic goal, however, is the development of a cooperative partnership between these two types of mental health facilities. Implicit in this is the intent that each facility should serve the function for which it is best suited.

The community mental health center is appropriate as the first line of community mental health resources. State hospitals can play a crucial role in development of the total system by appropriately focusing on specialized services which, for reasons of economy, geography, and manpower, can best be delivered by it. Specialized services can include long-term care, alcoholism programs, mental retardation programs, geriatrics programs, children's programs, and services for the mentally ill offender.

---

11   *Rollee Lowenstein,* J.D.

Affiliation Contracts—The Tie That Binds

The successful applicant for federal financial assistance in constructing or staffing a new community mental health center assumes a number of obligations to the federal government, and through their fulfillment, to the community, the center it will serve. The applicant must give "specific and detailed information" and "adequate assurances" that it, and all those affiliated with it, will comply with some very specific requirements set forth in federal regulations. These requirements are the operational expression of the basic principles that underlie the center concept. Although program design and organizational patterns may and do vary widely from one community to another, compliance with these requirements is "given" if the stream of federal dollars is to flow unchecked.

It is relatively simple to give the requisite assurances with confidence if the applicant agency is the sole provider of services. In over 70 percent of the centers funded to date, however, services are not provided by one autonomous organization in one free-standing building. The common pattern is a joint enterprise involving two or more organizations or agencies, each operating a separate physical facility located geographically throughout the community, and each clinging to its own corporate identity. Whether the official center applicant is one of the participating organizations designated by the others to act in their behalf or is a separately constituted board or center corporation, it must still guarantee compliance with federal requirements.

How can the applicant be sure that each of the separate and independent organizations providing the services of the center will play the game by the same rules? Dr. H. G. Whittington, participating in a conference on community mental health centers on November 19–21, 1968, remarked, "One model, and perhaps the most useful, is the interdependence model: if you scratch someone else's back, he will either scratch your back or stick a knife in it. The only way to coordinate all these separate efforts is to build an interdependency so that if one of them falls, the others fall." Translated into legal terms, Dr. Whittington was suggesting the necessity for a formal, and more important, a *binding* relationship between a group of organizations which share the same geographical area, perhaps the same bus line, hopefully the same treatment goals, and, whether they realize it or not, the same fate with respect to the continuation of their program if one of their number gets out of line.

The name of the relationship which makes these organizations no longer casual neighbors but a center is "affiliation" and the federal regulations require that this relationship be memorialized by a "contract or other formal written agreement." For years, applicants have been obediently shipping their documents to the designated federal offices duly labelled "affiliation agreement" or "contract between X and Y." It is now contended that they may not be worth the paper they are written on because they are not enforceable.

Fifty "contracts" or "agreements" between applicants for federal staffing support and one or more affiliates were selected at random for study. While they varied widely in clarity and in the number and comprehensiveness of the topics included, not one could be said to include all the legal elements of an enforceable contract.

Whether or not a document is a contract depends upon how the parties view it and upon some pecularities of local law. There are, however, some generally accepted basic elements which ought to be present in any contract. These elements are statements setting forth consideration, mutual obligations of the parties, the duration of the agreement, the effective date of the agreement, and the penalties for noncompliance with the terms of the agreement, unless the parties elect to rely solely on the general remedies available at law for breach of contract. Each of these elements is discussed below.

Why this emphasis on the proper contract content? Because without it, the document is merely an agreement to agree or a literary statement of good intentions. This may be perfectly adequate as long as the personal relationships between agency representatives remain cordial and the status quo is unchanged. But suppose an affiliate, for one reason or another, fails to live up to a specific assurance and all efforts at persuasion fail. The results are serious indeed for all the other agencies which make up the center. Among other things, the federal source of funding may be cut off and the entire future of the center may be in jeopardy. While in some instances it may be possible to replace the erring affiliate with another, more cooperative agency, as a practical matter this may not be a readily available solution. Surely these are reasons enough to be sure that all parties to the agreement incur a legal obligation to live up to its terms and that the various means of legal redress for breach of contract are available to compel performance in some instances or provide compensatory damages in others.

CONSIDERATION

Consideration is the cement that binds the parties to the agreement together; it is a statement of what each expects to gain in return for the services provided and obligations incurred. Each party to a center affiliation contract should be assuming his obligations "in consideration of," that is, in reliance upon a similar assumption of obligations by all other parties to the agreement. This mutual assumption of obligations may result in a federal grant and ultimately in a viable operating center program.

Not one of the documents studied recognized the importance of the interdependent relationship as a basic element of the contract. To be sure, twelve documents did set forth the "consideration" for the "contract." Each described it in terms of the funds which the fiscal agent would make available to the particular affiliate in return for the services the affiliate proposed to provide. If the affiliate failed to provide the service, the funds could of course be withheld. But where would this leave the other parties to the contract if the missing service was an "essential" service and if the entire grant was terminated because of the failure of one affiliate to live up to his obligations? The specific funding arrangements may, of course, be set forth in a contract or just as validly in separate letters of agreement between the center applicant and each individual affiliate. However, the interlocking reliances of all the parties upon the fulfillment of all stated obligations and requirements should be stated as consideration for the contract itself.

MUTUAL OBLIGATIONS

All the documents studied contained clear statements designating which organization or agency would be responsible for the provision of each service included in the program. Many of the documents stopped there, apparently well satisfied that the topic of mutual obligations had been thoroughly explored. No single document attempted to cover systematically all the federal requirements and assurances as minimal statements of mutual obligations, in spite of the fact that the very future of the grant could depend upon compliance with these obligations.

This is not entirely the fault of the applicant. The old federal staffing grant application listed a number of important assurances under Part IV of the application, but then it told the applicant that only the assurances designated as G,H,I, and J had to be evidenced by a formal agreement. (This statement has recently been revised in preparation for the issuance of an amended staffing grant application.) It was therefore quite natural for applicants to feel that other requirements, such as the provision of a reasonable volume of services at or below cost to indigents, arrangements for general practitioners to follow their patients into the center, or nondiscriminatory employment practices, could be ignored with impunity—at least as far as the agreement was concerned. This is a serious mistake. There is no hierarchy of requirements or assurances as far as the federal government is concerned. An affiliate's failure to observe any one of them may jeopardize the program for all the concerned agencies, but the aggrieved parties cannot enforce an obligation to which the agency at fault has never formally agreed.

At the very heart of the center philosophy is the concept of continuity of care for each patient. Operationally this means that a patient being treated in one service is automatically eligible for and must be trans= ferred for treatment to any other service component—or back again—when clinically indicated. This may mean a transfer of the therapist too, and it almost certainly involves a transfer of the patient's records from one treating component to the other. All these transfers involve important policy considerations. How strange, then, to find that of the forty-four documents which mention continuity of care at all, thirty-eight are content to parrot the language of the federal regulation that there shall be continuity of care and let it go at that.

To mention but a few potentially sticky administrative questions, one wonders where the decision to transfer a patient is made. Whose clinical judgment is determinative—the sending service's or the receiving service's? And is clinical judgment the only determinant? Six of the documents studied stipulate that a patient may be transferred only if adequate space, personnel, equipment, and financial arrangements are available.

It is axiomatic that medical data compiled about a patient in one element of a center is wasted if it cannot be made readily available to another element which is also undertaking to treat him. It is not surprising, therefore, that thirty-five of the documents studied require that a patient's record be kept on file at the service to which he has been admitted and that it be transferred with him when he is moved to another service. (Possibly the other fifteen centers considered this requirement too elementary to bother mentioning at all.)

But the unique structure, organization, and mission of a multiagency community mental health center raises questions with respect to sharing, storage, and maintenance of records not usually faced by the single agency center nor by the traditional hospital. For example, if essential services provided by separate, autonomous organizations are scattered throughout a community, how does a record get from essential service A to essential service B? Who will have access to these records en route? Who may read them within the new facility? How much of the record should be shared? Should all the information about a patient's past history—for instance, his sexual problems with his wife—necessarily be sent to the vocational rehabilitation unit that is preparing him for community employment? Where do the records ultimately come to rest for storage and how can they be reactivated? Is it necessary to obtain patient consent to transfer records from one center component to another?

There is no single answer to many of these questions. The old laws of many states pertaining to confidentiality of records were never designed to cope with the concept of continuity of care in a community mental health center and may well need to be overhauled. Moreover, the administrative arrangements worked out will necessarily differ depending upon the individual organizational pattern of each center or the particular laws of its home state—or both. The point is that whatever the solution devised, it should be made a part of the contract obligation of each of the parties. The consequences of noncompliance are too serious to leave this matter to inexact interagency "understandings."

Space does not permit a full discussion of all the other federal requirements which should be—but in most of the documents studied were not —included as contractual obligations. For example, only thirty-three of the fifty documents stipulated that there must be no discrimination on the basis of race, creed, or national origin in accepting patients. Only eleven documents required each affiliate to conform to the federal fair employment practice requirements. Only twenty-five documents stated that there may be no exclusion of patients on the basis of their inability to pay for services. Only twenty-four documents provided that general practitioners and other nonpsychiatric physicians must be permitted to assist in the care of their patients after the patient has been accepted in a center service. Finally, only six of the documents required that emergency services remain open twenty-four hours a day, seven days a week.

Without question, the federal requirements should be covered in any affiliation agreement. There are other topics, however, which are strongly recommended for inclusion in a binding contractual document.

One example is the important topic of patients' rights. Under this heading would come such matters as the right of a patient to be treated with dignity and compassion, the right to communicate freely with members of his family, with his lawyer, his private physician, and others, or the necessity of obtaining his informed consent before instituting an unusual therapeutic procedure. No center document mentioned any of these topics. Only twelve documents covered the subject of obtaining a patient release before making portions of his clinical record available to persons outside the center complex or otherwise providing information about a patient in response to outside inquiries. No one dealt with the sticky question of obtaining parental consent to treat minors. Two documents did go so far as to specify that every patient admitted to a center facility has a right to insist on treatment. In this connection it is interesting that no center to date appears to be willing to set down some minimum standards for adequate treatment, for instance, a required patient-staff ratio, although two of the fifty centers did set forth some specific staffing requirements and staff qualifications for each affiliate.

It should not be assumed that state laws are adequate to deal with all these issues. Even when these topics are specifically covered in state legislation, it is usually in the context of a hospital commitment law which may or may not be found to apply to patients in a community mental health center. It would seem the better part of valor not to wait for a lawsuit to test the applicability of these patients' rights provisions to center patients.

Another topic barely touched in any of the agreements studied is the question of who is responsible for a particular patient as he circulates through the network of services. Seventeen of the fifty documents did discuss admission procedures (but not discharge) and designated the admitting physician as the staff member responsible for the patient as long as he remains in the service to which he was admitted. Who is the decision-maker for a day care patient, for example, who is simultaneously receiving vocational rehabilitation services and family counselling from three different agencies—and then suffers an acute psychotic episode at home?

A related question is the legal responsibility of the center as a whole or of individual affiliates for negligence or malpractice on the part of one of its own staff or of the staff of another affiliate. Suppose, for example, that the occupational therapist neglected to read with care the cheerful old man's clinical record with its warnings about his suicidal tendencies because she was struggling with an overwhelming case load. She turns her back and he picks up a palette knife and kills himself. The family sues and joins not only the therapist and the agency which employs her but the other agency which referred the patient, the admitting agency, and the center as a whole. Who may be held responsible, assuming that negligence on the part of the therapist was established?

The answer depends upon a number of complex factors, not the least of which is the nature of the relationship between the center and the employee, between the center and each of the various affiliates involved, and among the affiliates with one another. Whether the affiliate may be considered to be acting as an agent of the parent center itself depends primarily upon the degree of control that the center is in a position to exercise over the actions of the affiliate and of its staff. In twenty-four of the documents studied, a board of directors was named to exercise overall administrative supervision of the activities of all affiliates. Twenty of these twenty-four documents provided that the board was to have access to the records and grounds of each affiliate at all times. (An injury arising from negligent maintenance of equipment might well be attributed to the parent center under these circumstances.) Fourteen of these twenty-four documents also provided that the center had the duty to supervise the employees of each affiliate. Potentially such a center is more vulnerable to liability for negligence than one in which each component acts as an independent contractor and shields its staff from any supervision but its own. Of course this also means that such an affiliate can hardly expect to share the burden of liability with the center under the circumstances.

We cannot fully explore at this time the complex topic of liability and immunity for negligence. Considering the fact that hospitals, facilities, and medical practitioners deal constantly with the vagaries of the human body and mind, it is indeed surprising and reflects great credit upon the healing professions that acts of negligence do not occur more frequently. Nevertheless, the problem of potential center or staff liability for negligent injury should not be minimized; it tends to get even worse as responsibility for patient care proliferates. The protection of adequate insurance coverage should be given serious consideration. The center should examine its insurance needs as an entity, rather than relying upon each component part to determine for itself which aspects of its operation to cover. It should take out a uniform policy covering all of its affiliates both for malpractice and liability, and perhaps also for fire and other types of protection. This will eliminate jurisdictional disputes between different insurance companies where multiple liability may be involved and might also result in a lower premium rate.

The details of such insurance coverage can be set forth in a separate agreement with the carrier, but the obligation to protect each affiliate and the center itself in this manner—if this is accepted as an obligation, of course—should be clearly spelled out as part of the affiliation contract itself.

OTHER MISSING CONTRACT ELEMENTS

The omissions already discussed are serious enough to raise doubts as to whether any of the documents studied in this survey should be dignified with the label "contract" at all. Just to complete the survey, it was found that only sixteen of the "agreements" stated the length of time for which the "contract" was to be in force; only thirty-two documents mention a date on which the "contract" is to become operative; and none of the documents discussed sanctions or methods of enforcement, although one agreement did provide that "in case of breach of contract, this agreement is subject to review and thirty-day cancellation."

It is not contended that an interagency agreement is the only instrument necessary to organize a community mental health center. While it can—and should—outline treatment philosophy, principles, policies, and mutual obligations, it cannot deal with every administrative specific necessary to implement the program. This section does suggest, however, that as a minimum, every program requirement listed in the federal regulations should be included in binding contractual language as mutual obligations to be assumed by all parties to the agreement. It has been further suggested that such additional areas as patients' rights, supervision of employees, access to grounds and records, insurance coverage, and treatment philosophy and policies also be included in the document. Finally, in view of the serious consequences of noncompliance to all concerned with the program, it is strongly urged that the parties sit down with competent local legal counsel, signify their intent to enter into a valid contractual arrangement, and allow him to draw up a document that can be enforced.

---

12 *Henry Weihofen,* J.D.

Confidentiality

Every center should promulgate, in a manual of rules or procedures or elsewhere, a set of instructions to govern giving out of information concerning patients. The following is therefore presented in a form that can be adapted for such a set of instructions. Adaptation will of course be required to conform to practices in the particular center and the law of the jurisdiction.

Professional ethics, strictly, protect only communications intended to be confidential, and not everything that a patient tells his therapist is so intended. But records of a mental health center should be presumed to be confidential. Indeed, a person may not want even the fact that he is receiving psychiatric treatment to be revealed.

All information and records concerning patients or other recipients of services are therefore to be regarded as confidential, and no such information and no access to records should be given except in accordance with the following instructions.

Confidentiality problems are involved not only in relations of the center with outside agencies and individuals, but also within the center itself. The former, however, are primary.

INFORMATION TO AGENCIES AND PERSONS OUTSIDE THE CENTER

Information will be given to agencies or persons outside the center only when doing so (1) will protect the interest of the patient; (2) is ordered by a court; or (3) is needed to protect the public.

INFORMATION GIVEN TO PROTECT THE PATIENT'S INTEREST IN GENERAL

Even when the communication presumably would be helpful or even needed, authority to release information to other agencies or persons should be given only if the following conditions are met:

1. Written consent has been obtained from: (a) the patient if he is of age and competent, or if he is an emancipated minor, that is, is married, or, if single, is living apart from and not supported by his parents; ° (b) the patient's parent or guardian, if he is an unemancipated minor; † (c)

° Patients of a mental health center often have been clients of a number of other agencies and the subject of numerous files and records. Not infrequently, no consent has been obtained for releasing information contained therein. Many of these people are not aware that they have any right to privacy. On the contrary, those in the lower socioeconomic strata tend to expect interrogation and prying by all social agencies, and even though they may resent it, they take it as one of the facts of life about which they can do nothing.

The center should not act on this assumption but should make clear that information given to the staff will, except in the special circumstances herein discussed, be kept confidential.

† On behalf of illegitimate, married, and other minors, consent may be given as follows:

1. A married minor, of whatever age, may legally request medical treatment for himself and may waive the privilege.

2. For an illegitimate, the mother may act.

3. For a child surrendered for adoption, the placement agency or adoptive par-

his legal guardian if the patient is mentally incompetent; (d) the executor or administrator of the estate if the patient is deceased.

2. The person giving the consent appears to have adequate understanding of what is being consented to.

3. The agency or person to whom the information is being given has adequate understanding and integrity concerning confidentiality.

Even when all these conditions are met, the information given should be only such as is needed for the inquirer's purpose. Thus if the inquiry concerns the patient's ability to hold a job, the response should be restricted to stating his strengths and weaknesses for the particular job, or stating the kinds of jobs he can or cannot handle. If the inquiry concerns competence to care for a child, the response should address itself to that. It should not say that a paranoid schizophrenic such as P is incompetent in general, but should deal only with the specific subject of the inquiry.

When a person is examined at the request of an agency, and the purpose of the examination is, in his opinion, not in his interest, ethics require that he be informed that the therapist will be reporting to the agency and that what the person reveals can therefore not be kept confidential. Examples of such situations are where a person is referred by a court to determine whether he is mentally competent to stand criminal trial or to be held responsible for his acts, or where a welfare client is referred to determine whether he or she may safely be allowed to have custody of children.

TELEPHONE CALLS AND INQUIRIES

When, by telephone or in person, someone inquires whether a named person is a patient of the center, or how a named patient is progressing, the proper response is, "Sorry, but we do not give out such information." The name and telephone number of the person calling should be obtained, and the patient told of the call. He can then return the call if he wishes. Sometimes the center is trying to find a relative. In that case, of course, information may be given. Needed information may also be

---

ents may act. Children placed in a foster home by a welfare agency are represented by the agency.

4. When parents are divorced or legally separated, the parent having legal custody is the one who can consent. If the parents are living together, or are separated by mutual agreement, the consent of either is sufficient, if the other has not specifically refused.

given when the request is by a known agency, at least in crises or emergency cases, but this should always be followed by a confirming letter, restating the information given.

WELFARE AGENCIES

Welfare agencies may be serving persons who are also patients of the center, or may refer such persons to the center for evaluation or therapy.

When a person is so referred, the referring agency should later be informed whether he has contacted the center, has kept his appointments, and so forth.

When the referral was for some purpose other than or in addition to therapy (as for evaluation to aid a determination the other agency needs to make), a report should be made to the referring agency. The person in such cases should be given to understand that report will be made and that what he communicates will, to that extent, not be confidential.

SCHOOL AUTHORITIES

A similar policy governs release of information to school authorities. If the person was referred by the school, a report should be made, but the person (or his parents) should be informed that this will be done. In addition, information will be released to schools if requested by the patient or his parents or guardian.

HOSPITALS AND PHYSICIANS

When a patient is being, or has been, transferred to another mental institution, relevant information concerning him should be transmitted. But except in emergencies or on judicial commitment, written consent of the patient, or his next of kin or guardian, should first be obtained.

The same policy applies when patients, or former patients, enter a general hospital or clinic, or when they consult a private physician who needs relevant background information.

ATTORNEYS

Information may be given to attorneys representing patients, if the conditions set forth above (informed consent of the patient himself, and so forth) are met. If it appears, however, that litigation against the center is contemplated, the center's legal advisor should be consulted before the information is released.

Attorneys representing other parties, including the patient's spouse (as in divorce or custody cases), should be given information only on subpoena.

A similar policy applies to other persons or agencies, such as credit bureaus, police, and so forth.

THE PATIENT OR PATIENT'S RELATIVES

Neither a patient nor any member of his family should ordinarily be permitted to see his record. The person who wants to see his record is often a paranoid patient whose condition would be aggravated rather than helped by the information.

The Judicial Council of the AMA says, "Whether the contents of the medical report are to be given to the patient rests with the decision of the doctor who knows all the circumstances involved in the situation." [1]

When in special circumstances inspection is authorized by the director of the center or his delegate, it should be on condition that the inspection be in the presence of the patient's attending physician.

Parents may demand information about their children that the therapist thinks they should not be given. This can usually be handled diplomatically, by telling them something, but not critical facts that may be inimical to therapy or to the parent-child relationship.

Things that the parents ought to know, but which the child refuses to tell them, may have to be told them by the therapist, but only after he has failed to induce the child to tell them, and only after he warns the child that he will have to do so himself.

Henry Weihofen

FORM IN WHICH INFORMATION MAY BE GIVEN

Even when release of information is proper under the restrictions above, such information should be given only as an abstract or summary.

The medical records themselves should not ordinarily be allowed to be taken from or sent out of the center (except on subpoena). An exception may be needed for neighborhood teams, but if they are allowed to take records to their neighborhood offices, they should be required to return them the same day, or at the latest, the following morning.

Authorization may be given to examine the records, in the center, but this should be permitted only with the patient's consent and the consent of the staff physician who treated him, and the inspection be permitted only in the presence of a member of the center staff competent to interpret the records.

If the person wishes to copy from the records, this may be allowed, under the supervision of the person assigned to interpret and supervise the inspection.

COURT ORDERS TO PRODUCE RECORDS
OF INFORMATION

A court subpoena ordering the center or a named member of its staff to produce medical or other records in court and make them available to a party, to a lawsuit, or to his counsel, must be obeyed. However, (1) the patient (or his attorney) should be notified of the subpoena; and (2) if revelation would jeopardize the patient's welfare, it would be proper, (a) to obtain legal advise on whether this danger should be called to the judge's attention before the records are produced; or (b) if legal advice is not available to the center, to call the hazard to the judge's attention before or at the time the records are produced, and request that they not be compelled.[2]

In at least thirty-five of the fifty states, confidential communications to one's physician are "privileged"; that is, the physician cannot be required, without the patient's consent, to testify in court concerning such communications or to produce confidential records.* In twenty-one

* Privileged communications statutes are of four main types: physician-patient, psychiatrist-patient, psychologist-patient, and psychotherapist-patient. States having each type are the following:

129

states, confidential communications to psychologists are now similarly protected. In most states, the doctor-patient relationship, and therefore the privilege, is held to exist in a hospital setting as well as in private practice. Where the privilege exists, the therapist should of course refuse to reveal such communications without the patient's consent. Administration of the law, however, is in control of the judge, and if he rules that the information should be revealed, the therapist must obey.

If the therapist is consulted by the patient on whether he should waive the privilege, the therapist may properly point out the implications of doing so, specifically that all relevant information available can then be inquired into, and that neither the therapist nor the patient can thereafter withhold particular items of information that might be prejudicial. Also, the therapist should consider whether the patient is able to give understanding consent; that is, whether he is mentally capable of making an intelligent judgment on the matter, whether he has an unconscious urge to disclose matters that will damage him, and so forth.

When a record is taken to court and left in the possession of legal authority, a receipt should be obtained and filed with the medical records department until the record is returned. When that is not done, records have been known to be lost.

BREACH OF CONFIDENTIALITY TO PROTECT
THE PUBLIC

A break in confidentiality is justified when there is reasonable cause to believe that failure to divulge the relevant information would result in death or serious injury to the patient, the therapist, or a third person. The procedure to be followed in such situations is:

Physician-patient, thirty-three jurisdictions: Alaska, Arizona, Arkansas, California, Colorado, District of Columbia, Hawaii, Idaho, Illinois, Indiana, Kansas, Kentucky, Louisiana, Minnesota, Mississippi, Missouri, Montana, Nebraska, New Mexico (venereal disease and workmen's compensation cases only), New York, Nevada, North Dakota, Ohio, Oklahoma, Oregon, Pennsylvania, South Dakota, Utah, Virginia, Washington, West Virginia, Wisconsin, Wyoming.

Psychiatrist-patient, four states: Arkansas, Colorado, Connecticut, Georgia.

Psychologist-patient, twenty-one states: Alabama, Arizona, Arkansas, Colorado, Delaware, Georgia, Idaho, Iowa, Kentucky, Michigan, Montana, Nevada, New Hampshire, New Mexico, New York, Oklahoma, Tennessee, Utah, Virginia, Washington, Wyoming.

Psychotherapist-patient, two states: California, Kansas.

1. If time allows, the therapist should consult the other professionals on the center staff, so that the conclusion of dangerousness will represent a consensus.

2. Such consensus should be reported to the center director with a recommendation that the information be given to the relevant authorities.

3. If feasible, the consent of the patient or of his next of kin or guardian should first be obtained.

In an emergency it may be necessary to take action without first completing all or any of the three steps above. Thus emergency hospitalization may be applied for, and confidential communications revealed, where the patient is likely to injure himself or others unless immediately restrained.

Particularly sensitive are problems of confidentiality in dealing with narcotics addicts. Here medical ethics are reinforced by the ethics of the addict subculture; "squealing" is a cardinal sin, and a criterion for separating the strong man from the weak sister; the strong don't squeal.

At the same time, factors that may call for breaking confidentiality are often more pressing than with other patients. The therapist learns that an addict patient is stealing to support his habit, or that he has syphilis, contracted by using a dirty needle. Unless treated he will infect others. If he refuses treatment, should the therapist report him? In states that have adopted the Uniform Narcotics Drug Act, physicians are required to report venereal disease cases they have treated. The general policy behind these laws is sound, but reporting will almost certainly destroy the narcotic rehabilitation program, with respect not only to the particular addict, but the entire addict population, for the word will quickly go out that the program cannot be trusted; its claims of confidentiality are untrue.

The privileged communications statutes typically do not protect requests made to the doctor to obtain narcotics illegally.

LEGAL LIABILITY

Confidentiality is primarily a matter of professional ethics. Under certain circumstances, however, a breach of confidentiality may violate the patient's legal rights and render one liable for damages. Possible bases for liability are libel and slander, and violation of the right to privacy.

Libel and slander are together called defamation. Libel is written; slander is oral. Defamation includes any statements that tend to injure reputation, that is, to diminish the respect or confidence with which one is regarded. Courts have held that imputing insanity or poverty is defamatory; so are statements that a person has attempted suicide, is a drunkard, a liar, or "queer," is having "wife troubles," or has made improper advances to a woman.

Truth is generally a defense, at least when the statement is made for good motives or for justifiable ends. Even if the statement turns out to be untrue, there is no liability if it was made for a proper purpose and in a reasonable way—for the safety of others, for example, or otherwise for the public interest. Consent, of course, is an absolute defense.

Highly objectionable disclosure of private facts, even though true and not such as to constitute libel or slander, may be ground for a damage suit based on invasion of privacy. But the cases allowing recovery have typically involved clearly unjustified publicity, as by publishing pictures of a person's deformity, or of his intimate anatomy. A center or a doctor revealing even confidential information about a patient to someone having a valid interest or a duty in the matter, would not be held liable.

CONFIDENTIALITY WITHIN THE CENTER

The center functions as a unity; the people it serves are patients of the center, not of an individual therapist. Cases may be handled by more than one professional, the therapist primarily responsible will consult other staff members, and the case may be discussed at staff meetings. Patients should be given to understand at the outset that this is how their cases will be handled.

Nonprofessional employees who are not as indoctrinated with the concept of confidentiality as professionals will also have access to information about patients. Secretarial and clerical employees should be instructed in the need for confidentiality. Patients may at times confide in such employees, or in kitchen or maintenance workers, and these too should therefore be instructed in how to deal with such situations. They should not only be warned against repeating such information to people outside the center, but should also be told to inform such patients that they will be obliged to pass on any relevant information to the professional staff—and to make this clear when the patient first begins to confide, instead of letting him unburden himself and then telling him.

Access to Records by Personnel   Specific rules should spell out which categories of personnel may be given access to inpatient and outpatient records, or parts of records. Trainees, for example, may perhaps be given such access by the trainee supervisor or chief of service. Employees having the task of carrying records from and to the records room should understand that they are not to read records.

Access to Records—Nights and Weekends   After regular hours and on weekends and holidays, medical records may need to be available for emergency cases. Access to the records should be given to a specific staff member, such as the resident or the charge nurse on duty. Care should also be taken that the person in charge does not lightly delegate the handling of the records to someone else.

Nonprofessional Mental Health Workers   Many, perhaps most, centers have a deliberate policy of employing indigenous nonprofessionals as outreach workers or as members of the treatment staff. Because they work in their own neighborhoods, they are known to a large number of people, and so is the fact that they work for the mental health center. When such a worker visits a certain address, the neighbors may recognize him as coming from the mental health center, and wonder who has "gone crazy" next door. When on a home visit he encounters someone who may be only a distant relative and the worker asks for Joe, the relative may learn for the first time that Joe is having mental difficulties. Or the worker sees a neighbor in the corridor of the center and recognizes that he must be there as a patient.

To teach nonprofessionals in a few weeks concepts of confidentiality that have been ingrained in the professionals' thinking over years of training and practice is not easy.

There is another side of the coin: the nonprofessional may have a sounder feeling than the professional for what is properly to be regarded as confidential in a given case. He may know that the patient is a member of a culture that is more mutually supportive than middle-class culture is, and that relatives and friends may properly be told how the patient is progressing because their interest is genuine and helpful. Much of the value we place on confidentiality may be the product of a middle-class culture, not necessarily applicable to people of a subculture in which people do more sharing of their troubles.

Group Therapy   Much of what is revealed in group therapy sessions may make choice gossip. Once it becomes known or suspected that information revealed in a session has been leaked outside of the group by other group members, patients are likely thereafter to be cautious about

133

revealing anything that may hurt them if repeated; and instead, present themselves only in a safely conventional light, which of course defeats the whole purpose.

Here again, the least that can be done is to (1) screen candidates for group therapy so as to keep out, as far as possible, those whose personality characteristics indicate a high risk that they won't be able to keep "juicy" information to themselves; and (2) emphasize to the group members the mutual interest in maintaining confidentiality if the project is to work. Once the group begins to function as it should, and participants do share with one another, the need for such confidentiality becomes so clear that violation becomes unlikely.

Expatients as Employees   Centers often make it a practice to employ expatients on the staff. When a young lady just hired for a clerical position is recognized as an expatient by one of the other girls on the force, the new employee may find herself isolated or shunned. Especially if she does not have the personality to win their quick friendship (or perhaps if she is seen as a sexual or other threat), she may be the subject of a whispering campaign: "She's an expatient, you know." On the other hand, if she is able to fit in, and the other girls come to like her, the "expatient" label may be discounted or forgotten.

Special Confidential File   Medical records of personnel of the center or of affiliated hospitals, or relatives of such personnel, who become patients of the center, had best be kept in a special confidential file separate from other records. The key to this file should be kept by the medical records librarian, and not made available to others. Entries in the records in this file should be handwritten or typed by the therapist himself.

Access to Records for Research   Professional persons conducting research, whether on the center staff or not, may be authorized to have access to records, but should be required to give assurance that any reports or publication resulting from such research shall adequately avoid identification of individuals. For cases where research necessitates removing records, rules should specify the number of days' notice that should be given to allow the requested records to be pulled, the maximum number that may be charged out at one time, and the length of time they may be kept.

NOTES

1. *American Medical Association News,* April 30, 1962.
2. The A.P.A. "Position Statement on Guidelines for Psychiatrists: Problems in

Confidentiality," approved Dec. 12–13, 1969, says: "In situations in which revelation of certain material may jeopardize the welfare of the patient, the psychiatrist may refuse to comply with a subpoena. However, this requires a special explanation to the judge and should be undertaken only with proper legal advice." *American Journal of Psychiatry* 126(April 1970) 187, 189. Except upon legal advice, it would seem more proper to request to be relieved from revealing harmful information, rather than to "refuse" to do so.

---

13   *Daniel Lieberman,* M.D.

A Community Mental Health Center and a State Mental Hospital in Partnership

The thrill and wonder of seeing your first patient, delivering your first baby, or removing your first appendix is multiplied a thousand fold when you encounter your first community of people for whom you plan to assume a high degree of responsibility for maintenance of mental health and treatment and prevention of mental illness and mental retardation. In becoming acquainted with our inner city community of 165,000 people the major problems were quickly identified—a large percentage of poor people, many on welfare; a high incidence of crime, drug addiction and abuse, juvenile delinquency, suicide, alcoholism, divorce; children without fathers (and sometimes without mothers); substandard housing, unemployment, educational deficiencies; and a large number of homeless, drifting, disenchanted, drug-using adolescents and young adults. We also recognized many community strengths which could be built upon—pockets of deep family ties, fierce loyalty to the neighborhood, citizen clubs and organizations, and public agencies performing their duties with skill and competence. We could see that the development of a structured system of communication among the various systems would assist all the service agencies to accomplish their objectives more effectively and would help many people to deal with their problems more productively.

Among the many systems we were concerned with, the Philadelphia State Hospital, which admitted patients from our community, was one that attracted our attention because we discovered that several hundred persons from our community were patients there. Fortunately, even before planning for the Community Mental Health Center commenced, meetings had been taking place between Jefferson's Department of Psychiatry and the director of the Philadelphia State Hospital for the purpose of developing a program of mutual assistance at the state hospital. Because the type of relationship suggested was so unique, portions of the original proposal by Jefferson in July 1967 are restated below:

Medicine, psychiatry and state mental health programs are changing rapidly today. In fact, the entire pattern of the responsibility for and delivery of mental health services has moved toward a model of the coordinated efforts of academic centers, federal, state and city programs, private institutions and community mental health centers.

No longer is it sufficient for these participants, if they are to be in the forefront in their fields, to catch up with the times; they must attempt in every way possible to stay ahead.

Schools of medicine and state mental health programs now should be able to accommodate many of the mental health needs of society since each is in a far better position today to approach the problems than at anytime in the past. More know-how, people, funds, and community acceptance are available now than ever before. The key ingredient, however, can be the design of comprehensive programs which will best utilize the accessible know-how, people, funds, and community acceptance to get the job done most effectively.

The material which follows presents a review and a proposal which relate to accomplishing the task of providing improved mental health services to the public in the framework of a joint program in which a medical school and a state mental health program would invest, to the fullest extent, their ideas, personnel, and energies toward a common goal.

Philadelphia State Hospital, because of its overwhelming size, structural arrangement and location, among many factors, has not been able to achieve the high quality program desired by its staff and administration. It is apparent that not only must the hospital decentralize and develop smaller workable units to bring about better care; at the same time increased investments of professional skills and leadership are essential to make such units capable of delivering better services.

The Department of Psychiatry, Jefferson Medical College, anticipates, as a major trend, an increasingly greater concern with programs which relate to public mental health. In order to better prepare its medical students and its psychiatric residents for the problems they are to face, and in order to more fully carry out its responsibilities in behavioral research and continuing education, Jefferson sees the need for a comprehensive clinical base which will provide the opportunities for services to patients, education, training, and research necessary to meet the challenges and responsibilities of psychiatry in our society today.

At present both the Philadelphia State Hospital and Jefferson Medical College have assets which could contribute much to a joint program, thus enhancing each, as well as the total endeavor. At the same time each has individual and particular deficiencies which would be overcome, in large part, by a workable close relationship between the two.

Philadelphia State is the largest hospital facility in the entire Commonwealth of Pennsylvania Mental Health Program. Administered under the Department of Public Welfare, its daily census now averages 5,500 patients, one of the largest concentrations of mentally and emotionally ill persons in the country. In addition to the need for more staff, the problems presented by very large numbers of patients, the many obstacles due to the physical arrangement of the plant, the geographical isolation, and the intellectual isolation all contribute to the difficulties of developing an adequate program.

Already the largest private medical school in the United States, Jefferson will further increase its medical student enrollment to 192 in the first year class, September 1967.

It must be pointed out that Jefferson, like many other medical schools, has been reluctant in the past to become involved in the sometimes overwhelming problems presented by an institution such as Philadelphia State Hospital. At the same time, it has been well established that massive infusions of training and research activities, more than anything else, enhance patient care in state mental hospital programs, even in the face of unpromising physical plants, inconvenient locations, obstacles resulting from large numbers of patients, and certain difficulties arising from an exclusively state-administered program.

It is anticipated that Jefferson's Department of Psychiatry can better meet its needs in training and research, and at the same time contribute significantly toward meeting the needs of Philadelphia State Hospital and those of the Commonwealth of Pennsylvania Mental Health Program in delivering better services to the community, by participating in a program proposed as follows:

1. The Department of Psychiatry, Jefferson Medical College, will operate a 950 bed mental hospital unit within Philadelphia State Hospital, to serve slightly less than one-fifth of the total existing patient census (5500). The program, experimental by design and operation, will be called The Jefferson Medical College Unit.

2. The administrative arrangements for the program will be planned so that the Jefferson Medical College Unit will be relatively autonomous, with` key professional staff carrying joint appointments at Philadelphia State Hospital (Jefferson Unit) and on the faculty of Jefferson Medical College. Qualifications would be met by all appointees. Through agreements with the Philadelphia State Hospital, certain basic services for the Jefferson Medical College Unit will be provided such as (a) utilities, plant maintenance, warehousing; (b) major medical and surgical services; (c) activities not now separately provided and not necessary to be so provided, for example, chapel services, large hospital community activities in the main auditorium, and so forth.

3. The existing East Unit of Philadelphia State Hospital, including buildings E1 through E8, plus the gymnasium, kitchen, O.T. shop, activities building, and laboratory facilities will be utilized as the physical facilities for the Jefferson Unit.

4. The Jefferson Medical College Unit will relate to certain established catchment areas in Philadelphia which geographically and functionally may be coordinated conveniently with the Jefferson program at Philadelphia State Hospital. Patients from areas in Region VII served by the proposed

Jefferson Medical College Community Mental Health Center in South Philadelphia and the proposed Northeast Community Mental Health Center in
Northeast Philadelphia will be admitted to the Jefferson Unit at Philadelphia State Hospital. In addition to the above catchment area services, patients from other areas of Philadelphia would be admitted and cared for,
when necessary, in the best interest of sharing the responsibility for the total
Philadelphia community, within the limits of the bed capacity and effective
programming of the Jefferson Medical College Unit.

5. The Jefferson Medical College Unit will provide a complete mental
hospital program for:

    (a)   general psychiatric patients, acute and chronic;

    (b)   special categories of patients, including separate activity areas
           for: alcoholic patients, geriatric patients, late adolescents, men-
           tally retarded, narcotic addicts, sociopathic individuals.

6. Educational and training programs will be conducted for medical students, interns, psychiatric residents, practicing physicians, student nurses,
and students in various fields of human behavior.

7. Appropriate behavioral research will be carried out with particular emphasis in the clinical areas directly related to those problems seen in a mental hospital setting.

8. Educational and training programs will be developed to benefit other
state mental hospitals.

9. The Jefferson Unit will assume the position of an *experimental hospital,* concerned always with trying and testing new approaches for developing
and evaluating effective models of care which may be fed back into Philadelphia State Hospital and also into the overall Commonwealth of Pennsylvania Mental Health Program.

10. The Jefferson Unit will utilize and test all available means and
methods in modern communications and transportation to facilitate the proposed program and bring about an effective working relationship between
geographic areas involving mental health personnel, patients, organizations,
facilities, programs, time, and money.

The opportunities for teaching and research in the clinical areas are clear
and apparent, but perhaps even more significant in their uniqueness are the
opportunities for training in mental health administration and of instilling in
mental health trainees a concept of the 'total perspective' in which they can
carry out their own fairly narrow specialized activity. This appreciation of the
total combination of services and their interrelatedness should do much to
make each participant in the program more effective. The feedback to the state
would be extremely valuable.

It is important that the proposed hospital unit be considered by Philadelphia State Hospital and by the Commonwealth of Pennsylvania Mental Health
Program as being a state service program, with the responsibilities and obligations of similar hospitals, but the medical school operated, with the explicit purpose of experimenting with program design, exploring new methodologies and
modalities, and conducting research and training in those areas throughout the
state system which need upgrading, improving and, in some instances, drastic

reshaping. In other words, the Jefferson Medical College Unit should be the experimental model seeking to develop an ideal model, with constant investment of both research and training into the total system of service for patients.

Although in the past medical school departments of psychiatry have shied away from the responsibility for the operation of public service programs, today there is justifiable criticism of this attitude and position. Psychiatry more and more is concerning itself with approaches other than the one-to-one therapeutic relationship. Teaching and research can be done best where there is responsible involvement for coping with the problems and responding to the challenges presented. Those who teach surgery, operate; those who teach medicine do so through evaluating and treating their patients. Psychiatry, likewise, must cope with the seriously ill patient as an individual, alone, and as a member of a group in a community, if we are to prepare our trainees realistically for what they will have to cope with in tomorrow's world with the increasing demands which society thrusts upon the health-science professions.

While this proposal was being discussed, detailed planning for the Jefferson Community Mental Health Center was underway. The state hospital administration unitized the hospital so that there were five distinct hospital areas which provided services to patients from five specific geographic areas of the city. One of these five areas contained patients whose residence was in the Jefferson catchment area.

The proposed director of the Community Health Center who was conducting the planning made arrangements with the state hospital to spend two days a week there for the purpose of organizing the hospital staff and beginning an intensive accelerated treatment program. However, an even more important aspect of this phase was the establishment of policies and procedures for rapid movement of the hospital patients into other services and facilities of the Community Mental Health Center. Arrangements were made for hospital staff to follow patients into the community as well as for Community Mental Health Center staff to participate in the hospital program.

For purposes of general orientation, several Community Mental Health Center personnel were assigned part-time to serve at the state hospital, and several hospital personnel were assigned part-time to the Community Mental Health Center. As an example, a hospital psychologist was assigned to the Crisis Intervention Unit of the Community Mental Health Center. Here it was demonstrated how working intensively with the mentally ill patient and his family (or other people significant to him) at the time of crisis for several hours could resolve a problem that otherwise would have required hospital admission and perhaps several weeks of inpatient treatment. Following the crisis intervention the patient (and his family) were followed by the psychologist for continued treatment as long as necessary in one of the facilities of the Community Mental Health Center.

Another example is that of the director of the Community Mental Health Center, Adult Outpatient Service, who spent one day a week at the state hospital conducting family therapy sessions with as many as thirty or forty employees in attendance. Here was demonstrated the importance of involving the family in the treatment and rehabilitation process as soon as possible and thereby uncovering some of the pathological communication problems which may have been operating in the maintenance of the patient's illness. This was also a good technique for preparing for the patient's early discharge from the hospital into the Community Mental Health Center. This was the first time that family therapy was used in the hospital setting.

Employees of both the Community Mental Health Center and the state hospital were encouraged to attend special teaching sessions that were held during the year. The state hospital personnel were particularly helped by the weekly research and training conferences at the Community Mental Health Center which focused on interesting new developments in the mental health field. Monthly case conferences were established and attended by personnel of both agencies on a monthly rotating basis with the conference being held at a different facility each time. Hospital therapists were encouraged to follow their patients as they left the hospital and entered into the community program. Regular days were established for follow-up patient contacts in the community's facilities.

Community Mental Health Center personnel concerned with aftercare and rehabilitation services were assigned to the state hospital to begin early work with patients identified as being good candidates for rehabilitation services. These people worked closely with the Bureau of Vocational Rehabilitation and it was possible to obtain an employee from the Bureau on an almost full-time basis at the hospital unit for the purpose of testing, evaluating, and recommending appropriate patients for vocational rehabilitation activities.

The director of the Jefferson Unit at the state hospital, an expert in the field of group therapy with geriatric patients, established a program in the Community Mental Health Center, on a one day a week basis, of aged individuals for participation in group psychotherapy. This stimulated the Community Mental Health Center staff to pay more attention to the therapeutic potential of therapy for elderly patients and the caseload of this category of patients increased rapidly.

Considerable effort went into the establishment of methods and procedures for patient referral with particular attention to insuring the rapid movement of patients and records from one facility to another as indicated. A coordinator for continuity of care attached to the Community Mental Health Center has full time responsibility for insuring that appropriate procedures are followed which are effective and efficient and that patients get what they need when they need it.

With the mixture of personnel from the two agencies an element of trust and affection developed which replaced the original suspicion and aloofness.

In April 1968, the Community Mental Health Center received its federal staffing grant and a contract between the Commonwealth of Pennsylvania and Jefferson Medical College had been signed and the program implemented. By July 1969, the 950 patients under care and treatment in the Jefferson unit of the hospital became 700 and by July 1970, the 700 became 500. We anticipate this will be 300 by July 1971, 100 by July 1972, and by July 1973, the community should no longer have need of the state hospital for general psychiatric patients. State hospital annual admission rates from the Jefferson catchment area have been reduced to thirty per 100,000 population, about one-sixth of what one would have expected just a few short years ago from an area of the character described.

Completely meeting the goals described above will be dependent upon the establishment of an adequate psychiatric inpatient facility for the Jefferson Community Mental Health Center which does not yet exist. At the present time there are thirty beds for adult mental disorders, and ten beds for mentally retarded children. It should be emphasized that the reduction in state hospital population is a function of improved inpatient service, availability of alternative modes of treatment in community based facilities and organization to provide for rapid flow of information, movement of patients and movement of personnel.

We have not documented the problems, disappointments, and frustrations which have accompanied this program since its onset. Suffice to say that the assets have far outweighed the liabilities and in the process many of us have become bigger and wiser.

An Information System for a Comprehensive
Community Mental Health Center

An information system for a community mental health center must encompass a relatively large number of input, storage, retrieval, and output activities to provide "interested parties" with data they desire concerning the various aspects of the center's operations. These interested parties are the information *consumers*. They range from *local* constituents (board members, county commissioners; contractors such as school superintendents; the administrative staff of the mental health center; certain clinical staff) to more distant constituencies (the state mental health agency; the State Health Department; the Regional Office of the Department of Health, Education, and Welfare; the National Institute of Mental Health).

Information has many uses, and what is relevant for one purpose (or group of consumers) becomes meaningless for others. The ideal information system would provide information in its most relevant and digestible form to each information consumer having a legitimate need for such data from the center. Moreover, it would provide this information immediately on request and in any depth required. Thus, such an *ideal* system could respond at once either to a request from a local board member concerning the unit cost of services or to a request from the state mental health agency for information concerning the percentage of time devoted to indirect services. The system could also provide expenditure data for the center administration and could provide program data for the clinical staff in regard to the use of the several services and in regard to patient characteristics such as diagnosis, age, and sex.

To round out the picture, let it be presumed that the center will have a reseach program. Research groups often become the most demanding of all information consumers in terms of the variety, depth, and accuracy of data which they wish collected and processed. They are most likely to desire extensive clinical data including mental status items, ward behavior ratings, nursing notes, and summary dynamic formulations. An *ideal* information system could meet each of these needs.

Figure 14-1 provides a diagrammatic presentation of an ideal information system in the setting of the total mental health center. It demonstrates in the broadest sense how information is interrelated with the various functions and activities of a center.[1] It seems clear, however, that few if any mental health centers are ready at this time to develop such an extensive information system. Neither the staff nor the board members have sufficient training or experience to develop or utilize such a system. Moreover, the cost of such a system is prohibitive because of the limited financial resources of the typical new center.

Accordingly, it seems far more reasonable for a center to begin the development of its information system by establishing a limited program rather than attempting to initiate a fully developed comprehensive system immediately. Whether the information is limited or ideal, however, it still can be developed on the basis of the theory and methods of operations research, an approach which was used in conceptualizing the

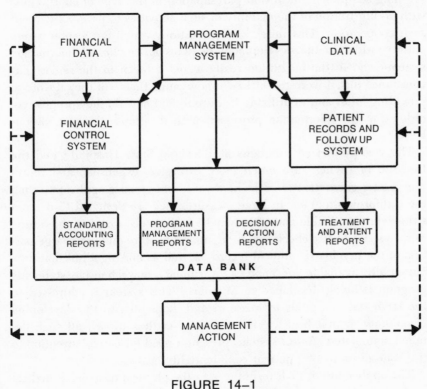

FIGURE 14–1
*Use of Information System
in Management—
Conceptual Model*

143

ideal system described above and one which has already been described in terms of its specific applications to mental health services.[2]

As an alternative to a total or ideal information system, it is possible to develop a system which is designed primarily to meet clinical needs. There is already a growing body of literature and experience regarding the establishment of clinical information systems in mental health settings.

One of the first and in many ways *the* pioneer effort in the development of a psychiatric information system, largely clinical, was a project conducted with very extensive federal support at a large California state hospital between 1962 and 1965.[3] It reached a rather premature demise but did demonstrate that the operations research approach of the early 1960's and the relevant technology could adequately collect, process, and display patient data from a large state hospital. Probably the most important outcome of this project was the demonstrated difficulty in developing adequate clinical staff participation in this type of effort, along with an illustration of the inability of such activities to progress without such cooperation. This raises major questions which any center group must consider in the development of plans for a *clinical* information system—who in the institution really wants it (even in the remote circumstance that it were to be "free"), how much time will they devote to providing input and in utilizing its output, and how do they propose coordinating the information processed with decision-making at various levels?

The well-publicized programs at Rockland State Hospital[4] and the Institute of Living[5] are much more extensive, expensive, and represent a later generation of both "hardware" and systems application than the California program. In large measure, they are designed to demonstrate what is possible and what may be feasible elsewhere in the future. Both systems utilize check-lists to input and to store on tape a large portion of the psychiatric clinical record, as well as making all of that data potentially available for analysis. A similar comprehensive statewide program is being developed in Missouri.[6] This system is addressed to the large state hospitals in Missouri and, hopefully, to the developing community mental health centers there. Needless to say, all such detailed, automated *clinical* systems present a need for careful attention to the issue of protecting patient confidentiality.

The application of such techniques to the physical or general medical evaluation of patients has been described by the Department of Medical Methods Research, Permanente Medical Group, Oakland, California.

They have developed systems whereby very comprehensive physical evaluations can be processed on a largely automated basis.[7]

Undoubtedly, the most ambitious development in the *clinical* information system field has been that directed by Lawrence L. Weed, M.D., and referred to as the "problem-oriented medical record."[8] Weed's original work was done at Western Reserve and has now been transferred to the University of Vermont where this very highly automated system for collecting clinical and related data is becoming *the* key tool in the education of physicians, nurses, and so forth. Some limited psychiatric data is included as part of the general medical evaluation. Obviously, a system such as this has tremendous potential but will only affect the individual mental health center rather indirectly during the next decade as a result of "spinoffs."

In order for medical and psychiatric records to become an effective part of an automated clinical information system, there has to be, in the words of one author, a great deal of "regularization and stylization" in medical and psychiatric workups.[9] Unfortunately, this often means resorting to checklists which are an anathema to many clinicians. An excellent review of the major approaches to reducing psychiatric and psychological information to standardized forms (check lists) is to be found in the published proceedings of a 1965 conference on methodology of classification.[10] The application of such standardized information to issues of diagnosis has been extensively developed by groups at Columbia [11] and Houston.[12] Those responsible for developing and directing new centers today will generally need to borrow heavily from existing clinical information systems, thus keeping their developmental costs minimal and making it possible to finance the system from the ongoing center budget and not from special demonstration or other research funds.

Examples of forms developed for the existing information system at the Northwest Community Mental Health Center, Bexar County Hospital District, San Antonio, Texas, can be obtained from the author of this chapter. Examples of other specific approaches can be found in publications of the National Institute of Mental Health.

When developing a new or adapting an existing information system, it is necessary that the staff of the community mental health center first determine their essential data needs. An excellent basis for beginning is to consult with personnel of both the National Institute of Mental Health and the state mental health authority in order to obtain from both agencies details about their requirements for information to be included in periodic reports. Using this material as a starting point, the staff can then review their own needs for information to be used for administrative and clinical purposes, and they can also determine the extent to which these needs will be met by efforts to satisfy state and federal requirements. The experience of many existing centers suggests that this required information is sufficiently detailed and comprehensive to assure that many more administrative and clinical questions can be answered with it than are generally asked.

A decision will need to be made as to the type of input forms and devices, the mechanism of storage, the procedures for retrieval, and the various output forms necessary. Will a computer be necessary for storage, retrieval, and output; if so, of what capacity related to volume and complexity of the information? How should the data be inputed? Will key-punched cards be adequate or will it be necessary to go to various mark-sensing devices? What are the problems and expenses involved in these and how do they relate to volume considerations? Is it possible that hand-filled forms, filing cabinets, manual search, and typed lists and tables will be adequate, at least for several years? It must be remembered that this information system is being weighed budgetwise against more clinicians or more support personnel of other types! The Western Interstate Commission for Higher Education has held a number of conferences on these and related issues and has two specific monographs available which are directly relevant to these bread-and-butter issues.

The purpose of this section has been to introduce the reader rather generally to the topic of information systems in community mental health centers. Current technology provides a potential for developing extremely useful methods for collecting and applying data to the operation of a center, but just as each center must adapt its program specifically to the unique needs of its catchment area, so too each center must adapt its information system to the unique needs of its program and staff.

NOTES

1. *Management Support System for the San Antonio Mental Health Centers*, Inteck Associates, Inc., Austin, Texas, May 1969.

2. H. W. Halpert, G. Horvath, and J. Young, *An Administrator's Handbook on the Applications of Operations Research*, National Clearing House for Mental Health Information, U.S. Printing Office, Washington, D.C.

3. R. Graetz, "The Computer—A New Tool in Psychiatry," *Hospital and Community Psychiatry*, 17(1966): 66–69.

4. N. Kline, and E. M. Laska, *Computers and Electronic Devices in Psychiatry* (New York: Grune-Stratton, 1968); E. Laska, "Scribe—A Method for Producting Automated, Narrative Psychiatric Case Histories," *American Journal of Psychiatry*, 124(1967): 82–84; M. Rosenberg, B. Glueck, and C. Stroebel, "The Computer and the Clinical Decision Process: I," *American Journal of Psychiatry*, 124(1967): 595; M. Rosenberg, B. Glueck, and C. Stroebel, "The Computer and the Clinical Decision Process: II," *American Journal of Psychiatry*, 125(January 1969): supplement 2–7.

5. J. G. Slettin, G. Ulett, et al, *Standard System of Psychiatry*, Missouri Division of Mental Diseases, Missouri Institute of Psychiatry, St. Louis, Missouri, January 1968; M. Collen, "Periodic Health Examinations Using an Automated Multitest Laboratory," *Journal of the American Medical Association*, 195(1966): 830.

6. Lawrence L. Weed, "The Problem-Oriented Medical Record," School of Medicine, Case Western Reserve University, Cleveland, Ohio, June 1969. Also, "Medical Records that Guide and Teach," *New England Journal of Medicine*, 278(1968): 593.

7. B. Gordon, "Regularization and Stylization of Medical Records," *Journal of the American Medical Association*, 212(1970): 1502.

8. M. Katz, et al, "Classification in Psychiatry and Psychopathology," *Public Health Service Publication No. 1584*, U.S. Government Printing Office, Washington D.C. (see particularly Zubin, 353–376).

9. R. Spitzer, and J. Endicott, "Diagno II: Further Developments in a Computer Program," *American Journal of Psychiatry*, 125, 7(January 1969): supplement 12–21.

10. J. Overall, and L. Hollister, "Computer Procedures for Psychiatric Classification," *Journal of the American Medical Association*, 187(1964): 583–588.

11. P. Person, "A Statistical Information System for Community Mental Health Centers," *Public Health Service Publication No. 1863*, U.S. Government Printing Office, Washington, D.C., March 1969; Community Mental Health Center Data Systems, *Public Health Service Publication No. 1990*, U.S. Government Printing Office, Washington, D.C., 1969.

12. *Establishing a Data Base for a Statewide Mental Health Program*, Western Interstate Commission on Higher Education, University of East Campus, Boulder, Colorado, February 1968; *Central Record Systems*, January 1968.

REFERENCES

American Psychiatric Association, Position Statement on Guidelines for Psychiatrists. "Problems in Confidentiality." *American Journal of Psychiatry* 126(April 1970): 187.

Bradley, J. C., Frank, A. R. "An Analysis of the Information and Referral Service of a Mental Health Association." *Mental Hygiene* 51(July 1967): 366–370.

DeWitt, C. *Privileged Communications between Physician and Patient.* Springfield, Ill.: Charles C. Thomas, 1958.

Gardner, E. A. "The Use of a Psychiatric Case Register in the Planning and Evaluation of a Mental Health Program." *Psychiatric Research Report American Psychiatric Association* 22(April 1967): 259–281.

Greenblatt, M. "Unitization Has Been a Catalyst." *International Journal of Psychiatry* 7(April 1969): 224–225.

Group for the Advancement of Psychiatry. *Confidentiality and Privileged Communications in the Practice of Psychiatry.* Report No. 45, 1960.

McNeil, J. N., Llewellyn, C. E., Jr., McCollough, T. E., "Community Psychiatry and Ethics." *American Journal of Orthopsychiatry* 40(January 1970): 22–29.

Miller, G. E. "The Unit System. A New Approach in State Hospital Care." *Texas Medicine* 65(September 1969): 44–51.

Moseley, R. W. "Interagency Planning for Aftercare of Mental Patients in the Community." *Public Health Report* 83(August 1968): 695–701.

Pugh, T. F., MacMahon, B. "Measurement of Discontinuity of Psychiatric Inpatient Care." *Public Health Report* 82(June 1967): 553–538.

Scherl, D. J., English, J. T. "Community Mental Health and Comprehensive Health Service Programs for the Poor." *American Journal of Psychiatry* 125(June 1969): 1666–1674.

Schulberg, H. C., Baker, F. "Unitization: Decentralizing the Mental Hospitalopolis." *International Journal of Psychiatry* 7(April 1969): 213–223.

Sifneos, P. E. "The Interdisciplinary Team." *Psychiatric Quarterly* 43(1969): 123–130.

Slovenko, R. *Psychotherapy, Confidentiality and Privileged Communication.* Springfield, Ill.: Charles C. Thomas, 1966.

Weihofen, H. *Legal Services and Community Mental Health Centers.* Washington, D.C.: Joint Information Service of the American Psychiatric Association and the National Association for Mental Health, 1969.

Zenoff, E. "Confidential and Privileged Communications." *Journal of the American Medical Association* 182(1962): 656.

V

Inpatient Services

EDITORS' INTRODUCTION

Inpatient services played a crucial role in the delivery of mental health services long before the community mental health center concept was initiated. In many respects, the history of organized mental health programs is a history of inpatient or hospital services.

The community mental health center has taken many of the basic principles of traditional inpatient care and has modified them in content and placed them in the context of multiple services. In the community mental health center concept, inpatient services no longer are considered to be the first approach to patient care. Rather, they are seen as being readily available for selected patients who require acute care with the implicit assumption that the direction of treatment will be toward returning the patient to the community as rapidly as possible and placing him in other types of services for continuing treatment.

Not understanding the place of inpatient services in the total community mental health center approach has often led many centers to overestimate the number of inpatient beds required in the local community to deliver necessary services. In fact, some community mental health center facilities have been constructed or renovated to include a higher number of beds than have actually been utilized. Consequently, in the course of continuing planning, many of these centers have had to find alternate uses for these inpatients beds such as night hospitalization.

The growing trend toward recognizing alcoholism and drug abuse services as part of the total community mental health center approach has also reflected on the utilization of inpatient services. In these areas, many center planners are now recognizing that hospital based twenty-four-hour services are not mandatory in all cases and that a different type of twenty-four-hour service, namely a detoxification center which is less costly and more efficient, can be developed.

Another important contribution of the community mental health center has been to stimulate thinking regarding other types of specialized inpatient services, especially for adolescents and children. As a consequence of the concept of acute care, the reduced demands for inpatient beds which will serve adults only can lead to the creation of inpatient services in the community which will meet the short-term treatment needs of some adolescents and children.

15　　　　　　　　　　　　*Donald P. Wilson*, M.D., *and*
　　　　　　　　　　　　　　John Guerrant, M.D.

Organizing Inpatient / Partial Care Services

Marin General Hospital opened the doors of its community mental health center in November 1968. Housed in a new building connected to the hospital by a bridge hallway, easy passage from the inpatient suites on the second floor of the center to the reception and emergency room areas of the main hospital is possible.

Each of the two inpatient units has single and double bedrooms for fourteen patients surrounding a large central living area which provides room for an additional twenty-five or more day patients. The center can therefore accommodate twenty-eight inpatients and fifty or more day patients without any appearance of crowding. Noise control has been successfully engineered to allow the formation of several groupings in the large central living spaces without interference from each other. Wall-to-wall carpeting allows groups to be seated on the floor without having to move furniture, providing an informality in which patients can feel more at home with the staff.

STAFFING

Not encumbered with an existing staff embedded in fixed ways of doing things, the center was able to attract a group of people who shared the desire to build an inpatient service where growth would take precedence over the more usual preoccupation with controls.

A heightening of the sense of the possible phase characteristically occurs when a highly motivated, freshly chosen staff comes together to build a new program. Unfortunately, this can be easily lost as the organization of daily work proceeds. We have postulated that deterioration into stale routines results from a failure of a staff to find a means for positive resolution of conflicts within itself. The staff then resorts to the avoidance of conflict by withdrawal and by stereotyping one another into prescribed roles and tight compartments.

The quality of the staff selected is crucial if this process is to be avoided. In our selection for the inpatient/partial care unit, the commitment to growth was so crucial that no applicant was accepted who was not willing or did not appear able to handle the pressures commensurate with active participation in building a new program involving new principles. Each staff member must be willing to examine his own feelings, especially those which signal an avoidance of conflict (for instance, boredom, depression, deadness, withdrawal, and so forth). In becoming aware of these feelings he knows when he is disowning responsibility for his own discontent. Only by accepting responsibility for the failures as well as successes of the program can there be a guarantee that a staff member will be moved to re-inject life back into the program when it has been momentarily lost.

Thus, in our system, each staff member is his own "chairman." He not only accepts the consequences of failing to follow procedural regulations, but is also assigned the responsibility to whatever consequences there might be of *not* breaking "rules." This principle is worth underscoring. It is not an empty or half-true slogan. Within our staff, anyone is expected to say anything he believes. While he is not guaranteed immunity from disapproval from his peers or supervisors, neither is he guaranteed protection from responsibility for whatever results from his failure to speak up when his opinion is in disagreement with those in authority. This insures the fullest utilization of available talent even in the presence of an authoritarian structure. We believe that full freedom of expression permitted by a guarantee that no administrative retaliation will occur effectively limits the abuses of authority as well as the "cop-outs" of those not in authority. At the same time, it avoids the tedious and often disjointed process of arriving at decisions by consensus.

Staff members are expected to express not only their ideas and criticisms, but also their feelings of hurt, anger, jealousy, admiration, affection, approval, and so forth. It goes without saying that we do not attain perfect openness, but we take this principle very seriously. All of us are convinced that the staff's willingness to communicate breathes life into the program and keeps it circulating among the members of our community, both staff and patients.

PROGRAM

The medical model for interstaff and staff-patient relationships is incorporated as a prominent thread running throughout the design of our program. In the definitive diagnostic work, in the necessary attention to medico-legal considerations, and in the management and reduction of symptoms through the use of medications, or (rarely) electroconvulsive therapy, the medical model for treating sickness and assigning responsibility is followed. We are not among those who wish to throw out this model entirely, but regard it as an essential dimension to our psychiatric service which is the only public resource for the care of major psychiatric emergencies in the county.

On the other hand, we consider such a model strikingly deficient when it precludes an appreciation of the familial and social dimensions of the problems which result in mental hospitalization and when it is used to absolve the patient of responsibility for himself. In this regard, we are firm in limiting the role we allow "sickness" to play in explaining what is happening to those who come to us for help. In the brief time people are hospitalized (ten days is average) we engage them in a variety of intensive here-and-now encounters. Through these, we encourage the patient to go through a series of discoveries, the most important of which is the breakthrough experience that occurs in making the connection between the unwanted symptoms they would have us rid them of and the hidden agenda that operates within them.

All, however, is not confrontation. Our staff has few inhibitions about offering comfort to someone who is hurting. For example, we rely considerably on medications which can abort a psychotic process.

In the end, it must be said that we consider ourselves most successful when a beginning sense of dignity is established with the discovery by the patient that he has a responsibility for his predicament and can now credit himself for the accomplishments he is making in his recovery. If he later finds himself in conflict, it is hoped that he will know where and how to reach out for assistance and will assume the responsibility for working to solve his own problems rather than make an impotent protest which can, in extreme form, result in an exacerbation of mental illness.

PROBLEMS

We have spoken so far of the theoretical approach of our program and staff toward inpatient services. It must be recognized that, realistically, the psychiatrists who admit their patients to the units are often by no means equally committed to our orientation. While the staff of the inpatient/partial care units were carefully chosen for their talent and ability to participate in the kind of setting described, many staff members in other services were largely transferees from an existing county program that had been far more traditional in its style.

Several months before the center was opened the director was hired and his initial task was to organize the new inpatient/partial care program and staff it prior to arranging for the administrative transfer of the previously existing county outpatient staff over to the center under his direction. Consequently, the inpatient/partial care staff had several weeks of orientation with the new center director and were on the way to becoming a vital team in which professional poses were discarded in preference for an open, spirited interaction between all staff members. The outpatient staff of psychiatrists, psychologists, and social workers, on the other hand, were used to working in a semi-isolated fashion, engaging patients primarily in one-to-one psychoanalytically oriented psychotherapy.

There were inevitable clashes. While many of the outpatient psychiatrists regarded the activities of the nursing staff as accessory to their individual psychotherapy, others came to appreciate their part in the overall regimen for the patient, limiting it to that which was necessary to maintain good medical practice and letting the programs on the units become the definitive treatment experience for the patients.

Unquestionably, the general hospital staff would also have preferred that we rock as few boats as possible and accommodate ourselves to the previous ways of doing things. Consequently, the freedom in dress allowed the staff, including the hip, disheveled fashion of youth today,

153

also set the stage of a long series of cultural shocks. The medical staff of the general hospital was particularly disturbed by the contrast which our center provided to the sedate, clinical ways of the rest of the hospital.

They also resented our admission policy which required a telephone screening with one of our staff rather than a simple telephone call to the general hospital admitting nurse who usually never challenged the appropriateness of the admission as long as there was an available bed.

Also troubling to the previously existing outpatient staff was our requirement that nonpsychiatrists must have a psychiatrist collaborator in the management of any case admitted to one of the units. Prior to this ruling, the nonpsychiatrists were setting up their own treatment regimens for patients which were often intolerable psychiatric practice and out of touch with the kind of program we offered.

We have chosen to describe some of these difficulties inherent in developing a new inpatient care concept to emphasize a very practical point. These difficulties need to be anticipated and the bases for prompt and full communication about them need to be established early. This means that the key people who plan to establish an inpatient service of this type, particularly the director, must be in the community for some time before the program begins operation. The freedom of an inpatient service to develop its own program and the survival of that program in the community depends upon an adequate explanation, preferably in advance, to the general community, especially to the health professionals and institutions, the social agencies, to the bodies exercising political and fiscal power, and to the police.

There are also other and more compelling reasons for the early selection of a director, notable among which are that he will have an opportunity to influence the construction (or remodeling) of physical facilities to be consistent with his program and to attract and orient a suitable staff. To be avoided, most definitely, is the situation where inpatient facilities are planned by one group of people, some staff selected and some parts of a center program put into operation by a partially different group; and then finally a director selected to lead a somewhat different group when the center begins full operation. This will lead to conflicts of philosophy between the director and some elements of his staff, and force the center into giving service before adequate education to its programs can be made even for the especially important groups mentioned above. Once the inpatient program is in operation, the work load of the staff, due to the demands for service and the need to cope with the effects of these misunderstandings, may make the community educative effort difficult and prolonged.

It should be remembered that once a vital program is set into operation as ours has been, the pace at which it proceeds is not altogether a matter to be deliberately decided. A staff and program have a life of their own and efforts to slow its processes to a rate acceptable to the community may cripple it as effectively as it may be crippled by the reaction of an outraged community to the faster pace. Sometimes a happy medium cannot be found. A program can move too fast for the community to accept but, if slowed, die of a failure to be true to itself. Most of the community, especially the patients and their families served by our inpatient/partial care services, have accepted our approach and sense its potential. Nevertheless, we continue to be under attack from some conservative elements of the community with regard to the issues which we have described. The outcome of the resulting struggle is still not determined, but the elements involved are, we believe, crucial in the development of a community oriented, short-term, inpatient service.

16

Henry Frey, M.D., *and*
David J. Muller, M.D.

Community Mental Health Center and State Hospital Collaboration through Busing of Twenty-Four Patients

An honorable and realistic concordat with its already existing state hospital is a significant concern to every developing community mental health center. At this still early stage of "The Fourth Psychiatric Revolution"[1] the relationships are often uncertain. One of the predictable and understandable effects of the community mental health center legislation was to create an atmosphere somewhat similar to that which has characterized the relationship between indigenous forces within "emerging nations" and the colonial powers which hitherto had been in charge of the "catchment country."

Levenson and Ozarin, in a paper entitled "The Future of the Public Mental Hospital,"[2] spoke clearly on many of the issues which are involved in the relationship between the community mental health center and the state hospital and which have specific significance for the program to be discussed here.

They asked, "What will be the future of public mental hospitals as community mental health center programs expand?" They suggested that their emerging role lies in joining the community's network of human services by adapting present organizational structures to permit flexibility and change. Mental hospital staffs can provide leadership and support to local, regional, and state mental health programs if they incorporate current scientific, technological, and social changes in their operations. They stated, "We believe that the inflexibility of the single model (the state hospital) over a century of time has been a crucial factor in producing nontherapeutic conditions in mental hospitals. The major characteristics of a community mental health center program is flexibility in use of staff and facilities to meet the needs of the community it serves. Designed to fill gaps in services rather than to duplicate them, the center organizational structure seeks to create community networks of institutions and agencies which together provide comprehensive mental health and related services . . . The future of the public mental hospital lies in the multiple opportunities for participation in the expanding network of community services . . . The establishment of a network of comprehensive mental health services that includes both community based and institutionally based programs must, however, insure a two-way flow with patients passing freely between the mental hospital and the community center. The public mental hospital should not be viewed as a resource for untreatable patients."

In January 1968, the Adams County Mental Health Center opened. Its philosophy was predicated upon a true joining with the Adams Team of the Fort Logan Mental Health Center (a state hospital facility) which had been the primary provider of inpatient and partial hospitalization services to the residents of Adams County for several years. The construction and staffing grant applications requesting federal participation in the Adams County Mental Health Center were prepared in collaboration with the Fort Logan Adams Team and with the encouragement and involvement of the senior administrative staff members of that hospital. Our collective objective was to bring about the creation of the best possible community mental health center program for Adams County, making every effort to avoid the duplication of meaningful existing services, through a program which would make possible the maximum participation of the state hospital in this newly created community mental health center. Our plan was to neither discard nor duplicate a Fort Logan's existing inpatient service.

With this in mind, the new community mental health center facility was designed so that a day hospital program could be provided in one of the three wings and be used for twenty-four-hour patients brought from Fort Logan each day, in addition to those patients coming directly from their homes.

This exciting new idea challenged us, but the obvious difficulties also evoked many uncertainties. We knew of no precedent in any of the developing community mental health centers, nor had we heard of anyone who had contemplated transporting the inpatient population from an existing state hospital program back to its community on a regular five-day-a-week basis.

SETTING

While there were some difficulties, this plan was technically feasible. The Fort Logan Mental Health Center is located in the extreme southwest corner of the Denver metropolitan area and is eighteen miles and a thirty to forty-five minutes drive from the Adams County Mental Health Center in the extreme northeast section of the metropolitan area.

Adams County, which is located directly north of and adjacent to Denver County, has a 1971 census of almost 195,000, an area of 1,246 square miles, and is the fourth most heavily populated of the sixty-four counties in Colorado. Approximately half of Colorado's population resides in the metropolitan Denver area and 8.5 percent of the state's population lives in Adams County. Our Adams County catchment area is contiguous to the City and County of Denver and it contains a broad spectrum of definable socioeconomic and psychosocial contrasts and variations. Today, as a result of an almost explosive increase in population, it has become a major suburban area containing a great proportion of the heavy industry of the metropolitan Denver area while still retaining vast areas devoted to farming and livestock raising.

HISTORY

Many factors argued in favor of an integral program linkage between Adams County Mental Health Center and Fort Logan. The community mental health program began in Adams County under modest and limited circumstances in 1958 as a small, part-time clinic conducted by a visiting professional team from the University of Colorado Medical Center. The program was a nonprofit endeavor supervised by a citizen Board of Directors.

In 1961, in response to the efforts of the Board of Directors and other interested community members, the clinic acquired a local staff of two full-time therapists and a part-time medical director. Coincidentally, the Fort Logan Mental Health Center also came into existence in 1961 as the second state mental hospital in Colorado; the other hospital being the almost eighty-year-old Colorado State Hospital in the City of Pueblo, 112 miles south of Denver.

Fort Logan was designed to provide treatment facilities for up to 3,000 patients gathered from the approximately one million residents of the Denver metropolitan area. The planners of this hospital looked toward a new type of decentralized program which would provide intensive full and partial hospital treatment with every effort being made to avoid long-term institutional care. Interestingly, the hospital only planned space for a maximum of 400 beds although the traditional ratio of beds to population served called for approximately 3,500.

Since the program's inception, the twenty-four-hour patients at Fort Logan have always been treated in the day care program along with day care patients coming to the hospital from the community. The primary treatment philosophy has revolved around the therapeutic community with consistent encouragement to patients to return to the community and develop "healthy behavior." It, therefore, was logical to assume that Fort Logan would take advantage of every realistic opportunity to align itself with developing comprehensive community mental health programs.

Prior to the opening of the new Adams County MHC in 1968, the data collected on the patient population of the Adams-Fort Logan Unit revealed an important point. Although the inpatient population on the Adams unit was proportionately similar to the population on the other two suburban county units, Arapahoe and Jefferson, the length of stay was longer. Of even greater significance was the small day hospital census on the Adams unit which tended to be only 25 percent of the day care program census on the "sister teams."

The major factors which explained these findings were the greater distance from the population center of Adams County to Fort Logan than exists for either Arapahoe or Jefferson County; the absence of a public transportation system in Adams County; and the very limited points at which the Denver Transit Authority bus system enters Adams County. Under the most ideal conditions, it would take over three hours for a person to travel from specific areas within Adams County to the Fort Logan Mental Health Center by public transportation. Such a trip would necessitate multiple bus transfers. Finally, the antecedent mental health clinic in Adams County had a smaller staff and a more limited treatment facility than the clinics in the other two suburban counties.

In summary then, and primarily for traditional and artificial reasons, Adams County residents tended to become sicker and more disabled before becoming recipients of service at the state mental hospital serving the area. Although the relationship between the Fort Logan–Adams treatment team and the staff of the antecedent Adams County Mental Hygiene Clinic was characterized by good intentions and mutual concerns, the geographical realities resulted in less than adequate cooperation in many areas, specifically intake and aftercare.

PROGRAM DEVELOPMENT

During 1966 and 1967, as we planned toward the new comprehensive community mental health program within Adams County, there was an understandable degree of ambivalence within the staff of the Fort Logan–Adams Unit concerning this proposed true decentralization into the community. Some of the resistance was attributable to the fact that many of the staff lived in the vicinity of Fort Logan and their commuting time and distance were, in some instances, quadrupled. This treatment team, all on the Fort Logan payroll and under the state civil service system, consisted of from thirteen to twenty-two mental health professionals (psychiatrist-team leader, psychologists, psychiatric social workers, psychiatric nurses, psychiatric technicians, and occupational, recreational, and vocational therapists).

Towards the final moments of "program truth," this ambivalence became detectable even within the senior administrative echelons of Fort Logan. Questions concerning the liability risks involved in the patient busing, the accessibility of a proper vehicle, the additional personnel demands which would be involved, and so forth, became matters of renewed concern. The overriding and inescapable value of the concept, however, pressured towards the resolution of these definable details and the associated resistance.

Finally, in the spring of 1968, our personalized version of therapeutic cross-town busing began. Since that time, a maximum of twenty-two inpatients have been bused on any single day, with up to three Fort

159

Logan staff members, in addition to the driver. The current procedure involved a microbus, which can seat up to eighteen, and when necessary a state owned car is used to carry up to four more patients.

On Monday, Tuesday, Thursday, and Friday, the bus leaves Fort Logan at about 8:30 A.M., and returns by 4:00 P.M. On Wednesday, the afternoon and evening program at the Adams County MHC is designed also to involve the families and associates of patients. Therefore, the bus leaves on that day at 12:30 P.M., and returns by 8:45 P.M. Laboratory tests, X rays, and various consultations for physical problems are performed at Fort Logan, and, whenever possible, are scheduled for Wednesday mornings so that patients will not have to miss any part of the regular program at the Adams County MHC.

This busing arrangement has been of significant benefit to the patient and his family. He has available to him a comprehensive community mental health center within his county, which now provides a total spectrum of psychiatric services. The proportion of day patients and their total number has increased consistently since the busing began. The length of a 24-hour hospital stay has also decreased correspondingly since the busing began and the Adams County team now has the largest day program of the nineteen Fort Logan teams. The patient now is provided with more contact with his home community, his friends, and relatives. Of obvious significance is the decrease in dependency upon the state hospital since the patient is "uprooted" from Fort Logan five days a week. In a sense, a person is not allowed to become "a state hospital patient" because, from the very beginning, his contacts are maintained with the mental health center within his own community. At the Adams County MHC there are no beds or private rooms to which the patient may retreat, and there has been unanimous agreement among the treatment staff that the twenty-four-hour patients are less disorganized in the bright, modern, community based center than they were at the Fort Logan Hospital.

The busing experience itself has also led to several interesting observations. The daily trip appears to lead to a greater sense of community and comraderie as manifested by the singing which often takes place on the bus. An illustrative example of the importance of this spirit concerns a particular hostile patient who seemingly could give nothing of himself to the patients or staff except his harmonica playing on the bus, which became very popular. The busing also leads to a clear and identifiable pressure upon the patient. The daily ride is a reminder that he is a resident of Adams County and that everyone's intention is that he will return to a better level of functioning and to his home as soon as possible.

In addition, as the bus and state car become more crowded, there is realistic pressure on the individual patient as well as upon staff for him to move towards day or outpatient status. Recently, a very dependent male patient asked the team psychiatrist for permission to go directly home at the end of a treatment day, rather than taking the bus back to Fort Logan for the night. In a more traditional hospital setting, this type of patient would be content to remain on twenty-four-hour treatment status.

The busing experience also affects the staff. It encourages greater flexibility by providing specific challenges and departures from daily routines. By working in their catchment area, the Fort Logan treatment team also becomes more involved in the various community systems which so strongly affect the patients. Home visits, family therapy, evaluations at the local jail and juvenile detention center, and contacts with various related county agencies are facilitated by working daily in the catchment area. In contrast, the more typical state hospital employee has less access to the patients' community and his family.

Working under the same roof with the outpatient clinic staff has also provided for greater continuity of care. The referral process between outpatient and inpatient care is now more direct and rapid for patient and staff alike. Often, after an outpatient is admitted to twenty-four-hour care, the outpatient therapist can visit the hospital program once or twice a week to maintain contact with the patient and facilitate his later resumption of the therapist's role.

Despite the absence of any untoward events surrounding the busing (there have been no accidents, traffic violations or elopements from the bus), certain small problems have attended its implementation. From two to four staff members must accompany and drive the patients from and back to Fort Logan five days each week. The presence of virtually all adjunctive services at Fort Logan, including medical care, dental care, diagnostic procedures and electro-shock treatment, results in a certain dilution of the regular treatment program at the Adams County MHC.

CONCLUSION

Now that we have entered into the fourth year of this program, we find that both patients and staff generally approve of the busing and no requests have been made to abandon it. Significantly better service is being rendered to the people of Adams County and the combined staffs of the Adams County and Fort Logan Mental Health Centers have found themselves working in a more professionally stimulating and rewarding program environment.

In this collaborative venture, we have shown that the best of the two public mental health delivery systems can be blended together to provide the best possible community mental health program.

The thoughts of Dr. Stanley Yolles, as he addressed himself to this matter in a presentation before the twentieth Mental Hospital Institute, held in the fall of 1968, are particularly relevant in summarizing this presentation. "None of us yet know what the future role of the public mental hospital will be, once the community-based treatment network actually becomes a nation-wide organization of services. But in many communities it is already evident that the state mental hospital, with improved transportation and communication facilities, and improved liaison with community agencies, is surmounting both its physical and professional isolation. Those developments are occuring simultaneously with the growth of preventive and maintenance techniques designed to keep the patient out of the hospital. It now appears that at least in the immediate future the public mental hospital and the community mental health center can and must complement one another." [3]

NOTES

1. L. Linn, "The Fourth Psychiatric Revolution," *American Journal of Psychiatry*, 124, 8(February 1968).

2. L. D. Ozarin, and A. I. Levenson, "The Future of the Public Mental Hospital," *American Journal of Psychiatry*, 125, 12(June 1969).

3. S. F. Yolles, "Social Policy and the Mentally Ill," *Hospital and Community Psychiatry*, 20, 2(February 1969).

Reducing the Need for a State Hospital Backup
to a Community Mental Health Center Inpatient Service

HISTORY

The plan to develop a comprehensive mental health center in Weber County originated prior to the passage of Public Law 88-164 and the birth of federally funded comprehensive centers. As early as 1961, C. W. Dalley, M.D., then director of the Unity Unit at Utah State Hospital, and his staff recognized the need to bring treatment services closer to the people who needed them, rather than removing disturbed persons from their home environments, natural habitats, and families. At that time, patients in Unity were from all over Utah so that adequate follow-up was a veritable impossibility. The staff was frequently faced with situations where the patient was helped to regain equilibrium and to return home, only to decompensate in the face of family pressures and circumstances in the community which precipitated readmission to the state hospital.

In 1962, the decision was made by the state hospital to redistrict the state along regional geographic boundaries. This transformed Unity into the Northern Utah Unit serving the eight northern Utah counties and their nearly 300,000 population. At that time, the unit had three inpatient wards, approximately 120 patients, and virtually no effective follow-up or aftercare program.

A follow-up clinic was established in Ogden in the fall of 1963 since roughly two-thirds of the Northern Utah Unit (NUU) inpatients came from there. That clinic, initially staffed by one social worker conducting three groups one evening per week under the auspices of the local, part-time mental hygiene clinic, proved to be the forerunner of the Weber County Comprehensive Mental Health Center. During the next four years, through the follow-up clinic and other efforts of the Northern Utah Unit staff, the inpatient census was reduced by about 25 percent. However, the problem of helping people to stay out of the state hospital after a period of inpatient treatment was still present.

In the late summer of 1967, the decision was made to recruit sufficient staff to expand the aftercare services and to establish better communication and coordination with agencies in the communities served by the Northern Utah Unit. Soon after, it was evident that Weber County had the potential to establish a comprehensive mental health center under P.L.88-164.

It was the largest of the counties served by the Northern Utah Unit with a population of 135,000 contained in just a little over 500 square miles. Weber's principal city, Ogden, is the state's second largest city, with a population of slightly over 80,000. Although Ogden is only ninety miles from the state hospital, it boasted a wide range of social agencies and two private hospitals with sixty psychiatric beds between them. In addition to five practicing private psychiatrists, Weber County also had a sizeable number of social workers, nurses, and psychologists essential to establishing a comprehensive center. Additionally, there seemed to be more interest here in a comprehensive center than in any of the other counties servied by the Northern Utah Unit.

While the state hospital's aftercare clinic had maintained continuous service from its inception, the Ogden Mental Hygiene Clinic had folded in early 1966, the victim of funding problems and local politics. Thus, Ogden had, for almost two years, been without locally supported public mental health services. Accordingly, the NUU staff began to lead the efforts to establish a comprehensive mental health center in Ogden, reasoning that such a center could assume major responsibility for aftercare of Weber County patients at the state hospital, thereby freeing the NUU staff to expand services in the other seven counties of the catchment area.

Within a few months, however, it became clear to the staff that no one in Ogden was prepared to spearhead the drive to establish a mental health center. This was due, at least in part, to the fact that local professionals were either busily engaged in private practice or had been traumatized by the demise of the mental hygiene clinic several years earlier. At that point, and in concert with the State Division of Mental Health, the NUU staff determined to capitalize on its prior contacts and investments in the community and to strive for a comprehensive center since the local Mental Health Advisory Council had resolved to have such a center at the earliest possible date.

Since NUU was already involved in the care of many clinic patients for whom local resources were insufficient, planning a comprehensive program to deal with all elements of the Weber County catchment area posed no unusual fears.

164

From the outset the plan was to take Weber County residents from the state hospital to the inpatient unit of the community mental health center when it became operational. Some of those chronic patients had been hospitalized for a long time. It was felt that they could be helped to live away from the hospital only if the resources of Ogden were close at hand so that partial hospitalization, for example, could be utilized in the transition to a nonhospital setting.

Further, research conducted at the Utah State Hospital had demonstrated that many persons admitted there could have been helped without inpatient care or through abbreviated periods of hospitalization if families, jobs, and familiar surroundings were close at hand.

Consequently, planning the services to be offered by the Weber County Center entailed not so much the concern for backup from the state hospital, but rather the alignment and coordination of community resources to preclude, to the greatest possible extent, the need for state hospital inpatient care and to provide an increased opportunity to return current state hospital patients to community life. An essential corollary, of course, was an efficient and pragmatic program to meet the needs of the rather large numbers of persons expected to have contact with the center after it opened.

The alignment and coordination of existing resources had begun some years earlier and was stepped up during the year prior to the opening of the Weber County Center. Major agencies such as the Welfare Department, Adult Probation and Parole Department, Public Health Department, Juvenile Court, and city schools were contacted. Consultation was made available to these agencies to help them deal more effectively with many of the difficult cases which often are labeled as mental health problems. This consultation was expanded to other agencies and continues today to be broadened as opportunities present themselves or can be engineered. This pattern of methodical alignment of agencies during the development of the community mental health center program helped to decrease the number of persons admitted to the state hospital thereby helping to achieve another of the goals essential to moving into the community with the patients from the state hospital—decreasing the inpatient census.

Another essential task in decreasing the inpatient census preparatory to opening the Weber County Center was to educate the public in general and local power people in particular—agency heads, newsmen, business and professional leaders, city and county government officials, church leaders, fraternal and service groups—about mental health problems and our specific approach to them. This latter was carried on through public speaking engagements, workshop participation, informal conferences over coffee, and any available vehicle.

PROGRAM PHILOSOPHY

The treatment philosophy espoused by the planners of the Weber County Center is primarily behavioral. It is based upon the assumption that the majority of these people exhibiting bizarre or abnormal behaviors are not "sick," but rather are under stress and out of phase with those around them. To quote Ullmann and Krasner:

An individual may do something (for example, verbalize hallucinations, hit a person, collect rolls of toilet paper, refuse to eat, stutter, stare into space, or dress sloppily) under a set of circumstances (for example, during a school class, while working at his desk, during a church service) which upsets, annoys, angers, or strongly disturbs somebody (for instance, employer, teacher, parent, or the individual himself) sufficiently that some action results (for example, a policeman is called, seeing a psychiatrist is recommended, commitment proceedings are started) so that the society's professional labelers (for example, physicians, psychiatrists, psychologists, judges, social workers) come into contact with the individual and determine which of the current sets of labels (for example, schizophrenic reaction, sociopathic personality, anxiety reaction) is most appropriate. Finally, there follows attempts to change the emission of offending behaviors (for example institutionalization, psychotherapy, medication).

The label applied is the result of the training of the labeler and reflects the society which he represents. The labeling itself leads others to react to the individual in terms of the stereotypes of that label (for example, "Be careful, he's a dangerous schizophrenic"; "Poor girl, she's hysterical").[1]

By adopting a nonmedical model, less emphasis is placed on "curing" patients and more on social engineering and involving them in changing those behaviors which bring them in conflict with others to the point that the need for treatment and/or hospitalization occurs. Therefore, a behavioristic reinforcement theory is generically applied with positive reinforcement for desired actions and negative reinforcement for undesirable behavior. Families and other important people are involved as much as possible, since maladaptive behavior patterns are generally learned in the matrix of family interactions. As family members become aware of their involvement in the patient's problem behavior and learn different ways of relating to and reinforcing it, the need for custodial care of the individual can be diminished. This behavioral philosophy is one of the keys to a small inpatient service and the lack of a general need for backup—sickness requires hospitalization and medical treatment, aberrational behavior may not.

Another important element of our program philosophy designed to reduce the need for long-term state hospitalization is emphasis on alternatives to inpatient care. Staff members draw on prior experience in welfare departments, public schools, juvenile probation, private psychiatric counseling agencies, child welfare agencies, the Bureau of Indian Affairs, V.A. and state hospitals, and public health departments. Accordingly, we are well apprized of the resources of local agencies, their workings, and the frustrations experienced by their workers. Armed with this information, we suggest alternatives to inpatient treatment, attempt to educate those staffs in how to make the alternatives productive, and at times even become very aggressive in demonstrating the effectiveness of a suggested alternative.

For example, a local agency recently wanted to send an eight-year-old Lebanese boy to the state hospital. The child had been adopted by a military couple who were later divorced, and he had experienced an all too familiar pattern of subsequent foster home failures and adoptive break-ups. At the time of referral he was temporarily lodged in a shelter home, and had lit a fire (one in a succession of fires in his history) in the home. After the child was seen by our psychiatrist and psychologist, the case was staffed with the other agency and we advised against commitment to the state hospital for a variety of reasons, foremost among which was our conviction that the child's aberrational behavior could be treated locally. Accordingly, a behavioral engineer worked with the child, the shelter home operator, and the child's caseworkers to map a program of reinforced behavior change. Despite the less than optimum conditions of the shelter home, the program was successful enough that our requests for joint conferences were soon met with the comment that they were unnecessary. After a short time, however, the boy set another fire, and a hue and cry went up to send him to the state hospital.

Encouraged by initial success when all were cooperating, we again advised against commitment to the state hospital, then backed our recommendation by involving a legal services attorney on the boy's behalf to block his commitment. In the staffings and court hearings that ensued, we suggested alternative ways of dealing with the boy and offered to make staff available to the undermanned agency unit to locate a suitable foster care arrangement where contingency management techniques could be utilized for the child's benefit. The upshot of the situation to date is that a home was found, the child has not been sent to the state hospital, and the other agency and the Juvenile Court judge are recognizing alternatives that were previously not open to them in the management of disturbed children.

From this example, it is clear that relationships with City, District, and Juvenile Courts are important in diminishing admissions to the state hospital inpatient service. Similarly, contact with the local police and sheriff's departments, the emergency rooms of the local hospitals, and the County Clerk (who is responsible for clearing all involuntary mental commitments) has allowed screening of many persons who used to be sent to the state hospital because they were a nuisance to the community. Through consultation, the courts are able to obtain a determination of the prisoner's psychiatric condition so that adjudication does not occur in a vacuum. Furthermore, the courts are often willing to direct prisoners to become involved in treatment (in essence making probation contingent upon their seeking help for the behavior which brought them into conflict with the law), thereby providing motivation, or at least a "handle" whereby we can begin to work with them. Since a large percentage of our patients at Utah State Hospital were involuntarily committed, since our approach is not based on traditional psychotherapeutic ideas, and since we have learned that exposure to our program often eventuates in real patient involvement, we do not hesitate to have people come to us initially against their will. Needless to say, we prefer to work with voluntary patients or clients, and have managed to keep involuntary commitments to a minimum.

RESULTS

Our original plans called for forty inpatient beds but we have never had more than twenty-nine full-time patients, including those transferred from the state hospital. Seventy percent of this latter group are currently outpatients and one of the remaining receives only night care at the hospital. The average length of inpatient hospitalization for new admissions is currently less than one week and is still decreasing. As the inpatient census has dropped, we have been able to involve personnel in day activities laying the foundations for further "outreach."

With the exception of two people sent during its first month of operation (one of whom was subsequently transferred back to the center), the only patients from Weber County to go to the state hospital were those for whom the center had not planned nor programmed. During the six-month period from January 1 to July 1, 1970, the Weber County Center's inpatient census declined from a high of twenty-one (half of whom were transferred from the state hospital) to an average of less than six during June.

CONCLUSION

To offer truly comprehensive service to all elements of the catchment area with minimal backup from the state hospital requires an aggressive program utilizing community resources to develop alternatives to inpatient hospital care. As the mental health team welds itself into a positive force and local agencies become increasingly comfortable and cooperative in working with "mental patients," the task becomes less than awesome.

NOTE

1. Leonard P. Ullmann, and Leonard Krasner, *A Psychological Approach to Abnormal Behavior*, Englewood Cliffs, N.J.: Prentice Hall, Inc., 1969, p. 21.

---

18 *Barcus B. Nunley, Jr.*, M.S.S.W., A.C.S.W.

A Community Mental Health Center Program to Provide Emergency Inpatient Services in a Rural Area

In September 1969, the Rio Grande State Center for Mental Health and Mental Retardation began receiving funds from NIMH for staff to deliver comprehensive MH services to an eleven county rural area. Specifically, two proposals outlined strategies whereby the five commonly agreed upon essential services of a comprehensive MH center could be provided in two of our rural catchment areas which were geographically distant from the parent facility and had not been adequately serviced previously. Although the grants made reference to the intent that all catchment areas in the region served by the original facility would eventually offer similar services, the focus of the grant proposals, and of the emergency services which were to be established, were the two rural catchment areas mentioned.

As originally conceived, the facilities created in the two catchment areas were to function as "satellites" of the "parent" center, the Rio Grande State Center for MH/MR. It was planned that four of the five elements of service (outpatient, partial hospitalization, emergency and consultation, and education) would be provided within the rural catchment areas themselves, although overall responsibility for provision of all services would remain vested in the parent agency. Long-term inpatient services which could not be supported in the catchment areas would be physically located at the "parent" center. "Satellite" staff, however, would have responsibility for participating in treatment, regardless of the length or location of hospitalization. The "satellite" centers were seen as being a type of "outreach" extension of the existing facility.[1]

Prior to the NIMH proposal, the areas served by the original facility were not broken into separate catchment areas, but were conceived of as one large catchment area, or a state hospital "region." The "region" was made up of twelve counties located in the southern tip of Texas and served a population of over one-half million. With the exception of a very few large towns, the entire twelve county area was either rural or semirural in characteristic and the demographic, social, and economic makeup of each county was, in general, similar to that of each of the other counties.

The two catchment areas selected for provision of services by "satellite" facilities together contained nine counties. The area encompassed was 12,464 square miles containing 191,825 persons. Five fairly large towns in the two catchment areas contained approximately 65 percent to 70 percent of the total population of the two areas, leaving the rest of the area with a population of approximately 61,500.

EMERGENCY INPATIENT SERVICES PROPOSED

In response to the need for emergency inpatient services in these two distant catchment areas, the proposal which was approved by NIMH stated:

Arrangements have been made with local hospitals to provide emergency hospitalization. Local physicians serving as part-time center staff in each county and the mental health field workers will be "on call" for emergency situations at night and on weekends. The local hospitals operate twenty-four hour telephone service.

In an emergency patients will be hospitalized to take care of the immediate situation and to give appropriate medical coverage. It is anticipated that this kind of hospitalization, which can be conceived of as a holding operation, will be needed only for overnight care or possibly weekend care with arrangements being made the following day for the patient to be taken to the inpatient unit (in the parent center) or transferred to the partial hospitalization program or outpatient services . . .

Within the framework of this emergency service the mental health field worker will have contact with the families of the patients and carry responsibility for continuity of care . . . the goal will be immediate attention in case of need . . .

At this time, the provision of "emergency" inpatient services was seen as being a major service need. In response to requirements that continuity and availability of care according to patient need be guaranteed, the above statement proposed a strategy aimed at discharging the responsibility to be immediately on call locally and to provide needed and fast developing treatment no matter what particular procedure might be needed.

The grant provided funds for added treatment staff roughly equivalent to twice the amount of treatment staff previously available in the entire eleven county region. Also, some extra state funds were allocated for expected increases in items such as travel, medicine, and office supplies necessary to complement the new treatment programs.

Office facilities were established in eight cities and towns and a total of forty-six newly created positions were filled. There were one psychiatrist, eight general practitioners (part-time), twenty-four field workers, three MSW social workers, four RN or LVN nurses, and six clerks or secretarial personnel. The majority of the extra treatment and supportive staff were initially placed in the various "satellite" centers or associated offices, while a few were placed in the parent facility and designated for coordinated treatment to satellite area patients.

The first month for each of the two sets of staff was spent in training at the parent center.

In the case of operations relevant to the provision of emergency services staffs were taught the nature of a psychiatric emergency [2]; methods of observation and evaluation of the emergency situation [3]; procedures for entering the situation and establishing a case [4]; procedures for involvement of other staff and facilities [5]; and the basic goals of the satellite strategy. Some general and nonspecific orientation was also provided relative to the concepts of comprehensive community services *per se*.

PROGRAM RESULTS

Training for the first staff hired began September 1, 1969, and for the second on November 1, 1969. Both facilities were in full operation by December 1, 1969.

In response to an assignment after six months of operation to explain to date the use of staff, consultant, general practitioners, and contract general hospitals in the provision of *emergency* services, one administrator reported:

I asked the staff how many patients had been seen in the general hospitals, either for emergency or inpatient services, and got the following report: 1. (Town)—one patient was arranged for overnight, another was referred for the first time from the hospital; 2. (Town)—one patient went to the emergency room on two different occasions and another patient has been an inpatient twice for a psychiatric problem, but the family and their insurance have paid for each of these; 3. (Town)—five patients have been seen on an outpatient basis in the emergency room and two of these have been seen more than once there; 4. (Town)—one patient was treated totally as an inpatient and this is the one you have been billed for. Three patients were seen on an outpatient basis and one of these patients was seen twice.

The other administrator reported:

Treated and released at (local hospital) 12 patients; Admitted to (local hospital) 3 patients; (local town) MH office—none; (local town) MH office—none.

The fashion in which emergency services were delivered is well exemplified in the following vignette:

The patient was an attractive teen-age girl living in a small town approximately 150 miles distant from the original facility in one of the rural areas eventually to be served by a "satellite" center. Prior to the establishment of the treatment resources in her home community, she had been referred to the parent center for evaluation and treatment as an outpatient. She was hospitalized after psychiatric evaluation had determined that she was suffering from an episode of acute illness.

In the course of hospitalization she achieved remission and a return of adequate functioning abilities. She was discharged as an active outpatient with the recommendation that she be seen weekly or more often if needed by a social worker, and periodically by the consultant psychiatrist.

There was no local treatment facility; therefore, the plan was modified according to the availability of resources to the extent that she would only be seen at the central facility once per six weeks for ongoing psychiatric evaluation and primarily somatic treatment. Shortly after returning to school in the fall, the symptoms which had been observed and treated to remission during the previous school year returned.

Symptoms returned during the same fall term that also saw the opening of satellite facilities in the patient's locale. When the local worker was contacted on the telephone by the girl's mother for help in handling an urgent problem, the patient could be heard shouting and screaming in the background.

Reassuring the mother that something would be done immediately, and promising to call her back, the mental health worker contacted the consultant at the parent center. The previous record was entered and suggestions were made, taking into consideration both clinical data and procedure. It was decided that the emergency treatment procedure should be utilized.

The local worker was notified to contact the local general practitioner and explain that immediate medical attention and the protective and supportive elements of hospitalization were recommended.

The mother of the patient was contacted and the plan was explained to her and her cooperation was assured. Both mother and mental health field worker then were able to calm the patient down and took her to the general hospital where she was met by the local physician and emergency admission was accomplished. A sedative was administered and the patient fell asleep peacefully.

In the morning, the patient was in normal control of herself. Later the local worker was able to determine that the girl had been confronted at school by some of her peers with some of the behavior which she had presented in the previous school year and she had reacted with panic.

As a result of treatment, after two days of local hospitalization under the care of a local general practitioner, the young lady was able to return to school. With her discharge from the local hospital it was planned that she would continue regular consultations with the doctor, and the local worker would continue the program of family and individual counseling that had already provided a new resource.

On her return, the girl was well received at school and she was, in general, regarded as having "become hysterical" rather than having had "a nervous breakdown."

The above sketch illustrates the concepts of local delivery of "emergency" inpatient services. The mental health field worker who was contacted by the family was primarily responsible for delivering outpatient services. However, since the worker was not bound to operate a "service," but to respond to the patient's needs, with consultation he was able to plan for and assist in delivering the more specific and technical services of emergency hospitalization under a physician's care.

After six months, the "satellite" served catchment areas were using inpatient care for only 4 percent of the patients treated per month, while the parent locale hospitalized 8 percent of those treated each month. This seemed to follow as the "satellite" locale staff matured and supportive procedures were set up by the parent center, and as the communities relearned where to refer problems. It seemed remarkable that newly served areas were having more patients seen than before but were hospitalizing patients seen at a rate one-half that of the rate of the parent served area. The conclusion was that the increased coverage and treatment contacts provided patients in the satellite locale was more comprehensive and appropriate to the patients' needs, and hospitalization, when used, was more specific to the need of patient or community.

EVALUATION OF THE DELIVERY OF "EMERGENCY" INPATIENT SERVICES

The "emergency" inpatient services component as conceptualized, given substance and practiced as one of five comprehensive services, was first and foremost a component of change in the "medium" of the previous provision of treatment in the entire eleven county area. Whereas services had been centralized, scarce, and provided by more or less rigid "programs" offered by one or more departments staffed by traditional professionals, this new service delivery system emphasized decentralization of facilities; dispersion of staff; and the provision of treatment according to the patients' needs, with a single person, the community mental health worker, responsible for having planned and delivered whatever treatment was needed. These changes did not, of course, involve simply the "emergency" inpatient service component of comprehensive services, but all five equally.

The idea of comprehensiveness, local delivery of services, and the multiple treatment responsibilities of the mental health worker all were radical departures from traditional state hospital elements of treatment service delivery. All had an effect on the delivery of "emergency" inpatient services, and the converse was true.

It was observed that, when local treatment resources were identified as the appropriate place for the community to bring urgent psychiatric problems, it, in effect, "locked in" the local facility with the responsibility of receiving problems of this type and discharging them adequately. As this occurred, it became impossible to overlook the necessity to produce effective treatment.

The idea of comprehensiveness and interchangeability of services was advanced by the conclusion that, just as an outpatient was not free of the risk of becoming an "emergency" patient, the institution responsible for the treatment of the patient could not consider itself free of the necessity of also providing "emergency" inpatient services. As in the example given, it made no administrative difference whether the mental health worker was to follow the patient in an outpatient service or on an "emergency" inpatient service; his responsibilities could not possibly have been discharged if resources were not available to him in the form of his being able to provide access to any and all services to each of his patients.

The role of the general hospitals should not be underemphasized although, as shown by the reports from the administrative leaders in the satellite areas, these hospitals were not used to as great an extent as had been expected. We strongly feel that their existence and utilization, even to a small extent, was quite significant in the development of total services. The commitment and availability of the hospitals gave substance to the commitment and availability of the "satellite" facilities and staff.

NOTES

1. Gary E. Miller, *Outreach Programs in Mental Health,* paper read before the Volunteer Services Council Workshop at Big Spring State Hospital, Big Spring, Texas, October 3–4, 1969.

2. S. Baxter, B. Chodokoff, and R. Underhill, "Psychiatric Emergencies: Dispositional Determinants and the Validity of the Decision to Admit," *American Journal of Psychiatry,* 124, 11(May 1968): 100–104; Jules Coleman, "Research in Walk-in Psychiatric Services in General Hospitals," *American Journal of Psychiatry,* 124, 12 (June 1968): 90–95.

3. H. Kritzer, and F. Pittman, "Overnight Psychiatric Care in a General Hospital Emergency Room," *Hospital and Community Psychiatry,* 19(October 1968): 22–25.

4. Raquel Cohen, "Intake Procedures at a Community Mental Health Clinic," *Community Mental Health Journal,* 2, 3(Fall 1966): 252–254.

5. Dorothy Aitkin, "Psychiatric Consultation in Social Agencies," *Canada's Mental Health,* 13, 6(November 1965): 45–50; Laurence Beahan, "Emergency Mental Health Services in a General Hospital," *Hospital and Community Psychiatry* (March 1970): 28–29.

REFERENCES

Arafeh, M. K., Gregory, M. D. "Linking Hospital and Community Care for Psychiatric Patients." *American Journal of Nursing* 68(May 1968): 1050–1056.

Beede, M., Radford, W. H. "How Existing Hospitals' Facilities Can Be Organized for Mental Health Services." *Hospitals* 42(February 1, 1968): 105–106, *passim.*

Brown, B. S., "The Role of the Hospital in the Helping System." *American Journal of Psychiatry* 124(January 1968): 972–973.

Wayne, G. J. "How Long, An Approach to Reducing the Duration of Inpatient Treatment." *International Psychiatry Clinics* 3(Winter 1966): 107–117.

175

VI

Partial Hospitalization Services

EDITORS' INTRODUCTION

In 1963, when the Community Mental Health Center Act was passed, the partial hospital was only just beginning to be recognized as a potentially important force in the total concept of mental health service delivery. By requiring that partial hospitalization be one of the five basic services of a community mental health center, the federal program for the development of centers has given tremendous impetus to the utilization and acceptance of partial hospital services.

As partial hospital services have been established, many community mental health center planners and directors have realized that partial hospital care can replace inpatient care as the primary backup resource for outpatient treatment. This is particularly true when the partial hospital program includes both day and night care activities.

Partial hospitalization programs can be organized in several different ways. In some instances, they are structured so that the day hospital and the inpatient service share the same space and the patients from the two units participate in the same therapeutic programs. Under such circumstances, there is little difference between an inpatient and a day patient except in terms of the overnight care provided for the inpatient. When such a program is properly structured, this relationship can stimulate the inpatient service to emphasize more rapid recovery and return of the patient to the community.

Partial hospital programs have also been structured and utilized to help in the movement of patients out of long-term care facilities. The unique adaptability of the partial hospital program to vocational and re-socialization activities has made it particularly useful in this regard. In addition, partial hospital care is also being increasingly recognized as having a particular usefulness in the treatment of alcoholics and drug abusers.

It should be noted that partial hospitalization programs continue to face special problems in their development. One of these is their dependence on adequate transportation in the community. Rural areas, in particular, face this problem and centers located in them must be particularly flexible in adapting partial hospital programs to meet local needs. Another special and unsolved problem facing the partial hospital is its legal status. Particularly noted are uncertainties concerning the licensure of partial hospitals and their potential role as facilities for the diagnosis of treatment of patients referred from the courts. Partial hospitals also come under significant financial stress because of their uncertain status in the eyes of insurance carriers. Many insurance policies cover inpatient psychiatric care but do not cover outpatient psychiatric care while the partial hospital service is often not considered at all. Moreover, even when insurance policies cover both inpatient and outpatient care, they often omit coverage for partial hospitalization and thus exert a bias in regard to the types of treatment which are realistically available to many patients.

Clearly, the partial hospital has been demonstrated in many community mental health centers to be a vital and successful part of the center program. If the partial hospital is to continue to develop as a potent force in the delivery of mental health services, it is essential that these programmatic, legal, and financial problems be resolved.

Partial Hospitalization and the General Hospital

BACKGROUND

This is the description of the day treatment program of a federally funded mental health center sponsored by a privately operated general hospital. The center program, as a whole, represents the first third of a three phase development and the staffing of each of the five required services was scaled proportionately. This plan stemmed partly from the fact that the center construction program had to be deferred for several years to await development of a new hospital building which will replace the present structure. It also resulted from the limited amount of county and state funds available to make up the difference between costs and federal funding.

As a consequence, the community mental health center consisted initially of ten open ward beds in the general hospital, two small houses across the street from the hospital (one containing the day-treatment unit), and four other scattered office sites (two in a high-risk neighborhood at a distance from the hospital). There is a total center staff of forty-five, including the three shifts of hospital personnel with day-treatment having a total of six who will be described later.

The day-treatment program is designed to be one which can be effectively implemented by staff members who are not clinical psychologists or psychiatrists. During the first year, the center's two psychiatrists have made themselves available to the day-treatment program on an as needed basis only. Ideally, this was done because it wasn't certain that a sufficient number of psychiatrists and psychologists would be available and to reduce total costs. It was believed that adequate psychiatric support could be given to the day-treatment program by the outpatient and inpatient psychiatrists, and if it didn't work out well with a large number of day-treatment candidates, the number could then be limited accordingly. The arrangement would add to continuity of care because the psychiatrists would already know many of the day-treatment program members from contacts with them as outpatients and inpatients.

In practice, it has worked out well because of the proximity and accessibility of the outpatient psychiatrist who can be called upon most informally and conveniently. The brief periods which he spends with day-treatment members and staff total about four hours a week.

The day-treatment program is also designed to provide specific correctional experiences instead of being a place for a group to come together just to do things and keep busy, even though this might provide a measure of nonspecific support. The program's general principles, treatment methods, and techniques (behavioral) are largely modeled after those presented in the report on the Day Treatment Center of the Veterans Administration Outpatient Clinic, Brooklyn, New York.[1] A social worker, with special training and experience in behavior modification therapy, trained the present day-treatment staff in this orientation while serving as the initial director of the day-treatment program.

Generally, the program offers a variety of experiences which can be used to effect a wide range of behavioral changes involving such characteristics as solitariness, competitiveness, noncooperativeness, motoric inabilities, and passivity. Through multiple opportunities for self-determination, there is enhancement of the members' ability to make the decisions necessary to live independently in the community at large. And, through activities and approaches rooted in realism, the program fosters improved reality testing instead of becoming a protective world separated off from life as it is. The recommended atmosphere of intimacy and cohesiveness is easily facilitated by the particular physical characteristics of the day-treatment program's setting.[2]

Within its own sphere, the day-treatment staff has had to cope with a number of ongoing challenges. There is the goal of having each program member feel he has one staff member to whom he can turn for individual assistance of any nature. At the same time, the staff wants the program members to see all of the staff as resources for support and guidance as an extended family accessible on an hour to hour basis for immediate concerns. When a given problem relating either to a program activity, or to a personal matter unrelated to the program, requires more intensive individual attention, the member is referred to his "individual" staff person. Borderline situations lead to ambiguity at times and require open and effective communication between staff workers to avoid detrimental effects on the program members.

The day-treatment staff has also had to repeatedly clarify the working relationships between the day-treatment service, the outpatient service, and the inpatient service. When day-treatment program members have been referred from the outpatient service, they may have been seen there for a lengthy enough period to feel quite rejected if the relationship with the outpatient therapist is altered too rapidly. Decisions as to how long and to what extent the referring therapist continues to be involved also require a high degree of cooperation and effective communication to spare the patient detrimental conflict and ambiguity.

Regarding the inpatient service, the day-treatment staff found itself in a particularly uncomfortable predicament. There had been an initial agreement that the day-treatment staff would provide an activities program for the ten-bed inpatient service. However, there are frequent occasions when only three or four of the inpatients are available to engage in the scheduled handicraft or recreational activities and it became an imposition to take one of the day-treatment staff away from a crowded day-treatment program to spend two hours with three inpatients. The inpatients, who rapidly develop a strong sense of cohesiveness, often felt different from the day-treatment members and were reluctant to simply join in with the ongoing day-treatment activities. The day-treatment staff also did not know the inpatients well enough to see their role with them as much more than providing diversions and this was not acceptable.

The problem was resolved by terminating the periods of activities to be furnished to inpatients by the day-treatment staff. Instead, inpatients who have improved sufficiently are now assigned to the day-treatment program on a full-time basis and have the same status as day-treatment members who are living at home. These inpatients have their meals on the ward and return to the ward at the end of the day. The new arrangement has increased the willingness of the inpatients to follow through as day-treatment members after they are discharged from the hospital.

As for relationships with the community, the day-treatment staff has gradually extended activities intramurally to take advantage of the practical kinds of daily living learning experiences which benefit program members. The staff and center director are also studying possible ways to promote development of supportive social clubs in the catchment area for chronically disabled members who have reached maximum benefit from the day-treatment program. The two settlement-house type organizations located in the catchment area have an activities program and a day-treatment staff that serve as program consultants while other center staff serve as case consultants.

SETTING

The center program was developed in the northern half of an urban area of 600,000 in which there were no psychiatric hospital beds or other psychiatric facilities. Almost all of the county's twelve private psychiatrists have offices downtown or south of town. The catchment area population is roughly divided equally between an indigent lower class group, a medically indigent lower middle class group, and a group who through insurance and other means are able to afford private care. Since the center has little capability to offer one-to-one therapy by a psychiatrist, many of the latter group seek psychiatric services from the private psychiatrists who use the psychiatric facilities at two general hospitals just south of the downtown area.

FACILITIES

The sponsoring hospital owned two six-room frame houses standing side by side across the street from its main entrance. One was assigned to the outpatient service and the other to the day-treatment service. The modest quarters inadvertently provided several of the environmental features which others have recommended for day-treatment settings.[3]

The small areas available for individual and group projects limit grouping to four to six individuals which results in a sense of intimacy and cohesiveness. The high degree of visibility of both members and staff impedes attitudes of withdrawal and avoidance and allows the staff to detect early any significant changes or problems which require special assistance.

The program is in a house and a homey atmosphere pervades throughout. The air of warmth and informality is devoid of institutional, authoritarian, and medical implications. Participants see themselves as program members and not as patients, a view which is enhanced by the day-treatment service director who is an occupational therapist and is not imbued with medical powers. However, any day-treatment program based in a house, with a kitchen, a living room with mantle and fireplace, and a pastel painted, well-lighted basement in which the coal bin has been converted into a workshop, would probably not be experienced as a medical setting even if most of the staff were psychiatrists.

In warm weather, gardening is done along the sides and the back of the house and croquet and volleyball are played on the small front lawn in full view of the people in passing cars. Along with these activities, members actively engage in multiple repairing and redecorating projects. A new building or a more expensive dwelling would not lend itself as well to such endeavors. Members gain a sense of ownership and belonging when they take part in altering the environment.

On the other hand, the small quarters become congested, noisy and malodorous at times from the mixture of cooking, baking, and perspiration. A few fastidious individuals have difficulty accepting the close body contact, especially with some of the chronically ill fellow members but some accommodation usually occurs.

The limited space is often frustrating when some must sit on the floor to attend a crowded meeting. Once, when a woman had a seizure in the basement, it was discovered that the stairs were too narrow at the corner to use a stretcher to remove her to the hospital. However, the smallness is forcing the center to decentralize into satellite programs at a distance from the hospital sooner than would have happened had more ample space been available. This is probably a healthy influence in the overall development of the center.

INTAKE PATTERNS

Fifty percent of the day-treatment referrals come from the outpatient service. Approximately two-thirds of the remaining 50 percent are referred by the center's inpatient service and the rest come from the catchment area unit at the Dayton State Hospital. There is no direct intake into the day-treatment service and the people referred there have already received a clinical diagnosis and often a prescription from a psychiatrist. Those receiving medication are periodically evaluated by one of the center's psychiatrists who is on call for the day-treatment program.

An average of fifteen new persons a month are admitted to the day-treatment service. It is apparent that both the outpatient and inpatient services could refer more people if the day-treatment program could absorb them. The additional referrals would be people who would probably benefit from the therapeutic milieu and a behavioral modification regime more than they would from group and individual psychotherapy. These are people who have a special need for additional socialization through the interactions possible in an activities program.

The criteria for admission are simple and liberal. Willingness to attend is the main criterion and ability to come is the other. Our experience has been that when such willingness is present, there is an almost complete absence of suicidal, disruptive, threatening, and other dyssocial behavior even when the person is grossly distressed. Both outpatients and inpatients have the opportunity to visit the program and meet with the day-treatment staff before deciding whether or not they are willing to attend. The day-treatment staff has the prerogative to refuse a referral, but has not found the need to do so. They have asked for an occasional brief moratorium on starting new members, but for the most part have been able to accept new people within a week of referral.

The two-thirds of the members who are on welfare or who are considered medically indigent pay nothing. A few of the remaining third are able to pay between five and twelve dollars weekly as determined on a sliding fee scale and the remainder pay five dollars a week or less. No charges are made for the psychiatrist's services to day-treatment members. In other parts of the center where the psychiatrist has a more active role, he bills separately on his own letterhead to conform with Ohio legal and ethical requirements.

CASELOAD

In contrast, for example, to a VA facility, many of the center's clientele are not chronically disabled. Many have severe acute and subacute disabilities which require the supports that inpatient or day-treatment programs can afford. Therefore, a number of referrals are made on a provisional basis to the day-treatment service by both the inpatient and outpatient services. In these cases, it is not known how long the person will remain so disabled that he cannot return to his usual employment

TABLE 19–1

Figures for Eleven Months of Operation

a.	Total admitted:	166
b.	Total terminated:	114
	one month or less:	21.5%
	one to five months:	66.3%
	six months or more:	12.2%
c.	Seventeen of fifty-two current members have attended more than six months.	
d.	Ten (known) day-treatment members have been hospitalized or rehospitalized after starting in day-treatment program.	

or how long a housewife will be unable to assume her usual responsibilities. As soon as an individual can return to work or a woman can remain at home and relieve the crisis of home care occasioned by her absence, day-treatment participation is often terminated. Earlier than expected return of ability to function results in some brief stays in the day-treatment program. A factor contributing to premature dropping out is a new member's inability to maintain or establish an individual working relationship with one person on the day-treatment or center's staff.

Attendance is from three to seven hours a day, two to five days a week, depending on need and ability to come. (See Table 19-1.)

The clinical diagnoses of those attending are nearly equally divided between psychotic classifications, neuroses (mostly depressions), and behavior disorders (mostly adolescents). Some of the psychoses and depressions are associated with chronic brain syndrome.

STAFF

The director of the day-treatment program is an occupational therapist with previous experience in a community mental health setting. Her staff consists of another occupational therapist, a social worker (group worker) and two mental health technicians (graduates of the local two year community college mental health technicians training program).

APPROACHES AND ACTIVITIES

Day-treatment members take an active role in formulating their own activities and schedules. If needed at first to help reduce severe symptoms, a reassuring structure is presented to a new member through a series of suggestions and specific instructions. When the actual distress is partially alleviated, the member is then required to begin making choices and decisions and to agree to work toward goals he helps formulate.

Within two weeks, the staff meets with each new member to establish a set of behavioral goals. The member's salient social assets and dysfunctional traits are listed on a blackboard which is brought into the living room meeting. The member is present at the meeting and joins the staff in contributing items to these lists. Lively discussions ensue when it is necessary to reconcile different opinions. A behavioral prescription is compiled which is designed to reduce the dysfunctional behavior by substituting more constructive responses and to exercise more fully the person's insufficiently utilized social assets. The prescriptions are recorded on cards and are referred to followup goal meetings and periodic evaluation sessions.

Examples of dysfunctional behavior are fear of trying something new, self-centeredness, helplessness, and bossiness. Examples of socially useful behavior include wanting to help others, creativity, and emotional warmth. The staff does not dwell on clinical diagnosis and prognosis since it is mainly concerned with what behavior is observable and potentially modifiable in the member's interest.

The tentative initial impressions and behavioral goals are repeatedly evaluated at goal meetings held twice daily and attended at least twice a week by each member. In these meetings, there is opportunity for each person to discuss his attempts to reach the goals set in the previous goal meeting. The goals are related to circumstances at home, work, and to projects and interactions at the day-treatment program. In the ensuing discussion, members exchange criticism and encouragement. Staff members who are present may occasionally find it necessary to demonstrate how criticism can reflect tolerance and acceptance. Unwillingness to share opinions and monopolizing the floor are behavioral manifestations of different life styles and are discussed when the opportunity arises.

Description of a completed task is not considered sufficient for the purposes of the goal meeting. The speaker is asked to explain how his example demonstrates some kind of change for himself. If he doesn't proceed to the next step, he is asked how the changed attitude or performance has relevance towards longer range goals of more independent, self-confident functioning.

Selective positive reinforcement for emerging socially constructive behavior usually takes the form of verbal recognition and approval from both staff and other members. This can be quite touching at times when a severely ill member surprises everyone by making a compassionate, sensitive observation about someone else's progress.

The reinforcement process is not a mechanistic one. First of all, the staff and other members must be able to establish trust and a feeling of mutual acceptance in the relationship with a new member. There is no contrived formula in doing this since it must be a reflection of genuine interest. The new member's willingness to learn new skills, manually and socially, is related to how successful others have been in establishing rapport with him. By the same token, the subsequent expressions of recognition and approval have only as much reinforcement value as the source of the reinforcement is valued.

A few people have been particularly difficult to reach, partly because of flattened affect, concretistic thinking, and general distrust. Gifts and coupons for gifts have helped break the ice in several cases and are provided through a small petty cash fund.

Daily staff meetings are held to plan and modify specific approaches for various members. Attempts to promote extinction of provocative behavior often requires staff unity and mutual support. For example, a member will attempt to make others feel guilty when no one responds to his dramatized helplessness.

Group projects are facilitated whenever possible as these are effective vehicles to promote desensitization and relearning. Group support is a potent neutralizer of anxiety as a person attempts to engage in feared social interactions, excursions into the community, or development of latent skills. When a staff person needs to assist a group to initiate a project, he fades back into the group and then out again as the member leadership emerges. The group is guided in the use of the principle of graduated steps whenever one of its members becomes overly anxious about a task or new situation.

As previously agitated, tense individuals learn to redirect some of their energy and as anxious, withdrawn persons begin to feel more accepted and secure, there is increasing emphasis on trips into the community, accompanied, at first, by staff workers. Home visits are made to apprise the family of signs of progress and to attempt to induce application of the new gains at home. Families also attend monthly meetings at the day-treatment house. Through the contacts with the family, it becomes easier to determine what kind of excursions have the most relevance and this knowledge is introduced into the activities planning discussions.

Staff members accompany anxiety-ridden individuals on public transportation until they feel able to go alone for shorter, then longer distances. Usually there is a reality oriented purpose for trips. Program members lacking in funds to practice shopping are given petty cash to purchase behavior rewards for themselves and others or materials needed for program projects.

Guidance in compiling shopping lists for home needs is a useful procedure and people are encouraged to start sewing and woodworking projects for their families and homes. Learning to iron and mend may be more important at times than creative art expression.

Staff members also accompany individuals to attorneys' offices, social security offices, physicians' offices, and job interviews when this is indicated. They also help program members join community clubs and recreational groups by going with them at first until the initial anxiety subsides.

A nursery is not available and on any given day there are usually two or three small children present whose mothers couldn't get baby sitters. Other program members have volunteered to help care for them and this has been beneficial to all concerned.

The community does not have a sheltered workshop specifically designated for the emotionally disabled. However, BVR and Goodwill Industries accept referrals from the center and the center's part-time vocational counselor helps locate job and training placements.

As yet, there is a lack of other facilities which chronically disabled individuals can use as a source of emotional support. Several members of the current day-treatment group have reached maximum benefit from the program and cannot be expected to show further gains. They are socially detached and have little in the way of family supports. When they feel pressured to try more independence, they often develop aches and pains and resume going on sick call at the hospital clinic across the street. Through conferences with the clinic staff, the day-treatment staff has been able to set limits on excessive "copping out" when this has been predictable.

Present plans include the development of supportive social clubs for such individuals.[4] This could be done, with assistance from the center's staff, at the church sponsored neighborhood activities programs and at some new nursing homes which have unused areas.

ADOLESCENTS AND PRE-ADOLESCENTS

At first, the few younger members were not scheduled separately. As their number grew to its present level, about one-third of the total day-treatment group, special activities were developed. Most of the adolescents are either out of school for various reasons or attending only part-time. Most attend day-treatment from one to five afternoons. In addition to group therapy, they participate in recreational interaction, play reading and role playing using the hospital's auditorium stage. They plan community trips and arrange pizza and dance parties at the center. About fifty percent have behavior disorders and the remainder have a mixture of neurotic and psychotic reactions.

CASE EXAMPLE: ADOLESCENT PROGRAM

L., 15 year old girl. Diagnosis: unsocialized aggressive behavior of adolescence. Suspended several times, parents separated, mother concerned and cooperative.

Initial Goals: Relating to peers without fighting girls or being provocative with boys; improving dress and general behavior to be able to return to school; and increasing verbal communication with mother and other adults.

After five weeks in day-treatment, meeting arranged with school psychologist, principal, mother, daughter, and two day-treatment staff, to negotiate returning to school part-time while continuing in day-treatment. Agreement was reached with specific guidelines written out for L., as well as a reinforcement schedule for each teacher to initial a note after classes in which L. behaved satisfactorily. This note was then brought to day-treatment daily as her "entry slip" and became the vehicle for much praise and recognition related to having attended school and behaving well there.

This worked fairly well for three weeks until she ran away for three days, voluntarily returned home, and returned to day-treatment. Currently, she is working on curbing impulses and assuming more responsibility in planning activities. She is becoming more verbal, able to compromise with mother, and another school attempt will be made in the fall.

THE ROLE OF DAY-TREATMENT PROGRAMS

Four primary tasks are usually associated with day-treatment programs.[5]

1. Alternative to hospitalization.
2. Transitional setting for re-entry.
3. Rehabilitation of the chronically ill.
4. Specific services to special groups.

This list should be expanded to include another category, namely, day-treatment as the setting of choice. Fulfilling this task requires providing the kind of support and therapeutic milieu which outpatient services cannot provide to patients who are usually hospitalized when a day-treatment program is not available. Day treatment should not be looked upon as an alternative to hospitalization when day treatment is the therapeutic mode of choice and hospitalization is the consequence of the absence of a day-treatment program. General hospital psychiatric wards abound with patients who not only could be treated in a day-treatment setting, but also with patients who present no more risks than the average outpatient and who should be day-treatment patients because it is the setting of choice. Hospitalization, in these cases, results in unnecessary dependency and regression with disruption of family and social ties.

A day-treatment program may also be a more economical treatment setting than twenty-four hour hospitalization. However, this fact should not obscure its role as the preferred treatment setting for many patients.

NOTES

1. Julian Meltzoff, and Richard Blumental, *The Day Treatment Center* (Springfield, Ill.: Charles C. Thomas, 1967), chapters 2 and 3.

2. Raymond M. Glasscote, et al, *Partial Hospitalization for the Mentally Ill*, Washington, D.C.: The Joint Information Service of the American Psychiatric Association for Mental Health, 1969.

3. Ibid.

4. Wanda Broadie Alexander, "The Development of a Therapeutic Social Club," *Hospital and Community Psychiatry*, 21(July 1970): 230–233.

5. B. M. Astrachan, et al, "Systems Approach to Day Hospitalization," *Archives of General Psychiatry*, 22, 6(June 1970): 550–559.

---

20   *Donald J. Morrison*, M.D.

Partial Hospitalization Programs
in Rural Mental Health Centers

It has been said that the partial hospitalization program was the white elephant hidden in the community mental health center program. It is imperative that the service be within thirty to forty-five minutes commuting time which is physically impossible when in a catchment area with a population density of two people per square mile. It is not financially possible to establish a multiplicity of such programs distributed throughout the catchment area to serve the needs of the population for partial hospitalization services. The only practical solution is for a community mental health center to establish a few partial hospitalization programs in one portion of the catchment area to satisfy the federal legislation and regulations.

Another difficulty is that partial hospitalization programs, as usually constituted, almost always lose money for the center. As the federal supporting grants decline many centers find that they simply can no longer support this service. There are very many patients whose families can ill afford the daily expense involved in this kind of care over a period of months. The problem is further heightened by the fact that very few insurance companies will provide third party payments for this type of psychiatric care. In short, a partial hospitalization program is almost always a liability for a community mental health center and especially so in a rural area.

The Northern Wyoming Mental Health Center has operated a variety of partial hospitalization programs whose success has been predicated on the absence of physical facilities owned by the center. Space had to be rented for programs. This led to a philosophy that it was the role of the center to help patients learn to use the facilities in the community rather than to teach them to function in our facility. Obviously the lack of physical facilities allowed our program to be quite flexible. The basic goal was to help people make the transition between inpatient care and outpatient care as well as provide services for patients where neither of these programs appeared to be terribly appropriate.

One of the earliest programs initiated was led by a recreational therapist. This was a program designed for young women in their twenties and thirties, who were unable to utilize the resources in the community and consequently spent a great deal of time at home alone. They were usually presented as being rather severely depressed young women who were borderline or ambulatory schizophrenics. The group met each morning at the recreational therapist's office in our outpatient clinic and then planned out their activities. They became involved in a variety of pursuits, such as working a day or two as volunteers at a local general hospital, retiring to one of the lady's homes to perhaps wash a rug or paint a room, going bowling or fishing, or perhaps decorating a Christmas tree at a nursing home. In a brief time, the women had been introduced to most of the service clubs, institutions, and agencies in the community. Many of them developed lasting attachments to these other organizations and ultimately dropped out of the program to pursue these interests on a continuing basis. As members of the group, they also had a chance to learn many skills such as dyeing materials, preparing gourmet meals, or sculpturing.

In addition to the recreational and educational activities, most of the women were also seen in individual counseling on a weekly or biweekly basis. A few that were more seriously disturbed were seen on a daily basis at intervals during their partial hospitalization. It happened that the recreational therapist and the psychologist providing the individual care were a husband and wife team and were able to compare notes daily on their patients.

The program was quite inexpensive to maintain since the only costs incurred were the recreational therapist's time, some expenses for mileage in traveling to the activities, and supplies. However, it should be noted that this was still basically a money losing proposition for the center since the recreational therapist's salary was more than four times the amount of money generated in fees collected from the recipients of the service.

Another program was designed to deal with young patients who were acutely schizophrenic. These young people were usually in a situation where they needed to be separated from their families for a period of several months, taught some work skills, and helped to continue with their education if it had not yet been completed. They were also in need of psychotropic medication and some individual supportive counseling. About half of the patients had previously been hospitalized for a period of a week in the inpatient program and stabilized on psychotropic drugs.

Arrangements were made with a nursing home to house these patients for extended care in a situation somewhat at variance with traditional partial hospital concepts but uniquely suited to a rural area. They were then seen almost daily for counseling and their medications were administered by the nurses on duty under the supervision of our psychiatrist or a local general practitioner. The nursing home encouraged these young schizophrenic patients to become involved in the care of the elderly people with the understanding that, if they were able to work any significant portion of the day, they would be compensated for their services. Most of the patients were able to put in an eight-hour day within two weeks and were given room and board, as well as a daily stipend for their efforts. In almost every case, they were able to repay the nursing home for the care received in the first weeks of living there. The patients tended to find that bathing and feeding and otherwise caring for the elderly was a very nonthreatening kind of employment and they were almost always seen as good employees by the nursing home staff.

Within a few months, most of them found better paying jobs in the community and moved out of the nursing home into apartments or boarding homes in the community and pursued their new jobs. Only one of these patients remained over a period of years as a permanent employee of the nursing home.

A similar arrangement was also made at a local dude ranch where patients could convalesce after an inpatient stay and ultimately work themselves into an employee status as either a domestic helper or an assistant in the kitchen. This program has not been as extensively used because the work is physically and mentally too demanding for most of our patients. Physically debilitated and senile patients are simply not as threatening to recovering mental patients, and the physical act of caring for the elderly seems to have some therapeutic impact in itself.

The remainder of our rural partial hospitalization programs have been highly individualized situations tailored to suit the particular needs of a client and cannot actually be called programs. For example, we have on several occasions made arrangements for patients to work as live-in babysitters and be lightly supervised by the couple employing the patient. These patients are almost always followed simultaneously as outpatients with supportive counseling and medication.

A few patients have also been placed at the local junior college under the auspices of the State Department of Vocational Rehabilitation. They are then followed jointly by a psychiatric nurse and the dean of women or dean of men in conjunction with outpatient psychiatric care. Other patients of all ages have been placed with foster families which are intensively coached and counseled in managing the patient's difficulties. This is usually accomplished by having a member of our staff meet with the foster parents in their home and discuss the patient's continuing care.

This overall approach to the problem of finding alternatives to traditional inpatient care is a far cry from the highly organized and institutionalized partial hospitalization programs that have been developed in urban settings. There is less emphasis on recreational activities since the major goal is to help the patient learn to live in the community rather than teach skills in an institutional setting. However, the basic goal is still the same, namely, to resocialize and rehabilitate the individual.

The traditional urban model of a day or night hospital is inappropriate in the rural area and a serious financial liability. If partial hospitalization programs are to be successful in rural areas, they must be innovative and geared to utilizing the existing facilities and services in the community. The truly successful programs in rural areas are those where patients can provide a realistic service to the community, for which they can be adequately compensated, and ultimately become financially independent individuals. Make work and purely recreational activities are generally not as useful to patients and do not seem to provide them with the same sense of dignity and self-reliance.

The backbone of most rural community mental health center programs is the outpatient operation closely followed by consultation and education services. Partial hospitalization programs should be planned to closely coordinate with these activities.

21

Jack F. Wilder, M.D., *and*
Stephen C. Caulfield, M.S.W.

Rehabilitation Workshops
in a Partial Hospital Program

Current conceptual approaches to psychiatric patients which stress treatment in noninstitutional milieus and early return of the patient to productive living in his family and community have contributed to the growth of both partial hospital services and vocational rehabilitation workshops. Nourished from common sources, the two programs tend to undergo a close parallel development, or more often one develops as an extension of the other. Some of the basic issues and problems concerning their functional relationships will be examined, using as illustrative case material the pattern of operation evolved by the Sound View–Throgs Neck Community Mental Health Center and its predecessor services. Five stages of development will be described.

A DAY HOSPITAL

In the late 1950s there was increased attention in the Department of Psychiatry of the Albert Einstein College of Medicine to social and cultural determinants of illness which stimulated the development of flexible and inventive modalities for prevention, diagnosis, treatment and rehabilitation. In 1959, the several research directions which had been pursued were organized into the Division of Social and Community Psychiatry, focused largely around an experimental day hospital and a walk-in clinic.

The day hospital was soon located in a three-story public health center on a quiet residential street, approximately a mile from the huge medical school–municipal hospital complex which houses a psychiatric inpatient service. The day hospital had a census of twenty-five to thirty men and women over age eighteen. Day hospital therapy was planned at three levels: individual, family, and group. A "therapeutic community" orientation was fostered by weekly community meetings and a patient government. Drugs and somatic treatment were prescribed when indicated.

In carrying out a number of evaluation studies, the day hospital admitted primarily patients with acute psychiatric illness. Patients were assigned upon admission to one of three activity groups of eight to ten patients. Small group cohesiveness was fostered by one-hour morning group discussions and a moderately structured daily group activity program. The activity schedule included a number of work activities for the day hospital, the Bronx Municipal Hospital Center, and community charitable organizations. For example, patients prepared lunch, operated a canteen, framed pictures, collated forms, assembled surgical supplies, and made toys. Patients were not paid for their efforts. Vocational counselling was available from a staff member of the New York State Division of Vocational Rehabilitation. The focus of the work activities was less on preparing the patients for eventual community employment than on providing the patients with meaningful activities for the utilization of small group processes. It was implicitly assumed that if the patients received multimodality treatment and were not subjected to the antitherapeutic influences of a total institution, they would recover and obtain jobs.[1]

A VOCATIONAL REHABILITATION WORKSHOP
AS AN ELECTIVE ACTIVITY

A two-year followup study of 189 patients who had been assigned to the day hospital and 189 patients who had been assigned to the inpatient service revealed poor family, residential, social, and vocational adjustments of many patients in both groups.[2] The work performance of patients was generally poor; more than the majority of "employable" men and women were not working full time at followup. The study seemed to demonstrate that day hospitalization is generally as effective as the traditional inpatient treatment program, but that keeping the patients home at nights and on weekends is not a magical treatment for psychiatric illness; not all of psychiatric illness is a product of institutionalism.

In 1964 a Work-for-Pay program was offered day hospital patients during the week's eight optional activity hours. It was the expectation that the workshop would improve the future work performance of day hospital patients. The program was structured to simulate a real work situation. A patient submitted an application for a job. Three references were required: from his doctor, his group nurse, and another day hospital person—staff member or patient. The applicant was then interviewed by the work supervisor (no one interested in employment ever failed to be hired). Contracts were obtained for light assembly work and workers were paid weekly on a piece-work basis.

Initially there was considerable resistance to this new program, primarily by the nursing staff. It was charged by some that the teaching of work skills as an end in itself and the paying of patients for work "were not therapy or treatment." The accusation that work was not therapy was a dubious one when a variety of other patient activities in the day hospital were labelled "therapy"; for example, "art therapy," "dance therapy," "music therapy." It was argued that the Work-for-Pay program be offered *after* day hospital hours and not during the week's elective activity sessions. Opposition to the program was overcome when it was agreed to house the workshop in a small room in the basement, off the premises of the day hospital, and to submit daily and weekly records of a patient's work habits and work production to the patient's doctor and treatment staff.

Despite the initial staff resistance, despite the two-to-one day hospital female-to-male ratio, and despite the large number of elderly patients, over 40 percent of the patients elected to work in the program at some time during their day hospital stay. Whether or not the work program was "therapy" or "treatment," it seemed to be helpful to many of the patients. It was also helpful to the nursing staff as even the sickest patients attended the program on their own volition and time was freed up for the nursing staff to complete needed paper work. The nursing staff soon requested that more activity hours be made available for electives in the Work-for-Pay program.

Jack F. Wilder and Stephen C. Caulfield

THE BEGINNINGS OF A VOCATIONAL
REHABILITATION SERVICE

The Work-for-Pay activity became an integral part of the day hospital program. It quickly became apparent that many patients, who were ready for discharge from the day hospital and who had demonstrated an ability to work in the program, were not employable in the community. Furthermore, many of these workers were not acceptable to formal full-time community rehabilitation centers or job training programs. Borrowing from their work with the physically disabled, the expectation of these agencies was total rehabilitation. Other patients were on waiting lists for such programs or were graduates of these rehabilitation programs but remained unemployable in competitive industry. Since the alternative after discharge for these patients was walking the streets or sitting in a park, the part-time work program was extended to include patients discharged from the day hospital.

The program consisted of four shifts of ten to twelve workers. A worker began on a two-morning or two-afternoon weekly schedule. With this part-time schedule, a single foreman was able to supervise forty to fifty workers. The part-time schedule structured the worker's week and maintained a supportive transference to the day hospital, yet it discouraged excessive dependencies. Earnings of six to eight dollars were never so great as to diminish the financial appeal of employment in the community. Although there was no time limit in the program, the vocational performance of each worker was evaluated periodically and, when ready, a worker was encouraged to move into more formal training or employment in the community.

The Work-for-Pay activity assumed increasing significance in both the day hospital and the outpatient clinic programs, especially the latter. With the increase in workers, more staff effort had to be assigned to obtaining contracts, record-keeping, and vocational counselling. Responding to the multiple needs of its workers, the workshop made available two additional services to help them in developing social skills and confidence. First, a course in self-improvement emphasized the acquisition of fundamental personality skills—grooming, posture, presentation—and offered concrete practice in a variety of job interview and social situations. Second, workers were permitted to attend a social club, the Keep-in-Touch Club, which met one afternoon and one evening a week in the outpatient clinic.

Slowly, around a focus on work, a vocational rehabilitation service had developed functioning in some ways similar to the day hospital. It was not uncommon for a decompensating former day hospital patient to be "admitted" to the outpatient workshop for his care rather than to the formal day hospital.

A COMMUNITY MENTAL HEALTH CENTER

The Community Mental Health Center of Sound View–Throgs Neck was established on June 1, 1967, to provide comprehensive mental health services to some 200,000 persons residing in the southeast Bronx. The center evolved from the limited model services of the Division of Social and Community Psychiatry, notably the day hospital and its allied rehabilitation programs, which were described above.

The center explicitly set as its primary treatment priority the comprehensive treatment of formal psychiatric patients, defined as persons with at least moderate psychopathology who manifest acute or chronic disability in major areas of functioning. Given this priority, rehabilitation services were formalized and expanded in three major areas: vocational, social, and residential. The three services represented auxiliary loci of care for patients whose overall therapeutic responsibility resided in staff members or the decentralized outpatient services.[3]

A continuum of vocational rehabilitation programs was developed by the center with the cooperation of relevant community agencies to meet the individual needs of patients. Programs were designed with increasing gradations of responsibility. For example, a patient might engage in unpaid hospital work, a part-time sheltered workshop, a full-time sheltered workshop, a specialized vocational school, a supervised on-the-job placement, community employment with supervision offered the employer, or community employment on his own. The enlarged center workshop moved to a site about a half mile from the day hospital location.

During the first year of the center's operation, the day hospital underwent two significant changes in attempts to fit this separate, singular unit into a huge complex of services. First, therapeutic responsibility for patients was reassigned from a core day hospital staff to staff members in the geographic outpatient services. For a variety of reasons described elsewhere, this change adversely affected patient selection, patient admissions, and staff morale.[4]

This change was followed by a more radical reorganization of the

198

program. It was apparent that at any one time about half the day hospital patients were at a stage of recovery where they no longer required comprehensive hospital treatment. This group of patients, subacutely or chronically ill, was assigned to a new Outpatient Social Rehabilitation Service. This day care unit was housed in the former community-based site of the day hospital. It offers flexible morning, afternoon, and evening programs to between 150–200 members. The outpatient status of the program eliminates hospital regulations regarding fees, extensive record-keeping, and strict nursing procedures. Therapeutic responsibility for patients in this program, as in the vocational and rehabilitation programs, remains with the staff of the outpatient services.

Patients who were acutely ill and who required only day treatment were assigned to a new fifteen census day hospital service established in its own quarters on the same floor as the center's inpatient services in the Bronx Municipal Hospital Center. The two hospital units are staffed by the same psychiatrists and social workers; the two units differ only in daily activity schedules. Although patients in both units are encouraged to start attending social and vocational rehabilitation programs on pass in advance of discharge, the two rehabilitation programs largely serve outpatients.

With the initiation of the center, the day treatment program evolved, as did the vocational workshop, into a major outpatient rehabilitation service.

A COMPREHENSIVE REHABILITATION PROGRAM

The social, vocational, and residential rehabilitation services now constitute a Division of Rehabilitation Services under one director. The division is undergoing four significant changes.

First, many psychiatric patients spend many months in the rehabilitation programs and become better known to the rehabilitation staff than to the staff members in the decentralized outpatient services. The latter staff also has additional functions; namely, providing services to other target groups, consulting in the human services network, and participating in community development projects. Plans are underway to establish a small aftercare unit in the Division of Rehabilitation, whose staff will have the therapeutic responsibility for the long-stay rehabilitation patients.

Second, increasing emphasis is being given to developing community rehabilitation resources to supplement the center's core rehabilitation program. For example, the Vocational Rehabilitation Service is expending considerable effort in setting up supervised on-the-job placements in community businesses and in developing consultation relationships with community businesses.

Third, there is increasing concern about the coordination of the various rehabilitation programs. A number of territorial issues have arisen. For example, what is the role of the vocational rehabilitation staff in the job supervision of patients working in a new center community thrift shop which is an outgrowth of a program of the Social Rehabilitation Service? Should the Social Rehabilitation Service and the Vocational Rehabilitation Service each have its own intake? Such issues are being resolved by consolidating rehabilitation components. For example, a common intake was instituted for all three rehabilitation services.

Fourth, the consolidation of the Social and Rehabilitation Services will be enhanced by their move from separate locations to a new three-story rehabilitation building in 1971.

A series of discrete programs, which evolved over ten years, are now regrouping into one organization unit and, through the five stages, have come full circle. The concept of partial hospitalization, as it was originally formulated ten years ago, has been expanded.

CONCLUSION

Day treatment programs have demonstrated their feasibility and efficacy, but it is not realistic to expect them to produce "lasting cures" for many psychiatric patients. Despite frequent hospitalizations, most long-term patients spend most of their lives living in the community where their social and work performances are often poor. Participation in social groups and employment are often essential to self-respect and productive community living. The expectation of total social and vocational rehabilitation for many long-term psychiatric patients is unrealistic.[5] Yet psychiatric patients can and will attend community social groups and work in community workshops.[6]

The authors suggest that day care centers will assume more of a social rehabilitation role for subacute and chronic patients and attempt less to treat the acute psychiatric patient. Day care centers will recognize the vocational rehabilitation needs of their psychiatric patients. In turn, vocational rehabilitation programs will recognize the social rehabilitation needs of their clients. In order to meet the total needs of patients, one program will evolve from the other or two operating programs will establish closer working relationships. Comprehensive rehabilitation centers will encompass multiple functions and patients will attend such programs for months, years, or a lifetime. It will become respectable to raise a patient to his optimal level of functioning and provide services which will permit him to function at that level.

NOTES

1. Israel Zwerling, and Jack F. Wilder, "An Evaluation of the Applicability of the Day Hospital in Treatment of Acutely Disturbed Patients," *Israel Annals of Psychiatry*, 2, 2(October 1964).

2. F. Wilder, Gilbert Levin, and Israel Zwerling, "A Two-Year Follow-Up Evaluation of Acute Psychotic Patients Treated in a Day Hospital," *American Journal of Psychiatry*, 122, 10(April 1966).

3. Jack F. Wilder, Gilbert Levin, and Israel Zwerling, *The Practice of Community Mental Health*, edited by Henry Grunebaum (Boston: Little, Brown and Company, Inc., 1970).

4. Jack F. Wilder, James Todd, and Koz Gabriel, *Partial Hospitalization: Problems, Purposes and Changing Objectives*, from the Forum on Partial Hospitalization held in Topeka, Kansas, by Ronald Chen, M.D., Executive Editor; James Healey, M.D., Co-Editor; and Howard V. Williams, M.D., Co-Editor.

5. W. S. Neff, and M. Koltuv, *A Study of the Factors Involved in the Rehabilitation of the Vocationally Disadvantaged Former Mental Patient*, New York: Institute for the Crippled and Disabled, 1967; Peter F. Briggs, and Frederick J. Kottke, *Factors Influencing Rehabilitation Potential Among the Psychiatrically Disabled*, Final Report, Washington, D.C.: Vocational Rehabilitation Administration, Department of Health Education, and Welfare, October 1963; Ladd McDonald, and Donald G. Miles, *Evaluation of Work as Therapy for Psychiatric Patients*, Final Report, Denver, Colorado: Fort Logan Mental Health Center, January 1969.

6. John H. Beard, Raymond B. Pitt, Saul H. Fisher, and Victor Goertzel, "Evaluating the Effectiveness of a Psychiatric Rehabilitation Program," *American Journal of Orthopsychiatry*, 33, 4(July 1963); Henry J. Meyer, and Edgar F. Borgatta, "Altro Health and Rehabilitation Services: Case Study of a Protected Work Shop," *Journal of Social Issues*, 16, 2(1960).

22

Edwin E. Fair, M.D.,
Chaplain William F. Gandy,
Thomas L. Foster, M.D., *and*
George Kreger

A Community Mental Health Center Alcoholism Program
with a Focus on Partial Hospitalization

BACKGROUND

Bi-State Mental Health Foundation is a rural community mental health center serving six counties in Oklahoma and one in Kansas. In July 1968, the foundation came into being through the Community Mental Health Centers Act, after having a ten-year history in the central county of the catchment area as a child guidance center. The geographical center of the catchment area is Ponca City, Oklahoma, a community of approximately 27,000 people, who have come to expect from the personnel of the foundation leadership in a program of mental health care. Although there was at least one Alcoholics Anonymous chapter in each of the counties presently served by the Bi-State Mental Health Foundation, there was no program for the treatment of the alcoholic in any of these counties prior to the origin of the program to be described.

In view of its involvement in community life, the staff of the foundation was cognizant of the need for a treatment facility for the alcoholic. This need was also recognized by the courts, law enforcement officers, clergy, physicians, business and professional people, industry, and most importantly, the alcoholic and his family. Though hospitalization for the acute alcoholic was available in the several general hospitals in the area, the usual reluctance to admit alcoholics to these hospitals was in evidence. Alcoholics in an acute episode were sent to one of the state hospitals for treatment removing them from the "pressure point" which was part of their drinking habits. It was recognized that this type of a treatment program was not the ultimate modality.

Because of the experiences which many alcoholics have had in Halfway Houses in surrounding states, it was thought that a Halfway House program would be the most logical and effective type of facility for this area. It also seemed most logical since this type of facility could provide a centrally located treatment point while enabling the alcoholic to maintain contact with his own community. People in the area are also accustomed to treatment facilities located in fairly close driving distance to their home base. Because of the rural nature of the catchment area, transportation, usually by private automobile, is a necessity rather than a luxury, and the location of a facility at the center of the catchment area was both logical and highly accessible.

As the Bi-State Mental Health Foundation moved toward a program for alcoholics, it got in touch with the several AA chapters in the area to serve as resources for planning the facility. In terms of the limited resources available, the treatment program must use as its base the program of Alcoholics Anonymous which, with several chapters started previously throughout the area, could provide a continuing contact and treatment point for the person after involvement in a Halfway House setting.

PROGRAM DEVELOPMENT

A meeting was held to present the problem and discuss the need and possible working relationship with the members of Alcoholics Anonymous. Alcoholics Anonymous representatives from Oklahoma City and Ponca City met with the County Medical Society to talk about needs and concerns and what kind of pilot program might be projected.

In April 1969, the Kay Council for Community Services sponsored a community-wide meeting that was open to the public. The invited visitors from outside the community included an industrial alcoholism counselor from Tulsa, Oklahoma, an alcoholism coordinator from Washington, D.C., and a member of the regional staff of the National Institute of Mental Health from Dallas. During the meeting, the Bistate Mental Health Foundation agreed to cooperate in the development of a program for the alcoholic with the assistance of Alcoholics Anonymous and with the support of the local community. As a result of the day-long meeting, a committee of interested citizens was appointed to study the feasibility of establishing a Halfway House in the community.

Very shortly, the nonpracticing alcoholics appointed to membership on this committee became dissatisfied with the time it seemed to be taking the committee to act. Distressed because there were two male alcoholics urgently needing help and shelter, one of these nonpracticing alcoholics on the committee rented a small, two-bedroom home to begin a Halfway House program for male alcoholics in Ponca City.

Almost immediately, men started arriving at the house seeking help with their alcoholism and showing a desire to achieve sobriety. The house was initially set up to accommodate five men. Within sixty days, ten men were in the house. In this venture, one of the authors (G.K.) and his three partners supported the operations of the house with the confidence that after starting, additional supportive help would be forthcoming. As they most adequately put it, "the Halfway House started on green stamps and prayer." After the house was rented and began taking people in, a second Alcoholics Anonymous group was begun in Ponca City which used the large front room of the house as a meeting place twice a week. This newly-established group, plus the twice-weekly meeting of the Alcoholics Anonymous group that had been in Ponca City for sometime, became the focal point from which the rest of the treatment efforts have developed.

As more men began to seek treatment at the Halfway House, it became evident that a better working relationship between the Halfway House and the Ponca City Hospital was needed. With the support of the Bi-State Mental Health Foundation, the Halfway House approached the administration of the Ponca City Hospital. With assurance and assistance from the Bi-State staff and the local Alcoholics Anonymous group with the acute alcoholic in the hospital, the administration of the Ponca City Hospital agreed to cooperate in the treatment of alcoholics on an inpatient basis as part of the total program. Both male and female alcoholics are admitted to the inpatient facility.

Very rapidly, the number of men applying for services at the Halfway House became so numerous that the available space was at a premium. At its inception, it was expected that the House could handle a maximum of twelve men, but within three months the house was filled with ten occupants. At times, there have been as many as fifteen men in the house. As it soon became evident that the original Halfway House facility did not provide adequate space to carry on the kind of program which was intended, a campaign was begun to raise capital funds to buy enlarged quarters.

During this same time, the Halfway House was approached by the Wichita Fellowship Club of Wichita, Kansas, seeking whether the ranch that they were developing eight miles south of Arkansas City, Kansas, might fit into the total program of the Halfway House. This ranch is a 120-acre site on the Arkansas River which had been begun by the Wichita Fellowship Club as a treatment resource for their Halfway House program. As members of the Halfway House investigated this program, they realized it could be useful as a place for alcoholics to begin their struggle toward sobriety by having the opportunity to spend time working out in the open in the company of other alcoholics, getting much needed rest, fresh air, and exercise. The ranch facility is complete with dormitory and eating area, a swimming pool, eighty acres of open land to walk over, dig in, produce crops, and meditate.

While these developments were occurring in terms of program expansion, there was still the acute need for additional facilities and space for the growing number of people who were asking for services at the local Halfway House. With the inclusion of the ranch in the program, the possibility of service to a larger number became possible, but this did not provide the relief to the original facility that was expected because the number of persons applying for services continued to grow. Under the leadership of the board of directors of the Halfway House, a capital funds drive was begun in the Ponca City area to attempt to raise 20,000 dollars to purchase a building that would provide more space. A significant portion of that amount of money has been raised and more spacious quarters have been purchased. This house provides more space for the present residents with more than adequate room to add to the capacity of the program. In addition, there is sufficient land to further expand in the future.

The program of the Halfway House consists of the following: When a person presents himself to the Halfway House for entrance into the treatment program, he is either sent to the inpatient facility at the hospital or retained at the house for a period of detoxification. As soon as he has become physically stabilized, he is sent to the ranch for a period of one week, during which time he gets a great deal of exercise, has four hours of classes concerning alcoholism and Alcoholics Anonymous, and participates in various work details on the ranch. At the end of a week, or longer if needed, the man is returned to the Halfway House at Ponca City. Upon his return, he immediately goes to work in various part-time jobs, often found for him through house resources, until he secures his own employment.

Upon admission to the house, each man is asked to pay 175 dollars for his first five weeks of residence. He pays 24 dollars per week thereafter as long as he remains in the house. During the time he is at the ranch or at the Halfway House, he is also attending a group therapy session one evening per week. These meetings are run by various volunteers, most of whom are nonpracticing alcoholics who receive assistance from consultation provided by the Bi-State Mental Health Foundation.

At the core of the total program is the interest, enthusiasm, and dedication of a number of nonpracticing alcoholics who provide many hours of service each week through individual and group meetings. They meet with the families of the men and sit with the acute alcoholic as he is being detoxified in the hospital.

SUMMARY

The Halfway House program in north central Oklahoma and south central Kansas began as a need and an idea, with the dedication and fortitude of four men and the cooperation and support of a comprehensive community mental health center.

At the present time, many services are brought to bear in the treatment of the alcoholic. The inpatient service provides the resources of psychiatry, psychiatric social work, psychology, nurses, nursing aides, and adjunctive therapy. The resources of the outpatient section of the Bi-State Mental Health Foundation program in Ponca City and Arkansas City, Kansas, provide psychiatry, psychiatric social work, psychology, pastoral counseling, and group work consultation. The two Alcoholic Anonymous groups in Ponca City, the cooperation with the Wichita Fellowship Club in providing the facilities of the ranch, the exposure of the men in the program to the alcoholics who are participating in the Wichita Fellowship Club program, and the resources of the time and talent of many dedicated volunteers, both alcoholic and nonalcoholic, provide concern and support in the community for those men seeking sobriety.

REFERENCES

Alpine, G. C. "Management of the Mentally Ill Alcoholic in Community Placement." *Mental Hygiene* 51(January 1967): 134–135.

Chen, R. "Prescription for Psychiatric Day Treatment." *Journal of the Kansas Medical Society* 67(September 1966): 456–458.

Harper, M. B., Mister, V. R., and Penrold, L. "Psychiatric Nursing in a Day Hospital." *National League Nursing Convention Paper* 1(1965): 14–20.

Hart, W. T. "The Treatment of Alcoholism in a Comprehensive Community Mental Health Center." *American Journal of Psychiatry* 126(March 1970): 1275–1281.

Lamb, H. R. "Chronic Psychiatric Patients in the Day Hospital." *Archives of General Psychiatry* 17(November 1967): 615–621.

Mohrnheim, J. E., and Butler, A. C. "The Rhode Island Medical Center Day Care Program. A Two Year Follow-Up and Evaluation. Day Care Program is Feasible and Effective in Management of Wide Range of Mental Disorders." *Rhode Island Medical Journal* 49(October 1966): 602–603.

Rubington, E. "The Halfway House for the Alcoholic." *Mental Hygiene* 51(October 1967): 552–560.

Rusch, K. H. "A Review of Wisconsin's Day Care Program for the Mentally Handicapped." *American Journal of Public Health* 57(December 1967): 2143–2148.

Shelly, J. A. "Daytop Lodge—Halfway House for Addicts on Probation." *Rehabilitation Record* 7(May-June 1966): 19–21.

Shelton, W. H. "The Day Hospital at the New Orleans Mental Health Center." *Journal of the Louisiana Medical Society* 120(February 1968): 76–78.

Silverman, M. "Community Attitudes to Psychiatric Day Care." *International Journal of Social Psychiatry* 13(Winter 1966): 67–70.

Vitale, J. H., and McDonough, J. M. "The Sheltered Workshop. An Experimental Study with Chronic Mental Patients." *Mental Hygiene* 50(1966): 270–275.

Weinstein, M. R. "A Program for the Rehabilitation of Socially Disabled Psychiatric Patients through Retaining." *Comprehensive Psychiatry* 8(August 1967): 249–264.

Wilder, J. F., Kessel, M., and Caulfield, S. C. "Follow-Up of a 'High-Expectations' Halfway House." *American Journal of Psychiatry* 124(February 1968): 1085–1091.

Wolfe, G. "Current Events Classes for Day Patients." *Hospital and Community Psychiatry* 18(July 1967): 217–218.

Wulff, M. H. "Experiences from a Sheltered Workshop for Discharged Psychiatric Patients." *Acta Psychiatrica Scandinavica* 42(1966): Suppl. 191, 232 ff.

Wulff, M. H. "The Evening-Patient. Experiences from a Rehabilitation Hostel for Psychiatric Patients." *Acta Psychiatrica Scandinavica* 42(1966): Suppl. 191, 250 ff.

VII
Delivery Systems for Outpatient Services

EDITORS' INTRODUCTION

New community mental health centers have often felt the initial impact of their existence most strikingly in their outpatient services and have had to be resourceful in developing innovative programs to meet these increased demands for service. As a result, community mental health centers have led the way in establishing new outpatient treatment methods which have included increased emphasis on group therapy approaches, greater use of paraprofessionals and indigenous personnel, and the development of systems and organizational structures which extend outpatient services beyond the confines of the traditional clinic setting.

The history of mental health services prior to the establishment of community mental health centers demonstrates an emphasis on individual as opposed to group treatment methods. In many instances, the acceptance and growth of group therapy approaches has been a result of the service demands made upon community mental health centers. Professionals have recognized that they cannot meet these demands solely through a reliance on individual approaches. These new group therapy efforts have included the utilization of group therapy techniques in conjunction with the dispensation of medication and the treatment of couples and multiple families, as a means of increasing the effectiveness of such adjunctive therapies as recreation, art, or music therapy.

209

The increased demand for outpatient services has also led to the development of new types of personnel to work in the context of innovative delivery systems. Recognition has now been given to the fact that many persons suffering from emotional problems will not come to the traditional clinic settings. For some patients, the reluctance to seek help has been based on distance and inaccessibility of services, while for others it has been a product of cultural barriers. Community mental health centers planners and directors recognize that often the center and its services must go to the patient rather than having the patient come to the center. The mechanisms used to bring the center to its potential patients have included the use of indigenous personnel drawn from the community served and also the location of the services themselves within facilities that are more closely identified with individual neighborhoods and communities. These have included storefront centers, community service centers, and neighborhood health centers.

This movement toward the community can be tremendously effective in increasing the availability and productivity of direct mental health services and can also have the effect of bringing the community mental health center into closer contact with other delivery systems which are attempting to serve different, but related, needs of the same community.

---

23   *Sister Mary Amelia*

Decentralized Outpatient Services in an Urban Setting

INTRODUCTION

In the fall of 1966, The Sisters of Charity of the Incarnate Word (a Texas nonprofit corporation), with the assistance of a federal staffing grant, undertook to organize the first community mental health center (CMHC) in the State of Texas.

During the first eight months of the center's operation, all staff were based at, and identified primarily with St. Joseph Hospital, one of the operating divisions of The Sisters of Charity of the Incarnate Word Corporation. The facility used consists of a four-story building, known as the Cullen Family Building, located across the street from the main St. Joseph Hospital Building. Just prior to the center's opening, this building served as a fifty-three bed unit for the St. Joseph Hospital Department of Psychiatry private inpatient service.

At this stage of the center's development, the above hospital facility was used for all inpatient, partial hospitalization, and outpatient services to CMHC patients, with the St. Joseph Hospital emergency room offering accommodations for psychiatric emergency care. CMHC outpatients were generally evaluated and treated in offices on the first floor.

By March 1967, all clinical services were in operation and patient case loads were increasing, particularly in outpatient service.

By April 1967, the need for additional outpatient facilities became quickly apparent and led to successful negotiations with St. Joseph Hospital's Outpatient Department to use its facilities certain days of the week. This was in addition to the facilities already in use on the first floor of the Cullen Family Building.

With clinical services continuing, and case loads mounting, the need arose to closely examine the extent to which the center was fulfilling its mandate as a community-oriented program, as opposed to a traditional clinical diagnostic and treatment facility. During this phase, the administrative director, as well as other professional staff persons, began to question the over-centralized, hospital-bound nature of services, and began to explore means of moving out to the community. It was evident that attempts to more directly extend services throughout the area would be a difficult task, but a necessary one, if the center was to become truly a community mental health center.

Thus, during the summer of 1967, the center's philosophy was undergoing change. This redirection of the center's philosophy brought about the decision to explore seriously new modalities of extending mental health services into the community, with the aid and cooperation of an already established and effectively operating social agency in the area—that being the Neighborhood Centers Association, which later became Neighborhood Centers–Day Care Association (NC-DCA).

St. Joseph Mid-Houston Community Mental Health Center Program, in conjunction with Neighborhood Centers–Day Care Association, decided to organize a

Service Delivery System capable of developing, relating, integrating, and coordinating delivery services and resources in such a way that an aggregate of services will be readily accessible and quickly available to families in a specific geographic area, and to assure that the services delivered are understood and utilized by these families effectively, maximally, and with continuity.

211

From the viewpoint of the community mental health center, the essential feature of this new delivery system was the development of a plan whereby outpatient and outreach services would be delivered through three "district centers" and eleven neighborhood "outposts." Each district center was designed to service a designated portion of the catchment area, and each neighborhood outpost was designed to serve an even smaller designated area. Definitive outpatient services are to be found at the district center, and in addition, health and welfare services provided by other community agencies are also available at the district center. Thus the district center is itself a multiagency, multiservice center, while the neighborhood outpost provides a walk-in point of entry for patients seeking mental health services and other community services. In addition, followup services can be provided at the neighborhood outposts and home visiting personnel operate out of the outposts.

In part, at least, the success of the community mental health center in developing a decentralized outpatient program is a function of its sharing a common philosophy of service with the NC-DCA. It is because of this common philosophy that the community mental health center was able to establish its first district center in the setting of an operating NC-DCA facility.

Even after the outpatient service had been moved into the NC-DCA facility, known as Ripley House, however, it was not operating efficiently and effectively until both agencies decided to develop another joint program. This is the Community Services Department. Funding was made possible through a federal growth grant with matching funds being provided by NC-DCA for almost all positions, as well as total expenses for other facilities and supplies for a period of one year. As a result, by working closely with the staff of the NC-DCA, the staff of the community mental health center has been able to develop and coordinate a network of decentralized programs for the provision of outpatient services.

DECENTRALIZED OUTPATIENT SERVICES

The establishment of the three district centers and the eleven outposts has greatly increased the scope and effectiveness of the outpatient services by making possible a variety of supportive services to the clinical team, the patient, and the patient's family.

Supportive services to the *clinical* team include:

1. gathering background information from the patient, his family, and other available sources;

2. giving supplemental information on a continuing basis concerning the attitudes of the family members, changes in family circumstances, and any additional background information;

3. interpreting the value of treatment to the patient and his family;

4. assisting the patient and his family to keep appointments and follow through on the recommendations of the clinical team;

5. arranging conferences with the family and providing an interpreter if necessary;

6. arranging conferences with other caregivers working with the patient and his family;

7. carrying out treatment recommendations—within the competence of the outreach worker—as requested by the clinical team.

Supportive services to the *patient* include:

1. helping him understand his need for treatment;

2. offering reassurance and understanding of his situation;

3. scheduling, reminding him of, and assisting him in keeping appointments;

4. providing transportation for appointments and obtaining medication if necessary;

5. supporting him in following through with the recommendations of the clinical team;

6. assisting him in relaying his needs and concerns to the family and the clinical team;

7. supporting and assisting him in interpreting his illness to employer, school, friends, neighbors, and so on;

8. referring him to other caregivers for physicals, financial assistance, employment, and so on, if needed;

9. making frequent friendly visits between appointments to offer reassurance, encouragement and information.

Supportive services to the *patient's family* include:

1. arranging screening and intake at a time and place convenient to the family;

2. assisting the family to evaluate and understand their total situation, informing them of available services, offering reassurance and under-

standing of their situation, and interpreting the need for and the value of treatment;

3. supporting the family in helping the patient understand and continue his treatment;

4. relaying the feelings and concerns of the family to the clinical team;

5. arranging for the family to talk with the clinical team and acting as an interpreter if necessary;

6. encouraging and supporting the family in attending groups as recommended by the clinical team;

7. referring the family to other caregivers for physicals, financial assistance and so on, if necessary;

8. assisting and supporting the family to interpret the illness to employers, schools, friends, neighbors, and so on.

ORGANIZATION

The Community Services Department (the Vehicle) was designed to achieve and maintain effective functional interrelationships between and among the agencies and all other participants in the delivery of services. The primary role of the Vehicle is managerial, but it also must assure the availability of all ancillary services. The Vehicle also initiates and operates short range experimental programs when needed and explores innovative ways of meeting current needs by utilizing all available resources of the neighborhood and community. Therefore, when in full operation, the Community Services Department involves the use of many methods and techniques. It has to be specialized in the areas of planning, coordination, experimentation, communication, neighborhood and community organization, group work, counseling, program development, evaluation, ancillary services, and anything else needed or available. The Vehicle must be free from the responsibility for delivery of direct, specialized services. But, even though the Vehicle does not provide or manage specific services, it provides an opportunity for the enhancement of those specialized services by making it possible for the services to be delivered within the framework of and supported by all facets of a comprehensive service program.

In order to perform its functions, the staff relies heavily on volunteers who live in the community. Volunteer leaders are involved in the program as members of the neighborhood committees in such areas as education, health and child development. These committees of neighborhood leaders represent the residents in planning, decision-making, evaluation, and operation of the programs. Being well aware of the needs of the residents, they are able to interpret needs, attitudes and concerns of the residents to agencies and other institutions. These neighborhood program committees are the main element in the development and delivery of neighborhood educational and enrichment programs, in the presentation and interpretation of services to the residents, and in the mobilization of neighborhood residents as participants in all programs.

In one district, for example, thirty-three different neighborhood program committees have organized during the initial stage of the program —these involve more than 500 resident volunteer leaders as committee members. Each neighborhood program committee draws its membership from nine different sections of the neighborhood it serves; thus, broad representation is assured of the residents in planning, organizing, and evaluation of all programs and services, as well as broad-based representation of the residents as participants in programs and in receiving services.

The work of the neighborhood committees is facilitated by the availability of staff members whose primary role is the development and support of neighborhood leaders. These staff members provide the neighborhood leaders with information about ongoing center programs, and they also conduct specialized training programs for the neighborhood leaders. These training programs emphasize such skills as those required for conducting meetings, undertaking community surveys, and disseminating information about center programs to residents in the catchment area.

Other staff members concentrate on providing crisis-oriented care for patients in the district or neighborhood. A screening and referral unit is responsible for establishing contact with patients in need of immediate care. The work of crisis intervention is made even more effective through an outreach unit, composed of indigenous workers who are known, trusted, and respected by their fellow neighborhood residents. The staff of the outreach unit are familiar not only with the customs and traditions of the neighborhood, but also with the nature of the services available through the several specialized agencies in the area.

One special feature of the program is the emphasis on the family unit as the focus of service. Because of the decentralized nature of the program, it is possible to maintain information about and contact with all members of a given family. To facilitate this, a central family record is maintained. This record includes not only standard identifying personal and social data but also information about jobs, health generally, school records, and the nature and extent of relationships within the neighborhood. The record also includes notations of all personal and telephone contacts with members of the family. The staff of the community mental health center thus have a considerable amount of information regarding each family and each family member, and as a result they are able to move very quickly and effectively whenever specialized mental health services are required.

24
Richard Stai, m.s.w., *and*
T. M. Atkinson, Jr., m.s.w.

Decentralized Outpatient Services in a Rural Setting

Our concept of the Psychiatric Mobile Team came into existence as an attempt to deal with several major problems in developing an efficient service delivery system in rural Appalachia. We asked ourselves several questions. First, in an area where transportation difficulties necessitate a decentralized program, how can we maximize the availability of scarce, highly trained, expensive, mental health professionals to both service receivers and service givers? Second, what will be our beginning service priority? Third, what staff composition is feasible in terms of cost and priorities? Fourth, how can we best utilize this staff pattern in terms of an administrative structure and in delivering services?

As issues presented themselves, both in grant development and in program implementation, consultation from NIMH and state officials led to the establishment of the following mobile team staffing pattern: one certified psychiatrist medical director, one supervising social worker, one certified psychologist, and one medical records librarian-stenographer. Although this staffing appeared minimal, it also appeared that we would be fortunate in filling even this meager pattern. Moreover, it was also clear that the extent of the staffing pattern had to be consistent with available long-term financial resources. As might be expected in a rural area, mental health services are very low on the local priority list for funding.

Our beginning priority was to deliver direct quality mental health services. This decision was based on several factors. First, there were no other professional mental health services available. Second, we felt that in order to establish credibility in a relationship with our oriented culture, we had to demonstrate directly our concern for people who were in immediate need of help. Third, this was what our staff was best trained to do. Fourth, we had to begin to develop sustaining income which is best done through direct services. Fifth, we had four hundred aftercare patients who were in need of followup care.

It was also decided that a multidisciplinary team headed by the psychiatrist-medical director would be most effective in providing a full range of mental health services throughout the region. The psychiatrist-medical director was felt to be essential in providing the needed medical attention for the team as well as the required legal and professional sanctions. As head of the team, the psychiatrist assigned the cases to local and mobile team staff members, developed treatment plans and priorities, and scheduled visits of the mobile team to local offices. In addition to his functions as head of the mobile team, he also served as supervisor of the partial hospitalization unit which entailed the supervision of the nurse in charge, prescribing medications for all patients, and establishment of treatment plans. The psychiatrist was available for consultation to local doctors regarding treatment of inpatients, and he also took direct responsibility for a limited number of inpatients in local general hospitals. In addition, he supervised all other staff members in regard to clinical matters.

The primary function of the certified social worker was training and supervision of professional and nonprofessional staff in the local offices. Basic to his supervisory functions was the implementation of an efficient information, screening, and referral system involving prescreening of patients by local staff and preparation of social histories for presentation to the psychiatrist.

The function of the psychologist was two-fold: diagnostic work and consultation to other agencies and institutions. Along with the psychiatrist and social worker, he was also involved in recruitment and screening of personnel.

The chief function of the medical record librarian was to assist in the maintenance of approved medical record standards. Also she served as a stenographer for the psychiatrist in such matters as psychiatric evaluations for social security and public assistance disability determinations.

The function of the mobile team was planned to fit the nature of the community mental health center and its catchment area. The catchment area consists of five rural counties in a mountainous area of Kentucky. Transportation among the counties posed a substantial problem, and the lack of professional personnel in the area made it impossible to develop independent programs in each county. Accordingly, limited full-time services were established in several scattered sections of the catchment area, and the mobile team was to provide backup and supportive services for them.

Five area teams were established to provide continuing services in each of the five counties. Each area team consisted of a social worker, a receptionist-secretary, and mental health workers (B.A. degrees). Their function was to operate an outpatient program for the patients of their section of the catchment area, and to assist them in this, they had local general practitioners available to provide medical supervision on an ongoing basis. Emergency services were available in general hospitals in three of the five counties, and the area team staff members and local medical consultants assisted hospital personnel in operating these services.

The mobile team's function was to visit each of the five county programs on a regular weekly basis. During these visits, the mobile team staff members could provide supervision, consultation to area staff and others in the area (teachers, clergy, and the general practitioners), and inservice training. They also provided direct outpatient services for both children and adults. Between visits, the members of the mobile team were available for telephone consultations at any time.

PROBLEMS

The functions of the mobile team were essential to the operation of the center, but the operation of the team as a coordinated unit presented a number of problems from the outset.

The most evident of these problems was the additional stress it placed on limited facilities. Sufficient office space was not available for the mobile team and the area team to be at the same place at the same time. Secondly, due to housing shortages in a small town, mobile team staff were not able to live in close proximity to each other making it difficult to travel as a unit. Furthermore, the variations of tasks to be performed at local offices necessitated availability of several automobiles. Practical problems such as road conditions, distance, and difficulties in getting the mobile team members together as a unit made it very difficult for the team to adhere to predetermined schedules. Continual difficulties were experienced in maintaining a coordinated system of scheduling patients for the mobile team because of the desire of each team member to maintain his own appointment schedule independently.

Service demands increased while primary case responsibility continued with mobile team members leaving no time for training of young professionals and generic mental health workers.

The chronicity of the above problems eroded the morale of the area team staff and necessitated a functional and administrative reorganization of the mobile team concept. Specifically, professional competence was not being developed at the local level. In addition, day-to-day decisions were being postponed until the arrival of the medical director. Menial services were being offered between visits of the mobile team psychiatrist. Furthermore, an untenable administrative situation was created by the discrepancy between administrative philosophy (local responsibility and accountability) and functioning (mobile team authority).

REORGANIZATION

The first step in reorganization was the disbanding of the mobile team. Instead of traveling and visiting local offices as a mobile team, each member visited offices independently according to schedules determined by each office. Appointment schedules for each former member of the mobile team were maintained through the local office.

In order to realize the administrative philosophy of local responsibility and accountability, it was necessary to restructure communication channels. The following changes were made. A Supervisory-Executive Council was established as a means of communicating to the administration both local and regional problems. This tended to standardize procedures in a formal way for the entire region. Furthermore, it provided an opportunity for participation of Area Team Directors in the decision-making process. The composition of the SEC is the Clinical Coordinator, Administrative Coordinator, Medical Records Librarian, Coordinator of Mental Health Specialists, Coordinator of Mental Retardation Specialists, and the Area Team Directors. The Medical Director and/or Executive Director participates on request from this committee. Formal minutes are taken.

One of the immediate results of this council was to call to attention the lines of accountability and responsibility and to prohibit random type decisions by traveling specialists. Opening up communication channels and allowing for participative management made it possible for all levels of personnel to be held accountable in their day-to-day activities. A further result of this council was the establishment of clearly defined agency priorities which tended to prevent individuals pursuing their own interests above agency needs. The immediate effect was role and status diffusion. However, once the normal group processes ran their course through the testing of new lines of authority, role delineation occurred and people became comfortable again with the new organization. During the testing period, there was an initial decrease in efficiency as reflected in our statistical accounting system. However, when both supervisors and supervisees became more comfortable with the realignment, direct patient hours, and income production, revitalized agency concern became evident. Subsequently, morale improved, there was a renewed emphasis on quality of services, and less internal conflict resulted in an out-reach to our community.

CONCLUSION

The delivery of services in a rural area requires decentralization. In pursuing this goal, however, numerous problems can arise which have been described. Most important is the maintenance of open lines of communication between the central administration and the area teams. Failure to clearly structure these relationships can undermine the primary goals of increased and more accessible services.

REFERENCES

Barnes, R. H. "Maintaining Chronic Patients in the Community." *Hospital and Community Psychiatry* 19(May 1968): 156–157.

Bauman, G., and Douthit, V. B. "Vocational Rehabilitation and Community Mental Health in Deprived Urban Areas." *Journal of Rehabilitation* 34 (Nov.–Dec. 1968): 28–30.

Berliner, A. K. "Bridging the Gap between Institution and Community in the Treatment of Narcotic Addicts." *Mental Hygiene* 52(April 1968): 263–271.

Blanco, A., and Akabas, S. H. "The Factory: Site for Community Mental Health Practice." *American Journal of Orthopsychiatry* 38(April 1968): 543–552.

Bonstedt, T., and Khalily, H. "Psychiatric Aftercare. A Discussion of the Importance of Predischarge Planning." *Ohio Medical Journal* 62(July 1966): 672–676.

Carhill, K. G. "A Community Placement Program for State Hospital Patients." *Mental Hygiene* 51(April 1967): 261–265.

Corney, R. T. "Screening Evaluation: A Solution to the Increased Demands for Outpatient Consultation in a Mental Health Clinic." *Mental Hygiene* 52(January 1968): 90–96.

Donner, J., and Gamson, A. "Experience with Multifamily, Time Limited, Outpatient Groups at a Community Psychiatric Clinic." *Psychiatry* 31(May 1968): 126–137.

Fabrega, H., Jr., Rubel, A. J., and Wallace, C. A. "Working Class Mexican Psychiatric Outpatients. Some Social and Cultural Features." *Archives of General Psychiatry* 16(June 1967): 704–712.

Frost, E. S. "Community-Hospital-Industrial-Rehabilitation-Placements." *International Psychiatric Clinics* 6(1969): 381–397.

Hallowitz, E. "The Role of a Neighborhood Service Center in Community Mental Health." *American Journal of Orthopsychiatry* 38(July 1968): 705–714.

Hogarty, G. E., Dennis, H., and Guy, W. "Who Goes There? A Critical Evaluation of Admissions to a Psychiatric Day Hospital." *American Journal of Psychiatry* 124(January 1968): 934–944.

Ingham, R. E., and Allgeyer, J. M. "Early Access to Clinic Treatment." *Hospital and Community Psychiatry* 19(December 1968): 387–388.

Koegler, R. R. "Brief-Contact Therapy and Drugs in Outpatient Treatment." *International Psychiatric Clinics* 3(Winter 1966): 139–154.

Komar, M. "A 'Therapeutic Community' for Outpatients." *Mental Hygiene* 51(July 1967): 440–448.

Levy, R. A. "Six-Session Outpatient Therapy." *Hospital and Community Psychiatry* 17(November 1966): 340–343.

Liederman, P. C., Green, R., and Liderman, V. R. "Outpatient Group Therapy with Geriatric Patients." *Geriatrics* 22(January 1967): 148–153.

Lipkin, K. M., and Daniels, R. S. "Programs for Discharged Patients. I. Community Activities Help Readjustment." *Hospital and Community Psychiatry* 19(March 1968): 76–77.

McAllister, R. J. "Open-Door Group Therapy in a Community Hospital." *Current Psychiatric Therapy* 7(1967): 162–163.

Ozarin, L. D. "Occupational Therapy Facilities in Community Mental Health Centers." *Hospital and Community Psychiatry* 20(September 1969): 289–290.

Pleasure, H. "Confrontation. Walk-in Centers Aid Mental Health." *Modern Hospitals* 111(December 1968): 180.

Rabiner, C. J., and Hankoff, L. D. "Satellite Neighborhood Clinics." *Hospital and Community Psychiatry* 18(September 1967): 282–284.

Seeman, K. "Multimodality Outpatient Group Psychotherapy." *American Journal of Psychotherapy* 22(July 1968): 443–459.

Straker, M. "Brief Psychotherapy in an Outpatient Clinic: Evolution and Evaluation." *American Journal of Psychiatry* 124(March 1968): 1219–1226.

Swartz, J. "The Outpatient Clinic." *International Psychiatric Clinics* 3(Fall 1966): 49–63.

Whittington, H. G., and Steenbarger, C. "Preliminary Evaluation of a Decentralized Community Mental Health Clinic." *American Journal of Public Health* 60(January 1970): 64–77.

Wiesel, B. "Outpatient Facilities and Services. Flexibility: Key to Planning of Psychiatric Services and Facilities." *Hospitals* 41(February 1967): 65–68.

GENERAL REFERENCES

Glasscote, R. M., Sanders, D. S., Forstenzen, H. M., and Foley, A. R. *The Community Mental Health Center, An Analysis of Existing Models.* Washington, D.C.: Publications Department, American Psychiatric Association, 1964.

Glasscote, R. M., Sussex, J. N., Cumming, E., and Smith, L. H. *The Community Mental Health Center, An Interim Appraisal.* Washington, D.C.: The Joint Information Service of the American Psychiatric Association and the National Association for Mental Health, 1969.

Glasscote, R. M., Kraft, A. M., Glassman, S. M., and Jepson, W. W. *Partial Hospitalization for the Mentally Ill: A Study of Programs and Problems.* Washington, D.C.: Joint Information Service, 1969.

National Institute of Mental Health. "Outpatient Services." Chevy Chase, Maryland: U.S. Department of Health, Education and Welfare, Public Health Service Publication No. 1578, 1968.

Ozarin, L. "The Community Mental Health Center—A Public Health Facility." *American Journal of Public Health* 56(January 1966): 26–31.

VIII
New Approaches to Emergency Care

EDITORS' INTRODUCTION

By virtue of its commitment to community based treatment, the community mental health center program has recognized that mechanisms must be provided to deal with acute problems at the time that they are occurring. Since patients generally come for help at a time of crisis, the commitment of the community mental health center to reduce the need for inpatient services must be accompanied by the development of effective alternatives to handle these crises when they are present. Consequently, the development of emergency services has been recognized as one of the five essential services of the community mental health center program.

A common problem which has been faced by many community mental health centers has been the development of these emergency services so that they are readily available on a twenty-four-hour basis, seven days a week. Traditional mental health facilities have not offered this kind of availability except in the context of a hospital setting. Since the development of a community mental health center program implies movement toward the community, it is also recognized that these emergency services must, for the most part, be placed within the community. Many community mental health centers have recognized this problem by the development of specialized services which are crisis oriented and which are identified to the community as resources during an emergency.

The identification of an emergency service can play an important role in the delivery of total mental health services. First, it can function as an entry point for all patients seeking mental health services. Diagnosis and evaluation can be completed and a disposition made to a different, but appropriate, service of the community mental health center. Second, and perhaps even more important, can be the utilization of the emergency service as the primary treatment modality for many patients who seek help. If the personnel who staff the emergency service are also trained to provide treatment, then the definitive care for many patients can be handled within the emergency service and referral is not needed.

In the context of this latter utilization of emergency services, many community mental health centers have designated certain members of the staff as specialists in crisis intervention whose work is solely within the emergency service. Personnel can be drawn from a variety of backgrounds and professional training provided that they all receive training in the special art of crisis intervention.

The availability of emergency services is further extended in the community by offering telephone contact on a twenty-four-hour basis as well as face-to-face contact. Recognizing the tremendous volume of service which can be provided through this type of emergency service, many community mental health centers have also reached into the community and recruited carefully selected volunteers to function alongside the professional members of the team and to receive the same training.

---

25   *Donald Weston,* M.D.

Development of a Psychiatric Emergency Service under the Direction of a Nurse

Since mid-1969, the St. Lawrence Community Mental Health Center Emergency Service has had a twenty-four-hour walk-in and telephone service in operation. This service has been operated under the direction of a psychiatric nurse, staffed by non-M.D. mental health professionals, and located outside the medical emergency service of the hospital.

The objectives of this service have been as follows:

1. To provide mental health crisis intervention on an immediate basis.

2. To provide individuals with an assessment of their mental health problems, recommendation for disposition, and amelioration of their problems through the various other direct services of the community mental health center with emphasis on alternatives to hospitalization.

3. To provide back-up and consultation services to medical emergency rooms of the hospitals in the community, to the East Lansing Crisis Center ("Listening Ear") and to other such facilities.

4. To provide emergency consultation to individuals, families, groups, or agencies regarding mental health problems.

5. To provide an emergency consultation resource to physicians in the community.

6. To serve as a training unit for students in medicine, social work, nursing, psychology, and psychiatry.

The development of the community mental health center included the concept of integrating the inpatient service into the total program, but at the same time it was considered important to effect a change in the established utilization pattern of the inpatient service. As a first step in this direction, it was decided to supplement the existing medical emergency room service with additional mental health personnel and to provide community mental health center staff members on an on-call basis during the night.

Here it is important to state that the center was strongly committed to the concept that many people in the mental health professions could carry out the roles traditionally reserved for the psychiatrist. Accordingly, from the beginning, we envisioned the utilization of psychiatric nurses, social workers, and clinical psychologists in the roles of primary therapists and emergency service staff. Psychiatrists and other physicians serve in the role of back-up doctors for consultation and the use of medication. Initially, the placement of center staff in the medical emergency room was welcomed by the regular emergency room staff. The latter perceived this as a means of speeding up the process of getting patients out of the medical emergency room and onto the psychiatric inpatient unit. Soon, however, because the center staff was spending as much as one to two hours talking with the patient and his family in an

effort to find alternative solutions to hospitalization, the center administration was requested to find separate space for these services. Secondly,
it was found that in the evenings when center staff was on-call, they
would tend to be called only when a patient was indigent, and did not
have funds for private psychiatrists; thus, it became obvious that any
impact the center staff was going to have on alternatives to hospitalization was limited primarily to the indigent population. Because of these
two overlapping problems, it was decided to establish a full-time,
twenty-four-hour, emergency service separate from the medical emergency room. This service was established under the direction of a psychiatric nurse and was staffed by mental health professionals from the
center.

The staffing of the emergency service is currently divided into two divisions:

1. *Day Service:* The primary therapist staff of the St. Lawrence Community Mental Health Center provides the manpower for the emergency
service Monday through Friday, 8:00 A.M. to 5:00 P.M. Each therapist is
on-call for a four and one-half hour shift (8:00 A.M.–12:30 P.M. or 12:30
P.M.–5:00 P.M.) approximately two or three times per month. This is
considered part of the regular work load for all primary therapists and
is therefore undertaken without additional remuneration.

2. *Night, Weekend and Holiday Service:* The fifteen-hour night shift
(5:00 P.M.–8:00 A.M.) during the week, the ten-hour shift (8:00 A.M.–6:00
P.M.) on Saturday and Sunday, the fourteen-hour shift (6:00 P.M.–8:00
A.M.) on Saturday night and Sunday night, and the shifts for holidays
during the year are all staffed by therapists who have been selected for
this service by the program coordinator and who are approved by the
medical director of the center.

The staff for the night, weekend, and holiday shifts receive seventy-
five dollars per shift. The manpower pool for night, weekend, and
holidays consists of a maximum of only fifteen participants in order to
insure that procedures and policies are implemented as uniformly as
possible. Regular meetings involving the day service staff as well as
night, weekend, and holiday service staff are held to review policies and
procedures and to discuss scheduling.

The emergency service also requires supplementary staffing during
part of the night shift. A male aide is utilized from 11:00 P.M. to 7:00
A.M. to provide assistance for the therapist. His duties include: (1)

seeing that families of the patient, police escorts, and so forth are attended to; (2) obtaining identification information from patients and/or families for emergency service assessment forms; (3) answering telephone calls when the therapist is not available; (4) being available to assist with severely agitated patients; and when necessary; (5) acting as an escort for patients to and from the medical emergency room or the inpatient unit.

A manpower pool of physicians is also available on an on-call basis to provide needed back-up services. This group of physicians is available to provide both consultation to the therapists and direct clinical services. This manpower pool consists of physicians from the Department of Psychiatry at Michigan State University and St. Lawrence Community Mental Health Center. The service is provided as part of their regular work load and is contributed without additional remuneration.

A psychiatric nurse was chosen to be director of the program for several reasons. The idea of a non-M.D. mental health professional playing an emergency role in a broad hospital setting was new to the community and it was felt that the R.N. would be the most acceptable liaison person. First, the physicians were accustomed to working closely with R.N.'s and psychologically were more conditioned to the concept of an R.N. dealing with crises independently. Second, a psychiatric R.N. has considerable experience in the area of psycho-pharmacologic drugs. Third, most of the other mental health professionals in our community had had very little experience with acutely disturbed patients whereas the psychiatric nurse had worked on the inpatient service prior to the establishment of the mental health center and had experience in this area. Fourth, there was a need to have a close working relationship with the medical emergency service for back-up resources for any mental health emergency which is overshadowed by a medical emergency, such as acute brain syndromes and suicide attempts.

TRAINING

All members of the staff are required to go through a training program to insure understanding of the procedures and facilities in the community and to acquire adequate skills in a role that is new for many of the non-M.D. professionals. Initially, they go through a period in which they spend time in the emergency service while a senior staff member is on duty. During this period they do not actually intervene with the patients, but rather they become familiar with the procedures and methodology used in the emergency service. This is a rather short period, usually limited to three or four evening sessions.

The second phase is a period in which they act as the primary emergency room therapist under the supervision of a senior staff member. No time limit has been set for this period in view of the different levels of skills that the staff bring to the agency and the various rates of individual learning. It is the responsibility of the senior staff member doing the supervision and the psychiatric nurse who is program coordinator for the service to determine when an individual has spent adequate time in this phase.

Even though the staff's ability to deal with most crisis cases was impressive, it appeared necessary to increase their sophistication in areas that are not always stressed in nonmedical mental health training programs. Therefore, there was developed a series of seminars conducted by staff psychiatrists and psychiatrists in the Department of Psychiatry at Michigan State University. These seminars have focused on the following areas.

Mental Status   There was a clear need for training in using a systematic manner of evaluating patients. (This was particularly true in having a systematic form of communication between the mental health professional on duty in the emergency room with the psychiatrist who is on back-up call.) Psychiatrists are trained to think in terms of mental status and frequently request the staff to report to them in this fashion. Though this was initially developed as a means of improving communication, feedback from the non-M.D. mental health professional has indicated that it has been helpful to them in organizing and conceptualizing the presenting problem in the emergency service.

Psycho-Pharmacology   Initially, this was a seminar focusing on the major psychotropic drugs, identifying indications for their use and major side reactions. At the present time, the staff is developing a much more intensive seminar with the objective of making the emergency service staff as knowledgeable about psycho-pharmacology as is a psychiatric resident.

Organic Syndromes   Though this is usually covered in the nonmedical mental health training program, it was felt that there was a need for a high level of sophistication in this area, particularly in a community where many people are questioning the use of non-M.D.'s in a traditional M.D. role.

Alcoholism   Though the community has another agency which has an active program in alcoholism, the center emergency service receives many patients with alcoholism as their primary problem. Many of these patients are those who have not responded to the other programs in the community. Because of this the staff felt the need for additional training and education in this area.

Drug Addiction With the increasing number of patients with drugs as their primary problem, and with many of the staff having never had training in this area in the past, it became quite important to educate the staff in the effects and side effects of the various chemical substances patients commonly use.

Finally, before any staff member is allowed to participate in the emergency service he must be reviewed by one of the staff psychiatrists or the medical director. This review focuses heavily on the areas of psychotropic drugs and organic syndromes. It usually takes the format of case presentations by the staff psychiatrist with the potential candidate for the emergency service indicating his approach to the problem, a differential diagnosis and a proposed disposition.

PROBLEMS

Probably the biggest problem in initiating an emergency service of this type relates to the medical profession's acceptance of other professionals in a role that has traditionally been reserved for M.D.'s. There was a period of approximately six months during which not only the psychiatrists but many of the nonpsychiatric M.D.'s in the community actively questioned and challenged the use of non-M.D. professionals both in the emergency setting and in the consultation role on the inpatient service. In part this was the result of the obvious alteration in the traditional private practice orientation of the community and the impact that the emergency service had on patients being admitted to the inpatient service. There were many fears expressed that the center, because it would be seeing all the emergency patients, might soon utilize all of the inpatient beds leaving none for admissions by private physicians. There did not seem to be any real belief that the goal was to cut down admissions rather than simply to follow the previous pattern of having almost all patients who were presented as emergencies being admitted to the inpatient service. Due to a continuing program of education, however, there has been a gradual acceptance of the emergency service. The fears that the inpatient unit would be dominated by community mental health center patients have now been allayed by the dramatic reduction in inpatient admissions.

The second major problem facing this type of emergency service is related to the legal limitations imposed on the non-M.D. mental health professional. As the psychiatrists on the staff and at the University have gained confidence in the competence of the emergency room staff, they now resent the continued need to fulfill the legal formalities of prescribing medication and hospitalizing patients. There appears to be no possible immediate solution to this problem, because such a solution would require a change in the licensure statutes.

EFFECTIVENESS

One of the major goals in the program was to find alternatives to hospitalization. Many patients were hospitalized under the old system because people did not look for alternatives. This has been dramatically shown in that the inpatient unit, which previously had forty-five patients and a waiting list of twelve to fifteen patients, has had an average census of approximately twenty-five patients for the past year. It appears that this is due to the combination of having a person available to intervene and having alternatives (such as day program, outpatient program, crisis groups, and contacts with other agencies) available to that person.

The program has been most effective both as a service and also in its role as a training ground for students in the various disciplines. When students from a variety of disciplines are placed in a role usually reserved for the psychiatrist, they begin very quickly to question what kind of skills are required to carry out a given task. Through training provided in this type of setting, graduates learn to be quite capable of functioning effectively either in the inpatient unit or the emergency service. Specifically, they seem to function better with the acutely disturbed patient than do new graduates coming out of more traditional training programs.

Development of an Emergency Listening Post
Manned by Ministers

Action for Mental Health, the report of the Joint Commission, very dramatically identified the minister, especially the pastor of a neighborhood church, as being the one person in the community most likely to be thought of as a resource by persons who have emotional problems. Additionally, the minister is sought *first,* in a very great percentage of cases, *before* the family physician, and certainly before a psychiatrist or clinical psychologist is sought.

The significance of this fact has been clearly recognized in the Meridian area since 1966. In that year the staff of the East Mississippi State Hospital began to offer classes in pastoral counseling for local clergymen, and since that year the services provided by the clergymen have become a vital part of the program of the Weems Community Mental Health Center. The classes were started in response to requests made by the local clergymen, who felt a need to increase their ability to answer the requests they received from their own parishioners and others who desired pastoral counseling.

Beginning in September 1966, classes for a maximum of twelve persons at a time were conducted for two hours each week over a period of twelve weeks. The trainees were helped through a variety of methods to become more effective in providing emotional support and counseling. Subsequently, two classes each year have been conducted at the hospital, primarily by the chaplain and clinical psychologist, and with the involvement of the hospital director-psychiatrist in orienting each new class. Great care was taken both to caution and to reassure the participants that no effort or inference of producing "junior psychiatrists" or "junior psychologists" was being attempted, but rather that the major effort was being directed toward helping them to become more competent and more comfortable in the counseling services which were already being requested of them. Perhaps equal or even greater emphasis was placed on the opportunity to learn when to refer a person with an emotional problem which might be too complex or too serious to be handled at the level of pastoral counseling.

As a greater and greater number of ministers in the area became trained through the program at the East Mississippi State Hospital, an almost inevitable and natural process began to take shape, in which a small group drawn from the larger total number began to consider the need and desirability of establishing a visible organization to facilitate the availability of the services which they had learned to provide.

Thus, on December 20, 1968, a new community service agency was established and incorporated, known formally as the Meridian Counseling Foundation, and more informally as The Listening Post. This organization, manned by seventeen ministers initially, secured office space in a downtown Meridian business building. Using second-hand donated furniture, a telephone, and a volunteer receptionist and secretarial personnel, they formed a free counseling agency. Very shortly thereafter, the local telephone answering service donated its services to cover those evening, night, and weekend hours when a secretary-receptionist was not in the office.

While such an organization might not appear to be of much importance or value in a community or population center blessed by numerous or sophisticated mental health services, it filled a real void in the Meridian area. Indeed, with relatively little initial publicity, it was utilized by troubled persons in significant numbers from the very outset of its establishment.

Since staff time was donated by local clergymen and volunteers from some of the local women's organizations, the necessary financial support was minimal. The organization had been established and incorporated as a nonprofit service agency, and hence it was eligible for tax-deductible contributions from individuals and organizations such as civic clubs, individual churches, and others. Also, since it was a legitimate service agency, it was eligible for inclusion in the group of civic organizations known in the Meridian area as the GLOW Fund Agencies, the local United Fund Organization.

While The Listening Post was developing and growing, the major efforts of the Director of the East Mississippi State Hospital had been toward the establishment of a community mental health center for the region consisting of the county in which the hospital is located and six other surrounding rural counties. Together these seven counties could make up a catchment area conforming to the federal regulations for community mental health centers. To establish the center, it was planned that the inpatient and partial hospitalization components required would be provided by the state hospital. A new building was to be constructed on state hospital land for the outpatient, consultation, and education services of the community mental health center.

Thus four of the five required services were to be developed by the state hospital. During the planning stage it became clear that the fifth required service, the emergency service, could best be developed through the newly created Listening Post, with its cadre of dedicated and trained ministers, its accessible walk-up office space in a downtown building, its secretary-receptionist on duty all day, and its telephone answering service already in operation for the evening, night, and weekend hours. The ministers were available for scheduled appointments for counseling during the daytime hours, and they also established an on-call system in order to be available to the answering service operators for emergency calls which came after regular office hours.

Since its incorporation into the community mental health center, The Listening Post has provided services mainly to three groups of people: first, those who might normally have gone to their own pastor for counseling, but who, for various reasons, were reluctant to do so; second, those who had no church affiliation at all, and therefore, no pastor to whom to go; third, those in emergency need or trouble, who would have no idea where to turn, or what to do, if it were not for the publicized availability of The Listening Post. Because of their awareness of those resources and services available in the area through other local agencies and individuals, the minister-counselors have been able to obtain definitive services for many persons who first sought help through The Listening Post. Their own counseling services have thus been supplemented by other human service resources in the community.

Statistics accumulated since the time of organization indicate some interesting trends. The service has been used quite freely by a very significant number of persons, totaling in excess of 300 in the first eighteen months of operation. On an average, there have been slightly over three appointments made and kept for each individual seeking counseling. The age range has been from children under the age of twelve, through teenagers, young adults, middle-age adults, and even a small number in the over-sixty category. The problems brought to the counselors in The Listening Post have included not only the expected kinds of emotional problems but also marital, physical, legal, and economic concerns. In those cases where it was obvious that assistance was needed in some area other than psychological, medical, or psychiatric, the knowledge and awareness on the part of the minister-counselor was put to good advantage in expediting a referral of the troubled person to realistic resources in the community. Of perhaps most significance is the fact that less than 5 percent of the persons seeking help through The Listening Post required referral for possible admission to the state psychiatric hospital. This would appear to support the inference of a tremendous need in the community for the type of service which The Listening Post provides.

It must be noted that persons other than the recipients of direct services of The Listening Post have also benefited from the establishment of this organization in our community. There are at least three identifiable groups of people, other than the counselees themselves, who have benefited through their involvement with The Listening Post. First, that significant group of local ministers, who have taken additional professional training in counseling, have been better able to serve their own church membership in addition to serving on the voluntary counseling staff of The Listening Post. Second, the officers and members of the churches represented by these ministers have had the opportunity to become aware of community needs and to help meet them through support of The Listening Post. Third, there is a general sense of satisfaction among all the citizens of the area in knowing that such a service is being offered by The Listening Post, available to literally anyone in need of help and without any cost.

Of perhaps even more global significance is the basic philosophy; namely, that of utilizing services and individuals that are available while avoiding duplication of services. Because of this philosophy, the community as a whole has been drawn closer together and has been given a commonality of purpose which could never have been achieved otherwise.

---

27   *Steve Walters*

The Use of Volunteers in the Amarillo Crisis Intervention Center

In early 1968, through the stimulus and concern of local professionals and lay persons, the Amarillo Mental Health–Mental Retardation Regional Board of Trustees began to explore the need for a Crisis Intervention Center in the Amarillo area which would be a twenty-four-hour-a-day emergency telephone answering service for people in emotional crisis. The opening of this new service in December 1968, was preceded by study and planning involving a multidisciplinary advisory board leading to many crucial decisions. One of these was to utilize nonprofessional volunteers who had been carefully screened and trained to answer the crisis telephone.

RECRUITMENT

Chad Varah [1] and his Samaritans discovered the great good that friendly, devoted people who cared could render to those in distress. This, in essence, is the lesson: that lay volunteers, properly selected, not overselected or overtrained, can learn and become the heart of an effective crisis center.

Varah also points out that good volunteers are found, not made. On this premise, volunteers for the Amarillo Center were recruited on an individual basis from various organizations such as the Ministerial Alliance, Junior League, University, College, public schools, professionals, and various community agencies. No public appeal was made for volunteers since other centers found many of those volunteering from a public appeal were persons seeking solutions to their own problems.

The first Amarillo group consisted of twenty-seven volunteers, twenty-two of whom are still active volunteers nineteen months later. This group included ten ministers, one director of religious education, two social workers, one mental health associate, one psychiatric nursing instructor, one psychology professor, one law-enforcement officer, and ten housewives. A review of the educational background of the housewives reflects that five had no education beyond high school, one had three years of college, three held B.S. or B.A. degrees, and one had a master's degree. Of the five original volunteers who are no longer involved in the program, one left for personal reasons, and the other four moved from the city. Twenty additional volunteers have been accepted into the program bringing the current total to forty-two.

Some of the basic characteristics searched for in recruits were motivation, maturity, responsibility, sensitivity, capacity for growth, stability, and ability to deal forthrightly with crisis situations. It was necessary for the volunteer to possess the capacity to function well in a group and demonstrate the ability to accept training and supervision.

The recruits were asked to provide the center with three references, clergy, medical, and personal, which were carefully reviewed. The recruits were then interviewed in depth by the director of the center. The service expected of a volunteer was explained fully to the recruit. Some decided against the program when the nature of the task became clear. Once accepted into training, the volunteers were told that, if they found they were uncomfortable with the work, they should feel free to drop out.

TRAINING

The initial training program followed very closely the outline provided in *Techniques in Crisis Intervention: A Training Manual*[2] available from the Los Angeles Suicide Prevention Center.

The training period consisted of thirty hours of lectures and role-playing. Realizing that some volunteers had no prior experience or training in mental health, the first session covered basic personality adjustment. Other sessions described the theories of suicide and the meaning of suicidal behavior. The major concepts presented were "communication," "the cry for help," "ambivalence," "significant other," "resources," "reactions to death," "helplessness," and "regression."

Training in the area of techniques included such things as how to conduct a telephone interview; how to evaluate suicide potential; how to identify and focus on the precipitating stress; available community resources; and how to use and mobilize these resources. These techniques equip the volunteer to define the problem of the callers and move toward appropriate solutions.

In the final phase of training, the NIMH recording, *First Training Record in Suicidology*,[3] was used. This proved helpful in giving the volunteers some insight into what actual calls were like. The good and bad points of each taped interview were discussed at length. At this point in training, the volunteers participated in role playing. This, at first, produced anxieties for them but with practice became less threatening.

Following the lectures and role playing, each volunteer began a period of on-the-job training when case records were reviewed. They observed calls being taken. Then, under supervision of the director, they began taking calls. Our experience has shown some relationship between the volunteer's anxiety and the length of time that elapsed before he received a call. Those who received calls soon after completing training were far less anxious than those who waited several days before receiving their initial call.

The initial training program as outlined above has been used with little modification with all subsequent volunteers. The Amarillo Crisis Center has steered away from overtraining the volunteer to the extent that he would think of himself as a therapist. The material offered is directed toward identification of problems and the professional resources available to cope with such problems. Patience, understanding, and awareness of the caller's inner suffering are required of the volunteer who listens, encourages dialogue, gathers necessary information, and makes proper referrals as he is trained to do. The dignity and worth of the man and respect for his life are the prime considerations in the volunteer's response. It should be particularly noted that no effort is made to limit the service to medical crises, psychiatric crises, or social crises. The response is to the total person who is calling for help rather than to some fractional aspect of his life. The focus is on the *individual,* helping him "to find himself," with encouragement for today and hope for tomorrow.

THE VOLUNTEER AT WORK

The Amarillo Crisis Center is operated administratively within the organizational structure of the Amarillo Community Mental Health Center. The volunteer office was located in the outpatient department. In retrospect, we see this placement as having been a most important aspect of the subsequent growth and acceptance of the Crisis Center. It gave the volunteer the opportunity to feel a part of something, to be "where the action is," and to be the back-up of the CMHC professional staff at all times. As a result, the Crisis Center has become a primary intake source for the CMHC and, as a part of the CMHC, its relations with other agencies, hospitals, and law enforcement were more easily established.

A special problem for the volunteers occurs when calls are slow in coming. When people volunteer to do a job, they need work to do. It is demoralizing when work is slow. Utilization of the volunteers' idle time in assisting with clerical work for various areas of the CMHC proved to be beneficial for all concerned.

The hours worked by the individual volunteers vary. From 8:00 A.M. to 4:30 P.M. Monday through Friday, the volunteers work regular three hour shifts per week at the center. Calls coming after these hours, on weekends, and on holidays are rerouted by the switchboard of the Community Mental Health Center to the residence of the volunteer on call.

237

This is done without interruption of the call or the caller being made aware of the switchboard location. The call is answered with, "May I help you?"

To assure a smooth flow of this part of the operation, the switchboard operators attended the Crisis Intervention training sessions to enable them to fully understand the nature of the center. An important aspect of the switchboard operators is that if the volunteer needs help, for example, police, emergency room, and so forth, a flash of the telephone button brings the operator back on the call. An example of this is the case of a young woman who called the center after ingesting a large amount of barbiturates. The volunteer flashed the operator who immediately had the call traced and alerted the police. This young woman lost consciousness before giving her address. Due to the operator being alerted, this young woman was hospitalized immediately and has subsequently recovered.

The volunteers on call at home, or on the Nightwatch as we call it, is an adaptation of the Nightwatch group at the Los Angeles SPC which has served as a model for this type of operation. An indepth description of their program can be found in *Suicide Prevention Around the Clock*.[4]

A *Repeaters' Bulletin* is sent regularly to all Nightwatch volunteers. This bulletin gives brief information on patients who call the center repeatedly to enable all volunteers to give the caller consistent recommendations.

OTHER CONCERNS

The Amarillo Crisis Center has, from the onset, extended beyond the somewhat arbitrary definitions of suicide prevention. It became evident that there existed a gap between the actual crisis and contact with the appropriate helping agency. We have attempted to focus our service into that critical gap where crisis intervention can effectively prevent emotional deterioration and facilitate appropriate referrals. The referral to private, city, county, and state agencies is a coordinating service that involves the whole community in a common concern.

From this community involvement came the opportunity for the Crisis Center volunteers to participate in a challenging drug abuse program. With the development of "Operation Drug Alert," the Crisis Center telephone service was advertised as a place where persons wanting information about drugs could call for accurate answers and where drug abusers could call for aid in securing medical assistance. In an effort to avoid confusing the public, the advertised number is the same as the original Crisis Center number. The trained Crisis Center volunteers underwent a comprehensive twenty-hour training course on recognition and identification of various drugs; physical effects of drug abuse; psychological effects of drugs; penalties of drug abuse and possession of drugs; the testimony of a heroin addict; the life of an LSD user. The above format was taught by local law-enforcement personnel, physicians, psychiatrists, attorneys, and drug abusers. The response to this telephone service has been overwhelming—620 calls received the first month. The young people of the community have been responsive to the direct, nonjudgmental approach of the volunteers. With the trust the youth of the community have developed for the volunteer, they are beginning to call with other problems—fear of pregnancy, venereal disease, parent-child conflict and the like. The Crisis Center is ever mindful of the responsibility to the volunteers and to the community at large to assure that a high degree of competence and skill is maintained at all times.

The near future will see our Crisis Center volunteers embark on an ever-widening scope of service to the community. The need for a central information and referral service for the Amarillo metropolitan area has been evident for some time. SPCI-ODA volunteers were already embarked on a course which included most of this information. A few additional hours of training, a few more sheets in the Volunteers' Manual, is making this a reality through the Crisis Intervention Center where the volunteers have accepted the challenge to "shorten the distance one has to travel to the nearest heart."

In the experience of this center, it has been proven that nonprofessional volunteers, trained in crisis intervention techniques, can and do play an important role in and make significant contributions to the mental health of the community. Of the 2,014 persons seeking assistance from this center since its beginning, none have taken their lives, many have received professional help, and others found their fears quieted by the friendly volunteers who cared enough to listen.

NOTES

1. Chad Varah, *The Samaritans,* London: Constable, 1965.
2. Norman Farberow, Samuel Heilig, and Robert E. Litman, *Techniques in Crisis Intervention: A Training Manual,* Los Angeles, California: L. A. Suicide Prevention Center, 1968.

3. *First Training Record in Suicidology*, available from National Institute of Mental Health.

4. Norman Farberow, Edwin Shneidman, Robert Litman, Carl Wold, Samuel Heilig, and Jan Kramer, *Suicide Prevention Around the Clock*, presented at the 1965 Annual Meeting, American Orthopsychiatric Association, New York City, March 17–20, 1965.

---

28   *Aaron Satloff*, M.D.

The Use of Boarding or Holding Beds
in the Emergency Service

INTRODUCTION

In many ways the emergency service of a community mental health center is the hub of the major activities of the center. It can also be viewed as the interface between the population at risk in the catchment area and the structure of organized supporting services within the mental health center proper. The emergency service thus becomes a kind of gateway to the host of alternative dispositions available to people in distress and, as such, occupies a position of great strategic importance. It has the power to affect markedly the complexion of the patient populations of the other components of the mental health center such as the day hospital, the inpatient service, and the outpatient clinics; and for this reason, it is imperative that there be close communication and cooperation between the emergency service and the rest of the community mental health center.

Many psychiatric emergency facilities are relatively new. Most of this numerical increase is due in large measure to the passage of the Community Mental Health Centers Act of 1963 (Public Law 88-164), which requires that an emergency facility be an integral part of every community mental health center. Emergency facilities, however, have been in existence prior to the advent of this legislation. One such long existing facility is the Psychiatric Emergency Division of the Department of Psychiatry of the University of Rochester Medical Center, in Rochester, New York, which now also serves as the emergency service for the University of Rochester's Community Mental Health Center. The setting of this emergency facility is the general emergency section of Strong Memorial Hospital, the main teaching hospital of the University of Rochester School of Medicine and Dentistry. The clinical service is open twenty-four hours a day and is staffed by psychiatric residents, backed up by senior residents and full-time faculty members. Currently, this emergency service is logging in excess of 4,000 patient visits per year.

In July 1968, the University of Rochester opened its Community Mental Health Center at Strong Memorial Hospital. The center is designed to serve a catchment area of somewhat in excess of 160,000 persons. The catchment area subsumes a portion of the inner city and most of the southern (both suburban and rural) areas of Monroe County. The catchment area served by the Rochester Mental Health Center (associated with the Rochester General Hospital) is roughly the northern quadrant of the City of Rochester and the corresponding suburban areas and towns.

From an administrative standpoint, the service is supervised by a clinical director, who is a member of the full-time faculty of the Department of Psychiatry. He is assisted by a third-year psychiatric resident who in turn directly supervises the work of the second-year residents, who form the backbone of the major clinical service activities. There is a full-time nurse-clinician, and a full-time psychiatric social worker as well as two secretarial assistants. In addition, many trainees serve on a regular basis. These include medical students, student nurses, psychology trainees, social work trainees, and nonprofessional staff preparing for work in the community mental health center.

In addition to teaching and clinical services, the emergency department also provides a rich locus for the conduct of research studies on the incidence and prevalence of mental disorders as well as the changing patterns of disorder in the community.[1]

One study, recently completed, involved an evaluation of the effectiveness of using short-term boarding or holding beds for patients who required more extensive observation in order to work out the proper disposition for them. Although this practice was the usual course of action when the normal dispositional channels were overloaded or when more time was needed to come to an adequate understanding of a patient's problem, this was one of the first times that there was any attempt at a systematic examination of this patient population.

The group under study consisted of patients seen in the Psychiatric Emergency Division of the Medical Center for two consecutive calendar years (1968 and 1969). Specifically, the study focused on all patients who were detained for more than six but less than forty-eight hours. These patients remained in the emergency facility and were cared for directly by the psychiatric emergency staff. These patients were all "problem patients" in that, at least at the time of the first contact, it was not possible to come to a firm judgment regarding a disposition for them. Thus, the responsible physician could not release them, nor could he refer them to any kind of outpatient care (whether clinic or private). Admission to a hospital would have been a safe measure in all cases and could have been utilized, but the boarding procedure itself was designed to avoid hospitalization when another form of care might turn out to be preferable. Therefore, since all these patients were potentially hospitalizable, a crude indicator of the effectiveness of the boarding procedure would be the frequency with which an alternative to hospitalization could be worked out.

The Psychiatric Emergency Division logged approximately 4,000 patient visits in 1968 and 4,400 in 1969. One hundred eighty patients (4.5 percent) were boarded in 1968 and 187 (4.25 percent) in 1969, bringing the two-year total to 367 patients. The drop in the percentage of patients boarded in 1969 in part stems from the fact that in the fall of 1968, an additional twenty psychiatric inpatient beds became available. In all other respects, the data for the two years are quite comparable and can, therefore, be grouped together.

The ratio of men to women seen in the emergency facility was 39.9 percent to 60.1 percent. This figure has shown remarkable stability over the years in this and in other emergency facilities.[2] As yet, no satisfactory explanation for this phenomenon has been forthcoming.

With reference to the diagnostic profile of this group of patients, it should be stated that the house staff were encouraged to base their diagnoses of patients upon *observed phenomenology* rather than upon inferential material or theoretical constructs. The APA Diagnostic and Statistical Manual (DSM-II) provided a standard classification for the study.

Table 28–1 shows the major diagnostic categories of the patients seen:

TABLE 28–1

PRIMARY DIAGNOSIS	NUMBER OF PATIENTS	PERCENTAGE
Alcoholism, Delirium Tremens, Pathological Intoxication, Alcoholic Hallucinosis	87	23.7%
Senile Brain Disease, Dementia	21	5.7%

TABLE 28–1 (continued)

PRIMARY DIAGNOSIS	NUMBER OF PATIENTS	PERCENTAGE
Non-affective Functional Psychosis, Schizophrenia, Reactive Psychosis, Paranoid Reaction	100	27.2%
Suicide gesture or attempt	51	13.9%
Character Disorder, Neurosis	43	11.7%
Drug Psychosis, LSD, Mescaline, and so forth	26	7.2%

As expected, the diagnostic profile of the group of boarded patients showed a much higher percentage of psychotic conditions (both functional and organic) than the total patient population seen in the emergency facility. Character disorders and neurotic conditions, for example, accounted for 56 percent of the total psychiatric emergency population but only 11.7 percent of those patients who were boarded.

Sixty percent of the boarded patients were eventually hospitalized while 40 percent were referred to a form of ambulatory care or unconditionally discharged. Even though this exceeded the rate for the total emergency patient population (48 percent), the boarding procedure itself must be viewed as having had a high degree of effectiveness because the incidence of major disturbance was much higher in this population of boarded patients. Furthermore, had the procedure not been available, many patients would have been sent to institutional care when perhaps it could have been avoided. The group of boarded patients who were not hospitalized (40 percent) was comprised diagnostically of the drug psychoses, character disorders and neuroses, suicide gestures, and approximately 40 percent of the alcoholics. Most of these patients were referred to some form of outpatient treatment.

NOTES

1. A. Satloff, "Patterns of Drug Usage in a Psychiatric Patient Population," *American Journal of Psychiatry* 121(1964): 382–384.

2. A. Satloff, and C. M. Worby, "The Psychiatric Emergency Service: Mirror of Change," *American Journal of Psychiatry* 126(1970): 1628–1632; J. Ungerleider, "The Psychiatric Emergency," *Archives of General Psychiatry* 3(1960): 593–601.

REFERENCES

Atkins, R. "Psychiatric Emergency Service." *Archives of General Psychiatry* 17(1967): 176–182.

Bill, A. Z., and Sample, C. E. "The First Psychiatric Emergency, Community Consultation and Education Service in Delaware." *Delaware Medical Journal* 40(April 1968): 115–118.

Bill, A. Z. "The Effectiveness of a Psychiatric Emergency Service." *Delaware Medical Journal* 41(August 1969): 241–249.

Blane, H. T., Muller, J. J., and Chafetz, M. E. "Acute Psychiatric Services in the General Hospital. II. Current Status of Emergency Psychiatric Services." *American Journal of Psychiatry* 124(October 1967): Supplement 37–45.

Gould, R. L. "Emergencies in the Outpatient Department." *International Psychiatric Clinic* 3(Winter 1966): 9–25.

Kritzer, H., and Langsley, D. G. "Training for Emergency Psychiatric Services." *Journal of Medical Education* 42(December 1967): 1111–1115.

Walk, D. "Suicide and Community Care." *British Journal of Psychiatry* 113(December 1967): 1381–1391.

Weiner, I. W. "The Effectiveness of a Suicide Prevention Program." *Mental Hygiene* 53(July 1969): 357–363.

Weisman, G., Feirstein, A., and Thomas, C. "Three-Day Hospitalization—A Model for Intensive Intervention." *Archives of General Psychiatry* 21(1969): 620–629.

IX
Consultation and Education Services

EDITORS' INTRODUCTION

A major contribution of the community mental health center program has been a recognition of the importance of delivering preventive mental health services in an organized fashion. The consultation and education service, one of the five basic required services, has been established as the mechanism for getting the community mental health center into the preventive role.

In reaching out to the community, consultation and education services have generally related either to other services in the community which relate to human needs and play an important role in development, such as the schools, or to community services which play a role in the handling of emotional crises, such as the police. It has been extremely difficult to establish measures to determine the impact of preventive services. Possible indices such as community change and the extent of mental illness within the community are often difficult to assess.

Most community mental health centers have either chosen to assign specific staff members to the consultation and education services or to make participation in consultation and education services a requirement which all staff members must fulfill. Either direction can present problems to the community mental health center if careful direction and supervision are not available. Some staff members may balk at the prospect of doing indirect service, a special skill for which they feel they have not had adequate training. In other situations, staff members who are totally committed to consultation and education services may become unwilling to deliver direct service when the demand on the center for this type of service becomes so great as to require their participation.

In most community mental health centers, the availability of consultation and education services has varied considerably. Some centers have designated direct service as their only mission, feeling that the needs of the community are such as to warrant their complete attention to this area. Personnel in other centers have had difficulty in understanding the concept of consultation and education and its importance. These situations can lead to difficulty when attempts are made to modify staff attitudes and to increase the skill of staff members in the delivery of indirect services.

Financial considerations have also played an important role in the variability of consultation and education services as they currently exist within centers. Most centers have had the experience that it has been necessary for them to pay for consultation and education services initially until the value of the services has been established to the agencies with whom they are consulting. Furthermore, the free availability of consultation and education services is often expected by the community and its other agencies. Many community mental health centers have also expressed a reluctance to charge for consultation and education services. Often, this reluctance seems to be derived from the fact that many community mental health centers depend on the same agency or government for their finances as the agencies to whom they are consulting.

Another complicating aspect in the development of consultation and education services has been its relationship to social action. In a specific community, the very acceptance of consultation and education services, as well as the center itself, can depend on the policy which is set by the directors and planners regarding the role which the community mental health center will play in social action.

If more community mental health centers are going to have an impact on their communities through consultation and education services, more time will have to be devoted in the planning of services and community mental health center strategy to this essential service and mechanisms will have to be developed which will allow the community mental health center to receive payment for consultation and education services.

29   *Thomas T. Glasscock,* M.D., *and*
Morton L. Flax, ED.D.

Programs for Consultation to Schools

The Arapahoe Mental Health Center was conceived as a general psychiatric outpatient clinic in suburban Denver in 1955. The public health nurses and teachers who assisted at its birth and who helped to nurse it through its early years were interested primarily in providing treatment services for children. This has remained a major concern of the citizens of the community who have served on its board. From the beginning, administrators of various school districts in the catchment area have served as board members.

PROGRAM DEVELOPMENT

In 1966, after the announcement of the staffing provision of the comprehensive mental health center act and after our first grant had been obtained to establish essential services, the possibility of providing more effective psychological services to the schools through a comprehensive mental health center "growth" grant was considered by the staff and presented to the administrators of two school districts who admittedly were having serious difficulties with personnel in the psychological services divisions. Until this time, each of the school districts had educational psychologists only and had never employed social workers. The plan, which the administrators accepted, was to obtain a grant to provide clinical psychologists, psychiatric social workers, and child psychiatrists to work in flexible, operational teams who would spend most of the time in the schools providing diagnostic and consultative services, but who would also spend a small amount of their time in the clinic doing direct therapy with children and their parents.

Three positions were created in the grant in addition to the psychological services teams. These were: (1) director of research (Ph.D. research psychologist) who would be responsible for developing and directing evaluations of new programs, especially in the schools; (2) a

247

coordinator of clinic services (a nonprofessional with an A.B. degree or equivalent in general education) who could coordinate the activities of the school personnel with the clinic services; and (3) a therapist for a special education class. The school administrators as well as the staff were painfully aware that the numbers of personnel for the school program provided under the grant were inadequate. As an example, we had provided two clinical psychologists and one social worker for the Littleton district with 16,000 children and we knew that by 1970 this district would have close to 20,000 children. Yet, it was felt inadvisable, in view of the decreasing federal funding, the potential school budgets, and the radical change in the nature of services to be provided, to put any larger program into operation at least for the first year.

It was like opening Pandora's Box. The school people were inundated with requests during the first year. Working in the school program was a more difficult, frustrating, and tiring task than working in a psychiatric outpatient clinic. The staff, divided loosely into teams with each member of the staff being able to give about four hours every other week to each school in the district which they served, responded to the schools' demand for a large number of evaluations augmenting the psychologists' testing with social work interviews with the parents. Since the social workers assigned to the schools were skilled in working with children, they were able to do many evaluations of families by themselves. Complex cases involving possible organic dysfunction where medications might be indicated were referred to the child psychiatrist. Each case was presented to the school people after evaluation with the intent of gradually increasing the amount of consultation done around children rather than evaluating individually every child referred. The major problem was educational, that is, helping the all-powerful principals to accept and use our staff appropriately.

In spite of the enormity of the problems faced by putting too few competent personnel into too many schools, the first year's operation worked well enough so that the remaining school districts in Arapahoe County requested that we provide these services for them. The two school districts already involved in the program requested more service. Therefore, a second grant request was written which was twice the amount of the first one (approximately 200,000 dollars).

Due to the demand for large numbers of psychological evaluations, it was decided in writing this grant request that staff psychologists at the master's level could be effectively employed as members of the teams. These personnel were more available than Ph.D. clinical psychologists; some of them were Ph.D. candidates who welcomed the opportunity to

248

get clinical experience in the program while working on their degrees. In addition, money for nonprofessionals to work as therapy assistants, particularly in the rapidly expanding after-school therapy groups and in the enlarged day camp program, was included. In view of the marked increase in complexity created by the contract to provide services to all of the Arapahoe schools, a new position of director for the total school psychological services program was also included in the grant request.

CONSULTATION

Slowly, the school program has evolved from a concern almost entirely with evaluating children referred because of various types of emotional-intellectual difficulties to a focus on individual and group consultation with teachers and the gradual inclusion of therapy programs directly into the schools. We now have increasing numbers of groups being held during the school day. These are part of the school curriculum in contrast to a clinic program of after-school activity groups.

School counselors, where they are present in the elementary schools, have been functioning as cotherapists in these inschool groups. Meeting with the children two times per week is more likely to produce a group identity and more effective group interaction within the school year than a once-per-week system. In all cases, there are at least two therapists in a group of not more than ten children.

Although there are many models available for a consultative team to use, the following general principles are followed in the five districts served:

1. The central administration must see the need for a total well-rounded mental health team to serve its school (psychologist, social worker, psychiatric nurse, and psychiatrist).

2. The principal and teachers at the local building level must see the team as not only interested in all phases of mental health, but particularly interested in stepping into the classroom and taking one difficult case and helping the teacher work through the ultimate resolution of that particular problem as a model for future independent action by the teacher.

3. Flexibility in a constant search for opening new avenues of communication between the team and the teachers. It is essential that the team assist teachers in talking among themselves, opening lines of communication which will eventually lead to teachers feeling free to talk to each

other, to their administration, and most importantly, to the children with whom they are working.

4. The avoidance of falling into the old model of having a case presented, testing or evaluating the child, coming back with some general type of consultation, and stopping at that point. The team must show that it is willing to take all cases but it must constantly be searching for ways of moving beyond the model of simply taking the troubled child out of the classroom; preferably, assisting the classroom teacher in dealing with problems which she has faced in order for her to effectively provide the environment within her classroom for the work which must be done. There will never be enough mental health workers in the public schools to actually help all of the children who are in need.

5. It is ideal to have a key person in the central administration who will provide leadership from within the school district and apply a philosophical attitude in developing the important function of providing an adequate base in budgeting for the team in the future. Each building principal should be able to indicate his desires and problems directly to the team. The key central office personnel should also be able to get additional overall feedback as to how the psychological needs of the district are being met.

6. There is a constant need to take well-trained clinicians and train them into being good school education consultants. The first task is to train them to utilize consultants around them since it is difficult to be a consultant unless one knows how to use a consultant. They must have a feeling of treating school personnel as equals; one professional talking to another. If staff members move into a building as experts having all the answers, their goal is lost even before they have an opportunity to begin.

7. A school consultative team must develop a thick skin, for not all schools will readily accept its services. Consequently, the team must be willing to present itself back time and time again until the school can accept the utilization of the services.

SUMMARY

The mental health personnel team must be willing to reach out to the schools even though the process has been a very slow and painful one. Education is now on the verge of entering into a new era of rapid change, of ideas and philosophies. Educators are willing, if the mental health field is, to enter into a marriage which can provide benefits to

250

both. This requires breaking away from the old traditions and entering into a situation where the needs of the children can be met most effectively—in the classroom, not in the clinic in play therapy or individual treatment rooms which typify most mental health programs. School consultants can no longer just sit back and simply run an evaluation and make recommendations for the schools. The key to successful programs is follow-up and constant re-assessment of the situation.

---

30   *H. Richard Lamb*, M.D., *and*
                                          Thurman McGinnis

Consultation to the Police

The words, "moving out into the community," roll off the tongue effortlessly when mental health professionals talk about what their priorities should be. This is all well and good when other agencies are seeking their services, even though a good consultant knows he must learn the system, the jargon, and the politics of the consultee agency before his efforts can be effective. But what if, in addition to the consultant's ignorance of the agency he is going out to "help," the agency does not know what a mental health consultant does, sees no way in which such a person can help, and is suspicious of the consultant and his motives. "That guy must be here because he thinks we're all unthinking, sadistic, and prejudiced," or, "He wants to analyze us and expose us." Exploitation seems like a possibility. "He's here to study us and write a book about us." This is a fairly typical description of what goes on at the outset when consultation is offered to a police department.

Is all of this oversensitivity, or paranoia? Perhaps, but a casual chat in many mental health circles reveals just as deep a distrust of the police.

Why this mutual distrust? There is no ready answer, but some aspects can be identified. Police and mental health professionals have little opportunity for contact, other than rather impersonal transactions, often by telephone, about missing patients, patients who have been arrested, and so forth. The police share a universal concern of the lay public that psychiatrists analyze people's every word and thus learn their innermost secrets. On the other hand, policemen are the epitome of authority; the

251

consultant must have a reasonable degree of comfort in dealing with authority. It should not have come as a surprise to the psychiatrist who openly advocated anyone's right to riot without police interference when his local police department informed him that his services as their consultant were no longer desired. A crucial factor is that mental health professionals, themselves being skilled at interpersonal relationships, apply their own standards of expertise in understanding and dealing with people to policemen who have little training in this area.

THE PROBLEMS OF THE POLICE

The public today is dissatisfied with the old image of the "cop on the beat." What is needed now is a skilled professional, one who carries out his duties with sophistication and restraint. As a skilled professional, the police officer must use a minimum of force, though be able to use force when needed—this is no job for the faint hearted. He must make use of the techniques of modern science. Yet becoming a professional, contrary to how it is defined in some quarters, means much more than simply making policemen more efficient and even more impersonal crime fighters and enforcers of the law.[1]

It also means having a working-level knowledge of basic concepts of psychology and sociology and an orientation that stresses the personal service and interpersonal aspects of police work. Professionalism, with all that it implies in terms of education and upward mobility of social class, may require a major change in identity for the policeman. He must no longer be an uneducated person who possesses a vocational skill, namely police work.

When the actual type of work that the patrolman in particular is called upon to do is considered, it becomes even more clear why emphasis on having knowledge of human relations is so important. Crime fighting comprises only a small proportion of the job of the policeman on patrol. In most communities crime fighting may be only 10 percent of the patrolman's work. In the inner city this may be somewhat higher, but probably rarely exceeds 25 percent. The rest of the patrolman's time is devoted to personal service—to keeping the peace and related duties. Further, in a police department, discretion as to how to handle problems that arise in the course of the day's work *increases* as one moves *down* the hierarchy.[2] Thus, the lowest ranking police officer—the patrolman—has the greatest discretion in deciding when and how to enforce those laws that are the least precise and the most ambiguous. Laws dealing with disorderly conduct are a good example of such ill-defined laws.

Having such wide discretion in vital matters in the community, the patrolman often finds himself not knowing what is expected of him. Some thoughtful patrolmen have verbalized this directly. Are they to enforce middle-class standards in lower-class neighborhoods and thus "enforce the law equally and similarly everywhere," or should they take into account the special nature of lower-class ethnic cultures and work differently in these neighborhoods than they would in an upper class suburb? Should they try and do something definitive to help resolve the situation in a family quarrel, or should they simply quiet the situation and "get in and get out as quickly as possible?" These questions are unanswered in the minds of most policemen, not only in terms of what they feel they should do, but what their superiors and the public want them to do.

Most patrolmen have strong feelings of inadequacy; they realize they are not sufficiently trained for the job expected of them. At times they come on stronger, with more overt self-assurance and authoritarianism than needed, as if to deny feelings of inadequacy and to prove themselves. They are concerned about not being adequately trained to handle the myriad of diverse situations such as collecting evidence, handling family quarrels, dealing with provocative minority groups and demonstrators. Their feeling that the general public holds police work in low esteem and their perception of their work as a working class job and not a profession further contribute to their insecurity and sensitivity to public criticism.

The police also often find themselves drawn into areas where pressure from various groups for social change is exerted. At times they find themselves in the unenviable position, not by choice, of being in the middle of demonstrations by radical groups where the conscious, avowed intent of the groups is to provoke the police and get arrested.[3] It should be noted, however, that while the actors are new the drama is not; the police, historically, have frequently found themselves in the middle.[4] A century ago it was the European immigrants on the one hand and "reform-minded" native Americans on the other who demanded that their own moral standards be imposed on their newly arrived neighbors. (Demands today from some quarters that the law be "equally enforced in black and white neighborhoods" show that a lack of appreciation of differences between subcultures is not a thing of the past.) Later it was the fledgling labor movement on one side and management on the other. And then it was the prohibitionists versus the majority of the public with the men in blue again caught between.

Many of these factors contribute to the easily observed fact that most policemen tend to see themselves as a persecuted minority group.[5] In this sense, the police and the black community share many similar feelings. Both groups tend to be suspicious and overly sensitive. Both feel they do not have an individual personality in the eyes of others. Because they feel like a persecuted minority group, policemen begin to associate only with other policemen and lose the opportunity for informal feedback from other members of the community, feedback that is needed by policemen for an impartial perspective of their job, their own attitudes and the community's needs.

THE CONSULTATION BEGINS

Our consultation with the San Mateo Police Department grew out of meetings with the San Mateo city manager and his staff to explore ways that the County Mental Health Division and the city could be helpful to each other. From this developed a program with the City Recreation Department which had many services to offer our patients and also a decision to provide consultation to the police department. The aim was to provide policemen with a meaningful, working knowledge of psychosocial concepts and how they directly relate to police work. San Mateo is a suburban city of 80,000 people with a police force of 107, not including ancillary personnel. To begin our consultation, we began by meeting with the top administration of the department.

After getting their support, we began a series of ten open-ended groups, one series with the day shift and another with the evening shift. Consultation with the police, as noted already, is complicated by their initial distrust for outsiders in general and psychiatrists in particular. The first few sessions were spent dealing with this initial distrust. It was especially helpful for the psychiatrist (the author) involved in this consultation to ride with the men on patrol about one night per week plus some daytime hours. This practice has continued throughout the psychiatrist's consultation with the department and is an essential part of the psychiatrist's task. He became a familiar figure around the station and came to know the men individually. Initial feelings of distrust were lessened as well as such feelings as "We're being analyzed by the shrink." In fact, occasional impromptu consultations were asked for. Most importantly, the psychiatrist gained a feel for the work of the patrolman that can be gained in no other way.

In the groups we talked about many of the issues which concern policemen—lack of respect by the public, having to deal with demonstrators and hostile people who called them m_ f_ pigs, low pay, and what they considered their bad treatment by the mass media. Emphasis was placed upon professionalism and the issues surrounding seeing police work as a profession. Though considerable interest was generated, these groups were only partially successful. One factor was that there was clearly a lack of formal training in many of the important concepts that would have made our discussions more meaningful. Further, the unstructured approach was very helpful for many of the men but the majority disliked the sessions and felt they were not really of value at this early phase of getting to know each other. In retrospect, such small informal discussion groups would probably have been much more accepted and useful *after* rapport had been well established between the consultant and the men. Further, presenting the issues clearly, as we have now come to understand them, would have clarified the purpose of the groups for everyone including the consultant. Finally, the consultant's lack of familiarity with police work at this point limited his effectiveness.

THE CONSULTATION PROGRAM

A different format was adopted. A formal course for college credit was started. This course included the basic concepts of psychodynamics and unconscious motivation, prejudice, understanding of different cultures, basic concepts of crisis intervention, and a description of some of the more common psychiatric disorders with emphasis placed on a practical understanding of them. Thus, what had been talked about in theory was being backed up by deed—the importance of increased professionalism and one of its prime prerequisites, more education. An attempt was made to hold psychological jargon to a minimum. The course was so structured that there was much time left for discussion and participation by the men. Forty-six men and one woman enrolled, including both relatively new and more experienced policemen. The latter were invaluable since it has been observed that policemen want to hear not just from "outsiders," but from experienced fellow officers who can report on the basis of their own experience that a positive human relations approach is both practical and desirable.[6]

One of the major purposes of this approach was to help the men become psychologically minded. Mental health professionals take being psychologically minded for granted and expect that others who deal with people will have the same attitudes. But the facts are that policemen have not had this training.

The initial resistance to psychological thinking was tackled head-on. The course leader, a psychiatrist, said, "I know you men have heard many jokes where the psychiatrist says, 'I wonder what he really meant by that?' This is the stereotype of the psychiatrist and on the face of it may sound ridiculous. But what I am trying to accomplish in these sessions is to get you as policemen to say to yourselves and to each other while on patrol 'I wonder what he really meant by that?' " Surprisingly, this idea was received quite well, as were the concepts of the unconscious and the doctrine of psychological determinism which holds that no act happens by chance or is completely fortuitous, that there is usually an underlying meaning in addition to the superficial meaning.

Consider, for example, the concepts involved in displacement, one of the mechanisms of defense. Mental health professionals learn about displacement and especially that form of it known as transference and countertransference in the first days of their training. It becomes accepted, taken for granted, and used almost by reflex. If a patient gets angry, psychotherapeutic work may have been successful. The police have not had this training and if someone becomes angry with them or calls them a name, they take it personally. Policemen are often lower class or lower middle class by background and orientation. Physical force, as an accepted and even usual way of handling conflicts in lower-class neighborhoods, may well be part of their life experiences. The police are told to exercise self-control, but the real rationale for this restraint is not made sufficiently clear to them. This is further complicated by the attitudes of working-class men that it is important to maintain one's self-respect, not to allow one's masculinity to be challenged, and not to take insults from anyone. The problem becomes worse if the man is insecure about his work or about himself.

Thus, an understanding of the concept of displacement can help the policeman understand that his uniform, in which he may (or may not) take pride, may symbolize hated authority or the hated white man. It is not he personally to whom persons are reacting with hostility, nor is it his manhood that is being challenged. This kind of insight does not make the job free from frustration, but it often does help make a difficult situation more bearable. Further, the concept of displacement, as we would use it in discussing countertransference, helps policemen, as it

256

helps psychiatrists, to develop some capacity for introspection. He must be able to differentiate appropriate responses to people from reactions that stem from his own inner needs, feelings, and background. All of this is vital, if the policeman is going to handle in a professional manner a situation where he is called a m_ f_ pig or if he is called upon to deal with the deliberate provocation of radical groups.

A phenomenon which illustrates this point is what policemen frequently refer to as the "attitude test" on traffic stops. On such stops the policeman's concern should be with the citizen's attitude toward the law and public safety, in addition to whatever he may have done that caused the policeman to stop him. Some policemen confuse the citizen's attitude toward the law with the citizen's "respect" toward the police officer. If the apprehended motorist has committed a borderline offense which does not necessarily warrant a ticket, the policeman should be concerned with the citizen's appreciation of the necessity to drive in a safe manner and not with the citizen's attitude toward the policeman. If he clearly is unconcerned about his own safety or the safety of others, a ticket may well be warranted, but the ticket is not warranted simply because the motorist gave the police officer a bad time or was disrespectful.

In order to help policemen better understand descriptive features and psychodynamics of mental illness, and also understand how mentally ill patients are handled by the psychiatrist, arrangements were made for the police to sit in on the psychiatric interviews of patients brought to the emergency room of the county hospital and to discuss with the psychiatrists afterward what had transpired. An added benefit of this arrangement has been increased contact and better rapport between the police and the emergency room psychiatrists.

Another aim of the consultation was to help policemen better understand the culture and points of view of minority groups so that they can better relate to and serve these groups. For instance, they need to be aware of the sensitivity of the black man who sees some routine police actions as disrespectful and as stripping away his dignity. It has been found elsewhere that black people's chief complaint about the police is not police brutality but rather what they consider the disrespect of stops and searches without cause.[7] The police need to know that it is the black man's feeling of insecurity and past injustice that makes him more sensitive to police actions that a secure middle-class white person might see as routine. Thus, aggressive preventive patrol may seem like good strategy to many white people and to the police, but it may seem like harassment to the black community. The patrolman needs to know that black people are suspicious of him, no matter how sympathetic to the black man's cause he may be, or how impartial or well intentioned he may be. The distrust may be based on past experience with police elsewhere which make black people feel that "cops are cops." Or it may be totally irrational and approach paranoia. Regardless of its cause, it is useful for the policeman to extend himself to win the confidence of the black man, as a psychiatrist might approach a paranoid patient. Both the patrolman on the beat, as well as community relations officers, need to go out of their way to explain police procedure and practice to the black community. Otherwise the possibilities for misunderstanding are endless. For instance, a group of black youths were standing on a street corner. A patrol car rounded the corner and shined its spotlight on the group. Immediately the group became uneasy and angry, wondered if they were being harassed, if a group of white men would have been treated in the same way. What they needed to know (and were not told) was that a robbery had just been committed a short distance away by a black man of whom the police had a description and that the police were checking this group out to see if it contained the suspect.

The policeman must understand that there are differences in the ghetto from his own values and way of life. For instance, he must recognize that one will never eliminate petty theft in the harsh world of the ghetto as long as it remains a ghetto. The policeman's first reaction to hearing this is, "It's wrong!" But he must go beyond this initial reaction and recognize that it is reality so that he can deal with it, not from the point of view of social outrage, but from the point of what practical approach can and should be taken.

The police must also understand that trying to enforce middle-class values in a lower-class community, either black or white, is going to lead to difficulty. This is a philosophical problem for police administrators and patrolmen everywhere. Does one enforce the law equally and in the same way everywhere, or does one take into account the different people with whom one is dealing and interpret the law differently in different cultures and neighborhoods? Many policemen believe this latter approach is practicing a "double standard" and that minority groups are thus being shown favoritism. However, it is not law enforcement that is the issue, but peacekeeping. That the law should be enforced uniformly with regard to felonies is not in question, but peacekeeping is not so easily defined. The level of noise that is the norm in one neighborhood may be intolerable in another. Groups on street corners may be the center of social activity in one neighborhood, but be seen as undesirable loitering by the residents of an upper-middle-class section a few blocks away. In the case of petty theft, a middle-class group may demand that the thief be arrested; a lower-class group may only want the police to help get the property returned and resent the thief being arrested. They do not want to see the offender get a police record and lose time from work for an action that they regard as "normal." One must also recognize different community norms with regard to the possession of potentially dangerous weapons, such as knives. In many lower-class neighborhoods carrying a knife is the norm; it is seen as necessary for self-protection and survival in a sometimes violent subsociety. If a person threatens a fellow citizen with a knife, the community wants the police to confiscate the weapon. They only want the person arrested if it is clear that he will not cool off and will remain a danger to others. In a middle-class neighborhood, the local citizens would expect the man brandishing a knife to be arrested; it is not the norm of the community. A black man from the ghetto would agree, "If whitey in that neighborhood pulls a knife, there must be something wrong with him and he should be in jail."

Reference has been made to the policeman's concern about his image in the eyes of the citizenry. That the policeman be seen as a helping person is important not only for his self-esteem, but also for his effectiveness. If people experience every contact with the police as an unpleasant struggle, it will adversely affect their trust of the police, their willingness to cooperate with them, or to call them when help is needed. On the other hand, people see the police in a different light if they know that policemen will stop to help them if their car breaks down on the street, that their calls for help will be responded to promptly and courteously, that the police are making a real attempt to understand them and their problems.

Policemen will listen to these points of view from the consultant if he has earned their respect and trust. They are interested in programs such as the one in a California city where the police undertook to find jobs for disadvantaged youth. Here young people came to see the police not as "pigs who will hassle you," but as men who were interested in and helpful to them. Likewise, it can be pointed out that, even when making an arrest, the policeman can do much to gain or lose community support. Seeming to have already prejudged the person as guilty is far different from courteously treating the person being arrested, helping him feel that he still has some dignity and not acting as if he, the policeman, already assumes guilt.

Another important part of our inservice training is modern crisis theory which stresses that in a crisis situation a maximum of change

259

may be possible with a minimum of effort, as compared with intervention in a noncrisis situation, and that this may take place with people who otherwise might not be at all amenable to therapeutic intervention.[8] These concepts introduced a major aim of our inservice training—to help the men see themselves as members of the helping professions, rather than solely as crime fighters and keepers of the peace. The policeman needs to be equipped with a basic knowledge of psychodynamics and interviewing skills. Thus, when he is called to a situation such as a family disturbance, he can do more than simply quiet the situation. Further, this knowledge gives him confidence that helps him try to resolve problems in what may otherwise seem like an unknown area. We should emphasize that we are not training the men to be family counselors or therapists although some thoughtful veteran patrolmen are already accomplished at this. Our goal was to point out to the police that they often are seeing people who have not been seen elsewhere, and may not seek help elsewhere in the future. Although they are not trained therapists, most policemen, with the proper orientation, can be helpful in these situations. The time-honored police method of coming into a home where there is a family argument going on is to separate the two parties, get the wife to go to bed, and the husband to go out to a motel for the night until things cool off. The whole philosophy has been of "not getting involved," of getting in and getting out as quickly as possible. But the policeman must see that there are other possibilities; some very simple measures can often be extremely meaningful to these people in crisis. First, if possible, the policeman can try to get the parties involved to sit down together and talk about whatever is happening. The policeman can point out that there must be a problem, can try to question and possibly clarify what this problem is all about, and get all parties to begin thinking that more is involved than the superficial issue that precipitated the dispute. The policeman can sometimes be instrumental in opening some closed minds in such situations and referring some of these people to appropriate agencies such as mental health clinics or family service agencies.

One example occurred on a call to a home to handle a family disturbance. When the police and the accompanying psychiatrist arrived, both husband and wife were sitting in the living room obviously having had too much to drink. The policeman's first inclination was to get them both to quiet down and go to bed so that the police could leave. Talking with the husband and wife, however, revealed that this was the husband's second marriage and was now of seven years duration. The marriage had gone well until five months before when the husband began to drink heavily. The drinking coincided with the death of the husband's twenty-year-old daughter by a former marriage in an automobile accident. It also, in the course of just a few minutes, quickly became apparent that neither husband nor wife had sought help elsewhere and that both desired it. A referral to the local family service agency was made.

The policeman often sees the adolescent who is heading towards major crime and the family that is in the early stages of disintegration. Helping his "clients" see that a problem exists and making a timely referral can route people to help while the problem is still soluble. But, the policeman must discard the previously traditional attitude of "I am not a lousy social worker." The role of the social worker is sometimes confused by the police with femininity or weakness or with a stereotype of the "bleeding heart" social worker.

Spending six hours with each group of rookies has also become an important part of the work of the consultant. A critical point in the career of a policeman is his first few months "out on the street." He naturally turns to the more experienced men with whom he is on patrol. A locker room indoctrination from men who are not oriented toward professionalism and who feel it their duty to "set these rookies straight" can form attitudes which may take much work to correct.

During this time spent with rookies a didactic approach with time left for discussion has proven effective. Much of this time is devoted to practical aspects of police handling of psychiatric emergencies. As an example, the men are encouraged to be honest with patients they are bringing to the hospital, to tell them where they are going and why they, the police, are taking this action. The importance in terms of establishing basic trust at the beginning of a patient's hospitalization is emphasized rather than bringing him to the hospital on the pretext of taking him elsewhere.

Also stressed is that disturbed patients, regardless of how they appear or how threatening they may be, are basically very frightened. Understanding this helps the policeman respond not to the threats but to the fear; for instance, he might say, "I am taking you to the hospital where you will be safe." The policeman must understand the concept of testing for limits; that despite a person's insistence that he won't go to a hospital, he may want to be firmly told that he has to go. In the face of such protestations, the inexperienced policeman may be reluctant to be "the bad guy." By discussing these topics in this way, the seeds are planted for psychological thinking, for looking beneath the superficial to understanding people and situations. Also covered is the concept of displacement, as described above, and the ways that policemen may play a crucial role as helping professionals in crisis intervention in family disturbances.

A primary task of the mental health consultant is to help the police to become and see themselves as professionals. Professionalization is taking place when the police see personal service as one of their major functions, equally important as crime fighting and the "good pinch." Professionalization is happening if police officers are psychologically minded, if they try to understand the different cultures with which they come in contact. The experience in San Mateo has been that mental health consultation can be extremely helpful in this process.

Consultation can also be useful to administration. To cite one example, when selecting new policemen, administrators may look for men who are least likely to embarrass the department with an ugly, newsworthy incident, who will not threaten their superiors, and who will follow orders. The result is that "safe" candidates are chosen. Unfortunately, safe can become synonomous with mediocrity and lack of imagination. To be sure, emotional stability is crucial in police work, but so is talent for working with people, intelligence, and creativity. Administrators need to be encouraged to "take a chance" on talented applicants, to see that stability is not defined as mediocrity.

What can be done for the future? There should be a requirement that all policemen should have or be working on an AA degree (equivalent of two years of college), with an emphasis on the social sciences. There should be a financial reward in terms of higher salaries for education for both two-year and four-year college degrees. At least as much emphasis should be put on human relations as on the scientific methods of police work. There should also be a board of police examiners, like the state boards of medical and nursing examiners, with the authority to grant and revoke licenses to practice police work. Thus, the police would truly be elevated to professional status with the same standards of self-policing as other professions. When this comes about, then perhaps even such things as civilian review boards will no longer be an issue.

NOTES

1. *The Challenge of Crime in a Free Society*, President's Commission on Law Enforcement and Administration of Justice, Washington, D.C.: U.S. Government Printing Office, 1967.

2. J. W. Wilson, *Varieties of Police Behavior*, Cambridge, Mass.: Harvard University Press, 1968.

3. S. M. Lipset, "Why Cops Hate Liberals—And Vice Versa," *Atlantic Monthly*, 223, 3(1969): 76–83.

4. T. J. Fleming, "The Policeman's Lot," *American Heritage,* 21, 2(1970): 5–17.

5. A. Niederhoffer, *Behind the Shield,* Garden City, N.Y.: Doubleday, 1967; J. H. Skolnick, *Justice Without Trial: Law Enforcement in a Democratic Society,* New York: Wiley, 1966.

6. L. E. Newman, and J. L. Steinberg, "Consultation with Police on Human Relations Training," *American Journal of Psychiatry,* 126(1970): 1421–1429.

7. *The Police,* President's Commission on Law Enforcement and Administration of Justice, Washington, D.C.: U.S. Government Printing Office, 1967.

8. D. C. Klein, and E. Lindemann, "Preventive Intervention in Individual and Family Crisis Situations," *Prevention of Mental Disorders in Children,* G. Caplan, ed., New York: Basic Books, 1961; G. F. Jacobson, D. M. Wilner, W. E. Morley, *et al,* "The Scope and Practice of an Early-Access Brief Treatment Psychiatric Center," *American Journal of Psychiatry,* 121(1965): 1176–1182.

---

31   *John Carver,* PH.D.

Behavior Modification in the Consultation-Education Element of Service

Multicounty Mental Health Center is a federally assisted program serving five predominantly rural middle Tennessee counties. The program of services is based on the belief that, given the size of the mental health problem to which we address ourselves, traditional direct services are in large part a waste of resources. In this program design, the use of indirect service delivery and the training of peer-professionals in the community to better carry out their functions related to human development and adjustment is most important. Approximately 80 percent of staff time is devoted to a consultation and education element of service; even the remaining 20 percent of our time given to direct client service includes counseling trainees from the community as often as possible.

In carrying out this community programming, several biases, such as the following, regarding community mental health determine the courses of action.

1. that in most cases maladaptive behavior may more effectively be viewed as a learned phenomenon rather than as the product of any disease process;

2. that psychotherapy by professional mental health workers is inadequate to meet the needs of community mental health primarily due to its inability to meet the volume demands;

3. that the chief mental health agency of the community is the school regardless of how well the school carries out this function;

4. that teachers, clergy, public health nurses, and others are the effecters of emotional development far beyond the ability of the psychiatrist and his colleagues;

5. that these community resources deal with most of the community mental health problems even if a large mental health center is available and that, therefore, mental health professionals have an obligation to aid them in serving more effectively;

6. that the most productive roles to be played by mental health centers are those of training, reconceptualizing, and acting as a catalyst for the enhancement of strength and resources already present in the community. (The mental health center, which is not attempting to work itself out of a job, is not fulfilling its professional obligation to the taxpayer.);

7. that the most economical approach to human behavior is oriented toward growth rather than pathology and is presented in terms which can be both understood and credible to the community.

With this set of biases we are easily led to behavior modification techniques as a strong component of our consultation-education program. The chief reasons for investing in these methods are their simplicity, high applicability to children, growth-orientation and cost-effectiveness.

The simplicity of behavior modification applies both to its conceptual framework and to its methods. The lack of complex hypothetical constructs which may be found in more psychodynamically based approaches is particularly useful when dealing with the average teacher, parent, or police officer. Although conceptual shifts are necessary for a trainee or consultee to adequately manage the methods, there is considerable appeal to common sense which lends some comfort of familiarity.

Since our own age emphasis is upon children, we are particularly in need of an approach to behavior that works well with youngsters. We have enjoyed good results in effecting change in child behavior with programs administered by parents, teachers, or other consultees. Environmental modification is, of course, more accessible when greater control of the environment exists. This is increasingly the case at the younger ages, rendering behavior management tactics more effective than with adults. The tremendous "leverage effect" of behavior change during the early years is most appropriate for our aims of primary prevention.

One of the more pleasing aspects of a behavioral approach to people is its conceptual inclination toward positive growth rather than pathology. The language of personality theory has so often been laden with pathological terms. Therapists and personality evaluators have been far more adept at seeing, talking about, experimenting with, and conceptualizing the negative than at dealing with joy, strength, and independence. The language of behavior modification is the language of learning, not of sickness, and facilitates an emphasis upon the positive which has too often been lacking.

With the size of our mission in community mental health and the lack of necessary funds and personnel, cost-effectiveness becomes a critical factor in our delivery of services. Services aimed at effecting community change in techniques and attitudes concerning behavior must be carried out with both human and monetary economics in mind. The simplicity of behavior modification assures its easy transferability to persons who can make the most use of these concepts. Its greater effectiveness for the younger ages and its positive, growth-oriented approach are important factors in the economics of service delivery. Persons being taught behavior modification can achieve relatively quick, observable results. This appeal to each consultee's need for success introduces a self-reinforcing element. By instilling early confidence in the recipients of such training, fewer training "dropouts" are produced lending further to the maximizing of community behavioral competence.

If it is assumed that behavior modification is a useful approach to the change of behavior in the development of positive growth and if it has been determined that working through existing community resources is the most effective way to multiply our impact and to approach primary prevention, then the chief question becomes how to disseminate these skills and to what target groups they might best be taught to maximize the mental health payoff from a severely limited professional staff.

This, of course, introduces the critical question of numbers. To teach a parent behavioral modification principles and aspects of healthy emotional growth would be both educative and preventive. But to teach one parent makes an insignificant dent in the great numbers to which effective mental health programming must address itself. Similarly, to give professional backup to a teacher in the handling of disturbed behavior and implications for more effective dealing with all behavior multiplies our manpower and is definitely preventive, but this too may be too small an approach. In considerations of this sort, a point is eventually reached which is beyond the capacity of a community mental health center. For example, it can be deduced that vast changes in teacher-training are necessary and that anything less can only be an impotent challenge to the size of the mental health problem. Certainly community mental health needs to speak to the problem of teacher-training inadequacies, but the individual community mental health center can devote little or none of its programming to this end, except through the consultation-education element of service. These points are made only to bring attention to the constant re-evaluation which responsible programming must pursue in regard to its obligation, its limitations and its overall effectiveness.

The largest caretaker group is parents. Behavior management is often taught to parents of dysfunctioning children in our direct, outpatient service. This has been extended to group teaching with a multiple number of parents in the education element of service. Under this guise, no registering as "patients" is necessary for either parents or their children.

Specifically, a time-limited series of six weekly evening sessions is used. Parents were originally contacted by a local school system because of the behavior problems seen in their children. The task of the community mental health center was to run a parent group during the summer while the schools were unable to act.

The school system made the original contact explaining the need; the community mental health center called each parent to detail the time, place, and expectancies. Only a small portion of parents thus referred actually attended which is a strong comment on parental motivation as an impediment to proper child care.

This series was held and to get more potential community good from it, four volunteers were included for training purposes. It was felt that, after sufficient exposure, the volunteers would themselves be able to run such groups with consultative back-up. The sessions began with an introduction to a way of viewing behavior and explanation of some principles of behavior. As much as possible these were made to "fit" previous common sense sets. Parents and trainees were shown how to pinpoint specific behaviors and each accordingly defined the single behavior of most difficulty with his disturbed or behaviorally disordered child.

The group was taught how to alter the immediately subsequent environment. Each decided upon a consequence deemed effective for his particular child before leaving the first session. All work with the children was carried out at home by parents. At no point were individual sessions given to children or to parents. The remaining several meetings consisted in adjusting behavior programs, generalizing applicability, and finally working on ways of providing a generally positive environ-

266

ment. The device used to facilitate the latter was to have the parents seek a rate of positive verbal reinforcement at least three times that of the negative.

Although this kind of service delivery has been successful with participants, it fails to influence sufficient numbers of people. In this regard with the potential of school systems to significantly influence community mental health should be noted. Working through teachers is a more readily available opportunity due to the pre-existing organizational framework. While this is somewhat offset by the cumbersome inertia encountered in school systems, there is still little doubt that the most striking changes in community mental health could most easily come through the schools.

Working with an individual teacher to teach classroom behavior management does have a multiplier effect sorely needed in our understaffed field and certainly it aims toward prevention. A teacher who has learned effective and useful means of conceptualizing and dealing with disturbed behavior is better equipped to deal with all behavior. Her skills thus developed are of use far beyond the single case upon which the consultation-learning experience may have been based.

We have found teachers to be considerably more receptive to new skills when they are concerned about an immediate child problem. The detached nature of most inservice training settings sometimes proves too sterile for an involved learning process.

In dealing with a group of thirty active children many teachers find themselves greatly concerned with order. In this setting, the child whose behavior disrupts the order is often faced with a confusing situation. Although the teacher verbally reprimands him and invokes punishments, she behaviorally pays off his disruptive acts with adult and peer attention. For the teacher an approach of continually responding to the negatively valued behavior becomes a way of classroom life which helps to produce and to maintain behavior problems and poor self-concepts.

One tactic is to offer the teacher some relief from this trap. Frequently, this entails explaining that this can be a self-defeating situation. The notion of behavioral payoffs must be conveyed; this one lesson alone is probably worth the cost of intervention. Then the teacher is helped to plan ways of dealing specifically with a behavior which is particularly troublesome.

Jim was a third grader who loved the attention of his peers. His behavior in class was such that the teacher felt compelled to correct or reprimand him several times each day. Various punishments and reasoning with Jim were to no avail; his behavior became more disruptive and more aggressive. The school had decided Jim's character was almost beyond its coping ability when a mental health consultant on the staff became involved.

The consultant asked that the teacher and principal abandon their trait concept of personality long enough to try a behavioral approach. With this vantage point, they could see that the classroom environment was literally teaching Jim the behavior pattern he had developed. The teacher was asked to keep a corner of the front blackboard set aside to count Jim's "bad" behaviors. She would explain to Jim that rather than fussing at him, she would put a mark on the board. Each day of the week a new count was taken and a list of days and behavior counts accumulated on the board for record. Because less social payoff was occurring for his disruption, this alone may have helped Jim. But due to the previous intransigency of the problem, another facet was added to harness Jim's need for peer attention. In order to provide for him a positive way to gain attention and to further detract from his propensity for disruption, the teacher made a bargain with Jim and the entire class. Whenever Jim's blackboard count by Friday was lower for the current week than the previous week, the entire class received an extra fifteen minutes recess time. Jim became the center of attention in this one regard, but only for the good results he was producing for his peers. The teacher had measurable behavior change in days and with occasional setbacks decreasing in frequency, she had significant change in several weeks.

Whenever possible we try to make even more general changes in the teacher's behavior by focusing on the behavioral aspects of a positive classroom. If the teacher can ignore as much of the negative behavior as possible and "catch the child being good" three to four times as often as she catches him being bad, changes occur which are far beyond the expectancies of most school personnel. A teacher's being able to change in this way is dependent upon several factors—her own flexibility, her principal's support and that of fellow teachers, and a regular and aggressive input from some source such as a mental health consultant.

Another link in the chain from mental health consultant to ultimate consumer is the guidance counselor.

One county school system employs an elementary guidance counselor whose job is to serve the guidance needs of six rural elementary schools. On all occasions, where mental health staff were called in for consultative assistance for elementary teachers in this school system, the elementary guidance counselor accompanied. It was the aim of these consultation visits to help the classroom teacher in the management of disturbed behavior which prompted the call since it is better to deal with such problems in the school setting rather than to accept children for therapy referral. This is based on the belief that the school is the chief mental health agency in the life of each child whether or not it desires to serve that function. Accepting therapy referrals from the schools tends to reinforce the same nonproductive thinking for which education and mental health facilities have been mutually guilty for a long time.

The elementary guidance counselor went along on all interventions. She was able to be exposed to classroom behavior management methods over a long period of time, becoming increasingly skilled in making these interventions herself with little or no aid from the mental health staff. The growth on her part meant that the mental health professional became decreasingly useful at any given level of problem complexity.

Lest there be any misinterpretation that the school person dealt with problems of a less serious nature than the professional mental health worker, an example might dispell that notion.

Sarah, an eleven-year-old fifth grade student is a bright child of concerned, intelligent parents. Prior to the counselor's work with the mental health consultant, Sarah's parents had spent up to $2,000 for psychiatric treatment for her over the previous two or three years. Sarah was indeed emotionally disturbed with very real physical illness and psychological disturbance revolving around school attendance. A mental health professional met with the guidance counselor and Sarah's parents on only one occasion. The remainder of the resultant plan was implemented by the parents and teacher under guidance of the counselor. The counselor conferred periodically with the mental health staff member.

The guidance counselor worked to align the behavioral environment both at home and at school to eliminate any possible payoff contingent for Sarah's "sick" behavior. Part of the plan had to take into account parental frustration, guilt, and temper which by this stage had become problem areas in themselves. Within three months, tremendous change was wrought and both home and school report "an entirely different child" this school year.

This was only one of many instances in which the counselor was able to apply behavioral skills learned in conjunction with a consultative program. This is the direction in which the entire program should progress.

CONCLUSION

The term "psychological services" with relation to our program in the schools is not used, preferring instead the term "behavioral services." The former has come to imply testing for intelligence or for psychopathology, both often useful but, perhaps more often, regressive ways of dealing with human lives. The professional staff members are not titled by discipline background, but are all called "mental health consultants," a term which may be less accurate than behavioral or adjustment consultant. These, of course, are mere semantic tools just as behavior modification is an action tool.

Behavior management is a highly effective, relatively simple, easily taught way to look at and to affect human affairs, but it is only a tool. The report of the Joint Commission on Mental Health of Children indicates that schools alone are dealing with fourteen times as many seriously disturbed young people than are mental health professionals. Behavior modification is an excellent tool, but as long as it stays chiefly in the hands of mental health workers, it is being put to inefficient use.

REFERENCES

Cowen, D. L. "Denver's Preventive Health Program for School-Age Children." *American Journal of Public Health* 60(March 1970): 515–518.

Ganser, L. J., Henry, C. M., and Fix, T. C. "A Mental Health Education Program in a Rural Area." *Hospital Community Psychiatry* 21(February 1970): 64–68.

Horn, E. A., Pollack, D., and Saint John, B. "School Mental Health Services Offered Without Invitation." *Mental Hygiene* 3(October 1969): 620–624.

Karp, H. N., and Karls, J. M. "Combining Crisis Therapy and Mental Health Consultation." *Archives of General Psychiatry* 14(May 1966): 536–542.

Kaufman, P. "Consultation Services." *International Psychiatry Clinic* 3(Fall 1966): 123–139.

Loeb, M. B. "Concerns and Methods of Mental Health Consultation." *Hospital Community Psychiatry* 19(April 1968): 111–113.

Millar, T. P. "Schools Should Not Be Community Mental Health Centers." *American Journal of Psychiatry* 125(July 1968): 118–120.

Parks, J. H., and Kimper, F. "A Group Method of Mobilizing Clergymen to Meet Community Mental Health Needs." *Virginia Medical Monthly* 94(March 1967): 170–176.

Rabiner, C. J., Silverberg, S., and Galvin, J. W. "Consultation or Direct Service." *American Journal of Psychiatry* 126(March 1970): 1321–1325.

Rockland, L. H. "Psychiatric Consultation to the Clergy. A Report on a Group Experience." *Mental Hygiene* 53(April 1969): 205–207.

John Carver

Stickney, S. B. "Schools Are Our Community Mental Health Centers." *American Journal of Psychiatry* 124(April 1968): 1407–1414.
Zegans, L. S., Schwartz, M. S., and Dumas, R. "A Mental Health Center's Response to Racial Crisis in an Urban High School." *Psychiatry* 32(August 1969): 252–264.

X

Specialized Services for Children

EDITORS' INTRODUCTION

In 1970, the publication of the Joint Commission Report on the current status of children's mental health services served to emphasize a problem which had been recognized within the community mental health center program for some time. Although community mental health center regulations have always required that services be delivered to persons of all ages, most centers have devoted the great majority of their resources to services for adults. Although more community mental health centers are now beginning to develop specialized services for children, they still continue to face many of the same problems that have precluded the development of children's services in the past.

One of these problems is the availability of manpower. Personnel are generally lacking, both in the sense that there are few people specifically trained to work with children and, also, in the sense that persons trained as mental health generalists feel inadequate when confronted by children's problems.

The second issue relates to the current organization of services for children. Whereas there are a number of agencies which devote attention to children and their problems, many of them do not consider themselves to be "mental health" programs and, therefore, are reluctant to take part in an organized program under mental health sponsorship. As a result, it has been difficult for community mental health centers to establish affiliations and cooperative relationships with currently existing agencies which serve children.

There are also special problems that accompany the recognition and handling of emotional disorders in children which have retarded the development of specialized children's programs within community mental health centers. For example, specialized inpatient services are required separate from those which are available more readily for the care of adults. Also, there are many children who require long-term treatment in residential type facilities and these are generally unavailable. Finally, basic difficulties in the diagnosis and evaluation of children can often lead to confusion with regard to the differentiation between mental illness and organic dysfunction.

For the reasons previously stated, the development of children's services can be quite costly. As a result, the development of adult and children's services simultaneously within a given catchment area is often a financial impossibility. Recognizing this problem, the National Institute of Mental Health has been encouraging community mental health centers to develop children's services on a regionalized basis. However, when community mental health centers do not exist in contiguous areas, the implementation of regionalized services is difficult.

---

32 *Sydney Koret*, PH.D.

A Community Mental Health Center for Children:
Issues and Problems

The Convalescent Hospital for Children was established in 1885 as the Infant Summer Hospital. At that point it was a summer tent hospital for children suffering from the then prevalent "infant summer fever." This illness was of the greatest concern of the City of Rochester and found its highest incidence in the immigrant areas of the city. From the outset, this organization was deeply involved in community concerns and its unmet needs. While infant summer fever had disappeared by 1890, the concern for the people of the slum areas had not. It was relatively easy to move from infant summer fever to dealing with other illnesses of children needing long-term convalescent care. Provisions were made to serve children with polio, rheumatic heart, and other debilitating illnesses of childhood. An informed citizen advisory group assisted in seeing that the Convalescent Hospital for Children move from a tent city to a permanent structure.

After World War II, the introduction of antibiotics, the advent of polio vaccine, and the psychological aversion to providing children with long-term hospitalization away from their families, led to a dramatic drop in the population of the Convalescent Hospital for Children.

In 1950, the Council of Social Agencies together with representatives from the University of Rochester Medical School organized a committee to study the unmet needs of children in Monroe County. They saw residential treatment for emotionally disturbed children as a prime need. Combining with representatives of the board of the Convalescent Hospital for Children, they engaged in an early form of community mental health planning. The recommendation that the Convalescent Hospital for Children enter into the mental health arena by opening a Residential Treatment Center took positive form in 1958.

By 1962, the Convalescent Hospital for Children was asked by the Council of Social Agencies and the County Board of Mental Health to sponsor an outpatient service. Shortly thereafter, a pilot day treatment service was also established attached to the inpatient unit. It then engaged in conjunction with the Council of Social Agencies in a detailed study which eventually resulted in a report recommending a full-flown day treatment program.

The deep concern of the staff for the problems of prevention and the terrible costs and investment of money and human life in residential treatment led to early trials in consultation. Having observed studies in the public school in early detection it had become clear that, by the first grade, children could already be selected who would present school behavioral and emotional problems by the third grade. This led to a venture in consultation and prevention in nursery schools. The close collaboration with the University of Rochester Medical School and Strong Memorial Hospital made emergency services readily available.

When the Community Mental Health Act became fact in 1963, the Convalescent Hospital for children had in an embryonic form all of the services needed to meet the provisions of the Act. It also had the emotional investment of a Board of Directors and a staff deeply committed to extending in aggressive fashion mental health services to the total community with emphasis on the disadvantaged.

The concept, however, of a community mental health center specializing in services for children and their families was totally alien to the initial administrators and planning bodies of the Community Mental Health Center Movement. The Residential Treatment Center met the requirements of an inpatient unit. The proposal of an expanded day treatment program met easily the qualification for partial hospitalization. The ongoing Child Guidance Clinic, particularly with its innovative aggressive fashion, made this a satisfactory outpatient service. Seeds had been sown for a widespread consultation program which could readily be implemented by acceptance of the plan proposed in a request for a construction and staffing grant. The suggestion was proffered that emergency services be offered by a contractual arrangement with Strong Memorial Hospital. In order to round out the comprehensive features, the contractual arrangement also provided for the treatment of adults at Strong Memorial Hospital where the Community Mental Health Center of the University of Rochester Medical School's Department of Psychiatry was later established. And finally, that formal efforts be made to add a research consultant to the staff. Thus, in structure, a community mental health center had been proposed, piloted, designed, and brought into being.

However, from the outset, moving this embryonic structure forward in a fashion consistent with the conceptualization of the community mental health center raised certain fundamental questions which demanded resolution. Since some of the services had been operational and offered to the total community for a period of years, withdrawing to new catchment area lines essentially meant withdrawal of services from a large portion of the population. Since other mental health centers were not yet available, and did not appear to be in the immediate offing to cover the total county, a serious ethical and funding problem arose immediately for the center as well as for the total community. From the viewpoint of legislators, people in the community, and private and public funding bodies, the total service area is the catchment area. That it does not coincide with the geographic one assigned to a community mental health center presented further problems.

For example, the principle of a children's residential treatment unit quickly comes into conflict with the catchment area concept and the conceptualization of continuity of care. The application of adult psychiatric principles to a children's unit is unacceptable. It is not feasible in terms of effectiveness, economy, or staff availability to have one children's residential treatment center in each catchment area. Since some mental health centers could not provide inpatient service for children, they had to utilize the residential unit in another center. For the Convalescent Hospital for Children, this meant that the residential treatment aspect would have to provide service to more than one catchment area. What then of continuity of care? Is it feasible for a staff in one center to continue following a child when he moves into an inpatient service in another center? Since this is generally a long-term stay and since the demands of a therapeutic milieu depend for satisfaction on close communication and day-to-day interaction by members of the staff, continuity of care in the sense of having the same worker follow a child throughout destroys the concept of continuity of care in terms of the therapeutic matrix within a residential treatment center.

A somewhat similar situation exists with day treatment. While here two centers provided facilities for children needing day treatment, strict adherence to this would leave one half of the area unserved. This ran into the same contradictions as occurred in residential treatment. Further, if a child was admitted first to residential treatment, but then was transferred to day treatment or the outpatient unit, would his treatment then revert to this catchment area in which he resided? Obviously this would be destructive to the principle of continuity of care while maintaining the principle of strict service by catchment area.

The total application of the catchment area principle for children also had to be scrupulously examined. The life style of a child and his needs does not adhere strictly to the pattern delegated for adults with the establishment of the Community Mental Health Act. A whole new set of circumstances are introduced when one starts delving into mental health problems of children. For example, many or most of the referrals, and many or most of the life problems of the child, center around school. This is the arena in which he spends most of his waking life. What then becomes the catchment area of the child, his school or his home address? Clearly the school a child attends may well be outside the geographic catchment area. Indeed, two children within the same family may go into different schools in different catchment areas. Is the family then divided and treated by several centers? When the child moves from elementary to high school, he may change catchment areas. What is the interpretation of the concept of continuity of care at this point since the child may well be in another center's catchment area? What may seem like the obvious in response need not necessarily be so. For example, the needs of the school demand that they not be deluged by representatives of several community mental health centers. It becomes utterly ridiculous to have one center see a child and another center offer consultation to that school. To offer effective service focused on the needs of the child rather than on a piece of geography requires some soul searching, questioning of the Act as it now exists as applied to children and the need to make quick therapeutic decisions.

Finally, the concept of the comprehensive nature of community mental health centers, including the provision of emergency services and services for adults, had to be resolved in order to provide services to a children's organization not attached to a larger psychiatric unit or general hospital.

Now let us examine each of these problems as they have been investigated, conceptualized, and translated into a therapeutic approach by the Convalescent Hospital for Children. Some implications are contained for revision of the Community Mental Health Centers Act if it desires to provide realistically the most effective treatment modalities for the children.

The primary problem presented is that of a unit or units within one mental health center servicing more than one catchment area. A basic difficulty is attempting to pattern children's mental health services in accordance with a format developed for adults. This became crystal clear around the utilization of an inpatient unit. The Community Mental Health Center in dealing with adults makes a presumption that the stay in an inpatient unit will be extremely short with a relatively fast transfer to day treatment or outpatient services. The total effort is devoted to returning the adult to his former level of functioning, and resumption of his position in the community. Thus each community mental health center can have a small number of beds and service a large population since the turnover is so rapid. When longer stays are needed, transfer is usually made to the state hospital while continuing to work on a therapeutic basis with the patient during his stay at the state hospital. In any case, they maintain constant knowledge of his whereabouts and if he is discharged, they may resume their therapeutic efforts.

When one deals with children, the situation is completely reversed. Children have no former level of functioning to return them to. Almost in every case the situation has existed since early childhood and it is its very chronicity rather than acuteness that leads to the referral to an inpatient service. Agency after agency has demonstrated that there really is no such beast as short-term treatment for seriously disturbed children. When this has been attempted, it has either collapsed around the frustrations of the staff or leads to a gradual extension of treatment when plans for disposition become ultimately unresolvable. The child is completely dependent on the support of an external environment and work with parents is a *sine qua non* of treatment. As a result of this compendium of factors, the residential treatment center must provide a child not only with all of the ingredients of therapy, but it must also provide basically rehabilitative child-rearing practices, a remedial education system, and a home to which to return, be it his own or another, since he is not able to establish an independent existence without the aid of collaterals.

It is apparent dramatically that the staff or staff members from one center cannot reasonably be expected to continue with the child after he has been admitted to residential treatment. The long-term nature of the commitment and the time involved not only in providing service, but in conferencing and constant communication becomes prohibitive. The very essence of an inpatient service for children demands the establishment of its own cultural pattern dependent very much on staff interrelationships, understandable communication, and instantaneous reaction to the needs of the child. Thus, within each residence, continuity of care establishes a matrix which prohibits the utilization of staff from other centers and is in direct contradiction to the traditional concept of continuity of care. Thus the conflict is between sound beneficial treatment and a doctrinaire statement of continuity of care.

In actual practice, the Convalescent Hospital for Children accepts referrals for its intensive services, residential treatment or day treatment, from the mental health centers in other catchment areas. Referring personnel then participate in the total intake process. This means they not only contribute what material they have to members of the Convalescent Hospital for Children but sit in on and engage in discussion around acceptance of the child and planning at the intake conference. They are then kept informed as to the progress and eventual planning for the child.

This frequently raises further problems since there is a strong possibility it could be a multiproblem family. In order to maintain a true continuity of care, to avoid overlapping and contradictory repetitiousness, the acceptance of a child into residence means the acceptance of the total family. Thus, from the time a child is accepted and as soon as it is practical while waiting admission, he moves into our outpatient clinic for therapeutic engagement. If other members of the family then need mental health services, they are seen as being within our catchment area regardless of their geographic residence. On discharge too, we continue to work with this child and his family as long as they need service with no re-referral to the referring agency. It would be well for those responsible for devising legislation and administrative fiats for our community mental health centers to redesign and reformulate the guidelines while thinking in terms of both experience and actual needs of children.

Day treatment too requires the same searching scrutiny as was applied to the needs of residential treatment. Again the wholesale application of the principles of adult care would be disastrous in the treatment of children. The prime function of a day treatment program for children is to provide them with a rehabilitative educational experience in addition to therapy, and make it possible for them to readapt to a public school situation. For most children who enter day treatment, public schools have been a farcical nightmare fraught with catastrophic episodes. Their experience of school failures, the inhibiting of their desire to learn or utilize the cognitive processes in educational fashion, and their perception of school authorities and teachers as the perpetuators of diabolical tortures has to be dealt with.

This is a long involved process. It would be unthinkable to take a child from one school, bring him into day treatment for three or four weeks, and then return him to the area which has epitomized his inadequacy and failure. Therefore, day treatment must also be conceived of as a relatively long-term process. Until such time as the political division is completely covered by day treatment units, it becomes the moral responsibility and the only sensible avenue for those day treatment programs that do exist in a community of this size to service the whole area. Further, since the problem is so inextricably interwoven with school, one must conceive of working with school districts and school mental health people even though they may at times cut through the geographic mental health boundaries as designed for the community mental health center.

A third fundamental question that has to be dealt with and perhaps re-examined is the concept of the "comprehensive" community mental health center. In order to provide this, the Convalescent Hospital for Children entered into a contractual relationship with the University of Rochester School of Medicine and Dentistry. Through the Department of Psychiatry, it was agreed that they would provide emergency services as well as all necessary services for adults. As part of the agreement it was stated that not only would the Medical School and the Convalescent Hospital for Children accept patients from each other but records would be mutually available to both staffs. Further as part of the concept of continuity of care, a therapist from one organization could continue to provide service while the patient was hospitalized in the other.

As with the above discussion regarding residential treatment, this becomes unrealistic and undesirable for both staffs and the need for the welfare of the child. The need for emergency services for children is so infrequent as to make the incorporation of such a unit in most children's mental health centers an expensive travesty on community mental health thinking. Eventually the University received approval for its own community mental health center. A mutual arrangement has evolved where adults are seen and provided service by that mental health center and children are serviced at the Convalescent Hospital for Children.

Sharing the same catchment area even if for two different age groups requires a close coordination. This has been arrived at by a liaison committee which meets every other week and is composed of three of the top administrative and policy-making personnel at the Convalescent Hospital for Children and their counterparts from the Community Mental Health Center at the University. In addition, a committee has been established of workers from each mental health center which meets weekly and deals with the problems of daily operation. The end result has been that in the inner city we share the same office space and now have joint records. Areas of conflict tend to arise around adolescents and consultation. These gray areas emerge in attempting to arrive at a clear definition as to where the primary function of one center ends and the other begins. It is not as easily differentiated as one might expect by merely selecting an age cutoff point. This is peculiarly true because of the mutual interest in adolescents. Any arbitrary division would tend to extinguish some of the enthusiasm in both staffs about a good portion of their work. It would also reduce the variety available. Nevertheless this has not been viewed as a major hazard. The quantity of available patients now and for the foreseeable future is so large that with this group it is possible to assign patients to both staffs.

This has been an eminently successful and rewarding experience. The contrast of the amount of service given to children in this catchment area to those in the remainder of the country points to one of the tremendous advantages in having a children's mental health center as administratively and even philosophically separate from an adult center. It seems inevitable that if the two function as one unit, the preponderance of effort will flow into the adult unit. In most cases, this has meant a virtual elimination of work with children. It is the old adage of the tail not being able to wag the dog. The utilization of liaison committees, ad hoc committees, and the joint confrontation on day-to-day issues has not only stimulated both staffs, but has made both more strikingly aware of administrative and therapeutic problems involved. This system does not seem to inherently engender any administrative or therapeutic inefficiencies nor does it appear to be more costly.

In discussing the theoretic considerations of a children's mental health center, one cannot escape problems of the current concept of geographic catchment areas any more than one could escape the inconsistency inherent in the concept of continuity of service. The present catchment area concept is based on a center accepting as its responsibility one clearly defined geographic area of a limited population. This works quite adequately with adults where the work centers about the adult's own functioning and that of their family's collaboration. The size of the catchment area seems quite reasonable.

In working with children the scene shifts dramatically. As has been mentioned above, no catchment area of this size can support some of the essentials of treatment for children. The concept of short-term inpatient service for children is a fantasy. When one begins to deal with a residential unit, the established size catchment area, particularly in urban areas, is far too small to maintain a residential unit either in terms of economics or effective program. The possibility or desirability of restricting children's units to precisely the same catchment areas as adult areas is questionable. In addition, the necessity of travel to reach the center is minimal in residential treatment. Thus the ability to walk a few minutes to the center or reach it very shortly with public transportation is not so monumental an issue.

Finally, a major portion of the involvement and work with children centers around the work with schools and teachers. Any catchment area concept which does not recognize the essential role of the school in the life of the child, and when necessary his emotional rehabilitation, is poorly construed. At the present moment, it would be a rare coincidence for the school district and catchment area to always coincide. Further, schools cannot effectively work with a diversity of mental health centers. The school rather than the geographical area should be included within the catchment area of a mental health center. This makes it possible to provide not only treatment and referral resources but consultation on an ongoing basis. Currently, if a family has children in two different schools which coincidently happen to be in different catchment areas, it would require treatment from two different centers, both working with the parents and both working with separate children. When a child becomes older and moves to high school, he then can move into a totally different catchment area since traditionally high schools cover a larger population than elementary schools. Strict adherence to the catchment area principle as currently devised leads to chaos. It would appear that a restudying and restructuring of catchment areas for children should be engaged in immediately. It would also be well worth considering the principle of separating children and adult units in terms of administration and operation.

---

33   *Roy J. Ellison, Jr.*, M.D.

A Children's Re-Ed Center as Part of a Community Mental Health Center

The Children's Re-Education Center in Greenville, the first of its kind in South Carolina, is located adjacent to the Marshall I. Pickens Hospital and Community Mental Health Center and represents a new concept in meeting the special needs of children.

Providing a five-day week residential treatment program for the education and re-education of the emotionally disturbed child and adolescent, the Children's Re-Education Center is quartered in handsome buildings of modern, open design on the Grove Road site of the community health complex of the Greenville Hospital System with living accommodations for a group of ten children and day care facilities for many others.

BACKGROUND AND PURPOSES

The purposes of the program are to provide a school treatment program that is educational in orientation for emotionally disturbed children; to return the child to his normal social system in the shortest possible time; to maintain a staff of highly qualified teacher-counselors and to develop a training program to implement the above staff and aid other schools and agencies in working with emotionally disturbed children; and to serve as a resource for the community mental health center and other agencies in the community working with emotionally disturbed children.

The mentally retarded, physically handicapped, and those candidates whose home background is considered insufficiently stable to support the Re-Ed program for the child are generally considered to be beyond

283

the treatment capability of the program. This program is especially well suited to children between six and twelve years of age.

Because of the location of this Re-Education Unit within a traditionally medical, hospital setting, certain unique advantages accrue, including the accessibility of medical consultation and services for more definitive diagnostic information, and for the development of appropriate medical management in certain cases.

The philosophy of treatment involves the use of intensive, educationally oriented techniques with an academic focus aiming at the remediation of academic disabilities and the improvement of motivation, and the quality of behavior in the child to make return to his home and the ordinary structure of the community feasible. It is felt that any and all appropriate professional services as offered by the mental health specialties can be effectively utilized in conjunction with the Re-Ed program. The Re-Ed program is seen not as a replacement for any community service, but as an adjunctive approach to problems of emotional disturbance in children. Within the Re-Ed program, it is the intention of the staff to maintain the greatest flexibility of approach, allowing especially for the creative or innovative use of new techniques with the individual child as they are felt to be applicable to his problems.

In addition to its primary purpose of serving emotionally disturbed children and their parents, the Re-Ed center serves as a demonstration project to the community by utilizing volunteers, subprofessionals, and students. Selected volunteers serve as teacher aides, reading teachers, physical education aides, and educational diagnosticians.

THE PROGRAM

A team of staff members works with each group of ten children. This team implements a closely coordinated and intensive program with its major goal as the improvement of the child's potential for living effectively within the structure of his family and community.

The Re-Ed residential team consists of four members: *the Day Teacher-Counselor* who has primary responsibility for the more formal academic aspects of the program; *the Night Teacher-Counselor* who has primary responsibility for the effective use of structured group experiences aimed at the fostering of more mature and competent behavior; *the Liaison Teacher-Counselor* who maintains the relationship of the Re-Ed program with the parents, the school to which the child is expected to return, and any other agencies directly involved with the child; and *the Residence Counselor* who lives in the residential unit and is responsible for the children during the night hours.

The Re-Ed day team consists of three members: *the Day Teacher-Counselor* who has primary responsibility for the academic part of the program, *the Liaison Teacher-Counselor* who maintains the relationship with the family, school, and referring agency, and *a Recreational Therapist* whose primary responsibility is for the effective use of activity hours aimed at group participation and cooperation.

In the Re-Ed concept of treatment, these team members are seen as the change agents. Working with each team to enhance their effectiveness are four consultants: a pediatrician, who is a member of the Greenville Hospital System medical staff; a clinical psychologist, who is a faculty member of Furman University; a curriculum specialist, who is a faculty member of Winthrop College; and a special educator.

A new admission to the residential program arrives at the unit on Sunday night where he and his family are met by the night teacher-counselor and the residence counselor. He is taken to his bedroom where he unpacks, meets his roommate, and prepares for the week ahead.

In the morning, the children get up and eat breakfast in the cafeteria. Afterwards, they return to their rooms to clean them up before class. At 8:00 A.M. classes begin for both residential and day programs. Each child has a daily assignment sheet which is prepared especially for his individual needs. The children in both groups spend the morning hours in class with their work emphasizing mastery of the basic academic skills and subjects. Classes are small enough so that each child is able to receive the individual attention he needs. At lunch both groups eat in the hospital cafeteria; during the warm summer months they often eat on the patio. After lunch, the residential group has a brief group therapy session known as a powwow. At this time, they discuss their behavior and performance during the morning and ways in which they can improve.

The children in the day program have recreational activities after lunch supervised by the hospital's recreational therapist and consisting of swimming, basketball, croquet, volleyball, and table games. After this period, these children also have their powwow and then go home for the evening.

The residential boys have a science class after their powwow where they work on both individual and group projects. After science, they have an arts and crafts period where they can express themselves creatively through semi-structured and unstructured projects. The remaining afternoon and evening hours are left for recreational activities and group living experiences which are designed to help develop the children's physical and social skills.

One time period is set aside for each group each week for what is known as Goal Trip. For the day program this is on Monday afternoon, and for the residential program it is Wednesday night. This trip is for those children who have earned it by meeting specific behavioral and academic criteria during the previous week. These criteria are determined by both the teacher-counselors and the children and are set according to each child's particular needs. The children who earn Goal Trip choose the nature of the activity which may be a movie, roller skating, flying kites, or miniature golf.

Concurrent with the child's attendance at the Re-Ed center, the parents are involved on a regular basis in either individual or group counseling. All parents are involved in a course which deals with principles and techniques of the management of children's behavior. It is here that the parents begin to take a closer look at the problems and recognize their responsibility to the system and the effect they have on their children's behavior. Parent conferences are scheduled routinely to handle special problems and discuss the child's progress and home behavior.

As each child reaches the stage where he is nearly ready to return to his family and school, the treatment team and his parents meet to discuss his progress and how to maintain his gains once he has left the structure of the Re-Ed center. Plans for placement are discussed and the parents are given the opportunity to discuss any part of the team's recommendations.

When placement plans have been finalized through special services, the liaison teacher-counselor makes a visit to the child's school to talk with the principal and teacher. The liaison teacher-counselor advises them as to progress made by the child, any remaining weaknesses, and methods which have been found effective in working with the child. At this time, a meeting with the principal and teacher is arranged for the child so that he can be more familiar with them and their expectations for him.

The liaison teacher-counselor maintains contact with the child's school system for a follow-up period of one year. This contact is primarily through visits with the child and his parents at home and visits to his school with him and his teacher. The referring agency or professional person also is available for continued support for the family once the child has left the Re-Ed center.

SUMMARY

The Childrens Re-Education Center, which has a capacity for twenty children (ten resident and ten day treatment) has served twenty-nine children. The average length of stay has been eight months, but with program development it is expected to drop to six months or less.

The cost of a re-education endeavor is not cheap, but it is the feeling of all concerned that the potential for reward is great and that the ultimate influence on treatment and preventive therapy is even greater.

---

34   *Irmgard S. Dobrow,* M.D.

A School Program for Emotionally Disturbed Children

The Meadowlark project, a school for emotionally disturbed children, was started because we recognized the limitations of conventional weekly outpatient visits to help emotionally disturbed children. The program was set up to provide help for those public school children who are so emotionally disturbed that they cannot be taught in a regular classroom or who are not able to realize their full growth potential even with the support of therapy alone. Many of them had already been expelled, suspended or otherwise restricted from school attendance because of interference with the rest of the class's learning.

The Jefferson County Mental Health Center provided a team to offer psychiatric, psychological, and social work services as well as recreational and occupational therapy. It also provided equipment, supplies, and office furniture not ordinarily related to a regular school program but related to the therapeutic needs.

Referrals were accepted from the school, the mental health center, private schools, other social health agencies, or private practitioners. These referrals were initially reviewed by a committee composed of representatives of the schools and mental health center staff. Guidelines used included:

287

1. The child was unable to perform and be maintained in regular school even with the supervision of the school nurse, social worker, or psychologist.

2. A complete social history and psychological evaluation must have been done and must have identified an emotional problem as opposed to organic difficulties.

3. The child must be of average intelligence or above.

4. He must be between the ages of five to less than eleven years of age at the time of admission.

5. Parents must be workable and motivated to participate in the program.

If the referral was judged appropriate, further psychological testing was done to clarify questionable points and a psychiatric evaluation by a child psychiatrist, and a review of the social history with the parent by the staff was conducted. When all this information was assembled and studied again, it was presented to the joint staff to make the final determination.

Problems were encountered from poor selection of the initial group. Teachers had been waiting for years for someone to deliver them from the worst problems and understandably these were the most urgent referrals. Thus, an initial group of "experienced trouble makers" was obtained who were difficult to manage. A group of passive-aggressive, anxious, acting-out children need a very definite structure and firm limits. The lessening of the staff's anxiety and better selection in composing the group improved significantly the efficiency of the program. It also took some time to educate the school personnel to portray the program in the right light and not to apply undue pressure to the parents for cooperation.

The staff consisted of two teachers and periodically placed student teachers, a part-time psychologist, two social workers, an occupational therapist, a recreational therapist, and a consulting child psychiatrist. The clinic director and the child psychiatrist shared responsibilities for the medical evaluation of the children, supervised therapy, and acted as consultants for the other staff members. A variety of treatment approaches have been used to fit the individual needs of the child and his family. All children are seen individually once a week for at least fifty minutes by the social workers or the psychologist. The parents are seen once a week in a group.

As skills were gained, many of the children's problems were handled in groups. Groups were also used to allow the children to participate in planning of activities, the handling of disciplinary problems, and as a source of feedback and reflection of what was peer-approved behavior and what was not. It was quite helpful to include the teachers in these groups.

The occupational therapist carried out her specialized therapy either in individual sessions or small groups. The children were encouraged to express themselves through the use of a variety of materials. The program offered woodworking, leather crafts, and artistic drawings. These activities provided for nonverbal expression and an atmosphere free of the structure and competitiveness of the academic set-up. The creative success might be the key to offset the many scholastic failures experienced in public school.

The recreational therapy program carried out activities to improve the child's physical skills. After his limitations were appraised, goals were set up to bring him up to age expectancies. Recreation activities offered unlimited opportunity to help the child relate to his peer group, improve his self-image and self-control, and accept his responsibility as part of the team.

During the summer months, academic programs are suspended, but the therapy staff carries out a therapeutic day care program three days a week. This program includes a few educational field trips but the main activities are exploration of the outdoors, hikes, and mountain climbs. The summer programs ended with a five day camp-out in an isolated area of the national forest. The sharing of enjoyable activities produced a group solidarity which does not come about in the classroom situation.

This is an ideal time to introduce new children into the program. Freer structure allows for easier handling of the "testing-out period" of the child and the generally pleasant activities facilitate the childrens' acceptance of the dreaded school change. By the time school starts in September, the child is well acquainted with his peer group and staff and is ready to tackle academic tasks.

From the results obtained we have been able to identify the following factors which appear to most effect satisfactory results: (1) the work has been far more successful with younger children; (2) the success of the program depended on the ability to involve the child's recognition of his ineffective behavior patterns and his motivation to change to more acceptable gratifying behavior; (3) progress was definitely related to the parents' ability and readiness to modify those psychological elements in the family that were hindering the child's emotional growth; (4) the success of returning a child to a regular public school has been greatly determined by the genuine acceptance of the child by the principal and the teaching staff, in particular, the teacher or teachers who would be directly dealing with the child; (5) if we found out that we had made an error in the evaluation and accepted a child whose primary problem was organic in nature, progress was very slow; children whose primary problems were emotional and who did not need specialized techniques did considerably better; and (6) consultations and on-going evaluations and modifications of goals were significant factors in determining satisfactory progress.

35

James H. Satterfield, M.D., *and*
Dennis P. Cantwell, M.D.

Development of an Evaluation and Treatment
Outpatient Clinic for Hyperactive Children

INTRODUCTION

Over a century ago a German physician, Heinrich Hoffmann, told the tale of a hyperactive child named "Fidgety Phil" in a children's book in verse.[1] The story told of the numerous activities of Fidgity Phil in pictures and doggerel verse. The succeeding years, however, have come to show that hyperactive children are in fact not humorous—not to themselves, their families, their companions, or their school teachers.

Several clinical descriptions [2] in the literature have outlined a syndrome that begins early in life, is more common in boys, and is characterized by a symptom pattern of overactivity, distractibility, impulsiveness, and excitability. Other areas of difficulty for the hyperactive child are: peer relations, discipline problems, and specific learning problems. Laboratory, psychological, and neurological studies [3] have as yet uncovered no single test or battery of tests which realistically and conclusively distinguishes the hyperactive child from the normal child.

Follow-up studies [4] indicate that while hyperactivity diminishes with age, other major handicaps persist into adolescence and adulthood. Disorders of attention and concentration remain possibly leading to a chronic and severe underachievement in school in the face of adequate intellectual resources. A significant proportion of hyperactive children still manifest psychopathology five to twenty-five years later ranging from emotional immaturity, inability to maintain goals, poor self-images, and feelings of hopelessness to overt anti-social behavior and psychosis. Family studies [5] indicate a high percentage of related psychiatric illness in close family members. Studies of results of treatment [6] have generally been short-term, uncontrolled, and have not used a double-blind procedure or objective measures of improvement. However, several well-controlled studies [7] using a number of variable tests of motor function, general intelligence, impulsivity, attention span, and perception given before and after a short period of drug therapy, suggested a small but significant improvement in intellectual functioning, perception, and impulsivity. Little is known about predictions of response to treatment of any type, but, in general, studies show that the earlier the treatment is instituted, the less disabling the disorder as the child grows older. Thus, it behooves all those concerned with the growth and development of children to learn to detect this rather common and potentially serious disorder early in the child's life.

SETTING UP A CLINIC

Various studies estimate the prevalence of the hyperactive child syndrome as better than 4–8 percent of the school age population. Therefore, one or two can be expected to turn up in (and disrupt) every classroom. Since it is in the classroom that the hyperactive child is best detected, it is evident that the main source of referral to the clinic should come from the school. Education of teachers, school counselors, school physicians and nurses, pediatricians, and general practitioners in the recognition of the hyperactive child is therefore crucial. This education can take place in several ways: (1) TV and radio programs; (2) talks to teacher and P.T.A. groups; (3) articles in local newspapers; and (4) direct mailing of educational materials to schools, local physicians, and P.T.A. groups. The last method has been found most effective in our clinic. A four-page descriptive brochure * has been prepared for teachers, physicians, and counselors: The brochure describes the salient clinical features of the syndrome; discusses treatment measures, both specific and nonspecific; and gives explicit recommendations to teachers to help manage the hyperactive child in the classroom. A similar five-page brochure has been prepared for parents. This brochure also describes the clinical picture and then discusses both general and specific

---

* All materials mentioned in this article are available from the authors.

measures that parents can follow to help their hyperactive child. A typical response of a parent after reading our brochure has been: "It was like reading something that was written about Johnny." In summary, we have found the use of these methods effective in educating the community in the detection of hyperactive children and thereby creating a demand for clinic services.

The minimum personnel needed to operate the clinic are: (1) a physician or physicians; (2) a social worker; and (3) a clinic secretary. It is helpful, but not necessary, to have the services of a psychologist. Volunteer workers are very helpful on clinic days in managing the children by keeping them busy with toys in the playroom. The physicians may be child psychiatrists, general psychiatrists, pediatricians or pediatric neurologists.

The secretary does initial screening, usually on the phone, and mails a packet to the parents consisting of: (1) the brochure for parents; (2) the brochure for teachers, physicians, and school counselors; (3) a physical examination form for the family doctor; (4) a structured rating scale for teachers; and (5) a structured rating scale for parents. When all of these materials have been returned, the parents are given an appointment for a screening interview with the social worker. The social worker completes part of the structured psychiatric interview and obtains the necessary consent and release of information from previous physicians and agencies with whom the family may have had contact. When these last mentioned materials are in the file, the parents and children are then seen by the physician who completes the evaluation.

The basic work-up of the patient consists of the structured interview with the parents; an interview with the child; and scoring of the structured rating form for teachers and for parents.

The structured interview with the parents consists of a fourteen-page interview covering: identifying data (13 items); symptom inventory (54 items); developmental and past medical history (22 items); family constellation and history of psychiatric disorder (15 items); description of parental home (14 items); and school history (9 items).

The purpose of the interview with the child is to determine the nature and extent of any abnormalities of emotions, behavior, or relationships shown by the child. The examiner must observe closely the child's behavior and emotional state throughout the whole interview with these categories and ratings in mind. However, the interview should be open ended and unstructured. The aim is to relax the child and to let him talk freely to assess the relationship he is able to form in such a setting, the level and ability of his mood, his speech pattern, and his behavioral manifestations.

The structured rating form for teachers consists of thirty-six items of classroom behavior arranged in check list form so that the teacher may check off each individual behavior exhibited by the child as not at all; just a little; or pretty much or very much. Following this are six questions inquiring whether or not the child has repeated grades, has been sent to the principal, has been suspended or expelled, has been referred for speech therapy or remedial reading, or has been referred to a psychiatrist or psychologist. The form concludes with an open-ended invitation for the teacher to make any comments she would like about the child. If the child has been seen by the school psychologist, results of intellectual and achievement testing are requested.

The structured form for parents consists of forty-five items arranged in check list form similar to the form for teachers. Following this section are five questions inquiring whether the main problem in the parents' view is behavioral, academic, or both, and whether there is any familial incidence of similar problems. The parents are then invited to make any comments they would like about their child. Both the form for teachers and the form for parents have the check list questions phrased so that a positive answer describes undesirable behavior. Each answer is scored.

A maximum score on the teacher form is 108 and on the parent form is 135. In clinical practice, a score greater than 50 on the teacher form and over 60 on the parent form is highly indicative of hyperactivity.

In addition to the basic work-up, neurological and psychological evaluation may be necessary. Neurological examination of the hyperactive child assists in identifying the child with organic brain disease who may require further diagnostic procedures and specific therapy; helps to clarify reasons why the child may not perform up to his expected level of achievement; and allays suspicion of organic brain disease in children with adjustment reactions of childhood whose overactivity and other symptoms may have mimicked the hyperactive child syndrome. Children with a suspicion of neurologic involvement on physical examination and/or history should be referred to a pediatric neurologist.

Certain psychological data are essential in all evaluations. These include a reliable estimate of general intelligence; an academic skill index; measures of perceptual functioning and other indices of language, learning, and behavior as indicated in the individual child.

TREATMENT

In the treatment of the hyperactive child, pharmacotherapy is the principal and most efficacious mode of therapy. This is not meant to depreciate the importance of the role of family counseling, environmental structuring, and remedial education as these are often needed in addition to chemotherapy.

There have now been many studies [8] documenting the usefulness of dextroamphetamine and other sympathomimetic amines. Several of these studies have been well designed and well controlled. Conners and Eisenberg [9] have demonstrated the efficacy of the stimulant drugs, dextroamphetamine and methylpenidate, for hyperactive children, children with learning problems, and emotionally disturbed children.

The enigma of how stimulant drugs produce a calming effect on hyperactive children has been with us since Bradley [10] first reported the usefulness of these drugs some thirty-three years ago. A recent study by Satterfield and Dawson [11] suggests that these children may have abnormally low levels of CNS excitability. If this finding is confirmed by future studies, it would explain the beneficial effects of the stimulant drugs since they are known to increase brain excitability.

There have been several reports [12] of the efficacy of tranquilizers, though other studies [13] report them to be no better than placebos.

The hyperactive child has been reported to be generally unresponsive to psychotherapy and this is consistent with our experience with these children.

STIMULANT DRUGS

Sympathomimetic amines or stimulant drugs should be tried first. About 70 percent of hyperactive children will get a good response from one or the other of these drugs. The dosage of methylphenidate is about .2 mg/lb and dextroamphetamine is about .1 mg/lb per dose. The drugs should be reserved mainly for school and, therefore, are given only five days a week. When starting medication, one tablet given before breakfast is utilized for the first three days of treatment. A second dose is then added and given before lunch. We have found that nearly all schools will cooperate in the giving of this second dose. Since the action of these drugs (especially methylphenidate) is no more than three to four hours, the double dosage schedule is necessary. The long-acting form of dextro-amphetamine can be substituted for the twice daily schedule and works well in some children.

In evaluating response to drug treatment we find that the teachers' rating scale is more useful than reports by parents or others. Although some halo or placebo effect can be expected to indicate improvement in the absence of a specific drug effect, improvement of more than 30 percent on the teachers' rating scale indicates a clear drug effect.[14] In general, parents can be told that a good response will be indicated by such things as improved attention span, better self-control, and less impulsivity resulting in improved relations with peers and adults and an improved self-image.

Dosage should be adjusted upward at approximately weekly intervals until a therapeutic effect is obtained or side effects prohibit further increase. This adjustment of dosage can usually be carried out by telephone reports from parents regarding changes in behavior at school. Patients should be seen at monthly intervals until the right dose of the right drug has been found and then they may be seen less often. As tolerance to these drugs develops in most children, it is necessary to follow them with the teacher rating scales to detect remission to former poor behavior patterns. When this occurs, dosage may be increased or another drug substituted. Some children respond well to either dextroamphetamine or methylphenidate and some to only one but not the other. In those who respond to both drugs, the child can be switched from one to the other, as cross-tolerance to these drugs does not usually occur. It is because of this tolerance phenomenon that the medication should be used for school only and not used weekends or during vacations.

The common side effects which these drugs produce include insomnia, anorexia with weight loss, gastrointestinal upset, crying, and headache. Most of their side effects diminish with continued medication. The most troublesome and most persistent of these are anorexia and insomnia. The insomnia can be combatted with Benadryl 50 mg at bedtime. Anorexia may persist for as long as a year or more but long-term stimulant medication has been found to have no deleterious effects on growth curves. As is true with all forms of treatment, the beneficial effects have to be balanced against the bad effects of treatment. We find, and most parents agree, that the benefits of drug treatment far outweigh the disadvantages.

TRANQUILIZERS

Those hyperactive children who do not respond to stimulant drugs should be tried on chlorpromazine or thioridizine, as many will have a good response to one or the other. The dosage of chlorpromazine and thioridizine is about .6 mg/lb per dose given twice to three times daily. Side effects are probably more common than with stimulant medication and include drowziness which usually abates after a few days, photo-sensitization of the skin and alterations in pigment metabolism. This latter complication appears to occur at much higher dosage levels than described here.

Neither the stimulants nor the tranquilizers mentioned above are addicting or habituating when properly prescribed for children. In over 2,000 hyperactive children reported in the literature, not one case of addiction has been reported. The same stimulants that produce a "high" in an adult do not have that effect in a hyperactive child.

In our experience, approximately one-third to one-half of hyperactive children can benefit from remedial education. Many of these children need educational therapy even after a good response to drugs. One of the reasons why many of these children require remedial education is the late age at which the disorder is first detected and proper treatment instituted. After a child has fallen behind two or more levels in one or more subjects, special education measures are needed and no amount of drug therapy can fulfill this need.

Parents can do much to help improve the hyperactive child by structuring the home environment, by developing realistic expectations of their hyperactive children and by finding activities at which they can succeed.

SUMMARY

The authors have described their experience in setting up an evaluation and treatment clinic for hyperactive children in a community mental health center. Recommendations are made for personnel, type of work-up, diagnosis, treatment and community educational programs to facilitate early case findings. Specific tools which we have used and found to be of value are described.

The vast majority of hyperactive children are neglected, undetected, and untreated. Since an effective therapy is available, there remains only one barrier to proper treatment—the development of programs. The availability of outpatient services for children with this disorder is an important function of a community mental health center children's program.

NOTES

1. Heinrich Hoffmann, "The Story of Fidgety Phil," *Struwwelpeter.*

2. M. A. Stewart, F. N. Pitts, A. G. Craig, and W. Dieruf, "The Hyperactive Child Syndrome," *American Journal of Orthopsychiatry,* 36(1966): 861–867; M. A. Stewart, "Hyperactive Children," *Scientific American,* April 1970; J. S. Werry, "Developmental Hyperactivity," *Pediatric Clinics of North America,* 15(August 1968): 581; R. S. Paine, "Syndromes of Minimal Cerebral Damage," *Pediatric Clinics of North America,* 15(August 1968): 779.

3. C. K. Connors, "The Syndrome of Minimal Brain Dysfunction: Psychological Aspects," *Pediatric Clinics of North America,* 14(November 1967): 749; Henry J. Mark, "Psychodiagnostics in Patients with Suspected Minimal Brain Dysfunction," Appendix B in *Minimal Brain Dysfunction in Children,* PHS Publication No. 2015, 1969; J. H. Satterfield, and Michael E. Dawson, "GSR Correlates of Minimal Brain Dysfunction," *Journal of Psychophysiology,* in press; J. S. Werry, G. Weiss, K. Minde, K. Dogan, A. Guzman, and E. Hoy, "Studies on the Hyperactive Child VII: Comparison of Neurological Findings between Hyperactive, Normal and Neurotic Children," presented to the Canadian Psychiatric Association, Toronto, June 1969.

4. M. M. Menkes, J. S. Rowe, and J. H. Menkes, "A Twenty-Five Year Follow-up Study on the Hyperkinetic Child with Minimal Brain Dysfunction," *Pediatrics,* 39(1967): 393–399; G. Weiss, K. Minde, J. S. Werry, V. Douglas, E. Nemeth, "The Hyperactive Child VIII: Five Year Follow-up," *Archives of General Psychiatry,* in press; E. M. Shelley, *Syndrome of Minimal Brain Damage in Young Adults,* presented at APA Annual Meeting, San Francisco, California, May 1970; N. W. Laufer, "Cerebral Dysfunction and Behavior Disorders of Adolescents," *American Journal of Orthopsychiatry,* 32(1962): 501; F. Quitken, and D. F. Klein, "Two Behavioral Syndromes in Young Adults Related to Possible Minimal Brain Dysfunction," *Journal of Psychiatric Research,* 7(1969): 131; D. P. Cantwell, *Hyperactive Children—Antisocial Adults?: A Study of One Hundred Brig Prisoners,* to be published; M. A. Stewart, N. Johnson, and W. Mendelson, *Hyperactive Children as Teenagers,* to be published; E. S. Greenberg, S. S. Bauman, E. B. Balka, and S. L. Werkman, *Brain Dysfunction in Adolescence—I Scope of the Research, II Life Styles, III Cognitive Functioning, IV Duplications of the Research,* presented at the annual meeting of the American Orthopsychiatric Association, San Francisco, California, March 1970.

5. J. R. Morrison, and M. A. Stewart, *A Study of Fifty Patients and Fifty Controls,* to be published; D. P. Cantwell, *Psychiatric Illness in the Families of Hyperactive Children: A Study of Fifty Patients and Fifty Controls,* to be published.

6. L. Eisenberg, "The Management of the Hyperkinetic Child," *Developmental Medicine and Child Neurology,* 8(1966): 593; J. G. Millichap, and G. W. Fowler, "Treatment of Minimal Brain Dysfunction Syndromes," *Pediatric Clinics of North America,* 14(1967): 767; J. G. Millichap, "Drugs in Management of Hyperkinetic and Perceptually Handicapped Children," *Journal of the American Medical Association,* 206(1968): 217; G. R. Patterson, et al., "A Behavior Modification Technique for the Hyperactive Child," *Behavior Research and Therapy,* 2(1965): 217.

7. C. K. Conners, and L. Eisenberg, "The Effects of Methylphenidate on Symptomatology and Learning in Disturbed Children," *American Journal of Psychiatry*, 120(1963): 1458; J. G. Millichap, et al., "Hyperkinetic Behavior and Learning Disorders III. Battery of Neuro-Psychological Tests in Controlled Trial of Methylphenidate," *American Journal of Diseases of Children*, 116(1968): 235; J. G. Millichap, "Studies in Hyperkinetic Behavior II. Lab and Clinical Evaluation of Drug Therapy," *Neurology*, 17(1967): 467.

8. L. Eisenberg, "The Management of the Hyperkinetic Child," *Developmental Medicine and Child Neurology*, 8(1966): 593; J. G. Millichap, and G. W. Fowler, "Treatment of Minimal Brain Dysfunction Syndromes," *Pediatric Clinics of North America*, 14(1967): 767; J. G. Millichap, "Drugs in Management of Hyperkinetic and Perceptually Handicapped Children," *Journal of the American Medical Association*, 206(1968): 1527; G. R. Patterson, et al., "A Behavior Modification Technique for the Hyperactive Child," *Behavior Research and Therapy*, 2(1965): 217; C. K. Conners, and L. Eisenberg, "The Effects of Methylphenidate on Symptomatology and Learning in Disturbed Children," *American Journal of Psychiatry*, 120(1963): 1458; J. G. Millichap, et al., "Hyperkinetic Behavior and Learning Disorders III. Battery of Neuro-Psychological Tests in Controlled Trial of Methylphenidate," *American Journal of Diseases of Children*, 116(1968): 235; J. G. Millichap, "Studies in Hyperkinetic Behavior II. Lab and Clinical Evaluation of Drug Therapy," *Neurology*, 17(1967): 467; W. G. Conrad, and J. Insel, "Anticipating the Response to Amphetamine Therapy in the Treatment of Hyperkinetic Children," *Pediatrics*, 40(July 1967): 96.

9. C. K. Conners, and L. Eisenberg, "The Effects of Methylphenidate on Symptomatology and Learning in Disturbed Children," *American Journal of Psychiatry*, 120(1963): 1458.

10. C. Bradley, "The Behavior of Children Receiving Benzadrine," *American Journal of Psychiatry*, 94(1937): 575–577.

11. J. H. Satterfield, and Michael E. Dawson, "GSR Correlates of Minimal Brain Dysfunction," *Journal of Psychophysiology*, in press.

12. J. H. Satterfield, unpublished results; H. R. Alderton, and B. A. Hoddenott, "A Controlled Study of the Use of Thioridizine in the Treatment of Hyperactive and Aggressive Children in a Children's Psychiatric Hospital," *Canadian Psychiatric Journal*, 9(1964): 239–247.

13. S. L. Garfield, M. M. Helper, R. C. Wilcott, and R. Muffly, "Effects of Chlorpromazine on Behavior in Emotionally Disturbed Children," *Journal of Nervous and Mental Disease*, 135(1962): 147–154; L. Eisenberg, A. Gilbert, L. Cytryn, and P. Molling, "The Effectiveness of Psychotherapy Alone and in Conjunction with Perphenazine or Placebo in Treatment of Neurotic and Hyperactive Children," *American Journal of Psychiatry*, 117(1961): 1088–1093.

14. J. H. Satterfield, unpublished results.

36

Sam D. Clements, PH.D., *and*
John E. Peters, M.D.

The Therapeutic Day School: A Service Strategy
of Partial Hospitalization for Children
with Learning and Behavioral Disabilities

The great majority of children and young adolescents who, together with their parents, come to the attention of mental health professionals seldom require services which cannot be administered by the ready availability of a variety of outpatient strategies and programs.

However, a small number of youngsters, frequently for the dual and simultaneous purpose of extensive diagnosis and concomitant treatment, are more conveniently served by programs of inpatient care and may require such intensive service until such time as nature and/or nurture has modified the entering condition.

There is yet another group of children, not so large as the former, and not so small as the latter, who derive maximum benefit from an intermediate type of mental health program. It is for this group that the therapeutic day school was designed and developed. The program is considered a component of the partial hospitalization category within the community mental health center array of services.

Priority placement in the therapeutic day school program is reserved for those children between the ages of five and fourteen years whose emotional, social, academic, developmental, and/or management problems are of a nature and degree that no existing school or mental health agency is able to provide the needed variety of services deemed necessary for adequate, consistent, and/or proper programs of intervention and amelioration.

A major objective of the therapeutic day school operation is to sustain an environment created to enhance the social, emotional, academic, and behavioral adjustment of the individual child. This personalized mental health programming is originally devised from the results of a comprehensive multidisciplinary diagnostic evaluation and is altered over time in harmony with the changing needs of the particular child and his family. It is a philosophy of the program that an essential element in the healthy growth or restoration of a child's self-concept is success in mastering the basic academic skills so much demanded by modern society.

Following an assessment of the cognitive, perceptual, motor, academic, and social skills of each child, a program of precision teaching is designed for him to be initiated at the level of his entering profile of functioning. His forward movement is calculated in small steps and adjusted to his emotional tolerance, span of attention, and activity level. Techniques for the reshaping of inefficient, self-defeating, and disruptive behavior are evolved for those youngsters whose adjustment requires such procedures.

The goal of the program is to return the child to the public school system in as short a time as possible with the ability to maintain himself independently and to compete successfully with his appropriate peer group, both socially and academically.

The therapeutic day school occupies the first floor of the three-story Child and Adolescent Unit of the Greater Little Rock Community Mental Health Center which is located on the campus of the University of Arkansas Medical Center. The companion Adult Unit building of the center is located on the adjacent campus of the Arkansas State Hospital. The combined services of the two units cover all categories of comprehensive community mental health care.

The school area consists of four individual units designed to accommodate ten students each. In addition to the classroom area, each self-contained unit includes a separate teacher's office, a restroom, and shares a supply and storage room with the adjacent unit. Each unit is bordered at the rear by an observation area which permits audio-visual surveillance of activity within the classroom. Entry into each observation room is by a separate main-corridor door so as to prevent interruption of the ongoing classroom situation by trainees and other observers. Adjacent to each classroom and accessible from it is a shielded outdoor patio area which is utilized for certain group recreational and educational activities. The offices of the Director of Educational Services for the center, the mental health nurse, teaching assistants, and mental health technician are located in the day school area, as is a large multipurpose auditorium which is used for indoor recreation, perceptual-motor training, physical education, and parent group meetings.

The furnishings and equipment for the four classroom units were selected to adapt to four general age groups of children: preschool and transitional; lower elementary; middle elementary; upper elementary and young adolescents.

In keeping with the concept of community involvement in mental health planning and care, an invitation was extended to and readily accepted by the Little Rock Public School System to collaborate in the development and operation of the therapeutic day school. A seven-member therapeutic day school planning committee consisting of representatives from the public school administration office and the Child and Adolescent Unit was formally constituted one year prior to the inauguration of the actual service. The major purpose of the committee was to establish guidelines for the various aspects of the therapeutic day school operation. Some of the specifics which evolved from the deliberations of this committee included: (1) selection criteria for student placement in the therapeutic day school program; (2) teacher qualifications and teacher selection criteria for the therapeutic day school; (3) systems for easy administrative transfer of the individual child from his present placement (public school, homebound, and so forth) to the therapeutic day school program and easy transfer, either transitional or complete, back into existing or future school programs; (4) methods of utilization of the therapeutic day school as a training and practicum placement site for teachers, counselors, school psychologists, speech therapists, reading specialists, special program supervisors, and administrators; (5) use of experimental educational curricula, methods, and materials; and (6) research programs in learning environments, personalized instruction, clas room management techniques, and use of nonprofessional mental health personnel.

The three major sources for referral of candidates for placement into the day school program are the diagnostic and treatment services of the Child and Adolescent Unit of the center, the public school systems, and the various mental health agencies which serve the catchment area. In the summer of 1969, all agencies were notified that referrals would be considered for placement in the program to begin in September. A priority list of children and young adolescents was accumulated by the day school staff and their records obtained from the referring agency. Prescreening of this list was accomplished by the staff, utilizing existing cumulative school folders, and reports from mental health agencies. Any records which indicated the need for additional investigation were categorized and processed for services to be delivered by the center.

A completed priority list of thirty-two youngsters was formed. Since each classroom unit in the day school area accommodated a maximum of ten children, a decision was made by the staff to limit the initial enrollment to these thirty-two children whose processing had been completed. In this way, two additional children could be added to each unit program over time. These two positions were held for emergency placements or for children in dire need of the service who were not yet known. All children referred for day school placement subsequent to the selection of the initial group were placed on a waiting list in priority order to enter when space was available.

During the first seven months of the program, forty children were admitted to the program. Over 80 percent of the children were males. Many had specific learning disabilities including reading disorders, hyperactivity, perceptual deficits, coordination deficits, language disorders, and central processing dysfunctions. Some children in the program, however, were diagnosed as having primary emotional problems.

The total staff of the therapeutic day school consists of fourteen people including special education teachers, teaching assistants, an education specialist, a social worker, a nurse, a language specialist, and a behavior modification specialist. One teacher and one teaching assistant are assigned to each classroom.

In addition to the regular behavior management and academic programs which serve all children assigned to the therapeutic day school, the following complementary services are utilized.

The academic program for each child is based on individual needs as derived from extensive psycho-educational assessment. The objective of this service is to enable the child to succeed in mastering basic and related academic skills commensurate with his appropriate grade placement for age group and intellectual functioning level. The major portion of the instructional program is administered in the classroom by the teacher and teaching assistant. Supplementary one-to-one precision teaching, when necessary, is done by the educational specialist.

When indicated, and as part of his regular program, a child may be seen for one or more hours per week in individual psychotherapy by a member of the Child and Adolescent Unit staff.

Each child in the therapeutic day school is assigned to an appropriate play group which meets one hour per week. Play group therapy is designed to increase the individual and group social skills and personal relationship capacities of the children through the use of semistructured small and large group activities. This program is under the direction of the behavior modification specialist.

Children with severe receptive, integrative, and/or expressive language disorders are seen individually or in small groups for specialized training in half-hour sessions three times per week by the language specialist.

An adjunctive program of chemotherapy is administered to certain children under the supervision of the nurse. This involves a close working relationship between the nurse and the parents of the children receiving this service.

Evening conference visits to the homes of families who have children attending the day school are paid by the social worker sometimes accompanied by the mental health nurse. These are often for the convenience of those families where both parents work during the day. Frequently, the major purpose is to observe total family interaction in the home setting as an aid in helping the parents with home management of the child.

Evening meetings are scheduled at nine-week intervals for all parents of children attending the day school together with all members of the day school staff. Parents visit the classroom of their child, talk with the teacher and teaching assistant, are shown samples of the child's daily work, and discuss any problems relative to the classroom program. All parents and staff then assemble in the auditorium for refreshments and an informal program consisting of special announcements relative to the day school, question and answer period, and the discussion of a pertinent topic by a staff member.

Weekly evening sessions of parent group therapy are offered to all parents of day school children. This program is under the direction of the social worker and the behavior modification specialist.

SUMMARY

The service, training, and research potentials of a therapeutic day school as a day-care strategy for disturbed children and young adolescents are limitless. The association of this program with a total community mental health center network strengthens opportunities for referral, continuity of care, and followup.

REFERENCES

Allen, B. H. "Dedication Of The Center for Developmental and Learning Disorders, Birmingham, Alabama." *Alabama Journal of Medical Science* 6(October 1969): 370–373.
Belmont, H. S. "Community Mental Health and Dynamic Child Psychiatry." *Pennsylvania Medicine* 71(March 1968): 53–56.
D'Amato, G. "Metamorphosis In A Children's Residential Treatment Center." *Psychiatry* 30(November 1967): 317–331.

Kessell A., Ridley, B., and Stamp, I. M. "A Seminar On Child Care As A Facet of Community Psychiatry." *Medical Journal of Australia* 2(December 1967): 1051–1054.

Kirman, B. H. "Advisory Service For Parents of Mentally Handicapped Children." *British Medical Journal* 5478(January 1966): 41–44.

Meyer, R. J., and Harvey, A. M. "Community Planning for Children with Developmental and Learning Disorders." *Journal of School Health* 38(April 1968): 246–247.

North, E. F. "Day Care Treatment of Psychotic Children." *Current Psychiatric Therapy* 7(1967): 32–35.

Rosenblum, G. "A Community Mental Health Center's Interaction With the Project Head Start Program." *Journal of American Academic Child Psychiatry* 6(July 1967): 410–414.

Shodell, J. J. "A Day Center for Severely Disturbed Children." *Journal of Rehabilitation* 33(July-August 1967): 22–25.

Tribbey, J. A., Louargand, E. M., and Allen A. "Sacramento's Day-Treatment Center for Autistic Children." *California Medicine* 108(March 1968): 201–204.

Weiland, I. H., and Berman, L. "The Child Guidance Clinic and the Mental Health Center." *Journal of American Academic Child Psychiatry* 8(April 1969): 290–305.

XI
Innovative
Approaches to the
Manpower
Problem

EDITORS' INTRODUCTION

Traditional mental health services have relied on four professional disciplines, namely, psychiatry, psychology, social work, and nursing, while the only nonprofessionals involved have been ward aides or attendants in hospitals. An additional problem in the past has been that professional groups have often operated in considerable isolation from each other. Thus, it has been difficult to integrate the work and approaches of different disciplines.

Some improvement in regard to this problem began to be seen even prior to the development of the community mental health center program through an emphasis on treatment teams whose members were drawn from all disciplines with the focus on coordinated patient care. The community mental health center has typically relied heavily on the use of interdisciplinary teams, and moreover, many centers have found it possible to extend the team concept into new areas. Thus, centers have been able to use teams in outpatient services as well as in the inpatient settings in which they originated.

Many community mental health centers have also extended the treatment team by adding a variety of new personnel. Many of these personnel are drawn from the ranks of nonprofessionals. The nonprofessionals are known by a variety of designations, including paraprofessionals, indigenous personnel, and simply as mental health workers.

The community mental health center has relied heavily on nonprofessionals, as well as professionals, for several reasons. One of these is the heavy service demand made upon the center by the residents of the catchment area. It has been necessary for centers to use available manpower in a way that makes it possible to meet large and growing demands for services of all kinds. Professionals to meet these demands have simply not been available and, as a result, it has been necessary for the centers to turn to nonprofessionals who could be trained within the setting of the center itself. In addition to extending the manpower capabilities of the center, the nonprofessionals provide the community mental health center with a route into the community and a means of establishing better and more solid communications between the center and the community it serves.

It should also be noted that the community mental health center has typically relied on volunteers as well as on paid staff. The volunteers again serve the center in more than one way. In part, they serve the function of providing additional needed manpower, but since they are also frequently drawn from the ranks of the financially well established of the community, they can provide a resource for financial support and community sanction.

Finally, it must be pointed out that the involvement of nonprofessional workers has presented problems for some of the centers. Moreover, the involvement of the nonprofessional staff members has also presented problems for some of the communities being served. Nonprofessionals frequently live in the catchment area while professional staff members more frequently live outside the catchment area. As a result, there have often been conflicts between the nonprofessional and professional members of the staff in regard to the assessments of community needs and service priorities. Moreover, even when professional and nonprofessional members of the staff live within the same community, they often represent different economic strata and consequently they may perceive the problems and needs of the community from different vantage points. Finally, it must be pointed out that, at least in some centers, the employment of nonprofessional staff members has served as a focus for conflict in regard to control of the center and its programs. This conflict over control is in part an outgrowth of the several dichotomies listed above, but is also a natural consequence of the movement of the community mental health center toward the community.

37

Donald R. Daggett, M.D.,
Loran E. Pilling, M.D.,
Mary Jones, R.N., M.S., *and*
Norman Segal, M.S.W.

Private Psychiatrists as Staff Team Leaders

St. Barnabas Hospital and Swedish Hospital are private general hospitals in Minneapolis which had been located adjacent to one another for many years and consolidated in October 1970, to become The Metropolitan Medical Center. Although neither hospital had contained a psychiatric unit as a part of its operating facilities, both hospitals had been attended by consulting psychiatrists. As hospitals with modern, progressive-minded leadership, they had long been aware of the need to provide psychiatric facilities to those patients requiring such care who came to the hospitals on referral by their family doctors. When a psychiatrist was called for consultation and recommended inpatient hospital care on a psychiatric unit, it was necessary to transfer the patient to another hospital which often interfered with continued participation in the care of the patient by the family doctor.

Late in 1964, it was discovered that each hospital was planning for the construction of a psychiatric unit within its separate structure. Since the hospitals had already been cooperating in many ways, the idea of a joint psychiatric facility was considered and discussed with appropriate funding authorities. After considerable review and planning, a National Institute of Mental Health construction grant was awarded. Ground was broken July 10, 1966, for the new construction containing the Metropolitan Community Mental Health Center along with other facilities which physically joined the two parent hospitals.

The Hennepin County Mental Health Board and the pre-existing Hennepin County General Hospital Community Mental Health Center entered into an agreement with the Metropolitan Community Mental

Health Center whereby the two centers would provide complementary mental health services to the community. Priorities for treatment at the Metropolitan Community Mental Health Center were established recognizing: (1) the relationship of the center to its catchment area; (2) the need to provide services and treatment for the intramural psychiatric problems occurring with patients already being treated at either of the two general hospital facilities; and (3) the need for service to the patients of physicians who had established practices at the hospital over a period of many years. The latter was important to encourage the family physician to participate in the patient's treatment to facilitate continuity of care when the patient is ready to return to his family and the community.

The first patients were admitted into the inpatient service of the newly organized Metropolitan Community Mental Health Center on November 11, 1968. A short time later, on December 16, the day care program became operational. The outpatient service and the service of consultation and education to the community began in June of 1969, and soon thereafter, a night care service was also initiated. The admissions to the inpatient service represented the culmination of years of planning and effort on the part of St. Barnabas and Swedish Hospitals to include an inpatient psychiatric facility as an integral part of the two hospitals already having a total number of beds in excess of 700 and now raising that number to 903 in the new hospital complex.

In this private-public interface system, it is possible to retain the following advantages of the private practice model: (1) the individual contract between the patient and his physician has remained a basic requirement and usually allows for ready and easy delineation of responsibility for care; (2) the patient understands who is taking care of him and from whom to seek advice, information, or counsel; and (3) the patient is traditionally free to choose and change his physician.

Several psychiatrists fill salaried positions on a part-time basis in the Mental Health Center while retaining their private practices on a more limited scale. The part-time salaried positions include the medical director, the clinical program director, and any psychiatrist on the staff when he appropriately assumes responsibility for organizing, supervising, or directing professional activities (teaching, in-service training programs, supervision of patient care by other professionals, research, and so forth) necessary to implement the program of the mental health center.

At the outset, the essential services of the mental health center were organized in such a way that each service was a separate, discrete entity. Gradually, we became aware of barriers to effective treatment and continuity of care. The most serious barriers encountered were communication problems between various staff members, staff rivalries between services, and the practice of labeling patients as "good" or "bad" based on such criteria as their service status (inpatient, outpatient, day care, or night care) and their verbal skills to participate in group therapy. To overcome these barriers, the clinical program was redesigned to integrate all services. This integration was accomplished by ignoring the classification of patients as inpatient, outpatient, day care, or night care. Instead, the clinical program was prescribed for them in accordance with their individual therapy needs resulting in a mixture of inpatients, outpatients, day care patients, and night care patients sharing the same setting, groups, and therapists. Following this change and a period of adjustment, improvement in staff morale occurred and an awareness of the comprehensive structure of a community mental health center and the holistic approach to patient treatment developed.

The various professionals responsible for the program design of the Metropolitan Community Mental Health Center had wide experience working in other mental health delivery systems, both private and public. The psychiatrists and their associates were familiar with and had worked in private practice psychiatric facilities in all of the hospitals in Minneapolis, St. Paul, and Rochester, Minnesota. The most familiar pattern of practice was for the psychiatrist to divide his time between treating patients in the hospital and in his office. Hospital visits and rounds were generally made three to six mornings per week, and it was customary for the psychiatrist to see the patient without a nurse or other staff member present. Varying philosophies and treatment modalities were prescribed and used by the psychiatrist with the hospital staff carrying out written orders for medications, physical treatments, and occupational and recreational therapy, and so forth. Communication between the psychiatrist and the hospital staff was always a problem because time rarely allowed for the psychiatrist to meet with the staff after he had completed his rounds, answered consultations, and prepared to leave for his office appointments. Written orders and instructions on the chart seldom gave the hospital staff enough information to realize and exercise the full potential of their therapeutic skills in working with the patient. Thus, it was generally agreed by the psychiatrists designing the program at the Metropolitan Community Mental Health Center that lack of communication was a barrier to the most efficient use of the hospital staff and to the growth, development, and increased morale of that staff.

From the beginning, the need to integrate and coordinate individual models or styles of treatment into a multifunctional approach was recognized. It was agreed that no single or particular philosophy or "school of treatment" would be encouraged or allowed to predominate. All ethical treatment modalities could be employed as long as the psychiatrist prescribing and directing treatment was willing and able to communicate freely with the staff about his plan for his patients and their progress in treatment.

The Minneapolis Clinic of Psychiatry and Neurology [*] utilizes the team concept employing coordinated treatment by psychiatrists, psychologists, social workers, and nurses and had found it to be successful over a period of several years. The professionals who were originally involved in the planning of the mental health center, including the director of professional services, were members of the staff of the Minneapolis Clinic of Psychiatry and Neurology. It was apparent that the private practice community was ready to accept treatment by the various professionals of the team when such treatment was directed and coordinated by a team psychiatrist. It was decided that the team approach would be used at the Metropolitan Community Mental Health Center.

A number of goals were established before planning and designing the staffing and program of the mental health center:

1. Through the involvement of private practice psychiatrists in a community mental health center, we would attempt to reduce the manpower shortage in psychiatry.

2. A dynamic therapy program would be designed using the incentives, skills, and resources of private-practice professionals. This program would be made available to private and public patients alike. Although the professionals had experience in working with patients in a variety of public practice settings, this mental health center would provide an opportunity for the "public-private interface" to occur simultaneously in the same setting and using the same professionals.

3. Private practice would become directly involved in the community, giving and gaining from the experience.

4. Preventive mental health needs would be identified and serviced.

5. Increased services to all patients in the community would be provided.

[*] The Minneapolis Clinic is a private practice specialty clinic with professionals in psychiatry and neurology working in all of the private practice hospitals in metropolitan Minneapolis.

310

Many problems were anticipated in designing such a program. The tendency to retain old models of treatment with which we were most comfortable had to be avoided. Flexibility was stressed. The need for change was recognized and considered whenever problems became apparent in our program and not ignored because of individual preferences or vested interests. One goal was to avoid splitting the staff into destructive, rivalrous teams as had been seen in other programs where the distinctions drawn between administration, inpatient services, outpatient services, and so forth, encouraged discrete empires to flourish and often led to alien goals, philosophies, and artificial barriers to treatment. Also clear was the need to establish continuity of care through preservation of key therapeutic relationships from one period of treatment to another. The staff also wanted to avoid the tendency to solve the problem of continuity of care through artificial means such as the use of the chart which followed the patient through differing treatment experiences with changing staff, implying that continuity of care was provided by the chart rather than by the relationship between the staff and the patient. Another potential problem was the fact that if the center succeeded, the demands made upon it would steadily increase, and as a result there would be a need to broaden the availability of mental health professionals, so as to provide better care to larger numbers of people in the community.

The multidisciplinary team, directed by the psychiatrist and employing group process, was identified as the system which would be used to attempt to avoid the problems of the past and meet the demands of the developing program of the community mental health center. A way had thus been found to effectively expand the therapeutic effort beyond the psychiatrist-patient relationship in a sensitive, responsive, and responsible fashion. Communication barriers would be reduced to those necessary to protect patient privilege as determined by the psychiatrist. The full impact of the patient's environment could be better understood, interpreted, and utilized in treatment. All mental health center workers, professional and nonprofessional, could now be used according to their ability, in the treatment of patients.

Each psychiatrist directs a team composed of a team leader (R.N.), a coteam leader (R.N., L.P.N., or psychiatric assistant), and a member of the evening duty staff (R.N., L.P.N., or psychiatric assistant). These team members have a relationship with every patient of that psychiatrist and have responsibility for carrying out his treatment plan. The psychiatrist determines what responsibilities each team member will assume

311

and depends upon them to coordinate each patient's care with other parts of the program. The number of patients each team serves varies widely from time to time. The members of this team meet regularly and frequently.

The Clinical Group Therapy Program, under which all the teams function and within which the patients are treated, is an intensive group program which attempts to use all of the group therapies that have proven to be helpful to patients with emotional problems. The group therapy staff is made up of registered nurses, L.P.N.s, and psychiatric aides with various practical or college experience who work directly with the patients under the consultative eye of social workers, psychologists, and psychiatrists who have group skills. These consultants, as well as providing direct consultation to the therapists working in the groups, have also undertaken the task of training the staff of the mental health center in a twelve-week long, four-hour-a-week psychiatric course which deals with all aspects of psychiatry but with special emphasis on the group process.

In addition, the psychiatrist meets on a regular basis (usually two times a week) with all therapists who work with his patients throughout the entire clinical program. The purposes of these meetings are: (1) effective program planning for the new patient; (2) review of each patient's progress; and (3) assurance that consistent goals are being pursued for each patient.

At present, there are eight teams, each headed by a private psychiatrist. Because all of the members of the team function as a coordinated unit, the patient sees each member of the team as important in his care and as an extension of the psychiatrist. This allows professionals, other than the psychiatrist, such as the registered nurse, to be more directly involved in the patient's therapy, including dealing with matters which in most settings are the exclusive domain of the psychiatrist. This approach thus gives the patient a team of therapists who, through their coordinated efforts, can help the patient deal with the emotional conflicts that led to his admission to the center. Within the clinical program each team functions as an independent unit, using the differing patterns, methods, and techniques of each psychiatrist. The psychiatrist must be willing to function within the group model, but he is in no way restricted in regard to the use of individual treatment modalities, such as electro-shock therapy, drug therapy, individual psychotherapy, or physical treatments of various kinds.

The total clinical program of the mental health center, however, emphasizes the use of group therapy approaches. All members of the staff are involved in the operation of the several types of groups, and all patients participate in a number of different group experiences. The groups are organized so that both inpatients and daypatients can participate in them. Each psychiatrist, together with the members of his staff team, leads a doctor's group, which is attended by all his patients. In addition, the other staff members lead psychotherapy groups, activity groups, special problem groups, and an orientation group for new patients. Every patient participates in his doctor's group, and participation in each of the other groups is determined by the psychiatrist in consultation with the members of his team, other staff members, and the patient himself. The roles played by the psychiatrist and the other members of the staff are perhaps best described through descriptions of the various groups.

The Doctor's Group   Each doctor's group is composed of the psychiatrist, his patients, team leader, and co-leader. The group meets three times a week for one to one-and-a-half hours. These meetings are followed by a postgroup session, attended by the team members after the patients have departed. The functional therapists may be any members of the team, and frequently the psychiatrist is not acting as therapist even when he is present. This group is the most heterogeneous of any of the formal groups. There is wide variation in the number of patients (usually eight to fifteen), age range, past treatment experience and general life experience. Many of the psychiatrists emphasize the importance of this heterogeneity and see their group as a microcosm of society. The majority of the patients in the doctor's groups are inpatients; however, some outpatients, depending upon their needs, are included. The psychiatrists work in these groups in a variety of ways, some emphasizing the group as a diagnostic tool, others using it as a treatment modality. In fact, some psychiatrists use these groups as their major treatment modality. The attendance of the psychiatrist at the group meeting depends upon the purpose for which he uses the group. Some of the psychiatrists attend on a regular basis at both the group and postgroup meetings. Other psychiatrists attend the group less frequently but attend the postgroup meeting on a regular basis.

Each doctor's group includes all the patients of one psychiatrist. All the other groups are composed of a mix of patients (inpatients, outpatients, day care, and so forth) of all the psychiatrists. The therapy staff for each of these other groups consists of two staff members, one of each sex, who work together as a team continuously. Each team works with a

313

consultant who has special group skills (psychiatric social worker, psychologist, chaplain). The amount of time set aside for consultation is approximately one hour per week for each group served by the team.

Psychotherapy Groups   These groups are composed of ten to twelve patients with two members of the therapy staff as co-leaders. They meet daily Monday through Friday for ninety-minute sessions. The determining criteria for placement are the needs of the individual patient and the group. There is no attempt made to have a completely homogeneous group in terms of specific problems. It is the general feeling that patients benefit from participation and exposure to group members with different problems and varying degrees of ability in verbal skills. Because the average length of hospital stay is approximately three weeks, these short-term groups tend to be crisis-oriented. At the end of his stay he may hopefully transfer new skills to the outside social groups to which he belongs. Inpatients and outpatients are broadly mixed in these group psychotherapy sessions. At present, there are seven such groups available, but the number can grow as more are needed.

Speciality Groups   Specialty groups are designed for patients with common psychosocial problems. These groups meet once or twice a week in hourly sessions, and they consist of eight to ten patients and two therapists. These are structured groups with specific goals associated with marital status, job, age, sex, and so forth. For example, there are specialty groups for single young adults, single older adults, parents, married couples, and so forth.

Activity Groups   Activity groups are designed for patients with common activity interests. These groups meet once or twice weekly in hourly sessions, and they consist of eight to ten patients and two therapists. These are structured groups designed to help patients develop better social relationships and achieve recognition for their accomplishments. These activity groups also provide another way in which staff can evaluate patients' strengths and provide new ways of expression for patients (other than verbal). For example, these are groups focused on music, dancing, art, grooming, nature, and outdoor activities.

Psychodrama Groups   Psychodrama is intended to help bring about expression through drama—to help "unfreeze" inhibitions of traditional patterns of relating by role-playing. Three psychodrama groups occur simultaneously so that all patients may attend and participate according to their comfort. Psychodrama groups vary in size from twelve to twenty patients, four therapists, and as many as three staff members in training.

Orientation Group   Generally all new patients participate in this group for a period of three to five days. Therapists for this group consist of a psychiatric social worker, a chaplain, and two nurse team leaders. One or more of these groups meet simultaneously for an hour each day, Monday through Friday. This group prepares patients for their participation in regular group therapies. This group also serves to help in the selection of appropriate groups for each patient.

Family Day The group processes are carried beyond the patient population to include significant people in the patient's life. Friday afternoon is set aside as family day when each patient brings one or more friends or relatives who are included in the group program. By including the "significant other" person on Friday afternoon, as well as in the evening group therapy program Monday through Thursday, the patient is able to begin to work through feelings and conflicts with people in his life. Through this involvement, the "significant other" person is better able to understand the patient, himself, and the affect their relationship has on the total problem. In this way we feel that we are not only bringing the patient with emotional problems closer to the community in which he lives, but we are also bringing the community closer to the patient. In addition, the patient and the community are brought closer together in another way. We have chosen to treat both inpatients and outpatients simultaneously in the same therapy program. This approach has solved many problems and contributed to the flexibility and effectiveness of our program. We believe that barriers between the community and the mentally ill have been removed by involving inpatients, outpatients, and nonpatient members of the community in the same group therapy program. We consider it a most important advantage of our program that the patient is able to return to live in the community as he improves and may continue in therapy as an outpatient with the same staff who worked closely with him as an inpatient. During the therapy process the staff draws upon community resources such as: vocational rehabilitation agencies, family and children services, churches, various public agencies, and so forth, so that they become integral parts of the patient's on-going treatment. This establishes continuity of care reducing the incidence of patient relapse and rehospitalization.

The emphasis on these groups and the reliance on staff teams are key elements in the operation of the community mental health center. Together these two features make it possible for the center to receive its medical direction from a cadre of private psychiatrists who function as only part-time members of the center staff.

Because group dynamics are always operating, our philosophy is not to question whether or not we have "group therapy" but rather how do we harness group dynamics to create the most effective therapeutic community for both staff and patients. In fact, a good deal of our success to this point is due to the ability of our staff to be flexible, open, and warm so as to create a therapeutic environment.

In our center, we are continuing to develop new means of facilitating communication, encouraging leadership, and improving decision-making procedures. We adhere to the basic premise that no person, community, or structure is static. In a therapeutic community the potential for constant change is essential. Therefore, it is necessary to relate to and understand group principles as well as to discover new principles and add to existing knowledge.

---

38   *Elmer R. Kramer*

The Volunteer vs. the Professional in a Resocialization Approach

There is considerable consensus that psychiatric disability is primarily an incapacity or failure at the interpersonal or social level of human functioning. The depressed housewife, the alienated adolescent, the deviant, and others with various neurotic and psychotic disorders often have an identifiable common denominator—social isolation. The jargon of mental health is replete with the concepts of relearning, rehabilitation, and resocialization as treatment modalities. Perhaps more relevant to the community mental health center are the processes of initial learning, that is, habilitation and socialization because the "proof of the pudding" of the effectiveness of psychiatric intervention lies in the eventual community performance and tenure of the mental health center client. Thus, "real" social learning may prove to be more "durable" when it is the result of a real people-to-real people relationship rather than that of the client-therapist relationship; in essence, the trained community volunteer.

The Community Institute utilizes the trained community volunteer in various areas, but four programs are unique in their methods to achieve —not *re*socialization—but socialization or initial social learning. These programs are yoga, music therapy, drug abuse, and partial care.

YOGA

Our yoga exercise program is staffed by a former patient, now a volunteer. The uniqueness of the program is interdependent with this unique individual who can present yoga as a philosophy and activity that everyone can accept. As she has stated, "It doesn't clash with religion or other philosophies of life."

Yoga is individual. The conscious relaxation, the repetitious breathing count, the concentration of separating each note from accompanying music, and, the chinning of an imaginary bar while holding the breath, all have the effect of "the naturalness of working off tensions." There is no confrontation or hostile response.

A group cohesiveness appears to form without verbal communication. Socialization is facilitated not only through joint exercises, but also through the wearing of leotards. Relaxation in leotards is achieved when there is the realization that "not everyone has a good figure." Group members feel more free, feel flattered, and "feel good about themselves when they stand straight." The volunteer leader expresses this in terms of self-image, "They look in the mirror and stand tall." What better self-image can one achieve in terms of positive reinforcement?

MUSIC THERAPY

The music therapy program has many of the same goals as that of yoga. Staffed by a professional musician as the volunteer group leader, the music therapy group achieves "honest communication through music." It facilitates a group relationship above problems and individual personalities. The volunteer leader recalls that when she first entered the group she anticipated that group members would relate only to her music abilities. After a short time in the group she states, "I realized that I was here to do my human thing," that is, establish sincere human relationships—for some, close socialization for the first time.

Subsequently, music means communication; provides a "common ground"; and, rhythmically, vocally, or in silence, the volunteer professional musician can tailor the music to the composition and mood of the group.

DRUG ABUSE

Our youth drug abuse program began with the request of two former patients and drug users for the use of a desk and a telephone a few hours a day. Within a few months, a fullfledged youth addiction program had blossomed.

As in the yoga and music programs, the vital catalyst and mover of the program are the volunteers—most of whom are past drug users—with two principal goals: to kick the habit and to prevent drug abuse. These youth volunteers have been able to establish a "grapevine" confidence not only with other drug users, but with other community groups, parents, and citizens.

The program operates on the basis of creating a "friendly" atmosphere rather than an "observing" one. The more experienced volunteers are assigned three or four "patients" with whom they become friends. Some of their simple rules for breaking the habit are: (1) environmental change, that is, "move out of the old clique"; (2) "become an active volunteer rather than a passive drug abuser"; and (3) after-hours' socialization of having fun without getting "stoned."

Thus, initial socialization is again achieved through what the youth coordinator of the program calls "normal functions" such as motorcycle riding, shows, and so forth. In his words, "Normal functions and learning to enjoy them are quite a trip for us."

At present, the youth addiction program has eleven active committees. These are: emergency telephone; case workers; speakers; speaking committee; secretarial duties; telephone; employment; transportation; fund raising; slush fund; and, an advisory council committee.

The enthusiasm, dedication, and innovation shown by these youth are something to behold. Their ability to serve as "consultants" to the professional staff has been exceptional. Many drug abuse grants, professional steering committees, and even modern clinical approaches to drug abuse appear wasted when compared to these youths in operation.

PARTIAL CARE

The concept of partial care in itself is not new; however, its implementation can be broadly unique. An example is the philosophy of volunteer utilization within the program. This means an acceptance by the professional adjunctive therapist that it is easier for patients to work with, and relate to, volunteers. Volunteers appear to be able to keep the group in a better social context. Also, there is a consensus that the participating volunteer can more accurately assess the group member's interests and needs than the professional. This is accomplished by the volunteer's attention to the individual through home visitations in time of crises; contact when the group member misses a session; or, simply being able to work individually with the group member as a "real" person.

In one recreational group, for example, two volunteer therapists are used to "counterbalance" each other, based upon their unique personalities. One is the "lady" in the group while the other serves as the "clown." The negative feelings and impulsive emotions are taken out on the "clown," while the "lady" establishes more sincere relationships and often serves as the mother figure who gives approval when necessary.

Thus, partial care embodies a variety of activities, but the common denominator remains one of learning to establish initial human relationships and socialization.

TRAINING THE VOLUNTEER

All volunteers are chosen through routine procedures, that is, by written application, interview, and skills and interests; however, two principal criteria are emphasized in their training: (1) maintaining the unique laity of the volunteer, and (2) training in communicative listening in a group setting.

The primary objective in the training of volunteers *is not* to overtrain them. The laity of the volunteer is unique and this uniqueness must be maintained in the interpersonal and socialization process. Subsequently, our volunteers are minimally trained in order to maintain the lay relationship with the client. Within this premise is the assumption that volunteers bring their own life experiences to the interpersonal relationship with the client. We do not seek to professionalize these experiences. As a result, the bulk of the volunteer's training is on-the-job training, under supervision, with concomitant formal training in communication.

The communications training is accomplished within a group setting composed of volunteers with an experienced group professional conducting the group. The number of group sessions is usually six to eight on a weekly basis. Training basically consists of "communicative listening," that is, the perception of communication in terms of how the client communicates meaning rather than interpretations based on the listener's

319

values and judgments. This is achieved through both interaction and confrontation within the group and through role playing. In summary, the group training strengthens the volunteer's sensitivity to underlying meanings rather than perceiving only surface verbalization.

SUMMARY

In preparing this article, six volunteer group leaders presented some of their impressions of various critical factors in the use of volunteers in any resocialization type program. The factor discussed most spontaneously by all six group leaders was that of the volunteer versus the professional.

The argument from the volunteer is that the professional is not "real," principally because he is paid. All six volunteers referred to this as "the natural barrier of the professional." Thus, by using volunteers, particularly in the resocialization process, there is an accomplished universality which comes from taking away the professional barrier. The volunteer feels that the professional barrier is one of confrontation; or, that the patient senses an "analyzing" approach which is not conducive to the establishment of those relationships required in the socialization process.

This, however, does not downgrade the importance of the professional because the volunteers emphasize both the importance of training by the professional as well as the consultation role and clinical understanding which the clinician provides.

Thus, the resocialization process in our program is not one of re- *per se*, but more so a program of initial learning, socialization, or habilitation. In this process, then, both the volunteer and the professional need to take a social stance which is "down-to-earth" in order for real socialization to take place, and the trained volunteer appears to work the best.

---

39   *George A. Lopes*

Development and Delivery of Mental Health Services to Seven Rural Counties in North Dakota

In 1969, North Dakota had the distinction of receiving the American Psychiatric Association's Gold Award for exceptional progress in the expansion of its community-based services and state hospital program.

From one state hospital and one state psychiatric clinic in 1965, mental health services have improved so that more than three-fourths of North Dakota's population is within an hour's drive of one of five mental health centers. There are now five well-established and securely financed mental health centers, with plans for three more, serving sparsely populated rural regions. The success of the program can be attributed to good leadership and good planning, but especially through participation of hundreds of individuals in each of the eight mental health regions and the involvement of community volunteers in planning, programming, and delivery of services.

The North Central Mental Health and Retardation Center, probably the most rural mental health center in the most rural state of the nation, is an accomplishment of many concerned community members from seven rural counties. Businessmen, professionals, farmers, housewives, and students worked sometimes cooperatively, sometimes individually, and perhaps sometimes selfishly, to provide mental health programs to a region where there was only one private psychiatrist to serve a catchment area of approximately 150,000, and where the nearest state assistance could mean more than 300 miles of travel. This is a region where people live mostly on farms and usually commute to towns, whose populations are between 50 and 1,000, for their immediate needs.

To best understand how and why the North Central Mental Health and Retardation Center developed the services as it did, it would help to know something about the state of North Dakota, its people, and how its problems are unique as compared to the other states of the union. The following excerpt from a study of the Great Plains environment, contributes to an understanding of the needs of North Dakotans: [1]

North Dakota is a comparatively young state. The Northern Great Plains was one of the last portions of the 48 contiguous states to be settled. Some of the original pioneers are still living and most of the population is only one or two generations removed from the original settlers. The close of the settlement period for North Dakota is generally considered to have occurred about 1915.

Since the close of the settlement period, North Dakota's population has changed very little from one census period to another. Since 1930, the trend has been slightly downward, from 681,000 in 1930 to 642,000 in 1940, to 632,000 in 1960. While the state was experiencing a net decrease of 7.1 percent between 1930 and 1960, the total United States population increased 35.7 percent. North Dakota is the only one of the 50 states that had a smaller population in 1960 than in 1920.

American Indians comprise the only sizeable racial minority in North Dakota. The proportion of Indians among the total population accounted for less than 2 percent of the total population in 1960. About 85 percent of the Indians are concentrated in nine counties in which the four Indian reservations are located.

North Dakota has a larger population of its work force employed in agriculture than any other state. In 1960, 32.8 percent of the employed persons were engaged in agriculture, compared with 6.6 percent for the nation as a whole. Only 4.7 percent of those employed are in basic industries, compared with the national average of 28.3 percent. A very large part of the economic activity in North Dakota consists of providing goods and services to farmers, and especially those items used in the farm-production process.

Mechanization has enabled farmers to operate larger acreage, and to reduce the amount of labor they need. The average size increased from 462 acres in 1935 to 975 acres in 1964.

North Dakota's per capita income has been below the national average because farm incomes have been low compared to nonfarm incomes. Moreover, there has been a lack of industrial job opportunities in North Dakota, and the chronic surplus of unskilled and semiskilled labor has had a depressing effect on wage rates.

Villages and small cities comprise an important part of the agricultural economy of North Dakota. These 'farm towns' are where farmers market most of their production and buy the commodities needed for household consumption and machinery, and services used in farm production. Also, farmers are turning more and more to these towns for social, recreational, educational, and religious services for their families.

Everything said above for all of North Dakota is basically true for each region of the state, although population and industry does decrease from the eastern border to the western border of the state.

Minot, a city of 35,000, is in approximately the center of the north central region which is one of eight mental health regions in the state. Minot is the largest center of culture, industry, or trade between the Red River Valley and central Montana and is 225 miles west of Grand Forks, on the Red River, with a population of about 34,000; 115 miles directly north of Bismarck, the capital, whose population is about 37,-000; and about 260 miles northwest of Fargo, a city of 46,000. In between these four cities are many small farm towns and villages.

The official region served by the Minot Center consists of seven counties, Burke, Bottineau, McHenry, Mountrail, Pierce, Renville, and Ward. Minot is located in Ward County. Ward's population is approximately 45,000. The county with the next largest population is Bottineau, with 11,315, and Renville has the smallest population, with 4,698.

A further impression of the sparsity of the population and the distances that have to be traveled by individuals to and from Minot can be obtained by a comparison of the county seat populations and distances from Minot. The city of Bottineau, 2,600, is eighty miles northeast of Minot; Bowbells, in Burke County, 687, is seventy miles northwest; Towner, in McHenry County, 948, is forty-seven miles east; Stanley, in Mountrail County, 1,795, is fifty-nine miles west; Rugby, in Pierce County, 2,972 (the second largest city in the region), is sixty-seven miles east. The total catchment area population is approximately 120,000.

PLANNING FOR THE CENTER

At the time of preliminary discussions in 1965 concerning the area's mental health problems, there was one private psychiatrist in Minot to serve the entire region, and the state hospital in Jamestown, located 180 miles from Minot, was the only public facility available. There was no other psychiatrist or psychiatric facility in the entire northern region of North Dakota, with the exception of Grand Forks on the eastern border.

The problem was then how to provide mental health services to a sparse population spread over a very large area. The decision was made to rely heavily on volunteers and community participation.

The first use of volunteers for the North Central Mental Health and Retardation Center was in the planning stage.

Members of this region are traditionally interested in local problems, and have always solved them through co-ops, township meetings, boards, clubs, and other cooperative efforts. Because communities are small, almost anyone who wants to participate can. Residents live in an environment where the cleaning woman calls the director by his first name; after all, there is usually some problem in the community in which they have a common concern and may even be on the same committee.

The first region-wide mental health survey was conducted in 1964 using volunteers. While meetings continued during 1965, legislation was passed making state monies available for mental health centers if the community would tax itself with a mill levy to an amount not to exceed three-fourths of one mill.

If the people of a community wanted to work hard enough and would show their desire by voting for a tax, the state would assist with funds not to exceed more than 40 percent of expenses. It is important to note that many of the legislators who supported this bill were members of one of the many volunteer committees.

The first group to try for a mill levy was from Ward County (Minot).

More volunteers were recruited, a speakers' bureau was established, funds solicited, and petitions circulated. In September 1966, the mill levy was voted on and passed by a two-to-one majority.

After the victory, many of the volunteer workers felt their job was done, but, fortunately, a small group stayed together to work with the Ward County Commissioners to plan the initial steps necessary to establish a center. Since this was a new experience, no one was quite sure what to do. They did, however, solve one problem immediately in a very traditional manner by forming a board of directors.

The original board members were all volunteers and were a Lutheran minister, a farm wife, an attorney, a businessman, and a hospital administrator. This group began to meet in early 1967, hammering out policies and plans, and in August of that year added two medical members, the private psychiatrist in the community, and a general practitioner.

As a member of the Air Force, stationed at Minot Air Force Base, I had been one of the original volunteers and committee chairman during 1964 and 1965, and, although transferred from the community, I was asked in 1967 to return and take over as an administrator. The board felt very strongly about the volunteer origin of the program and wanted one of the original laymen volunteer participants as director.

At the same time that I returned to Minot in November 1967, a psychiatrist, Dr. Rosalie B. Kryston, arrived in town as a dependent of a newly assigned Air Force medical officer. Dr. Kryston was hired as clinical director, and subsequently a secretary and social worker were added to the staff. Facilities were found in a medical clinic and an outpatient service opened on January 15, 1968, to anyone in the region desiring services.

THE USE OF VOLUNTEERS IN CENTER PROGRAMS

During the first few months of operation, the center did not initiate any formal volunteer programs. However, those volunteers who had been active during the planning and mill levy campaigns were kept informed of the center's progress through the news media, articles, and direct contact with staff members.

Fifteen days after the official opening, an open house was held for all members of the community. Special invitations were sent to state and national dignitaries, and especially to those who had been active in the formative planning and campaign. Volunteers were used to decorate the center, to plan the program, to furnish refreshments, and to draw posters depicting the mental health story. Many groups were involved. The Minot State College Council for Exceptional Children provided young ladies to act as guides; students from Bishop Ryan High School drew the posters; children from the Minot School for the Mentally Handicapped made cookies (with much help from parents); a local company provided soft drinks; and the American Legion provided coffee. Air Force officials from the base and state dignitaries were on hand for the ribbon-cutting which was done by State Senator Herbert Meschke, who represented Governor William Guy.

In order to keep the community involved, and the center involved in the community, members of the staff joined several organizations in the seven-county region. The clinical director participated in the Alcoholism Information Center Advisory Board, Minot State College Speech Therapy Department, Dakota Boys Ranch, and became the second member on the Mental Health Committee of the district's medical society.

I, as the administrator, became a permanent member of the Consultants Committee, and the Special Educational Regional Advisory Board, as well as a member of the Board of the Minot School for the Mentally Handicapped. To make the center's services more known to the community and to assist in community planning, I also became a member of the Elks, Sertoma, American Legion, Knights of Columbus, the North Dakota Mental Health Association, and the Great Plains Association for Retarded Children.

Because many members of other community agencies had been active in the original mental health committees, it was relatively easy to establish good rapport with all the medical, social welfare, educational, rehabilitative, and law enforcement agencies in Minot, and also in some of the other counties where members had participated. We made it a point to visit each agency and explain what we hoped to do.

We also asked for and received volunteer assistance from nonmental health and health organizations such as the Northern States Power Company, Montana-Dakota Utilities Company, the Y.W.C.A., North Hill Bowl, the Coca-Cola Bottling Plant, the Minot City Library, and Trinity Hospital. These organizations made it possible not only for the center to provide almost all of the services and activities that can be found in a large mental institution, but also provided patients with real community contacts and activities.

The Northern States Power Company cooperated in the first formal volunteer program attempted by the center. Like most modern, expanding industries, NSP has a good public relations program. One of these programs utilizes a complete home economics classroom, which, not surprisingly, is furnished with all of the electrical appliances that can be fitted into a contemporary kitchen. In charge of this program is a home economist who occupies her working hours giving instructions and demonstrations to housewives so they can find more uses for their kitchen equipment. Miss Opland volunteered to provide this service as a therapeutic activity to patients of the center.

The girls in our first adolescent therapy group were soon baking pizza pies, engaging freely in group therapy, and communicating again with their community. During the North Dakota State Fair, the girls, much to our surprise, volunteered to decorate a booth for the North Dakota Association for Mental Health and to distribute literature.

Other volunteer groups were formed and activities added according to the patients' needs. Bowling at North Hill Bowl and swimming in the Trinity Hospital swimming pool were soon included in the activity schedule. Professional bowlers at the bowling lanes volunteered time to assist patients, and a full-time swimming instructor with the Red Cross donated time to act as a lifeguard and swimming instructor.

In the fall of 1968, we decided to test the possibilities of having the other counties within our region place a mill levy vote on the November ballot. We first contacted those people who had done volunteer work for the center and who, we knew, were interested in our program. In counties where we were not acquainted with anyone, we asked those people whom we knew from other counties in the region if they were acquainted with anyone who could introduce us to someone in the county we wanted to approach. If the original contact showed no enthusiasm, we asked him if he might know of someone else who would probably be interested. This afforded him an opportunity to "get off the hook" and provided us with another contact. Many phone calls were made and we soon had at least one person in five of the counties who volunteered to assist us in some manner.

We then contacted all of the clubs in the five counties, such as Jaycees, Kiwanis, American Legion, and asked if they would assist us and if we could have an opportunity to speak to their group. We did this also with such groups as PTA, Homemakers, Farmers Union, and the Farm Bureau. In a month's time, we had a network of volunteers in each county who were willing to assist us in a mill levy campaign and no one was more amazed than we were.

Before the campaign began, we asked our volunteer in each county to accompany us on a visit to the county commissioners to help explain the program. First, however, they made the initial contact with their commissioners, whom they knew personally, and then invited us to a meeting with them.

We received volunteer assistance in preparing mailing lists, radio and TV broadcasts, and newspaper articles for each of the weekly county newspapers. Implement dealers, farmers, educators, and a recovered alcoholic made tapes for spot announcements on radio and TV. Many sandwiches were eaten and many gallons of coffee consumed during local meetings in these communities.

When the returns were counted, thanks to all of the assistance of the many volunteers and groups, four of the counties voted two to one in favor of a mill levy, and the fifth county voted three to one in favor of the levy.

After the successful mill levy campaign, we again contacted the volunteers who had assisted us and asked them for more help in setting up direct services to their communities. Again, when they couldn't help us, we would ask for another name of someone else who might. All of this communication led to the discovery of many people who needed service and confronted us with two problems—the transportation for some patients from farms to town and finding suitable places to hold interviews.

Although we had some ideas where we would like to meet with patients in each town, we decided to involve our volunteers as much as possible, and to seek their assistance in finding a suitable meeting place. We began by visiting two of the largest populated areas furthest away from Minot—Bottineau (2,613), eighty miles northeast, and New Town (1,586), seventy-five miles southwest. On alternate weeks our chief social worker, and our psychiatric nurse, traveling as a team, visited these towns. In Bottineau, they were furnished office space in a small community hospital, and in New Town, they were provided with an office in a rather modern nursing home.

At the same time, in New Town, training was given to the nursing home staff both formally and informally so that ongoing therapy would continue during the absence of the team. Activities were suggested and volunteer programs planned. In Bottineau, the majority of our work was with the high school and a small community college. Group therapy was conducted in both places.

As so often happens, as our programs expanded, so did the needs of the community. Consequently, another psychiatric nurse was hired specifically to travel to the rural communities of all the counties to determine the need and the programs that would be most feasible using community volunteer assistance.

327

She traveled to the three counties not covered by the psychiatric team and enlisted the help of the Mrs. Jaycees and other groups, to furnish transportation and other assistance to patients. In one town, she formed a group for therapy of former state hospital patients who, with the help of volunteer drivers, met once a week in a church near Columbus.

Certainly, not everyone can be treated by a visiting therapist or counselor. Those who can't are asked to come to the center. Intake procedures are conducted, however, in the individual's community either by the center traveling staff member or by a county nurse. If transportation is required, arrangements are made with one of the volunteer drivers.

About the same time, a member of Alcoholics Anonymous also offered his services. He was a certified alcoholism counselor who, in his earlier years, had been a fast-traveling alcoholic carrying out his sprees throughout most of the region. He was concerned with the number of alcoholics in the small towns and especially about those who had been to a treatment center, but weren't getting any follow-up care.

He began work on a volunteer basis traveling throughout the region forming new Alcoholics Anonymous groups, and assisting those already formed. He also conducted alcoholism education classes in the schools and churches of the north central region.

The volunteer program in Minot has been organized under a volunteer coordinator. The volunteers assist with programs such as the Community Day Care program, providing transportation, and assistance with activities. They also provide baby-sitting services for patients. A nursery in a downtown church has been donated to the center for use at anytime during the week. Occasionally, volunteers will also assist with special events. One example was a drug education program sponsored by a local citizens group. Volunteers from the center obtained NIMH and Blue Cross literature and distributed about 3,000 copies of each.

Two major projects organized in Minot with mental health center personnel and volunteers acting as catalysts, and completed during the last year are a comprehensive sheltered workshop and a Community Information Center.

The workshop began as a joint project between the Ward County Director of Special Education and center personnel. Mr. Robert Carlson, Ward County Director of Special Education, and I began by seeking out available funds, visiting workshops, and attending state meetings to convince everyone that Minot was a likely place for a sheltered workshop. With the special education program in the county, Minot State College's emphasis on special education, and the facilities of the mental health center, we felt that the city was in a position to establish a quality program.

Eventually, we were notified by the State Mental Health Administration that federal funds could be made available for staff. Mr. Carlson and I began putting together a grant application.

For several years, the board of directors of the Minot School for the Mentally Handicapped, to which we both belonged, had been trying to get the Minot School System to fund the school and make it a part of the system. Mr. Carlson explained to the school board the necessity of redirecting its voluntary resources to the more ambitious program of sheltered training and employment. The school board voted to incorporate the students of the school for the mentally handicapped into the public school system, and the board of the Minot School for the Mentally Handicapped applied for a federal staffing grant to establish a sheltered workshop. The Sertoma Club voted to sponsor the workshop as their fund-raising project.

Meetings were then held in Minot in the same manner that the original mental health center meetings were held. Planning committees were formed with professional and lay personnel, special advisory boards formed, and individuals were asked to volunteer their time, and at times, their money.

A director of a successful workshop in Canada was hired to become the executive director of the Minot Sheltered Workshop. A volunteer committee, consisting of local businessmen who previously had not been on any mental health committees, was formed to find a suitable location. This type of a project appealed more to businessmen and bankers because of the industrial possibilities and their familiarity with the business organizational process.

A supermarket that had been closed was chosen as the best location. However, a railroad company which held a binding option and was not fully aware of the sheltered workshop program, did not desire to rent to an organization such as this. After five tries, and many phone calls by many groups and some of the most prominent individuals in town, the lease was signed.

The facility, now being remodeled, will eventually provide for work and training for 250 handicapped individuals. Thanks to the participation of other professional individuals, such as vocational rehabilitation personnel, several new grants have been received by the workshop. A classroom has been built in the workshop and the Minot School System has leased it to train students for what was formerly the Minot School for the Mentally Handicapped.

During this same period of time, the entire medical clinic in which is housed the North Central Mental Health and Retardation Center, went out of practice due to ill health of the director-owner. A second floor would be vacant and a large pharmacy with a store front entrance was also included in the lease.

A group of agency representatives for the various service agencies was formed to discuss utilization of the pharmacy. It was decided to turn it into a Community Agencies Information Center to provide information and literature concerning all of the helping agencies in the region. Shelves, paint, and other materials were donated and volunteers converted it into such a center. Volunteers also assisted in the remodeling of the medical clinic to make it more suitable for mental health center purposes.

Presently, the Community Agencies Information Center is staffed by volunteers of Recovery, Inc., an organization originally formed by patients of the center. Center funds were used to send two patients to Chicago for training in Recovery, Inc.

In addition to an information center, the old pharmacy will also be used as an outlet store and coffee bar for the workshop. It will give patients of the workshop an opportunity to deal directly with the public. A sublease with the Ward County Mental Health Association provides rent for this portion of the mental health center.

Present planning for the Minot volunteer programs include training volunteers to assist more fully in the day care program, such as participating in group therapy and providing after-hours contacts with patients.

It is our hope that during the fall semester at Minot State College, we will be able to recruit students to man an emergency telephone in the information center and to provide a nonpunitive contact for students who seek drug information, or just want to discuss their problems.

CONCLUSION

We feel that in two and one-half years the center, through its participation in community programs and because of all the assistance provided by individuals throughout the seven counties, can point to some notable achievements. None of this could have been accomplished without assistance from volunteers.

I think it is evident that community participation, as we see it, does not present the problems that one might find in a larger urban area.

George A. Lopes

There is no minority group within the region, and there are no deep ethnic conflicts. The majority of the population is farmers and those who provide services and goods to farmers. Although the poor farmer may feel some resentment and inferiority to the successful farmer, they are both farmers and have similar problems that differ only in the degree of individual hardship.

In towns of several hundred population, people have a regard for one another and a knowledge of each other's activities. In a region where temperatures go to forty below zero sooner or later, someone is going to need the assistance of his neighbor. Not everyone belongs to the same club, but they do belong to similar clubs and, because of lack of population, most have an opportunity to participate in them. A man may belong to the Elks, the American Legion, the Farmers Union, and the Senior Citizens Club, or maybe all four, but there is something for everyone. There is structure and security in the township meetings. The county agent, the farmer's home administrator, and the county auditor, are common points that touch all men's lives in a rural county and bring them together for common purposes.

Decisions are made usually through the democratic process of a discussion, a vote, a majority rule. Men normally make their decisions in accordance with what they see as traditional Christian ethics and the Golden Rule.

How successful is our program in terms of serving a sparsely populated rural area? In terms of salaries and reimbursement, it is probably costing more than other rural area programs where the patient must bear the burden of traveling to the center to seek assistance. In terms of public relations and community cooperation, it has been excellent. There is almost unanimous support for the center's programs throughout the seven counties being served.

In the last two and one half years, we have been very busy developing programs, and have not conducted a scientific evaluation of our procedures. We also feel that we are in the developmental stage, and that the final program has not fully evolved. At some future date, a scientific evaluation, comparing our program with other mental health center programs in North Dakota, will be made.

We do feel, as most everyone else must certainly believe, that our seven-county community of rural citizens deserves as much service as is required to serve the population's needs. We consider that ours is one experiment that should be tried as an attempt to solve the delivery of services problem.

Each of the eight mental health regions in North Dakota includes

331

about 100,000 people. If these people were living in a city of 100,000, there would be many services available to them. We have come to see our region as a community of 100,000 individuals who deserve to receive the same services that would be available to them in a modern, progressive city of the same population. Volunteers have provided us with the resources to achieve this goal.

NOTE

1. Stanley W. Voelker, and Thomas K. Ostenson, *North Dakota's Human Resources: A Study of Population Change in a Great Plains Environment,* Fargo, North Dakota: Department of Agricultural Economics, Agricultural Experiment Station, North Dakota State University, in cooperation with Economic Development Division, Economic Research Service, U.S. Department of Agriculture.

---

40   *Vernon C. Bohr,* M.D.

The Use of Students as Employees in a Community Mental Health Center

Ingleside is a mental health center in Rosemead, California serving a catchment area population of approximately 170,000 persons. Because of historical precedent, it also serves many individuals from a much larger geographic distribution, including referrals for inpatient treatment from all over Southern California as well as from a number of other states.

In order to discuss the impact that employed undergraduate and graduate students have had upon our programs, it is necessary to give a brief review of the history and development of the organization. Ingleside was initially founded in 1926 by Jean McCracken, one of Los Angeles' first social workers. Its purpose at that time was to treat elderly indigent alcoholic males. As the years progressed, this purpose broadened to include the treatment of other psychiatric disorders in a broad age group including adolescents.

Approximately twelve years ago, Ingleside began to contract with the Los Angeles County Probation Department to care for a certain number of adolescent delinquent males. This was the beginning of Ingleside's involvement with the treatment of adolescents. Shortly after instituting an adolescent program, the treatment emphasis of Ingleside sharply changed to being a primary treatment facility. Within the past decade a whole new physical plant has been built including three separate ward units to house adolescents exclusively. However, at the beginning of the building program, Ingleside was like many inpatient psychiatric facilities insofar as it provided humane care that was largely custodial. As with many custodial inpatient facilities, the staff had a low level of psychological sophistication and worked primarily on the medical-custodial model which included maintaining clean facilities, feeding patients, dispensing medications, and generally providing control for the patients. Much of the treatment was organic-somatic and very few structured milieu programs existed. The existence of custodial programs, in itself, leads to a type of "vicious circle." When an organization is custodial in its outlook, it generally does not attract a higher quality ward attendant or higher quality nursing help. In turn, this seems to further aid in maintaining the custodial nature of the institution. Also, as with any private institution with limited endowment, it is difficult to hire high-quality personnel who have psychological sophistication.

In the mid-1960s, the picture at Ingleside began to change. At that time, the adolescent program had grown to include both boys and girls. Also, the overall institution continued to experience growth in both its inpatient as well as outpatient and consultative services. As a result, two key employees were added to the staff. These were a medical director and a director of adolescent services. Both of these physicians were trained psychiatrists with extensive experience in hospital psychiatry and milieu therapy. They entered their tasks enthusiastically with the goal of changing custodial services to quality treatment services. This necessitated recruiting staff at all levels, including expansion of the attending medical staff, particularly attracting capable, younger psychiatrists who were interested in dealing with inpatient adolescents as well as doing general hospital psychiatry. How that task was accomplished will not be the subject of this particular discussion.

However, I would like to discuss a specific method for developing a high-quality adolescent ward staff which could bring to its task enthusiasm, sophistication, and an *esprit de corps*. It was apparent that, with the salaries we were able to pay, this type of staff could not be acquired by hiring older persons with family responsibility. The decision was made by the director of adolescent services and the medical director to explore the hiring of students from local colleges on a part-time basis. Ingleside is in the fortunate position of being located within short driving distance of several junior colleges as well as one very large state college and several private colleges. By the nature of several of these institutions, it is common for students to seek employment while working toward degrees on the undergraduate or graduate level. It was felt that such persons would be particularly desirable to attract to Ingleside as employees. Because students are desirous of getting jobs which will not conflict with their academic hours, we made the decision to be flexible in assigning shifts which were built around the students' academic time. Students in turn will work for lower salaries if they are allowed to pursue their academic careers under these conditions. However, two additional problems presented themselves.

Some students beginning their college programs proved to be too immature and too close to the turmoil of their own adolescence to work effectively with disturbed adolescents. They would tend to overidentify and be easily manipulated. Secondly, a college student will generally not work unless there is job gratification involving some type of intellectual and emotional stimulation as well as a strong program of inservice training. A factor in job gratification was to make the job one of significance and to make the student-employee feel that he has a key role in developing programs and in the overall treatment program. How these problems were approached will be discussed subsequently.

We found that by employing a number of college students, many of whom were pursuing part-time jobs, it was not difficult to get coverage on all shifts since the students all had individual academic programs with differing free times. A chief counsellor was employed who would work with the student-employees aiding them to schedule their work time within the framework of their academic time. It also became apparent that the minimum work week for any student would be set at twenty hours per week, and preferably twenty-four hours per week. It also was felt initially that students hired should show evidence of maturity and stability, and preferably be students in the social sciences or physical education (since many of the milieu activities involve physical activities). Each applicant was screened by the director of nurses, the chief counsellor, and the psychiatrist who was director of the Adolescent Unit.

It should be noted that since the general medical model of nursing conceptualizes an attendant as being dressed in white and with certain types of personal grooming (without mustaches, beards, and so forth) and generally presupposes full-time employment, this concept of employing part-time college students was not initially accepted wholeheartedly. Also, many anxieties arose that these were persons with no previous hospital experience and hence might not be able to perform hospital tasks. If these indeed were liabilities, the assets that these young people brought to their tasks were enthusiasm, youthful vigor, good grounding in psychological matters, and a willingness to learn and help.

Immediately upon acquiring a director of adolescent services, an active inservice training program was begun. Each attendant had a minimum of one administrative meeting per week with the psychiatrist in charge. Additionally, each ward had a clinical case conference each week reviewing the management of a difficult patient. Sensitivity training programs were set up for both nurses as well as for the counsellors to acquaint them with their own problems involved in dealing with patients and to give them further awareness as well as to give some formal education in psychological matters. In addition, ward government meetings were instituted on each ward on a twice-weekly basis at which time all of the staff as well as the administrative psychiatrist attended. Other training functions were established including training films, pertinent guest speakers, a weekly hospital grand rounds, and a daily ward rounds with key persons from the adolescent area. Not only did these programs increase the psychological sophistication of the staff, but they seemed to increase job gratification and make the jobs more interesting and rewarding.

In addition, with the help of the director of the adolescent services, each ward set up their structure and milieu with the whole staff participating. It was agreed by the attending staff doctors that matters involving privileges, passes, and so forth would be decided by the ward staff in toto, dependent upon the patient's behavior that week. The ability of the students to participate in making significant decisions regarding the structuring of the milieu as well as the facets of treatment of the patient involving passes, and so forth, greatly increased their morale and made them feel valuable members of the team.

Initially, many problems were encountered. As with any hospital attendant, each of these college students brought with him his own background and biases. Tendencies to overidentify, be over indulgent and over permissive, or to be overly restrictive or punitive were all encountered. These attitudes were discussed on an ongoing basis in sensitivity training meetings as well as ward staff meetings. Possibly one of the most rewarding facets of this program has been to see the great psychological growth of the staff and to watch them pursue their individual careers in their respective fields.

In the three and a half years that this program has been in effect, a goodly number of our ward staff have completed undergraduate as well as graduate degrees. A number of them have chosen to continue to pursue their doctoral work. Also, a number of them have been licensed under California law as marriage, family, and child counselors subsequent to acquiring their master's degrees in their respective social science. As these persons have finished their educational objectives, many of them have moved to other positions within the mental health center including positions in the outpatient clinic, social services department, and so forth. Thus, not only has this program been rewarding to Ingleside in the sense that these students would increase the awareness of Ingleside to their respective academic departments in which they were working (which constitutes valuable public relations), but also they have provided a source of recruitment from the ward staff to higher positions within the institution as they acquired more training.

In summary, the difficulties initially involved in the program consisted of integrating a psychologically sophisticated group of young people into a medical hierarchy in which they often had to work cooperatively with a nursing staff that had less psychological education than themselves. It also caused significant administrative anxiety that their grooming was more typical of the present day college generation than the grooming usually demanded by most nursing service departments. Also, many of these young people brought considerable theoretical knowledge to their job without any actual practical experience in dealing with psychological problems. Many times this was refreshing, insofar as it generated new ideas, but occasionally it was an impediment, since many of them held preconceived biases that had to be overcome. Some of them proved too immature to work with patients who were just slightly younger than themselves. However, by and large the majority showed great ability to grow with the job through sensitivity training as well as inservice training. They brought vigor, freshness, and enthusiasm to an existing lethargic staff. At times they even brought political agitation to the institution. However, it must be emphatically stated that their enthusiasm, fresh outlook, rapidity of learning their tasks, and dedication in their tasks, as well as ready ability to identify with the adolescents and to relate, far outweighed any difficulty or disadvantage of the program.

41

C. Allen Roehl, PH.D.

The Indigenous American Indian Mental Health Worker: Evolution of a Job and a Concept

American Indians comprise a small but noteworthy minority in the catchment area of the Panhandle Mental Health Center. The center's area comprises about 14,500 square miles of ranching and range country in western Nebraska. Evidence of human habitation dates from 7,500 B.C.; prehistoric humans were replaced by the plains Indians, who lived with the land before the advent of the white settlers and who are currently having a difficult time adapting to the way of life which is being imposed upon them.

Whereas battles, disease, and massacres took the lives of many, the survivors have faced various alternatives. Some chose to remain on the Pine Ridge Reservation, which borders the northern portion of the center's catchment area, and is the second largest Indian reservation in the country; a few have been absorbed into the mainstream of American life; and a sizable number (about 1600 of the 93,000 people in the catchment area) have drifted into a type of existence which is peripheral to the reservation, an existence with some unique and special problems. The plight and habitus of the reservation Indian has been well detailed elsewhere.[1] Those peripheral to the reservation cause the greatest concern to the mental health professionals at the Panhandle Mental Health Center. Their problems are those of other identifiable minority groups —poverty, prejudice, lack of educational and job opportunities. The Indian's reaction to this situation is reflected in the incidence of alcoholism, * lack of school achievement, and low income.[2]

In spite of their social and economic problems, very few American Indians were seen by the professional staff at the mental health center when it first opened. Those few who were seen were referred either by the courts or by the county welfare department. The probability of "mental health problems" seemed so high and yet there was practically

---

* During the first nine months of 1970, the arrest record for drunkenness in the city of Scotts Bluff lists 126 Caucasians, 9 Negroes, and 130 Indians.

no utilization of professional services. In an attempt to try to determine what barriers or screens had been set up to prevent the Indian from availing himself of these services, the concept of the Indigenous Indian Mental Health Worker was generated.

The worker was recruited from a community which has a sizable Indian population and is fifty miles distant from Scotts Bluff. Several candidates were suggested by the welfare director and by a VISTA volunteer working in the community. The worker was selected from these candidates, primarily through interview assessment.

The professional staff showed their anxieties and concerns. Would he be able to talk to professional people? Would they be able to talk to him? If his salary were too high, he would become middle class and draw away from the people he should be working with. What kind of report writing and record keeping would be required? Could he do it?

Because the worker did not have a high school diploma, he could not be hired in his proposed position under the state merit system. It did not matter that no American Indian had graduated from high schools in this particular town since 1939 and that a high school diploma was not even part of the job qualifications. This problem was solved by transferring the source of funding to another agency.

The worker continues to reside in his home community, fifty miles from the center. He works out of his home, and has contacts with other center staff only about once a week. Formal record keeping is not required, but brief narrative records are logged. An example of the log for one week follows:

MONDAY

At 8:00 A.M. I went to Police Court. I then attended a ministerial meeting where Reverend Bill was present and conducting the meeting. This meeting was about how the minister could be effective in family problems. The rest of the day I spent talking with A.B., an alcoholic who was in DT's all day off and on but did not want any doctor's care.

TUESDAY

Today I again became involved with A.B. He is an American Sioux Indian, 56 years of age, and has over one hundred arrests for intoxication. A.B. is a very sick man, mentally and physically. I keep urging him to get medical help. He walks around in a state of DT's. At 11:00 P.M., A.B. called me to say he could not go on by himself so I immediately called a doctor. The doctor gave him medication but did not advise hospitalization. A.B. stayed in the City Jail. I left the jail at 1:00 A.M. Wednesday morning. A.B. had gone to sleep.

WEDNESDAY

I made an appointment for A.B. at the Panhandle Mental Health Center. I went to the City Jail to get A.B., but he had left. I met him on the street, but he started to drink again and refused to go to the center. I was contacted by Mrs. C.D., an Indian woman married to a white man. Mr. D. is an alcoholic. He has been in Hastings State Hospital two times. He has been drinking for six months, one a day. He has become violent and threatened his wife and children. Mrs. D. wants to commit him to Hastings again but fears her husband so much she will not go to the courthouse. I will continue to work with Mrs. D.

THURSDAY
I went to the county courthouse and waited for Mrs. C.D. She was not there. She told me she would be there at 8:30 A.M. I looked for Mrs. D. but could not find her. I spent the rest of the day at the Community Mental Health meeting.

FRIDAY
I was called by E.F. of Crawford. She has no job and wants to become a client of our Rehabilitation Service. I drove to Crawford and interviewed E. She has a high school education but cannot find work. I also talked with the Director of the Neighborhood Center. He told me that jobs were not available in Crawford. I also talked with Reverend Billy R. who does a lot of work with the Indian people.

The worker's activities include the following: social action, case finding, therapy, follow-up, community consultation, and the role of ombudsman. The ombudsman role takes on aspects of being patient advocate and, hopefully, community advocate. In these roles, the worker has been caught up in some of the conflicts which impinge on community mental health centers, conflicts expressed in the dilemma of a commitment to direct treatment versus a commitment to social change.

Throughout the training and supervision, the staff was continually conscious of its endeavors not to "over supervise" the worker, transforming him into a person with the same mental health commitments and techniques that the professional staff had. Instead, the goal was to help him find his own way, relying more on the needs of his community and his sensitivities to it, rather than direction from the center. Because of this, training and supervision, especially at first, were minimal.

There were some bad things about this approach. The initial message to the worker was to go back to his community and do his thing. There was too little structure and not enough time was spent in outlining the goals and philosophy of self-help and community improvement. Although it is felt that a worker of this type should not be given a good deal of direction in specific things to do, there should have been more guidance in the types of goals and overall community trends which are important.

As a consequence of this lack of direction, several problems arose.

339

The worker felt guilty if his work was not immediately directed toward "mental patients." For example, he was reluctant to report on a project of clearing some land for a ball park and perhaps a little embarrassed about this. The project involved organizing a group of Indians to clear junk and debris from a piece of vacant land owned by the city so that it might be used for a ball park in the area where most Indians lived. The city allowed the use of this land, and furnished a truck for hauling, but the labor was provided by the Indians. The worker needed reassurance that, in spite of the fact that this type of activity may be controversial and give rise to some questioning of his role, it was eminently related to the kinds of things the center wanted him to do since projects which related to self-help and to enhancing self-esteem fit in with the overall goals for improving the mental health climate of the Indian population. The worker even became marginally paranoid about the staff and his position and only later was able to express his feeling that he had been hired solely for "window dressing" as a political move.

His work has often been incongruent with any traditional model, and so his activities may be best explained by citing a few examples of programs which have been developed. Two of these, which were begun before he had been hired, were the organization and leadership of the American Indian Committee and an Alcoholics Anonymous group.

The American Indian Committee was formed as a civil rights committee to help effect action and reform in the community. The worker himself describes it as a "gripe and bitch committee." The AA group developed from an obvious need which became more urgent when Indians would come to the American Indian Committee meeting drunk. Although the Caucasian Alcoholics Anonymous Committee ostensibly welcomed Indian members, there was considerable resistance on the part of the Indians to become involved in this type of meeting. Not only did they feel out of place in a middle-class home, but the highly verbal and intellectualized material that was sometimes presented at these meetings left them out in the cold because of their lack of education. The Indian mental health worker borrows heavily from AA literature during his meetings, but the structure is much less formal and most of the meetings are held in the local dialect of the Sioux language. Meetings are attended by approximately fifteen people at each session.

Another program involved voter registration. There were nine registered Indian voters in the county in question at the time the worker was hired. Helping to organize a voter registration drive resulted in the registration of 88 more Indians, out of a total of about 200 eligible adult voters. This program is continuing, and fifteen more have been registered recently. As a result of this, local politicians are more sensitive to the needs and aspirations of the Indians and spend some time in talking with and to the Indian community.

The worker feels that one of his most important activities is attending court sessions. He is able to pick up potential clients, to act as a resource to the court, and sometimes as an interpreter. Problems which are not dealt with directly are referred elsewhere and often the referral comes to the personnel of the Panhandle Mental Health Center. Several who have been identified as town bums or the town drunk have had extended periods of sobriety. This has had a tremendous public relations effect and resistance toward obtaining these services has been wearing down.

Twenty-three Indian people are now in a rehabilitation program under the Department of Vocational Rehabilitation. Previous to the collaboration between the worker and the vocational rehabilitation counselor, there had been no Indians in this program. In this instance, then, the worker is seen as an effective source of referral and encouragement to the Indian people.

In conjunction with a social worker, the worker has organized community meetings which are held every two weeks. Although these are similar to the meetings of the American Indian Committee, they are open to all residents of the area and increasing numbers of Caucasian people come to the meetings. An increase in community understanding and communication has evolved from these. A member of the chamber of commerce may explain job situations and economic conditions in the community. The welfare office may discuss programs and benefits.

From these meetings evolved a program of free medical care for all poor people in the community. An office is staffed by volunteers, from church groups and elsewhere, who keep records and provide transportation. Persons screened by this group are immediately eligible for care by the participating local physicians. Prior to this, poor people, especially Indians, were reluctant to make office calls for any but the most serious physical problems. Although the physicians sincerely felt that they were standing by to offer medical care to all who needed it, they were probably unaware of the reluctance to approach the carpeted middle-class office, to undergo the embarrassing stares in the waiting room, and possibly the screening comments of the office nurse before seeing the physician. The results of this program of medical care have been eminently successful. Not only does the program tie into concepts of self-help and self-improvement, which have been the overriding theme of this program, but also reports from the local physicians have verified the value of the program. The physicians, aside from recognizing the beneficial aspects of this as an approach to preventive medicine, have become aware that their middle-of-the-night calls to the emergency room of the hospital have decreased. Prior to the service, minor problems would become acute and severe, requiring the only type of help most Indians were willing to get, emergency care at the emergency room of the hospital.

An important means of contacting Indian families and working with them is the Boy Scout troop. The worker helped to organize this "Indian" scout troop, and presently he is acting as the scout leader. This troop accepts all boys, and there are three Caucasians and two Spanish-American boys as well as about a dozen Indians. Scout activities have proven to be a means of reaching some families which were hard to contact. All parents of scouts are visited. The worker feels that some of the benefits from the scout meetings are filtering into the homes and feels there is an increase in sobriety and job stability on the part of several parents, directly related to the fact that the boy in the home has been a member of the scout troop. Also, two fifteen-year-old scouts with incipient alcoholism have improved as a result of the sobriety requirement at scout meetings.

Two practices characteristic of the Indians in this community are especially relevent for working with them. One is a long-standing cultural pattern of the Sioux. If an Indian has any substance, he is expected to share it with his extended family, whether the substance is a pot of stew, a side of venison, a welfare check, or a check from the sale of Indian lands. Since there are always some impoverished people in the friendship and relationship, this practice makes it almost impossible to accumulate material possessions. There may be other implications, such as the survival value for the group, perhaps more pertinent during the days of migratory hunting. Another implication might be the decreased emphasis on immediate family life.

Another custom or tradition has origins which are more obscure. It is a self-leveling process which extends from school performance (ostracism for good grades) to job advancement (too much display of personal wealth means a person is getting too fancy for his friends). It is an example of the extreme contrast between a typical off-reservation Indian and a member of the Caucasian middle class, although parallels exist among other subgroups. It is especially a problem for an alcoholic trying to avoid drinking. An Indian with an alcohol problem, and there are many of these, finds it much more difficult to quit drinking because of the tremendous pressure exerted by his cronies. The pressure goes beyond the typical razzing, enticing, seducing. There have been incidents of severe beatings and of wrecking a person's "shack" (home) because of his attempt to stay away from liquor. The usual result is that the person who is trying to reform goes back to drinking. It is a matter of conjecture whether this lack of ability to "fight the system" is related to the hazing and harassment and lack of power which have characterized the Indians' life for the last hundred years.

A problem being given highest priority is the development of effective lay leadership in the community. So many programs, such as the Boy Scout troop, have fallen back on the worker for leadership and direction. The necessity of encouraging and developing other leaders is recognized. However, recent history has not provided reinforcement for leadership behavior, but has rather encouraged apathy and a simple hedonism.

A retrospective evaluation of the worker's effectiveness would touch on the following points. As has been found in programs elsewhere, a native to the area and a person familiar with a subgroup is more effective in communicating with the people for case finding and in offering direct counseling and advice.

The center's worker has also been especially helpful in seeing needs which probably would not have been visible to professional staff people. One example is the importance of attending court sessions as a source of case finding. Other programs which were started by the Indian mental health worker and probably could not have been implemented by the professional, included community improvement projects such as the clearing of the land for a ball park.

Disagreement exists about whether functions such as this are legitimate and appropriate for a person salaried from a mental health center. Our conclusion that these activities feed into an overall improvement of the mental health atmosphere of the community seems ample justification.

NOTES

1. "Baseline Data Study. Some Notes of School Dropouts," *Pine Ridge Research Bulletin,* Pine Ridge, S.D., 11(January 1970); *Look,* New York, N.Y., (June 2, 1970); Eileen Maynard, "Community Portrait No. 4—Manderson Community," *Pine Ridge Research Bulletin,* Pine Ridge, S.D., 11(January 1970).

2. *Nonprofessional Personnel in Mental Health Programs,* Chevy Chase, Maryland: National Clearinghouse for Mental Health Information, November 1969.

REFERENCES

Abrams, A. "Nurses Supervise Family Care." *Hospital Community Psychiatry* 19(May 1968): 154–155.

American Medical Association, Council on Rural Health. "Models for delivery of health services in rural areas." Mimeographed. Chicago: American Medical Association, 1969.

Anderson, W., and Lennbach, M. A. "The Volunteer Program and Community Relations." *Mental Hygiene* 47(1963): 380–383.

Atwood, R., and Joregenson, C. Paper presented at the Washington State 10th Annual Research Meeting, held in Seattle. *The Volunteer Psychotherapists' Journal*, 1969. Spokane, Washington: Steptoe Selfhelp Publications.

Bettis, M. C., and Roberts, R. E. "The Mental Health Manpower Dilemma." *Mental Hygiene* 53(April 1969): 163–165.

Birdman, A. J., and Spiegel, A. D. *Perspectives in Community Mental Health.* Chicago: Aldine Publishing Co., 1969. Chapter references:

Chapter 8: Graving, Frank T. "Basis and Plan for more effective use of community resources in mental health."

Chapter 10: Dorken, H. "Behind the scenes in community mental health."

Chapter 11: Halper, H. P., and Silverman, C. "Approaches to interagency cooperation."

Chapter 16: Hallock, A. C. K., and Baughan, W. T. "Community organization—a dynamic component of community mental health practice."

Chapter 17: Goldson, S. E., "Mental health education in a community mental health center."

Chapter 19: Friedman, M. H. "Community mental health education with police."

Chapter 32: Hobbs, N., and Smith, M. B. "The community and community mental health center."

Chapter 35: Birdman, A. J., and Klebanoff, L. B. "A nursery center program for preschool mentally retarded children."

Chapter 36: Plaut, T. F. A. "Some major issues in developing community services for persons with drinking problems."

Brockmeier, M. J. "Nursing in Two Community Health Settings." *Nursing Outlook* 16(April 1968): 55–58.

Bulbulyan, A., Davidites, R. M., and Williams, F. "Nurses in a Community Mental Health Center." *American Journal of Nursing* 69(February 1969): 328–331.

Cantor, E. M. "The Challenge of Volunteer Services." *Child Welfare* 47(1968).

Chaplan, A. A., Price, J. M., Zukerman, I., and Elk, J. "The Role of Volunteers in Community Mental Health Programs." *Community Mental Health Journal* 2(1966): 255–258.

Chen, R., Healey, J., and Williams, H. V. *Partial hospitalization: problems, purposes, and changing objectives.* Proceedings of the Topeka State Hospital and State of Kansas Division of Institutional Management sponsored Forum on Partial Hospitalization at Topeka.

Cole, J. P., and Cole, W. E. "Volunteers Helping Families of the Mentally Ill." *Mental Hygiene* 53(April 1969): 188–195.

Cotter, M. D. "The Public Health Nurse and Community Mental Health." *Nursing Outlook* 16(April 1968): 59–61.

Cowne, L. J. "Approaches to the Mental Health Manpower Problem. A Review of the Literature." *Mental Hygiene* 53(April 1969): 176–187.

DeMarche, D. F., Robinson, R., and Wagle, M. K. "Community Resources in Mental

Health." In *Joint Commission on Mental Illness and Health*. New York: Basic Books, Inc., 1960.

Depaul, A. V. "The Nurse as a Central Figure in a Medical Health Center." *Perspective Psychiatric Care* 6(1968): 17–24.

Ehrenwald, J., and Kloth, E. "General Practitioner in Community Psychiatry. Experimental Treatment Project." *New York Journal of Medicine* 69(June 1969): 1739–1743.

Hallowitz, E., and Riessman, F. "The Role of the Indigenous Nonprofessional in a Community Mental Health Neighborhood Service Center Program." *American Journal of Orthopsychiatry* 37(July 1967): 766–778.

Hershenson, D. B. "A Requirement of Our Times: The Community-Centered Counselor." *Rehabilitation Record* 8(September-October, 1967): 6–7.

Huessy, H. H., Marshall, C. D., and Lincoln, E. K. "The Indigenous Nurse as Crisis Counselor and Intervener." *American Journal of Public Health* 59(November 1969): 2022–2028.

Lamb, H. R. "Aftercare for Former Day Hospital Patients." *Hospital and Community Psychiatry* 18(1967): 342–344.

Lubin, B., and Wallis, R. R. "Psychology Positions in Comprehensive Community Mental Health Centers and Community Clinics." *American Psychology* 24(September 1969): 878–879.

May, A. R., and Gregory, E. "Participation of General Practitioners in Community Psychiatry." *British Medical Journal* 2(April 1968): 168–171.

Maylor, H. H. *Volunteers Today—Finding, Training, and Working with Them*. New York: Association Press, 1967.

Minnesota Department of Public Welfare. "Community Planning for Psychiatric Patients." Proceedings of Joint National Institute of Mental Health—University-State sponsored institute for hospital and clinic social workers, field representatives, and volunteer services coordinators at Minneapolis, Minnesota, June 20–22, 1960.

National Commission on Community Health Services. Action Planning for Community Health Services. *Report of the Community Action Studies Project, 1967*. New York: American Public Health Association.

National Commission on Community Health Services. Community Structure and Health Action. *Report of the Community Action Studies Project, 1968*. New York: American Public Health Association.

National Institute of Mental Health. *Mental Health Services in Sparsely Populated Rural Areas*. Proceedings of the National Institute of Mental Health Program Development Conference held at Phoenix, Arizona, April 2–5, 1968.

Pasamanick, B. "The Development of Physicians for Public Mental Health." *American Journal of Orthopsychiatry* 37(April 1967): 469–486.

Pretzel, P. W. "The Volunteer Clinical Worker at the Suicide Prevention Center." *Bulletin of Suicidology* 6(1970): 19–34.

Rieman, D. W. *Organization, Operation, and Extension of Consultation Services*. Austin: Division of Mental Health, Texas State Department of Health, 1965.

Ross, M. G. *Community Organization*. New York: Harper and Brothers, 1955.

Ryan, W. "Citizens in Mental Health—What Are They For." *Mental Hygiene* 50(October 1966): 597–600.

Ryan, W. "Community Care in Historical Perspective." *Canada's Mental Health*. (April 1969): Supplement.

Savino, M. T., and Schlamp, F. T. "The Use of Non-Professional Rehabilitation Aides in Decreasing Re-Hospitalization." *Journal of Rehabilitation* 34(May 1968): 28–31.

Schulberg, H. C. "Future Steps in Implementing Mental Health Plans." *Community Mental Health Journal* 2(1966): 157–162.

Shachnow, J., and Matorin, S. "Community Psychiatry Welcomes the Non-Professional." *Psychiatric Quarterly* 43(1969): 492–511.

Staton, E. E., Tiller, C. B., and Weyler, E. H. "Teens Who Care: Potential Mental Health Manpower." *Mental Hygiene* 53(April 1969): 200–204.

Torre, M. "The Physician and the Community Mental Health Center." *Journal of the Louisiana Medical Society* 119(July 1967): 278–283.

Ujhely, G. B. "The Nurse in Community Psychiatry." *American Journal of Nursing* 69(May 1969): 1001–1005.

Wellner, A. M. "A Statewide Survey of Community Needs for Mental Health Technicians." *Mental Hygiene* 52(April 1968): 204–206.

Whittington, H. G. *Psychiatry in the American Community.* New York: International University Press, Inc., 1966.

XII
Providing for
Staff
Development

EDITORS' INTRODUCTION

The development of the community mental health center program with its emphasis on innovative methods for service delivery and the utilization of additional manpower resources beyond the traditional mental health disciplines has presented an increasing need for emphasis on training. The centers have had to develop their own training programs, in part because of their need to develop new nontraditional services and in part because of their need to develop additional manpower drawn from the community itself. Both of these factors have required community mental health centers to develop a variety of inservice training activities.

Most professionals who serve in community mental health centers have not been trained to perform many of the tasks that they are called upon to undertake in the community mental health center setting. Traditional professional training has emphasized the care of individual patients rather than group approaches. It has emphasized direct services rather than preventive approaches and it has done little to prepare the professional for work with community groups. As a result, the community mental health center must provide its professional staff members with training in those areas in which they are lacking.

Moreover, the center must provide training for those nonprofessionals who come to the center without any previous training or experience whatsoever. These nonprofessional staff members must be trained to perform a variety of functions and they must be trained to work in the specialized setting of the mental health center.

In developing these needed training programs, the community mental health center faces several problems. One is the availability of resources to support training activities. Although these training programs are essential, it is often difficult to justify training activities to those agencies that provide financial resources for the center. Moreover, it is also quite difficult, at least in many settings, to find appropriate people to conduct the training programs. The techniques of community mental health center operations are still quite new, and as a result there are still few people, at least on a relative basis, who have either training or experience in their application.

A second problem relates to the utilization and training of nonprofessionals, particularly those who reside within the community itself. In part, the value of the nonprofessional to the community mental health center arises from his being a member of the community in which the center is located. Unlike the trained professional, who often lives outside the community, he is not set apart from the others who live in the community. Once he begins to receive training, however, one of his principal functions in relating the center to the population served is perhaps compromised, for he no longer can see himself and he no longer can be seen simply as another resident of the community. Instead, he becomes identified with the center and identified as a person who is somehow different from the other residents of the community.

Still another problem facing the center and its nonprofessional staff members is the issue of career lines. Many of the nonprofessional staff members who receive training within a particular center rapidly begin to acquire the goals, sets, and skills of many of the professional staff members. As a result, they often wish to obtain additional training outside the setting of the center so that they can achieve higher professional status and better financial security. This then confronts the community mental health center with the need to turn over nonprofessional staff on a continuing basis. Moreover, this constant turnover may disrupt the relationship of the community mental health center and the community it serves.

42

Stephen R. Perls, ED.D.,
Jerome Levy, PH.D., *and*
Robert A. Senescu, M.D.

A New Professionals' Career Program

A key factor influencing the development of the Bernalillo County Mental Health Center program is the tri-cultural population which lives in the catchment area. The proportion of Spanish-Americans to white or Anglos and blacks is quite high. The unique cultural and social-psychiatric background of the Spanish-American made it quite apparent that different techniques for the effective delivery of mental health services had to be developed. People with an intimate knowledge of the culture would have to become a key part of the delivery system.

Since few professionals with the desired cultural beckground were available, a plan to train forty indigenous individuals was undertaken. The Albuquerque Concentrated Employment Program's New Careers Program was beginning and, after negotiation and planning, a two year program to train new professionals in the mental health field was agreed upon.

RECRUITMENT AND SELECTION

The program at Bernalillo County Mental Health Center is multifaceted with an inpatient facility, a partial hospitalization program, a children's service, and community-based sustained-contact teams. To develop a manpower pool for each of these service units, the following number of trainees was requested: (1) inpatient, twelve; (2) partial hospitalization, eight; (3) children's service, ten; and (4) sustained-contact teams, ten.

To be eligible for the New Careers program, individuals had to reside in the Concentrated Employment Program's (CEP) target area which was in the catchment area; had to be heads of households earning less than 3,000 dollars per year; had to be able to read and write English; and have no criminal action pending.

An initial group of sixty-five people were referred from CEP and a selection committee of mental health center staff picked the first group of ten trainees. The basic criteria for acceptance into the program were an interest in working in the helping services; an ability to communicate warmth and acceptance; and an expressed interest in working in the community. After the initial selection, some members of the first group of trainees assisted in choosing the remaining thirty trainees.

THE TRAINING PROGRAM

Each training week consisted of forty hours divided into twenty hours of on-the-job training; ten hours of skills training; and ten hours of educational enrichment. On-the-job training was spent in direct contact with patients or community agencies, initially under close supervision but with a rapidly increasing degree of independence.

Each program unit differed in its specific expectations for the trainee during the on-the-job-training period. The inpatient section utilized trainees in basic nursing activities including physical care, and therapeutic interacting. Trainees developed and acquired interviewing techniques. Each trainee spent time working on the three different nursing shifts and on both wards, the crisis unit, and the longer stay rehabilitation unit.

The partial-hospitalization section trained eight people as activity therapy specialists. Utilizing a therapeutic community approach, the trainees learned to interact with groups of patients in specific work areas such as maintenance, house-keeping, kitchen-canteen, and arts and crafts. They participated in group therapy sessions as well as sensitivity groups.

The childrens' service trained ten child care workers who learned various techniques such as behavior modification approaches to autistic children. After an initial period of close supervision, they developed their own therapeutic programs and carried them out on the pediatrics ward of the county hospital, in local kindergartens, in Head Start programs, and in special education classes for exceptional children.

The ten sustained contact team trainees (community mental health workers) learned to make home visits, acquiring entry skills and knowledge about the role of the interviewer in a home setting. They also developed skills in crisis intervention and the diagnosis and assessment of family interaction. The walk-in clinic was also a training ground to acquire knowledge about record keeping, referral procedures, and scheduling. Group techniques were also taught for use in treating alcoholics and patients with poor social skills.

Skills training varied within service units. The inpatient group learned first-aid, basic physiology and anatomy, and the psychodynamics of behavior. Trainees on the childrens' service studied human growth and development and had workshops on the use of games and arts and crafts in the treatment of children. Partial hospitalization trainees concentrated on techniques of group interaction with a specific focus on the concepts of behavior modification and the therapeutic community. Trainees working with the sustained-contact teams concentrated on learning interviewing techniques with individuals and families through the process of role-playing and role-reversal. Psychodynamics of behavior, side effects of commonly prescribed medications, normal and abnormal growth and development in the child and adolescent, and community development techniques were also covered during the training program.

The "educational enrichment" experience initially emphasized exposure to different aspects of work, such as salaries, credentials, expectations of supervisors, training, labor market, and mobility. Later trainees chose to spend this time studying the ethnology of the Southwest and broader community, state and national problems that affected all Spanish-Americans, black, and Indian cultures.

Trainees entered the program at all levels of educational achievement ranging from fourth grade to one year of junior college. To help each trainee obtain at least a High School Equivalency Diploma, a special tutoring program was arranged through the College of Education. Fifteen of the trainees did not have their high school degree at the start of the two-year program. Only four remain who still have not completed all requirements. Specific tutoring for university courses was offered through the College of Education with an emphasis on developing library, research, and term-paper writing skills.

In order to enhance knowledge in the social sciences and humanities, many trainees have enrolled in introductory college courses such as sociology, psychology, speech, and anthropology as well as more specialized courses such as "Creative Art in Elementary Schools" or "Child Clinical Psychology."

Concurrent with the institution of this program came the development of the first Associate of Arts degree offered by the University of New Mexico, which was open only to people who participated in the New Careers Program. This Associate of Arts degree in Human Services requires sixty-nine credits for completion. The degree includes twenty-four hours of credit for college class work, nine hours for generic training and thirty-six hours for on-the-job-training. At this time, only the college courses are transferrable to a B.A. degree though this is expected to change in the near future.

The A.A. degree is optional and is not required for participation in the program. It is offered solely as an opportunity to assist the new careerists' personal and educational development.

Finally, a group guidance and counseling experience was begun to help trainees deal with the many new and varied pressures. Held for two hours once a week, these "rap sessions" helped in information sharing, dispelling of rumors, and working through personal and interpersonal difficulties.

THE CAREER LADDER

The mental health worker is a new career in the State of New Mexico and no job description or salary scale was available at the beginning of the program. After reviewing other training programs, a tentative job description was developed for each of the four service unit areas. After one year of experience with the program, the following career ladder was developed (Table 42–1):

TABLE 42–1

JOB TITLE	ANNUAL SALARY RANGE°	MINIMUM QUALIFICATIONS
Mental Health Worker I	$3582–4943	No specific type of experience required; aptitude for working with disturbed persons, particularly in the lower income groups.
Mental Health Worker II Community MHW I	$3933–5467	Six months progressive and successful experience and training at the MHW I level or its equivalent.
Mental Health Worker III Community MHW II Activity Therapy Assistant I	$4318–6045	Twelve months progressive and successful experience and training at the MHW II, CMHW I level or its equivalent. (People who complete the N.C. program will start at this level.)
Mental Health Worker IV Community MHW III	$4741–6685	Eighteen months progressive and successful experience and training at the MHW III, CMHW II and

TABLE 42–1 (continued)

JOB TITLE	ANNUAL SALARY RANGE °	MINIMUM QUALIFICATIONS
Activity Therapy Assistant II		ATA I level or its equivalent.
Mental Health Worker V Community MHW IV Activity Therapy Assistant III	$5200–7393	Two and one-half years of progressive and successful experience. An appropriate AA degree may be substituted provided it furnishes equivalent skills and knowledges.
Community Mental Health Worker V Child Care Associate I	$5716–8174	Serves as team coordinator, after having demonstrated ability to work without supervision and is able to establish priorities, supervise lower level Mental Health Workers and obtain cooperation from others.

° These positions are re-evaluated each year and the pay grade is changed according to rises in the cost of living, prevailing pay scales in the community, and job responsibilities.

Two of the job descriptions, Mental Health Worker II and Community Mental Health Worker V are as follows:

TITLE: Mental Health Worker II

ORGANIZATION: Department of Psychiatry, Mental Health Center.

DUTIES: This position is an advanced learning and development situation. Participates in various classroom courses (including college), on-the-job training and group discussions.

Training includes theories, concepts and techniques of intervention, interviewing, counseling, various therapeutic approaches and methods, observation and recognition of patients' conditions, recording and reporting patients' conditions and behavior, motivation, safe practices and development of a degree of self-understanding through self-exploration.

Training is designed to furnish the trainee with skills and knowledge needed to provide proper physical and psychological assistance to patients without the close supervision of professional personnel, but following prescribed treatment or instructions.

In some cases, develops and carries out initial and follow-up care for patients.

Serves as patient advocate.

Makes recommendations for community involvement

through contacts with appropriate resources, groups, associations, and so forth.

Work and training assignments may cover all or most of specialized areas within the mental health center, such as inpatient activities, rehabilitation, children's services and others.

Employees may progress from general assignments into specialized areas at higher grades as training progresses and experience is gained.

Responsible for the physical and psychological welfare of patients to whom assigned.

Works closely with more experienced employees and professional personnel who guide and supervise learning processes.

KNOWLEDGE
REQUIRED:
Basic concepts of working and communicating with disturbed persons and therapeutic applications.

SUPERVISION:
Administratively supervised by a unit or team supervisor or coordinator and technically by personnel to whom assigned for training, guidance and/or performance. Supervision is close except in some areas where skills and knowledge have been developed sufficiently for performance with minimum supervision.

MINIMUM
QUALIFICATIONS:
Progressive experience or training which clearly demonstrates aptitude and ability to work with disturbed persons. Six months progressive and successful experience and training at the Mental Health Worker I level or equivalent will meet this requirement.

TITLE:
Community Mental Health Worker V

ORGANIZATION:
Department of Psychiatry, Mental Health Center.

DUTIES:
Performs duties similar to Mental Health Worker IV with the following additional responsibilities: schedules, sets up priorities and coordinates all Sustained-Contact Team activities. Supervises and provides training to lower level clerical personnel and community mental health workers. Provides liaison with other teams, units and other organizations.

KNOWLEDGE
REQUIRED:
Therapeutic practices and concepts of communicating and working with disturbed persons and ability to coordinate and schedule work of a team and establish priorities including training of subordinate team members.

SUPERVISION:
Supervised by a program coordinator or administrator. Works with minimum to no supervision following prescribed treatment or instructions with authority to make changes within predetermined limitations.

MINIMUM
QUALIFICATIONS:
Progressive and successful experience in addition to appropriate training which clearly demonstrates ability to work without supervision, establish priorities and schedules and supervise, train and obtain cooperation from others.

Generally, two and one-half years or directly applicable progressive and successful experience and/or training is required.

An appropriate A.A. degree may be substituted provided it furnishes equivalent skills and knowledges. A resident of the area of assignment is preferred.

PROBLEMS ENCOUNTERED

Although experience has shown that the mental health worker program has been basically successful, several problems have been encountered. The greatest problem was funding. Obtaining the local share of this federally supported program was extremely difficult since community financial resources were negligible. After months of negotiations, a small grant from the Model Cities program defrayed approximately 25 percent of trainee wages. The rest has come from the mental health center's budget utilizing funds made available by the resignation of other staff who were not replaced.

A second financial problem was the obtaining of a salary increase for the trainees in the middle of the contract year. Additional funds for a twenty-cents-per-hour increase were ultimately obtained through the Department of Labor and the University of New Mexico School of Medicine, Department of Psychiatry.

The final fiscal problem centered around obtaining funds for permanent employment. Since the mental health center was experiencing fiscal difficulty itself due to decreasing federal support, the board of trustees was understandably reluctant to commit themselves to supporting additional staff members. Since only thirty to thirty-five of the original forty trainees completed the program and because of their demonstrated effectiveness, the board finally approved an operating budget which permitted employing all trainees who successfully completed the program.

Another type of problem which presented itself was the changing self-concepts of the trainees during the initial four to eight months of the program. Each trainee went through a stress period which was caused by conflicting expectations of family, community, and self. Most of the trainees were able to deal with this although frequent concomitants were missing work, getting into arguments, and threatening to quit.

Another problem area which has been noted in this New Career Program is the conflict between the "old" and the "new" professional. The problem did not come from specific occupational groups, but from individuals who were not comfortable with themselves and their abilities. They included nurses, social workers, psychiatrists, and others. What made the basic program work, however, was a commitment to the concept of the indigenous worker by the top administration and key staff members in all aspects of the center program.

SUMMARY AND CONCLUSIONS

The New Careers Mental Health Worker training program at the Bernalillo County Mental Health Center has developed into a meaningful training program that has helped build a bridge between the culturally depressed community and the mental health professional community. This has been done by encouraging participation in a comprehensive training program, yet letting the trainee utilize his own skills and knowledge about his culture and community without imposing value judgments.

It takes approximately 60,000 dollars to train a physician. It took nearly 10,000 dollars to train each mental health worker. Was it a worthwhile investment? Since most of the trainees were unemployed and receiving welfare assistance at the beginning of the program and are now taxpaying citizens, the investment will be repaid to the community within a few years. The type and quality of crisis intervention among our target population has also significantly changed since these workers arrived on the scene. Preliminary indications are that a significant impact has also been made in the crucial areas of trust and acceptance of mental health practices by the community.

43
George G. Meyer, M.D.,
Margaret Speicher, M.S.W., *and*
Robert E. Buxbaum, S.T.M., M.S.W.

Training the Mental Health Assistant

The Northwest San Antonio Community Mental Health Center began operation in January 1969, facing the tasks of developing a program of services to the community and of recruiting staff competent to deliver them. It is the first of its kind in the San Antonio metropolitan area which has a population of nearly 800,000.

Professional staff is scarce in the area. Psychiatrists in private practice are fully involved with their patients; clinical psychologists are associated with some of the local colleges, with a few community facilities, and are engaged in private practice; social workers are in high demand by local agencies which compete for the graduates of the local Worden School of Social Service. Some professional staff are associated with military establishments and not available to civilian agencies.

The opening of the University of Texas Medical School at San Antonio in September 1968 brought additional psychiatric staff to the city. Since the operation of the Northwest Community Mental Health Center was directly related to the Department of Psychiatry of the medical school, recruitment responsibilities for psychiatrists fell to that department. However, the clinical psychologist and social worker on the planning staff realized that the recruitment of professionals from their fields would not be as easy. Furthermore, recruitment from outside the area could not be considered as a feasible alternative since the salary scale of the center compared unfavorably to other areas of the country.

Recruitment of less-trained, subprofessional staff seemed to be the next most feasible approach. None of the local colleges, however, conducted an undergraduate program in either social work or psychology which was clinically oriented. Therefore, B.A. or associate degree level staff were not available to supplement the limited professional staff. Since totally untrained staff could not be employed and expected to render direct patient care, the only other alternative was to employ staff without professional training and to provide inservice training to prepare them for work with patients. Work with local colleges to accredit and develop training programs was simultaneously undertaken. This paper presents and discusses these developments.

PROGRAM DEVELOPMENT AND RECRUITMENT

Service needs called for personnel who could work with trained staff in the evaluation and treatment of patients. A job description was developed which revolved around the key phrase "assists the professional staff in the evaluation and treatment of patients." The job title Mental Health Assistant underscored the key element of the job description within the setting of the mental health center. The mental health assistant would be expected to work in the intake and treatment section of the community mental health center and would be supervised by the social work staff since he would be mostly engaged in functions traditionally assigned to that discipline. The mental health assistant, however, was also trained in the administration of some psychological testing material and was under the supervision of the clinical psychologist when engaged in this activity.

What qualifications would candidates for these positions need? The following were considered essential: (1) sufficient intelligence to enable the person to participate in an intensive training program including lecture material, independent study through reading, and workshops and seminars; (2) experience in working with people so that the candidate's ability to work in interpersonal relationships could be evaluated; (3) personal maturity; and (4) a high school degree with some college courses in addition preferred. The latter was required to insure that the candidate had had exposure to didactic learning experiences and could involve himself in training. A commitment to complete college work was not required, although it was encouraged.

Recruitment efforts were directed toward persons who had worked with people and their problems. The center contacted neighborhood centers, church groups, settlement houses, and medical clinics with the expectation of locating persons who had not had many educational opportunities but had shown an ability and interest in working with troubled people.

It was anticipated that women who had returned to work after raising their children would be interested in these positions. This expectation was not borne out. Instead a group of people in their twenties sought the positions and were employed. They were mainly: (1) those interested in the behavioral sciences who had to interrupt their college careers for financial or personal reasons or who had enrolled in part-time college work and did not wish to work in clerical or technical occupations while completing their education; (2) those who had earned B.A. degrees in the behavioral sciences with the intent of entering professional schools but had found themselves unable to implement such plans; and (3) those who had a few years of experience in another field which they did not wish to pursue as a career but were financially unable to enter directly into training for a new career. For each, the mental health assistant position was viewed as a stepping stone into one of the disciplines of the mental health field.

TRAINING PROGRAM

The proposed training program was discussed with the faculty of the Worden School of Social Service at Our Lady of the Lake College, in San Antonio, which had just completed plans for an undergraduate program leading to a B.A. degree with a major in Social Welfare. However, this program could not be adopted in its entirety for several reasons. The community mental health center needed personnel whose training placed more emphasis on understanding normal and abnormal behavior and personality theory than was included in the undergraduate social welfare curriculum. The academic calendar of the college did not meet the mental health assistants' need for a period of intensive training prior to their being engaged in work with patients.

The center's screening of applicants was comparable to the college's screening of candidates for admission and the training program offered by the center covered many areas of the material normally included in the courses in the social welfare sequence. Moreover, the staff involved in teaching the community mental health center course met all of the criteria of the college for academic faculty. Therefore, when the center's curriculum, discussed in detail below, was completed, it was submitted to the academic council of the college which granted twelve semester hours of undergraduate credit to the program. Then credits could be used by the mental health assistant in completing requirements for his bachelor's degree.

The curriculum of the center's program attempted to provide the types of learning experiences that would be helpful to the mental health assistants in their work with patients and in their understanding of and communication with other mental health workers. The format of the program was conceptualized as offering several different types of learning experiences that were serialized but timed to coordinate with each other as they intertwined; much like the threads of a rope. Their strength was increased by their complementary nature.

A good example of the curriculum content which would be basic to similar programs in other centers was the lecture series on Personality Development and Psychopathology (Table 43–1). These lectures were delivered by the clinical and teaching staff of the medical school's department of psychiatry, some of the staff of the community guidance center, and two of the physicians on the staff of the San Antonio State

359

TABLE 43–1

Personality Development and Psychopathology

The History of Medicine and Psychiatry   (3 lectures)
Normal Personality Development   (9 lectures)
Psychopathology: Psychiatric Nosology
Psychopathology: Psychoneurotic Reactions   (2 lectures)
Psychopathology: The Brain Syndromes
Psychopathology: The Character Disorders
Psychopathology: Homosexuality and the Sexual Deviations
Psychopathology: The Addictions
Psychopathology: Suicide and the Affective Reactions   (2 lectures)
Psychopathology: The Psychoses
Psychopathology: The Geriatric Disorders
Psychopathology: The Psychophysiologic Reactions
The Major Medical Symptoms
The Major Medical Considerations

Hospital. It provided the students with an introduction to the soil of the field in which they would be working.

A second lecture series introduced the student to some of the issues involved in the practice of social work (Table 43-2) by beginning with an intensive study of the people who make up the treatment team. An honest appraisal of the contributions and limitations of the psychiatrist, psychologist, social worker, and nurse helped the student to more clearly identify the nature of his role and the place he occupied within the team. Lectures by a sociologist on the hospital as a social system, an exposure to the social welfare system, and an emphasis on the structured and unstructured health and welfare resources within our own commu-

TABLE 43–2

The Social Work Practice Lecture Series

Introduction to the Treatment Team: The Social Worker
Introduction to the Treatment Team: The Physician
Introduction to the Treatment Team: The Psychiatrist   (2 lectures)
"Our Work in Bexar County; An Overview"
Introduction to the Treatment Team: The Psychologist   (2 lectures)
Introduction to the Treatment Team: The Nurse
Administrative Concerns of Social Work Practice   (2 lectures)
The Social Structure of the Hospital   (2 lectures)
Introduction to the Social Welfare System
Contemporary Systems of Economic Maintenance and the Patient
The Network of Structured Community Health and Welfare Resources
The Network of Unstructured Community Health and Welfare Resources
The Family and Its Community   (4 lectures)

---

nity were also included. Observation and discussion of team family intake helped to concretize the foregoing material by focusing upon the family and its community.

A series of seminars and experiences were provided, with a focus upon the contemporary situational and cultural influences that help shape the lives of the people whom the center serves. We proposed that the mental health assistants become able to see the patient as a person within systems that created and fed into his intrapersonal dynamics and interpersonal relationships (Table 43–3). Trinity University made available their Director of Urban Studies for two seminars that introduced the student to the field of urbanology and focused on the stresses, tensions, and conflicts created by urban living. The chairman of the University's Department of Sociology and Anthropology led a discussion on the culture of poverty and its practical implications. Two afternoons were spent with the pastor of one of the city's black Baptist churches. The trainees watched the feature films *Raisin in the Sun* and *The Pawn-*

TABLE 43–3
Contemporary Situational and Cultural Influences Series

Life in the City	(2 lectures)
The Culture of Poverty	
Life in the Black Community	(2 lectures)
Life in the Barrio	(2 lectures)

broker, which provided the bases for their discussions of the many issues that are currently finding expression in our society. The group's insight into the minority viewpoint was enriched when it experienced rejection first hand as one of the militant brown power groups refused to keep a meeting that had been set up between them.

Social work methods were taught through the use of recordings which received individual verbal and written supervision from the program's coordinator-supervisor. Problems with interview methods; an understanding of the interference created by the injection of personal concerns; and a study of the ways in which natural sensitivity, feelings, and personal strengths can be utilized for both understanding and treatment of the persons seeking help were emphasized. Trainees listened to tape recordings and videotapes of interviews done by professionals and discussed their own interviews in group supervision. These experiences gave the students the opportunity for participant observation and the chance to evaluate their own methods in comparison to those employed by staff with more training and experience.

The student's involvement in an evaluation of both the program and himself were vital parts of the program's concluding phase. A written evaluation of each student was offered by the program's supervisor, discussed with the student and with the person who would become the student's supervisor when he returned to full-time clinical work. This became the starting point for the student's continued learning and supervision. In order to recognize the significance of the completion of the program and to establish its proper importance in the center's work, each student received a certificate from the Bexar County Hospital District at a graduation luncheon. Upon presentation, these certificates became the proof necessary for the awarding of credit hours for academic work at Our Lady of the Lake College.

PROBLEMS

As we fully expected, there were some weaknesses which became apparent during this pilot program. These were discussed with the students and faculty and will be used as bases for modification of future training programs. Several major problem areas were noted.

1. Twenty-four hours a week were devoted to training time and sixteen to clinical practice. The necessity of continuing clinical practice while an intensive training program is in progress is vital. It provides the clinical material for learning and helps to keep the program goals relevant. However, the division of time presented a problem; three days a week in the program and two in the clinical setting. Lecture scheduling prevented the carrying out of this plan and the result was conflict between clinical and learning obligations. It would probably be preferable to schedule lectures only in the mornings and to devote each afternoon to clinical work.

2. The "visiting lecturer" approach in many parts of the training program provided resources that would have otherwise been unavailable. However, it also led to considerable repetition. While this aroused some resistance within the student group, it is probably unavoidable without impoverishing the program. The coordinator's presence and willingness to engage the speaker in discussion can minimize the problem.

3. Experience has convinced us that the student–supervisor ratio (eight to one) was too great for the provision of good supervisory experi-

ence. Individual and regular supervisory conferences are an important teaching method that the program had to forego.

4. Faculty committees in other local colleges contacted tended to resent pressures from "outsiders" on their guarded curriculums, and the acceptance of new courses and new policies tends to get tabled in various committees as proposals get passed along the academic hierarchy.

5. The faculty of additional colleges approached are threatened by the advent of more and more part-time students and fear the "cheapening" of degrees and academic credit. Relaxing admission criteria to accept less academically qualified students into courses has been a difficult concept to sell, except in the original cooperating school.

6. Trained personnel tend to be recruited away by other programs. Therefore, entry level training courses need to be repeated at least yearly and possibly twice yearly.

7. The training program must provide the actual dollars for tuition and books as well as support for items such as baby-sitting and car fare. Even motivated and capable trainees can lack the ability to absorb these costs.

SUMMARY

The goal of the training program's curriculum can best be formulated in response to the question posed by the brothel owner in the movie *The Pawnbroker* when he asked the pawnbroker: "Masserman, are you that kind of person? Are you? The kind of person who closes your eyes to what's going on around you and doesn't feel?" Our ultimate purpose was to help our students open their eyes to the lives of the people they serve and to enter these lives with feeling. We believe that people who can see and feel are therapeutic instruments in the lives of the troubled persons who seek help.

---

44 *Margaret M. Taylor*, R.N.

The Training of Nurses: The General Hospital and the Community Mental Health Center

The emergence of community mental health centers has created the need for the development of new roles and functions for mental health professionals. The uniqueness of each community influences the types of services which are needed and the professional roles and functions that are developed to provide them.

Traditionally, the majority of psychiatric nurses have functioned as nurse administrators, educators or quasitherapists with rather prescribed functions. In contrast, the role of the nurse in the community mental health center is evolving to include different dimensions. This article discusses the evolving role of one psychiatric nurse as a trainer for nursing staffs in three general hospitals affiliated with the community mental health center for the provision of inpatient services.

SETTING

The Community Mental Health Center of Escambia County, Inc., a private nonprofit corporation which began operation in July 1968, serves a one-county catchment area of approximately 200,000 people. The center provides the following services: outpatient, a 24-hour crisis intervention program, day treatment (or partial hospitalization), education-consultation training, aftercare services for patients returning from the state hospital, and special programs in the areas of alcoholism, drug abuse, and learning disabilities. Also housed in the center is a full-time vocational rehabilitation counselor and the mental health association.

Since there are inpatient psychiatric units with a total of eighty-three beds in the general hospitals, a unique cooperative agreement has been made with each hospital to provide for continuity of care and the transfer of records. The utilization of these general hospital services reduced the initial building cost of the center, eliminated the on-going cost of administering and maintaining inpatient facilities and their staff, and promoted cooperation and coordination of mental health services in the community.

THE ROLE OF THE NURSE

During the planning stage of development, the psychologist director of the center, the community psychiatrist, the three directors of nursing of the general hospitals and the state mental health nurse consultant discussed the role of psychiatric nurses in community mental health. Two positions were created in the day treatment program for nurses who would function in essentially therapeutic roles with patients.

This group also requested a third nursing position. This employee would develop an inservice educational program on the psychiatric units of the three general hospitals. The job description called for a nurse with a master's degree in psychiatric nursing who would function as a coordinator, educator, consultant, and liaison between the center and the inpatient services. The salary for this position was the shared responsibility of the three hospitals and the center. Administratively this "mental health nurse coordinator" was responsible to the director of the center.

This direct administrative line from the director of the center is accompanied by staff lines from the directors of nursing of the three general hospitals. Conflicts are avoided through a Nurses' Coordinating Committee for Mental Health which was formed during the planning phase of the center. This committee meets monthly to discuss problems and to share information. The members of the group include the three directors of nursing of the general hospitals, the director of nurses of the U.S. Naval Hospital, the director of public health nursing, the director of the community mental health center, the community psychiatrist, the three psychiatric nursing supervisors, the psychiatric nurse in day treatment, the mental health nurse coordinator, and a psychiatric social worker. The meetings are used to coordinate activities that involve the nursing staffs of the three hospitals such as classes or workshops and to present the ideas and plans of the coordinator for discussion.

INSERVICE EDUCATION
WITH THE GENERAL HOSPITALS

Originally the mental health nurse coordinator had thought that a combined inservice program for the three hospitals for nursing personnel might be feasible. However, during the orientation phase, this idea was rejected. The three hospitals and psychiatric units were quite different and different staffing patterns posed problems for a centralized inservice education program. The competitiveness that existed among the three hospitals was an additional factor negating a coordinated program.

Each psychiatric unit had its own assets, problems, and learning needs. For example, one hospital had applied for federal construction funds to expand the unit from eighteen to thirty-eight beds to include an adolescent treatment program. Therefore, many new nursing staff at all levels had to be employed and trained with a special focus on adolescents. More knowledge about normal growth and development was required.

365

Functioning as a consultant to the director of nurses, the psychiatric nursing supervisor, and hospital administrator involved in planning the program for the new adolescent unit, suggested additional changes. A recreational program was started using two students from the physical education program of the University of West Florida. The hospital provided a station wagon for transportation to activities outside of the hospital and recreational equipment. A psychiatric social worker was employed to interview families and provide counseling services. The mental health nurse coordinator participated in the interviewing and selecting of the social worker. Patients were given more responsibility including making their beds, eating in a central dining room, and caring for their personal belongings. Nurses wore street clothes if they desired.

Another hospital had the newest psychiatric unit with the least experienced staff in psychiatric nursing. Since the head nurse of the unit was relatively unsophisticated about psychiatric nursing theory and practice, it was necessary for the mental health nurse coordinator to develop a relationship with her before attempting changes. Crisis situations were especially useful to the mental health nurse coordinator in establishing herself as a helpful and supportive person and in teaching. During a crisis, the nursing group was more receptive to new ideas, to problem-solving, and to trying out suggestions. As they began to achieve success with crises, they started to initiate requests for help with other problems.

The third hospital had the oldest and largest psychiatric unit and the psychiatric nursing staff had the most experience. The nursing supervisor had been involved in the original request for a mental health nurse coordinator. The relationship that has developed emphasizes consultation more than teaching. The therapeutic milieu received the major emphasis. Group meetings of staff were held to demonstrate the use of interpersonal skills. As this consultation progressed, staff members became more comfortable in their interactions with patients and allowed them to have a more active role in the planning of therapeutic activities.

CENTRALIZED EDUCATIONAL PROGRAM

Many practical nurses are employed on the psychiatric units who have had limited educational and clinical experiences in psychiatric nursing during their basic practical nurse training. The coordinating group agreed that there was a need for developing the therapeutic skills and competencies of this group. Classes were offered by the vocational section of Pensacola Junior College. Fifteen practical nurses enrolled for a thirteen-week course. Classes were actually held in the day treatment center at the community mental health center. It is interesting to note that some of the practical nurses, who were motivated to attend this class for thirteen weeks on their own time, would not attend inservice educational programs held at work during work time. It appears that the practical nurses, as students, expected to enroll, attend class, and have homework assignments. In a work role, however, they expect to work and to perform various assigned tasks related to patient care. Many of them did not consider work as a learning experience and felt that they could only learn outside the work situation.

Two one-day workshops on Planning for Nursing Care were held for the registered nurses. The workshops consisted of small group discussions about specific nursing care problems and administration.

After the day treatment program began to emphasize behavior modification techniques, the mental health nurse coordinator attended several workshops on behavior modification. Several classes were then held for the psychiatric nursing staff of the three hospitals to acquaint them with the theory and some of the techniques. Since that time the mental health nurse coordinator and the nurses have developed some nursing care plans using this technique which has been useful in motivating very withdrawn patients.

LIAISON WITH DAY TREATMENT

Partial hospitalization is needed for many patients to work through the transition from the full-time hospital to the community. The mental health nurse coordinator was in a strategic position to assist in this transition since she was part of the full-time hospital units and day treatment. She interviews patients in the general hospitals who have been referred to day treatment and presents her recommendations to the staff of day treatment for their consideration.

At times, problems arise because of conflicting philosophies about mental illness and its treatment. The hospital psychiatric units are often operated in accordance with the concepts of the medical model where the individual has a disease which the doctor diagnoses, treats, and arrests if not cures. The patient is expected to cooperate by being a passive recipient of care from the expert and his assistants. The day treatment program of the community mental health center views patients as being able to be active participants in seeking different solutions to their problems. The mental health nurse coordinator can play a very important function in resolving these conflicts for both patients and staff.

GENERAL HOSPITAL CONSULTATION AND EDUCATION

The mental health nurse coordinator is also utilized on a limited basis for both consultation and education in the general hospital. Some of the educational activities have included lectures on Emotional Aspects of Intensive Care Nursing of the Acute Cardiac Patient, Emotional Aspects of Seriously Ill Patients, and the Traditional Problems of Patients Being Transferred from Intensive Care to General Floor Care.

PROBLEMS ENCOUNTERED

Inservice education on psychiatric units of general hospitals is a difficult job. Issues which must be faced include the heterogeneity of the group with differences in education, experience, and age; the rotation of shifts and days off; the rapid turnover; the pressure of work; and antieducational attitudes.

Nursing personnel consist of registered nurses, practical nurses, aides, and orderlies. The experiences of the group are as varied as their educational backgrounds and create challenges in designing and carrying out meaningful general inservice programs. To approach these problems, group discussions have been frequently employed keeping the focus centered on a particular patient or nursing problem and soliciting the observations and ideas of everyone present. Assigned or suggested reading materials, while not effective in general, have proven to be helpful to some nurses in providing for individual learning and professional growth. Giving specific reading assignments to individuals along with the responsibility for presenting the material to the group is more effective than just suggesting that people read for their own interest. Films have also been effective tools especially if the films are scheduled for repeated showings to small groups at staggered hours. Bringing in outside speakers stimulates some enthusiasm and interest in the group as well as increasing the nurse's general fund of information especially about community resources and programs. Providing a flexible and varied program is more stimulating to everyone involved than relying on one method or one person for inservice education.

The turnover of personnel and the rotation of shifts poses problems in planning content and in providing for continuity of learning. Unless a specific program can be scheduled for multiple times, only a limited number of nursing staff can be involved in a single program. Keeping records of who attended what programs is helpful in planning inservice programs designed to meet specific learning needs. Audio-visual methods of teaching can contribute to a solution of this problem. A lecture or conference can be taped so that it can be heard by people on days off or on different shifts and saved for future use as the need arises. Two of the hospitals are currently using closed-circuit television for inservice education programs.

A high percentage of the hospital nurse's time is spent in dispensing medication, admitting and discharging patients, transcribing orders, making rounds with doctors, and transporting patients to various areas in the hospital for diagnostic procedures. These activities often have higher priority than interacting with patients. This presents a challenge to the person responsible for inservice education to be creative, flexible, innovative, and reality-oriented in designing and activating programs. The content of the programs must be practical and relevant if it is to be effective in promoting improved nursing care and interaction with patients.

SUMMARY

If the mental health of a community is to be promoted, community resources, agencies, and professional services must be utilized in more creative, flexible, and innovative ways. It behooves nurses engaged in helping to provide mental health services to examine, change, and expand their roles and functions so that the services they provide are relevant to the needs of a community. Traditional practices must give way to changing times. Each nurse needs to develop her knowledge and skills so that the services she renders directly or indirectly promote the mental health of the community. The employment of a mental health nurse coordinator has proven to be a useful method for stimulating change toward more effective patient care on the inpatient psychiatric units of general hospitals associated with a community mental health center.

369

REFERENCES

Christmas, J. J., Wallace, H., and Edwards, J. "New Careers and New Mental Health Services: Fantasy or Future." *American Journal of Psychiatry* 126(April 1970): 1480–1486.

Errera, P., Bellis, E. C., and Coleman, J. V. "The Training of Residents in a Community Psychiatric Clinic." *Mental Hygiene* 51(April 1967): 270–274.

Fischer, A., and Brodsky, C. M. "Training Medical Residents: Lessons for the Coming Manpower Crisis in Psychiatry." *Comprehensive Psychiatry* 10(May 1969): 173–180.

Fredrick, C. J. "Future Training in Psychotherapy." *International Psychiatric Clinic* 6(1969): 379–401.

Gaskill, H. S., and Norton, J. E. "Observations on Psychiatric Residency Training. Community Psychiatry." *Archives of General Psychiatry* 18(January 1968): 7–15.

Grosser, C., Henry, W. E., and Kelly, J. G., eds. *Non-Professionals in the Human Services.* San Francisco: Josey-Bass, Inc., 1969.

Grosser, C. *The Role of the Non-Professional in the Manpower Development Programs.* Washington, D.C., U.S. Department of Labor, 1966.

Harris, M. R., Kalis, B. L., and Schneider, L. "Training for Community Mental Health in an Urban Setting." *American Journal of Psychiatry* 124(October 1967): supplement, 20–29.

Kern, H. M. Jr., Spiro, H. R., and Kolmer, M. B. "Preparing Psychiatric Residents for Community Psychiatry." *Hospital Community Psychiatry* 17(December 1966): 360–362.

Kvarnes, R. G., Rittelmeyer, L. F. Jr., and Schneider, I. "The Associated Faculties Program in Community Psychiatry." *Hospital Community Psychiatry* 21(February 1970): 62–64.

Levenson, A. I., Beck, J. C., and Quinn, R. "Manpower and Training in Community Mental Health Centers." *Hospital Community Psychiatry* 20(March 1969): 85–88.

Lynch, M., and Gardner, E. A. "Some Issues Raised in the Training of Paraprofessional Personnel as Clinic Therapists." *American Journal of Psychiatry* 126(April 1970): 1473–1479.

Mandeville, P. F., and Maholick, L. T. "Changing Points of Emphasis in Training the Community's Natural Counselors." *Mental Hygiene* 53(April 1969): 208–213.

Minuchin, S. "The Paraprofessional and the Use of Confrontation in the Mental Health Field." *American Journal of Orthopsychiatry* 39(October 1969): 722–729.

Pearl, A., and Reisman, F. *New Careers for the Poor: The Non-Professional in the Human Services.* New York, Free Press, 1965.

Peck, H. B., Levin, T., and Roman, M. "The Health Careers Institute: A Mental Health Strategy for an Urban Community." *American Journal of Psychiatry* 125(March 1969): 1180–1186.

Rosenblum, G., and Hassol, L. "Training for New Mental Health Roles." *Mental Hygiene* 52(January 1968): 81–86.

Schwartz, D. A., and Schwartz, M. "A Preceptorship in Community Mental Health Administration." *Comprehensive Psychiatry* 8(February 1967): 53–61.

"AA Degree in Human Services for New Careerists." *New Careers Bulletin* 1(May, 1969): 1.

"A Suggested Course Outline for Introductory Generic Training." *New Careers Perspectives* 2(January 1970).

370

Margaret M. Taylor

"Impact of the Indigenous Non-Professional on the Professional's Role." *New Careers Perspective* 9(June 1969).

"Roles and Functions for Different Levels of Mental Health Workers." A report of a symposium on Manpower Utilization for Mental Health. Atlanta: Southern Regional Education Board, 1969.

XIII
Critical Issues for Community Mental Health Centers

EDITORS' INTRODUCTION

Born in 1963, and currently in its ninth year, the Community Mental Health Center Program can no longer be considered as being in its infancy, with more than 400 centers funded and approximately 300 in operation. Nevertheless, it is clear to all those who have surveyed the situation carefully that growing pains are definitely in evidence as a result of many of the issues which have been discussed throughout this book.

In reviewing and assessing the total scope of the program, however, four broad areas clearly reflect the current critical state of the community mental health center program and are responsible for much of the anxiety which is felt by those who support its development and growth. Stated generally, these are the areas of community, administration, manpower, and financing. Each of the articles in this final chapter addresses some of the basic and most critical issues which are facing the current planners, developers, implementers, and supporters of community mental health centers.

The Concept of Community

DEFINITIONS

A serviceable definition of *community* is given in a textbook on sociology by Leonard Broom and Philip Selznick: [1]

A community is a comprehensive group with two chief characteristics: (1) within it the individual can have most of the experiences and conduct most of the activities that are important to him; (2) it is bound together by a shared sense of belonging and by the feeling among its members that the group defines for them their distinctive identity. Theoretically, the member of a community lives his whole life within it; he feels a sense of kinship with others who belong to it; and he accepts the community much as he accepts his own name and family membership.

Communities are usually based on locality—a village, city, or nation. The geographic area and a sense of place set the boundaries of common living and provide a basis for solidarity. However, without respect to geography, one may speak of the 'Catholic community,' in the sense that there is a unique set of Catholic activities and institutions which, taken together, permit many Catholics to live out much of their lives within boundaries set by religious affiliation. . . .

Writing on community some fifty years ago, Eduard C. Lindeman [2] quotes C. C. North's statement that members of a community "are bound together by the necessity or convenience of fulfilling certain essential needs in a cooperative way." North goes on to say, "Local government is probably the most distinguishing feature of a community." This last remark is worth bearing in mind.

A definition of *Gemeinschaft* (community) by Ferdinand Tönnies likewise harks back half a century: "Whenever, by institutionalized means, men are bound to each other through their wishes and answer affirmatively to each other, there a community is existent . . ." [3] The requirement that they "answer affirmatively" adds significantly to a somewhat comparable definition recently offered by Donald C. Klein, that community consists of "patterned interactions within a domain of individuals seeking to achieve security and physical safety, to derive support at times of stress, and to gain selfhood and significance throughout the life cycle." [4]

The "seeking" that Klein emphasizes provides the theme for a profound and prescient book by Robert A. Nisbet, *The Quest for Community*, published in 1953.[5] Nisbet regards the modern preoccupation with community as "ominous," seeing it as "a manifestation of certain profound dislocations in the primary associative areas of society, dislocations that have been created to a great extent by . . . the present location and distribution of power in society." He states that these current dislocations and deprivations have driven men, "in this age of economic abundance and political welfare, to the quest for community, to narcotic relief from the sense of isolation and anxiety."

Within such groups . . . as the family, the small local community, and the various other traditional relationships that have immemorially mediated between the individual and his society . . . have been engendered or intensified the principal incentives of work, love, prayer, and devotion to freedom and order.

This is the area of association from which the individual commonly gains his concept of the outer world and his sense of position in it. . . . It contains and cherishes not only the formal moral precept but what Whitehead has called 'our vast system of inherited symbolism.'

Feelings of moral estrangement, of the hostility of the world, the fear of freedom, of irrational aggressiveness, and of helplessness before the simplest of problems have to do . . . with the individual's sense of the inaccessibility of this area of relationship. In the child, or in the adult, the roots of a coherent, logical sense of the outer world are sunk deeply in the soil of close, meaningful interpersonal relations . . . we are learning that many of the motivations and incentives which an older generation of rationalists believed were inherent in the individual are actually supplied by social groups.

Nisbet comments that "A vast amount of attention has been given to such phenomena as marital unhappiness, prostitution, juvenile misbehavior, and the sexual life of the unmarried, on the curious assumption that these are 'pathological' and derive clearly from the breakdown of the family."

But it is not disorganization that is crucial to the problem of the family or of any other significant group in our society. The most fundamental problem has to do with the *organized* associations of men . . . in an economy and political order whose principal ends have come to be structured in such a way that the primary social relationships are increasingly functionless, almost irrelevant, with respect to these ends.

Although it is important for the kinds of primary group relationships that characterize *community* life to be meaningfully linked with the dominant *organizational* structures of the society, each being "relevant" to the other, I believe it is worthwhile to make a clear conceptual distinction between these two sorts of entities. Those structures of relationships that have the quality of *community* exist and are valued for their own sake, as ends in themselves. Social *organizations,* by contrast, are valued for their usefulness and productiveness with reference to one or more specific objectives. In principle, organizations exist *only* for the sake of the goals they achieve, the functions they perform, the purposes they fulfill, and the goods they produce. In actual fact, however, once an organization has become established it begins to take on certain attributes of *community.* As this occurs, the organization's continuing existence then becomes important for its own sake, quite apart from considerations of its effectiveness in achieving its stated goals.

From this standpoint there is no such thing as a strictly "functional" community, consisting of people bound to each other simply and solely by the fact that they practice the same profession or occupation, or work for the same organization. If functions alone are the reason for being, there must be continual validation of the actual usefulness of activities carried out by their members. Thus, what Murray Ross [6] calls "functional communities" are more accurately designated as *organizations* (or systems of interrelated organizations) and not as communities at all.

Communities in the strict sense do *not* have to have their usefulness demonstrated, any more than do nations, religions, fraternal orders, families, or human individuals. One does not seriously pose William James's question, "Of what use is a newborn baby?" nor does one ask comparable questions concerning social entities that have the quality of community. The significance of the newborn baby and of the community lies in the mere fact of their existence, in their heritage from the past and their prospective development in the future; not in their functional usefulness. Such functional groups as the medical profession, for example, readily take on these attributes of community as ties that can be described as "fraternal" are cultivated among medical colleagues. As these ties develop, it indeed does become appropriate to consider physicians—or trade union members, or students enrolled in a college, or members of an ethnic minority—as constituting a "community within a community." [7] These groupings serve to define their members' distinctive identity, and provide a basis for solidarity quite different in its nature from that which springs from the pursuit of utilitarian goals.

Thus I would differ from such writers on the community as Roland Warren,[8] who considers that specialized interest groups and organizations fulfilling specific technical functions are essential—and increasingly dominant—aspects of "community." Rather, following Nisbet, I would maintain that the effect of these organizations has often been, in Stein's [9] phrase, to *eclipse* community; to encroach upon its domain. It is this encroachment upon the realm of community by the dominant organizational emphasis on specific functions, interests, and products that has led, in my opinion, to the current widespread and uneasy "quest for community," the search for those aspects of human social life that are to be valued and nurtured in their own right and for their own sake, rather than for the supposedly useful or productive things they accomplish.

In defining community, Talcott Parsons [10] treats "community" in an analytic sense, as an *aspect* of social structure. Community, in his view, is to be considered "not as a type of concrete social unit, but as an *analytic* category" for designating one aspect "of *every* concrete social collectivity or structure." As he remarks, this mode of definition departs from much recent sociological tradition—the tradition followed by those who regard *all* structured human interactions occurring within a community's boundaries as constituting that community. Similarly, I have urged that community be considered as an analytic concept, rather than identified with concretely existing aggregations of people. "It can then be seen as a *dimension* of human behavior, a *component* of man's view of himself and his fellows."

But Parsons restricts "community" to "that aspect of the structure of social systems which is referable to the territorial location of persons . . . and their activities." In my view, the aspect which is distinctive of community is not simply territorial, but rather consists of a symbolically expressed "sense of common destiny, a common envisaging of situations that are going to arise," a sense of interrelatedness in the face of this common destiny, and a knowledge of what community members can expect of one another.

"Destiny" is a word that seems well suited for use in a definition of community, for it combines connotations of a fate that befalls people (either from the outside or as a consequence of their own actions) with connotations of a direction in which they are moving, a destination they seek. [11]

By this definition ethnic, religious, or other "fraternal" (and sororal) sorts of affiliations can be as central to the concept of community as territorial boundaries. The concept is still an analytic one. Thus, *every* collection of human beings and their patterned activities, *to the extent that* participants share and express a sense of common destiny that is shaped by the past and oriented to the future, *to that extent* constitutes a community, according to the definition I have proposed.

Some of the young people of today who are in the vanguard of the so-cial and cultural revolution that is currently taking place—largely in re-bellion against (in Nisbet's words) "the present location and distribution of power in society" and against such idealized images as that of "the organization man"—have a succinct term for characterizing community that seems fitting—they call it *tribal*. I think they are correct in regard-ing the tribal aspects of social living as having crucial—and recently much neglected—significance. In my opinion it is these aspects that most clearly define, in current terms, precisely *where community is at*.

APPLICATIONS, ISSUES AND PROBLEMS

The catchment area assigned to a community mental health center may bear little or no relationship to "community" as defined above. If this is true, what can the staff of a community mental health center hope to do about it?

For one thing, the center's staff can attempt to *create* a community, starting, if need be, from scratch. To individuals living within the area who come seeking help for psychological problems, the center indeed represents their common destiny. It is their destination—and may be the only resource available to them—when they apply or are brought for the help they need. A center's staff should remember, however, that serving as a functional resource to which psychologically distressed peo-ple can turn is hardly enough of a basis for building a community, espe-cially one designed to embrace the catchment area as a whole. This can, however, be a starting point.

Communities of Patients With regard simply to patients who come for treatment, there are certain steps in the direction of "community" that a mental health center staff can take. If the center includes facilities for inpatient and/or day hospital care, a therapeutic community of the sort described by Maxwell Jones [12] and others [13] can be created. For ex-hospital patients, or those not hospitalized, there can be "therapeutic so-cial clubs" of the kind inaugurated by Joshua Bierer [14] more than thirty years ago.

A decentralized "unit" serving a mental health catchment area can be created at the state hospital that customarily receives patients from the area, if that hospital can be persuaded to adopt the unit plan rather than continuing—as some still do—to classify and segregate patients ac-cording to the behavior expected of them. The older model of a large, centralized, hierarchically organized public hospital has been tellingly described by Stanford H. Simon [15] under the title, "Maximizing Thera-peutic Inefficiency." The newer model of a "unitized" mental hospital or of a community mental health center is presumably more therapeutically efficacious, though its effectiveness has not been fully documented. Ac-cording to this model, all staff members, and patients as well, function as members of the "treatment team." Rather than a narrow and easily blocked chain of command, there is widespread democratic participa-tion. Roles within the organization are flexibly defined, and, within lim-its, tend to be interchangeable; therapeutic responsibility is widely dif-fused. The recent college graduate, the secretary, the gardener, the attendant, the "new career" subprofessional, the volunteer, or the fellow-patient—any of these may prove to have therapeutic skills at least rivalling those of the physician-psychiatrist, or those of the nurse, the psychologist, or the social worker.

The unit or center is, furthermore, accessible to people within the area it serves, and contacts in patients' behalf can be far more readily made with a finite number of community caregivers located within spec-ified geographic boundaries than with the virtually infinite number of potential resources in the large territory a public mental hospital may serve.

There are a number of ways in which staff of the decentralized mental hospital unit or mental health center can extend a "therapeutic commu-nity" approach beyond the walls of the center itself. These include con-tacts made to facilitate patients' entry into treatment, to plan for their discharge, and to provide further aftercare or follow-up. They also in-clude activities designed to prevent hospitalization: mental health educa-tion—especially for such key people as the police, school teachers, and welfare workers—the provision of outpatient care, "crisis intervention," walk-in clinics, 24-hour-a-day emergency services, and—increasingly—visits to the patient at home.

This last often involves other members of that small community, the family, in the treatment process. Family treatment also can take place in a clinical setting. A team of therapists may work with the family as a whole or with its members separately, or alternate from the group to in-dividuals. Recently, as Speck and Rueveni [16] have described, family therapy has been extended to include other kinfolk, friends, and neigh-bors. Dramatic results have apparently been achieved when all who are involved in the local "tribe," including its formal and informal leaders, are brought in to participate in the treatment of a disturbed tribal member. This indeed *is* community psychiatry, on a scale larger than that simply of the family but much smaller than that of a catchment area. (It is in fact quite possible that catchment area boundaries could arbitrarily *exclude* strategic members of the tribe, whose place of residence might require that they relate only to the staff of a different community mental health center from that which serves the overtly disturbed member of the tribe.)

The Broader Community—Is This Where the Psychiatrist Belongs? Maxwell Jones [17] has recently suggested that the social worker, rather than the psychiatrist, should be the leader of the "community team." Pursuing this thought further, one may wonder whether psychiatrists will perhaps move toward relinquishing the community role that they have so recently been learning to assume. Perhaps, indeed, they will also give up much of their role as psychotherapists, permitting others to whom they have imparted these skills to carry them out, practicing under general psychiatric supervision. Primarily psychological, sociological, or sometimes political functions would then be left to persons whose training to carry them out would have been less circuitous, not to say "absurd," [18] than that of community psychiatrists.

Recognizing increasingly the extent to which a variety of physical illnesses and injuries are psychologically determined, realizing the extent to which "mental" patients suffer from physical ills, and also recognizing the importance of medical and neurological approaches to the treatment of mental disorders, it may well be that psychiatrists will presently move toward rejoining the medical fraternity in order better to deal with illnesses for which psychosocial modes of treatment do not suffice. Through closer association with their medical colleagues they might begin to participate much more extensively in the treatment also of patients for whom strictly medical modes of treatment are insufficient, perhaps because psychosocial considerations have been overlooked.

Nonpsychiatric physicians have been described as the most important undeveloped resource for mental health that exists in the community, and it would seem to be high time that this resource was cultivated, rather than continuing to be neglected. Most people with psychological problems in fact turn first—and perhaps solely—to a nonpsychiatrist M.D. For their part, such physicians are becoming increasingly concerned about the "delivery" of their services to persons in need of them. Plans that are being developed for comprehensive health insurance coverage give promise of rendering adequate delivery of health services a reality. One wonders how mental health services will fit in. *Will* they fit in, or will they remain isolated from and alien to the rest of medicine?

Other Health Provisions Often mental health catchment areas have been drawn up without reference to resources for general health or medical care. *Public* health services traditionally have been closely linked to units of local government, as well as to government at state and federal (and sometimes metropolitan and regional) levels. Presumably, as insurance coverage grows, public health agencies will stop providing their own, usually second-class, direct services to the indigent and instead will seek to apply a single set of standards to all health care resources. They can then concentrate on establishing standards for, inspecting, and securing accountability from, other resources that provide direct services, meanwhile focusing their own direct efforts upon controlling environmental hazards to health.

Public *mental* health officials *might* follow a similar pattern, focusing on social and other environmental hazards to mental health, working closely with private or voluntary agencies and institutions, with business and industry, and with local and other government agencies to see that these hazards are removed or minimized. They could encourage and assist these agencies in carrying out basic mental health functions of their own through education, counseling, screening, "first aid," and appropriate referral practices. At the same time they, too, could establish and enforce standards and insure accountability.

In the nature of the case, such public officials cannot effectively impose standards on themselves. Yet generally, in the mental health field, *they* are the ones who are the providers of service. Herein lies a crucial problem, and one that is generally overlooked. It is as if a local health officer became so discouraged with the poor standards of cleanliness and sanitation in his town's restaurants that he decided to have the health department itself take over all the restaurants in order to keep them really clean! It might work, for a while. But soon his restaurant managers would grow lax or develop irrelevant preoccupations—and there would be no one left with responsibility to enforce standards on *them!* Diners might be unhappy—but since a government monopoly would have been established, they would find there was little they could do. Political action might lead to increased budgetary appropriations, or to putting a new health officer in charge—but these steps might well leave the situation fundamentally unchanged.

Residents of the town who had no need of restaurants would not suffer hardship and the wealthy could patronize private dining facilities of their own. Their response would doubtless be somewhat apathetic. Poorer residents in need of service would, however, *have* to rely on this one monopolistic resource, or else go without. And especially if they could not be accepted as patrons outside the local catchment area, one could expect consumers' protests about the restaurants' inadequacy to be of little, if any, avail.

This, unhappily, parallels the situation of people whose mental health needs to be restored. Imposing catchment areas *and* developing what amounts to a state monopoly of mental health resources thus runs the danger of depriving less privileged consumers of a choice, and hence of a voice, concerning the services they receive. Accountability is lessened, not increased, when a monopoly exists. And this situation reinforces, rather than eliminates, a dual standard of care—one for the well-to-do and another for people of average income or less.

Monitoring Functions What has been said above suggests that public mental health authorities might best restrict themselves to what can be called monitoring functions. They would then see to it that mental health resources of good quality were available to people who needed them; assist in the development and maintenance of high standards of care; and work toward the elimination of mental health hazards, together with the formulation and espousal of new programs based on these studies' findings. This last would be accomplished through consultation and education on the one hand and through fact-gathering epidemiological and evaluative studies on the other hand. Public mental health authorities would not themselves try to provide direct services to people, for they would recognize the impossibility of monitoring what they themselves do. They would instead encourage others to assume responsibility. Who would these others be?

Presumably they would be persons in positions of community leadership—and these communities might or might not be wholly located within the geographic boundaries of catchment areas. They would include local government officials, trade union officers, business executives, college administrators, officers of voluntary associations or professional organizations, clergymen, and so on. For the most part they would be heads of corporate groups who could legitimately speak for their members or constituents or parishioners, and who were concerned for the latter's well being. Either informally or formally, they would consist of that "most distinguishing feature of a community"—local government.

These agents of various sorts of communities—some geographically defined, some not—would be encouraged to make contracts to supply their corporate members with mental health services offered by service providers who would themselves generally be organized as corporate groups. As an alternative, some communities might prefer to contract for the services of individual practitioners, employing the latter as members of their own staff. In either case, if services proved inadequate, the contract could be terminated and another provider of services could be found. This is the kind of pattern that has developed in the field of college psychiatry, and that has been adopted also by a few industries and unions.

The usual procedure is for the "community" in question to employ its own psychiatric or counseling staff, usually in association with the medical staff. Alternatively, contracts for these services can be made with an independent group of clinicians who may serve a number of corporate "communities," as the College Mental Health Center of Boston, Inc., now does with some twenty-five member colleges.[19]

Performing a monitoring function in such a way as to encourage others to fulfill their responsibilities for meeting mental health needs as adequately as possible, rather than "taking over" as if to say that other people *never will learn* to be responsible, seems to be the most constructive course of future development for the field of community mental health. This represents the rationale of mental health consultation,[20] which maintains and reinforces the consultee's responsibility for his client's or patient's well-being. It is in fact the rationale of clinical practice quite generally: physicians (including psychiatrists) have learned that patients may be harmed rather than benefited if their lives are managed for them so that they are deprived of opportunities for exercising their capacities and of encouragement to do so.

But the general thrust of the community mental health center movement in this country has largely been in the opposite direction. Those charged with governing local communities have been bypassed and ignored. Their responsibilities for mental health have been denied, restricted, or taken over as H. G. Whittington has recently stressed.[21] Often, it is true, local officials or leaders are included among the members of an area mental health center's board of directors or advisors, but in this position they are not directly charged with responsibility for their own constituents' mental health. Instead, they—with others—simply try to make their voices heard. Often, within the monopolistic and bureaucratic structure of state services, no one seems to be listening.

Is It "Community" Mental Health? Some Current Shibboleths   It is ironic that mental health services bearing the label of "community" should so thoroughly ignore actual communities that exist, and that they should so much tend to "take over" in ways that fail to respect and reinforce local responsibility. The boards established for catchment areas do represent an effort to transform these areas into communities. Ignoring

383

the boundary lines of existing political units, as catchment areas do, however (and as they must, to stay within the legally specified population limits of 75,000 to 200,000), area center staff often are deprived of opportunities to foster the responsibility of local governmental bodies for the well-being of their citizens. Significant opportunities to intervene from a preventive or "health maintenance" standpoint, by working with and through the structure of local government, are missed.

The persisting separation of mental health from the mainstream of health and medical care threatens to exclude psychiatric treatment from national health insurance plans that are now being devised in an effort to deliver adequate health care to every community's citizens. As a consequence, the conclusion from UAW experience [22] that "basic" health insurance coverage should include mental health, and that it can do so at modest cost, is in danger of going unheeded. The denial of free choice to consumers likewise runs counter to provisions likely to be included in federally supported health plans of the future, just as they now are in the Medicare and Medicaid laws. Meanwhile the ardently contemptuous rejection of the so-called "medical model" by many community mental health professionals does little to foster collaboration with local medical practitioners who might otherwise rank among mental health's strongest allies.

One reason for the distrust of local government is its concern with aspects of people's well-being that do not immediately have to do with mental health. Yet concern with a decent sewer system, with public transportation, with police protection, or with attracting new industry to town, may actually prove to have a good deal of relevance to the community's mental health. A community is a social and ecological system, wherein changes involving any part affect the whole. A single-minded focus just on mental health, especially as it is defined by professionals linked with a state-level bureaucracy, can hardly be expected to transform a catchment area into a community. By recognizing others' concerns, however, important progress can often be made, as through the essentially political process of "cross-commitment" that Starr and Carlson have described.[23]

Not content with the kind of educational and consultative activity that can foster responsibility on the part of others, mental health center staff often feel the urge to "coordinate" the activities of other resource people within their catchment area as a supposed means of creating community. It is, of course, quite possible for improved coordination to be achieved when people are brought together to consider common problems and objectives. But resentment and conflict, rather than collaboration, can result when mental health staff arrogate to themselves the task of coordinating the activities of people whose position in the community may be more firmly established than their own.

Those who are concerned with "coordination" also talk frequently about doing away with "duplication" on the one hand and "fragmentation" on the other, while they advocate "comprehensiveness" and "continuity" of care. Yet many who urge the latter and deplore the former seem to work against their own stated goals. Comprehensiveness and continuity are lessened—and fragmentation is increased—when, for example, mental health is kept separate from other forms of health and medical care. As for "duplication," it is well to bear in mind that a monopoly can exercise a deadening influence, leading to inefficiency and unresponsiveness, while competition—and this includes competition among non-profit organizations—can serve consumers' interests. When those who receive service are free to choose among competing resources, they choose that which suits them best and which entails least cost. No one complains about "duplicated" restaurants in a given locality, for each new one helps to keep the others alert and concerned with serving their own customers well.

Activities in the fields of consultation and education are often claimed to be "preventive." So they may be though their preventive efficacy remains to be proved. But people who live in areas where emphasis is placed upon preventive mental health programs are sometimes unhappy with them. They want direct treatment resources to be available *now* for people suffering from mental disorders, rather than measures that may or may not prevent such disorders in the future. Their unhappiness may well be justified from the standpoint of prevention itself. A parent whose disorder remains untreated can harm the mental health of his or her children to a tragic degree. Providing effective treatment for such parents may have more impact in preventing disorders in the next generation than a wealth of educational and other "preventive" programs possibly could though mental health professionals may enjoy the latter activities more. *Not* to provide services people demand and obviously need hardly manifests nor encourages the sense of responsibility for others which would seem to be the most essential element of preventive mental health.

"Specialized" services also provoke problems. In many instances it seems to prove beneficial to mix together various categories of patients. Bierer, for instance, remarks,

We are often asked how we select the patient membership for a specific club. Visitors are surprised to see that Cockneys and patients with very cultured backgrounds belong to the same club; brilliant scientists are put in a club with mentally retarded patients; strictly raised churchgoers and criminal psychopaths and sexual offenders; young people from 16 to 18 and grandparents from 60 to 80; and patients suffering from a wide variety of mental illness—all get along happily in the same club.[24]

But some categories of patients evidently do need to be handled in special ways. Children may be one such category though it can be argued that they are best dealt with in the context of their own families which, of course, include adults. Those whose pattern of life activities constitutes essentially a separate culture can perhaps best be treated by others who are conversant with the same culture, be it that of Skid Row, the drug scene, or the gay world. These, too, represent distinctive communities for which, through self-help activities, members (or exmembers) with a capacity for leadership can have a responsible and constructive role to play.

In theory, the staff of an area mental health center is responsible for meeting *all* the mental health needs of *all* the people residing within the area. Responsibility is theoretically assumed for this *total population*, rather than only for the selected individuals who in the past have found their way to, and been accepted by, mental health treatment resources. The recent push to translate this theory into practice has wrought dramatic positive changes and accomplished highly praiseworthy improvements.

But through its failure to deal explicitly with entities that to the highest degree possess the qualities of *community*, whether these are territorially or otherwise defined, the community mental health center movement has jeopardized the achievement of its own theoretical goals. A government authority can require and help others to meet their responsibility for offering assistance to all needful individuals within their respective communities. But a governmental mental health authority cannot effectively impose this sort of requirement upon itself. And as long as the tendency to "take over" persists, rather than to rely on procedures that foster responsibility on the part of both "local governments" of communities and those who agree to provide them with the mental health services that those legitimate leaders of the community choose—so long will community needs for mental health services fail to be adequately met.

NOTES

1. L. Broom, and P. Selznick, *Sociology*, 4th edition. New York: Harper and Row, 1968.

2. E. C. Lindeman, *The Community*, New York: Association Press, 1921.

3. F. Tönnies, *Gemeinschaft und Gesellschaft*, 6th and 7th edition, Berlin: 1926.

4. D. C. Klein, *Community Dynamics and Mental Health*, New York: Wiley, 1968.

5. R. A. Nisbet, *The Quest for Community*, New York: Oxford University Press, 1953.

6. M. Ross, *Community Organization*, New York: Harper, 1955.

7. W. J. Goode, "Community Within a Community: The Professions," *American Sociological Review*, 22(1957): 194–200.

8. R. L. Warren, *The Community in America*. Chicago: Rand McNally, 1963; R. L. Warren, ed., *Perspectives on the American Community*. Chicago: Rand McNally, 1966.

9. M. R. Stein, *The Eclipse of Community*, Princeton, N.J.: Princeton University Press, 1960.

10. T. Parsons, *Structure and Process in Modern Societies*, New York: The Free Press, 1960.

11. L. P. Howe, "The Concept of the Community: Some Implications for the Development of Community Psychiatry," in Bellach, L., ed., *Handbook of Community Psychiatry and Community Mental Health*. New York: Grune and Stratton, 1964, pp. 16–46.

12. M. Jones, *The Therapeutic Community*, New York: Basic Books, 1953.

13. E. M. Bonn, and A. M. Kraft, "The Fort Logan Mental Health Center: Genesis and Development," *Journal of the Fort Logan Mental Health Center*, 1(1963): 17–21.

14. J. Bierer, "The Marlborough Experiment," in Bellach, L., ed., *Handbook of Community Psychiatry and Community Mental Health*. New York: Grune and Stratton, 1964, pp. 221–247.

15. S. H. Simon, "Maximizing Therapeutic Inefficiency," *Mental Hospitals*, 12(April 1961): 22–23.

16. R. V. Speck, and U. Rueveni, "Network Therapy: A Developing Concept," *Family Process*, 8(1969): 182–191.

17. M. Jones, "From Hospital to Community Psychiatry," *Community Mental Health Journal*, 6(1970): 187–195.

18. M. P. Dumont, *The Absurd Healer: Perspectives of a Community Psychiatrist*, New York: Science House, 1968.

19. L. P. Howe, "The Application of Community Psychiatry to College Settings," *Counseling the College Student*, D. L. Farnsworth and G. Blane, eds., *International Psychiatry Clinics*, 7(1970): 263–291; P. Solomon, *et al.*, "A New Approach to Student Mental Health Center," *American Journal of Psychiatry*, 124(November 1967): 112–115; L. P. Howe, and V. D. Patch, "College Mental Health: Problems and Solutions," to be published in Bellach, and Barton, eds., *Progress in Community Mental Health, Volume II*, New York: Grune and Stratton, 1971.

20. Caplan, G., *The Theory and Practice of Mental Health Consultation*, New York: Basic Books, 1970.

21. H. G. Whittington, *Balkanization of the City—An Unresolved Consequence of the Community Mental Health Center*, paper presented at the Annual Meeting of the American Orthopsychiatric Association, March 1970.

22. M. A. Glasser, and T. Duggan, "Prepaid Psychiatric Care Experience with UAW Members," *American Journal of Psychiatry*, 126(1969): 675–681.

23. R. Starr, and J. Carlson, "Pollution and Poverty: The Strategy of Cross-Commitment," *The Public Interest*, 10(Winter 1968): 104–131.

24. Bierer, "The Marlborough Experiment," pp. 221–247.

46   *Alfred M. Freedman*, M.D.

The Role of the Administrator

Recently, there have been many discussions of the crushingly burdensome role of medically trained psychiatric administrators who are trying to cope with the major issues of the day. At times one might think he was hearing the conversation of undergraduates as stories of "he's copping out" or "so-and-so is opting out" or "he is being destroyed and will have to get out."

Admittedly the task is very difficult; it would be gratifying if the administrator were sure at least of the high regard of his colleagues for his administrative role or of his own self-respect for the job he is doing as an administrator. Both are very often lacking. How often have you heard of an acquaintance being dismissed by remarks such as "Oh, yes, Joe was a promising researcher (or a superb clinician), but now he's wasting his time being an administrator." Or the notion that administration is not "real" work.

If the administrator's image in the professions is eroded, his self-image generally as an administrator is even more diminished. This seems especially true of physicians and psychiatrists, who become administrators. Their career patterns, their training, and aspirations have generally been toward clinical work, teaching, or research. Those are "respectable" fields. It is not unknown for an administrator to come home and when asked by his wife, "What sort of a day did you have?" to say, "It was a complete waste of time. I spent three hours with the Community Mental Health Board and then two hours with the Assistant Commissioner of Hospitals in regard to our affiliation contract, and spent the lunch hour with the site-visit team in order to lend my weight to a member of the department whose research application is being reviewed, and then an hour negotiating between the service group and the teaching group in regard to a program, and on and on and on. A complete waste of time." Perhaps the truth is that this is the most difficult and most important task of the day—the managerial task. Few people have the sensitivity, the strength, and the perspective to see it through.

This is the sort of "corridor talk" that one hears at any large meeting where there are a large number of administrators of hospitals, chairmen of departments of psychiatry, and directors of community mental health centers. It is often tied with comments about the difficulty of getting senior responsible individuals to accept administrative posts in governmental offices and the fact that many positions for mental health administrators have long been vacant.

There are indeed many cruel pressures that beset administrators. What follows is only a brief sampling of the total range of problems.

Most prominent of all the obstacles is the very nature of the world today. Issues are ambiguous. They never really are resolved. There is no certainty of rules; the rules themselves are unknown; all that is known is that they change constantly. This certainly holds true for much of the mental health administrator's work. New issues emerge but old issues are never settled. Each day begins back where it started from but a little more difficult and something new added.

Another cause of distress is the multiplicity of responsibilities for which the hospital administrator or community mental health center director is accountable. He is responsible for both training and service and very often research. This is rarely seen in industry where training, service, production, and research are distinctly separate and there is very little necessity for an administrator to negotiate between one and another. In medicine, in general, teaching and service are closely interwoven. One is constantly preoccupied with setting up priorities, undertaking negotiations, making trade-offs, and even at times setting up relationships. Steadily escalating expectations and demands for service by the public particularly in regard to community programs have made mandatory not only being responsive to such requests but actually anticipating them in order to avoid disastrous confrontations.

Another problem arises because of the effects that the pluralism of American society has had upon the organization and implementation of psychiatric services in the United States. This issue cannot be over emphasized in its contribution to the despair and confusion of psychiatric administrators. The mental health administrator is not at the head of the pyramid as so many utopian and unreal flow charts would indicate. Rather he is at the center of a three-dimensional matrix with forces impinging upon him from above and below, from the side, from the front and the back. He not only deals with various levels of the government, often competing or in conflict, but in addition to the public sector he must negotiate with the private sector, foundations, voluntary hospitals, citizens groups, agencies, and politicians. It is not only that skill is necessary in dealing with these groups but the hours required in order to touch all the bases is beyond that which is physically possible.

Moreover, the administrator finds himself heading up larger and larger, more and more complex organizations, ironically enough at a time when there is a distinct breakdown of respect for authority, particularly among junior staff members, trainees, and students. This has been ascribed with great justice to failure of the adult generation to have produced a world of tranquility, cleanliness, rationality, and peace. There is much questioning of the wisdom of senior administrators. As a result there is more necessity for explanations, prolonged discussions, and negotiations. Certainly from an historical view grave doubts concerning the credibility and competence of leadership in all areas has been steadily increasing since World War I, during which agony, catastrophe, and crisis have followed one another steadily. The observation of Lord Gray in 1914 that "the lights are going out all over Europe and will never go on again" might have been more prophetic than many wish to acknowledge.

Even if one wishes to remain small, narrow, and parochial, it is often impossible. Pressures are exerted from above and below that are compelling in nature. Rational planning and the necessity to play a public role requires an enlargement of commitment. One hopes by such enlargement to introduce economies of scale, but the decline of funding more than offsets economies that may be produced by more rational structures.

One special situation that makes the role of the psychiatric administrator in many institutions even more difficult is the fact that many of the professionals have ready access to private practice, and to incomes that may exceed salaries. Thus, one is clearly negotiating with independent entrepreneurs.

One could go on and on listing the perturbations that beset the psychiatric administrator. Of even more significance is the need to seek solutions. One might say that someone whose primary training is medicine does not belong in an administrative post. Thus, some have suggested that administrative posts should be turned over to the pure administrative types, the managerial experts, while the doctors stick to supplying clinical services, or teaching other doctors, or doing research. However, this purely managerial approach is fraught with dangers. One of the major issues of the day is the dehumanizing effect of bureaucracy and technocracy. One who looks upon the delivery of health services purely in terms of managerial skills and cost-benefit analysis tends to lose the last semblance of human consideration that's involved in the field.

It is essential to have people in administration who have first-hand, immediate knowledge of what it means to be ill and to treat someone who is ill, and what it means to aim for health and the difficulty of achieving it. The mere possession of an advanced mental health degree is not a guarantee of competence. The ineptitude of some mental health professionals in important posts is clear. It appears equally clear that unless we can develop a cadre of outstanding administrators drawn from the ranks of mental health professionals, we will see these posts filled by the "pure" managers who hopefully will respond to input by the professionals. To develop these new administrators, however, it will first be necessary to make the job of administrator much more respectable and attractive.

The obstacles and the constraints are clear indeed, but it is equally clear that a psychiatrist or other mental health professional can function successfully as an administrator. To do so, he must understand the processes and practices of administration just as he understands the nature of clinical services. Moreover, he must understand the nature of the task which confronts him as the administrator of a specific type of program.

The very first essential is for the administrator to comprehend in explicit detail the great importance and uniqueness of his role. It is his efforts and energies that make possible the work that goes on, and without his activities all will come to naught. It is the peculiarity of medicine and science in general that the administrator and the generalists are often scorned. In other fields, the generalists and administrator receive great respect. Unfortunately, many professionals have been brought up and trained to believe that in any rank order the administrator will end up very low.

Having looked at himself, the administrator must look upon the larger organization about him, that is, the community mental health center. He finds that he is not just looking at a large organization or one that was larger than before. It is different, and as he looks at it, he sees that it is in reality a complex of systems, that the organization is a pattern of simultaneous, parallel, and sequential work operations, that an individual's contribution is of less value except insofar as it is made at the right time and place, in the right order and sequence. Further, it is an organization imbedded in other organizations, for example in the medical center or the medical school. As a result, if the administrator is to be effective, the dynamics of the system must be known, and the forces and processes of such a system's dynamics must be effectively channelled. Moreover, the administrator must realize that he is in charge not of individual workmen but a system or complex of systems.

The administrator of such a system cannot always proceed to a solution directly. He must look at the organizational structure and the processes from which solutions emerge rather than at any individual result. Thus, when results generally are unsatisfactory, he must ask what kind of process is producing it and what kinds of steps might change the process.

In this way, the role of the administrator begins to emerge. Whatever he does affects all groups. If he acts, all groups must react and they must make adjustments. If one group moves wisely or unwisely, he must make compensating moves on behalf of the rest of the system. As a result, the administrator must constantly be running around making new agreements, new commitments, and new assurances from those to whom he had made another commitment just a short time before. In this way, decision making is not a discrete simple event. It is a continuous and intricate process of brokerage or negotiation. The heart and soul of an administrator's task is his skill in negotiation. He plays the role of the broker, and as a broker he sees that the making of organizational decisions consists of a going back and forth, constantly making trade-offs, for example, between personality and job design. The administrator must be able to deal not with an ideal situation but with "how do you make do." The administrator constantly asks himself at each stage of an unfolding situation or about each alternative he is considering, "What is a fixed constraint and what is something that is variable, and how do I work within this combination of fixed and not fixed variables?" Leonard Sayles has pointed this out very well in his book *Managerial Behaviour*. "The manager who does not recognize this iterative pattern can in fact anticipate failure. He does not comprehend the modern organization, but, instead, sees things in 'blacks' and 'whites'; he expects to have available all the resources he needs, when he needs them, to do what he has to do (that is, the 'authority'), and he expects others, upon whom he depends, to do their work so as to effectuate his activity. In reality, solving problems in a modern organization is a matter of flows, of processes. Decisions are the product of actions through time on the part of many people. People are not responsible for compartmentalized specific functions or actions but for participating in and influencing a series of relationships.

"The individual manager does not have a clearly bounded job with neatly defined authorities and responsibilities. Rather he is placed in the middle of a system of relationships out of which he must fashion an organization that will accomplish his objectives. There is no standard interface: rather, the relationships differ, depending upon the objectives and the position of the other groups with whom he must achieve a working pattern of give and take."

The question is then, how does one give some stability and some regularity, in the effort to provide service in the pressure-filled setting in which the community mental health center must operate. Since the leadership is almost by definition obliged to operate in close connection with political and other agencies, there is need to comprehend the matrix, to identify the priorities as the first step in developing answers. A demographically complex community, a professionally dedicated work force, a politically alert urban official and a distant set of bureaucratized overseers are at best curious allies and at worst aggrandizing spokesmen for sometimes contradictory interests. The administrator needs a logic by which he orders activities that would otherwise seem like encroaching and tedious relationships. It is essential that the director discover early on that what he takes to be nuisances that interfere with orderly expenditure of time and energy are indeed the core of his work in his extraorganizational tasks, and that these tasks can and must be ordered by the attentive administrator. Just as business leaders have discovered that their appointment books are crowded with demands on their resources working at all the intersecting boundaries of their organizations with others in their external environment, so too, the mental health center director must discover the precise nature of the matrix in which he is imbedded and the options he has for shifting the lines that otherwise would circumscribe his activities and his potential for decision making. Further, he must distinguish jobs that require special skills or particular expertise, and those that are by their nature, of unusual difficulty. In other words, he must realize that some jobs are difficult unless a person with some special skill is found, while other tasks are simply difficult by their very nature.

An administrator must be constantly involved in inventorying. He needs a complete inventory of professional manpower, subprofessional manpower, beds, laboratories, the current objectives existing manpower is now working for or looking for, what can be made attractive to professionals and subprofessionals, the interests he is likely to be conflicting with, what undernourished professional aspirations are there to which appeals can be built, and existing services. One important outcome of such inventorying is to be able to predict jurisdictional conflicts. Sometimes even if they are predicted, they cannot be avoided. Every new community organization overlaps other jurisdictions. One can expect efforts by an older organization to protect its territory. Success by the newer organization will encourage plundering in direct proportion to this success. But if there are any sudden changes, there follow unanticipated consequences; and here it is necessary to keep one's options open, to keep a reasonable amount of fluidity and flexibility.

One of the most troublesome problems of administrators is the delegation of authority, which is very different from the abandonment of responsibility. The administrator remains responsible and accountable and must see that the objectives originally decided upon are carried out.

Progress toward achieving these objectives is often obstructed or prevented by the constant need to put out "brush fires" inside and outside the organization. The brush fires consume one's energies and pre-empt time. One may delegate authority or eschew personal participation, yet it is the nature of a brush fire that it requires all hands to put it out, particularly those of the chief administrator.

Progress through long-range planning is also undermined by the constantly shifting scene and the variability of support. One cannot be assured of the continuation of anything. One must have sets of alternate and contingency plans constantly available. Not only must one anticipate the foreseeable consequences of any action, but steel oneself in preparation for the unanticipated consequences.

Physicians are accustomed to being solution oriented. Someone is sick —he is treated, but such an approach is no longer feasible in the large, complex organizations that are dealt with in community mental health centers. Individuals have tenure, are members of unions, they have contracts or they are in the civil service. Residents and students stand together and insist upon due process. Even if one were able to react in a simplistic fashion, however, it is questionable whether it is advisable. One is not simply supervising the work of a number of individuals. The administrator is dealing with a whole complex system, and he must look for solutions in the process of organization, not in the mere shifting of individuals. It has often been said that the administrator plays a parental role, but, in viewing the organization as a complex of systems, his delegation of authority must conform to the organizational pattern, not to individual relationships. It would be impossible for the administrator to view himself as the immediate supervising or parental figure. Rather he is the negotiator, the broker between the various subdivisions, and his primary purpose is to maintain the regularity and pattern of the processes underlying the division of work. The administrator's most important role thus is holding the organization together. He does this through constant negotiation. The administrator must dismiss the myth of single lines of authority and clear-cut relationships. These were possible at one time, but in the complex organizations of today they are rarely seen. Modern administration must be non-Euclidean. Any two points can be connected by any number of straight lines. There are multiple bases for decision.

Many of the lessons and experiences in industrial management appear to be relevant to problems in community mental health centers, but in the latter they are perhaps even more difficult. Professor Sayles has listed a series of "old wives' tales" of management theory—rules which simply are not applicable in modern organizations, especially in community mental health centers. Among these can be included the following:

1. A manager should take orders only from one man—his boss. (Most managers, in fact, work for, that is, they respond to the initiations of, many people who are customers for the services they render or who are in a position to make demands upon them.)

2. The manager does work himself only under exceptional circumstances; the good manager gets all his work done through the activities of his subordinates. (The manager himself must carry on many of the relationships with "outsiders" in order to negotiate for the materials and services he receives and to participate in the procedures by which his activities are evaluated by specialized groups in the organization.)

3. The manager devotes most of his time and energy to supervising his subordinates. (The need to interact with many groups outside his own keeps the manager away from his subordinates a significant portion of the time.)

4. A good manager manages by looking at results. (The modern organization has so many interdependent parts that the manager could not wait for results if he wanted to; others who are being affected would be at his door. But even without these pressures the costs of waiting to find out "how things are going" until the results are seen would be enormous. Furthermore, most results are joint products and cannot be assessed against a single individual. Consequently, methods of continuous information feedback are required.)

5. To be effective, the manager must have authority equal to his responsibility. (A manager almost never has authority equal to his responsibility. He must depend on the actions of many people over whom he has not the slightest control.)

6. Staff people have no real authority since they are subsidiary to the line organization. (Staff groups have very real power.)

395

As Professor Sayles states, "Management principles have been based too heavily on organizations that no longer exist or at least are diminishing in importance."

This has been a brief survey of the role of the mental health professional as administrator in a complex organization such as a community mental health center. Certainly, with the steady development of community-centered neighborhood-center facilities, with the increasing involvement of the government in the delivery of health services, and with the possibility of national insurance or health programs looming on the horizon, such problems of administration will be even more prevalent and more complex. In his role and in his decision making, the administrator will have to be prepared for steady as well as sudden change. Thus, the administrator must be surefooted in modifying his behavior as he detects changes in his surrounding world, in legislation, and within his own staff. He is in a state of dynamic equilibrium if he is lucky, balancing or trading favorable responses in one sector in exchange for stress and hostility in another. Equilibrium is constantly changing and the administrator must be presenting countervailing forces to some of these changes and facilitating others based upon his objectives. Thus, he is constantly making marginal decisions. He certainly can rarely afford to make a decision and stick with it come what may.

This has been summed up very well by Harlan Cleveland, a former assistant secretary of state for international organizations: "This increase in the extent to which each individual is personally responsible to others is most noticeable in a large bureaucracy. No one person decides anything. Each decision of any importance is a product of an intricate process of brokerage involving individuals inside and outside the organization who feel some reason to be affected by the decision, who have special knowledge to contribute to it. The more varied the organization's constituency, the more outside veto groups will need to be taken into account. But even if no outside consultations were involved, sheer size would produce a complex process of decision. For a large organization is a deliberately created system of tensions to which each individual is expected to bring work ways, viewpoints, and outside relationships markedly different from those of his colleagues. It is the administrator's task to draw from these disparate forces the elements of wise action from day to day consistent with the purposes of the organization as a whole."

47

Charles F. Baltimore, M.D., *and*
Jack A. Wolford, M.D.

The Nondegree Community Mental Health Worker
and the Community

INTRODUCTION

The process of developing a community mental health program in the center of an urban complex where the constituency presents many unique situations not totally within the ken of the professional poses problems. The communications barriers that exist are due to many factors. Among the significant are "strangerhood situations" which can occur due to differences in the black and white culture and socioeconomic level barriers which preclude adequate understanding of the presenting situations.

The nonverbal and verbal signals which are exchanged often are not well understood or are misinterpreted and preclude the effective exchange which is so necessary to the interaction needed in the helping situation. Since the primary educative experience of the majority of treating mental health professionals centers around the "psychotherapeutic or talking model," major gaps in treatment and prevention programs will be apparent unless special attempts are made to surmount these difficulties. Too little attention has been paid to the various ethnics that abound in most center city areas and, in fact, may still live in small enclaves retaining much of the "old world" cultures and value systems. With the knowledge that behavioral science and social psychiatry have made available, it seems untenable to plan programs for treatment and prevention without considering the sociocultural and socioenvironmental factors.

The selection of catchment areas in community mental health programs has been largely on the basis of population and not on criteria of community. This has undoubtedly been necessary due to our inability to clearly define community or to delineate with any accuracy the boundaries of a given community. Even when we talk about a community, we are aware that it can be further subdivided. The "community" that we wish to address ourselves to in this section is, in fact, several communities. In any city there is no such thing as *a* black community. Rather, there are many areas and ghettos where black persons are sequestered but inside each may be many communities and, in some sense, all of these areas are part of a total community of blacks.

Due to these factors we arbitrarily subdivided our catchment area, not into communities but subcatchment areas. One was populated predominantly by black citizens (98 percent), 40,000 in number. This area, for the most part, was characterized by the term "urban blight" and in some sections could only be described as a slum. A second section, although rimmed by poverty, contained many middle-class families and even some from the upper socioeconomic level. This is the "cultural center" of the city. The third subcatchment area, also designated a poverty area, has many ethnic groups and about one-half middle-class families. The ethnics are Hungarian, Polish, Czechoslovakian, Italian, and Irish. The fourth area is made up predominently of middle-class whites with the largest ethnic group being Jewish. This area is also the scene of the youth drug culture, although many persons come from outside the area to congregate here. There are also many persons of great wealth living in this section.

This section will focus on the first mentioned area known as "the Hill District" and discuss one approach to the utilization of the "indigenous nonprofessional." His interaction with the professional and an institution whose primary purpose until the advent of the community mental health center was to educate and train the professional will also be examined.

PROFESSIONAL OR NONPROFESSIONAL

In our program we started with the use of the terms "indigenous worker" and "nonprofessional" but soon abandoned them. The reasons were that the use of such terms put these workers at "the bottom of the totem pole" or "last in the pecking order" even though in certain areas they already had greater expertise about the community than the "professional." This knowledge was unrecognized and not verbalized and could be communicated only when we "professionals" began to listen carefully. Their skills were in the areas of understanding the concept of community, the true culture and values, community organization (for instance, how to get a meeting organized) and communication. This knowledge led us to the early abandonment of the above terms which had pejorative connotations and to the adoption of the terms "community worker" or "community mental health worker."

398

Charles F. Baltimore and Jack A. Wolford

Although the majority of personnel in a community mental health center can accept in theory the term nondegree professional versus degree professional, it is difficult for everyone in the total complex to accept this concept. A recent survey [*] attempting to evaluate this phase of our program elicited many negative responses, particularly from lower echelon staff who felt community mental health workers were not well enough trained and lacked adequate supervision. Judged by the stereotype of professionalism the community mental health worker may not be professional, but is this stereotype the proper measuring rod? We think not. Should the diploma and degree weigh more heavily in determining the status and value of the individual than the ability to perform the required task or work? We feel that excellent performance must receive recognition and reward regardless of how the knowledge to attain it was obtained.

Furthermore, those who suggest "new careers" for these people in "schools of the allied health professions," "community colleges," "vocational schools," and "hospitals" have a tendency to pattern their programs for roles that supplement or augment existing tasks of the professional which, due to manpower scarcity, are no longer deemed to require the excellence of the professional. In our opinion, this blurs the value and significance that a community mental health worker (to use our term) can bring to the mental health team and its program.

COMPOSITION AND RECRUITMENT

The original objective in developing a "Hill Team" was to have a mix of degree-professionals and community mental health workers who would deliver direct services to the community as well as provide consultation, education, community organization, and community development where indicated. In the beginning, we saw the community worker as the one who would be primarily concerned with providing the bridge between the community and the degree-professional. We saw the degree-professional in his traditional role as the person providing definitive care. We have subsequently changed this view and our community mental health workers today are involved in a collaborative team effort in *all* facets of treatment, both direct and indirect, and prevention. They also continue to have a bridging function.

[*] This material is taken from a study of our Hill Team titled "Re-Thinking Community Mental Health Care Functions: A Working Paper on an Evaluative Program Sponsored by the Maurice Falk Medical Fund." Task Force members included Carolyn Carter, Frank G. Pogue, Daniel Stern, Otto von Mering, Jack A. Wolford.

399

We began with a white psychiatrist as team director. He was devoted to change in our mental health care delivery system and had a particular interest in the Hill District. His entrance to the community had been through a narcotic addiction program he had developed in the city. His ability, charisma, and advocate role were extremely important in the development of this team. In this first phase, he recruited three black male social workers, two black female nurses, and later a black psychiatrist to form the degree-professional group. Nine community mental health workers were also recruited.* In the beginning, the selection was carried out primarily by the professional staff with the team director having the final decision-making power. Over the past three years this has changed to a policy where community mental health workers recruit and hire other community mental health workers.

Criteria for employment as a community mental health worker included a knowledge of his community and an ability to communicate with members of his community as well as the degree-professional. Hopefully, he would be able to communicate with the white as well as black staff members in a fashion that would result in a mutual exchange of ideas and information and would be educational to the white staff, a reciprocal learning experience. We had many brushes with the university personnel department around job classifications, pay scales, felony arrests, school records, and "satisfactory" references from previous employers. Some of these problems still exist but over time university policies have changed and more rational and reasonable decisions are easier to obtain.

A remaining area of major difficulty has been the question of an adequate salary range to enable us to avoid an administrative cul-de-sac and leaving the community mental health worker in a dead-end position.

EDUCATION AND TRAINING

We had consulted the literature in an attempt to determine a curriculum which would prepare the community worker for his role. In spite of the many helpful suggestions in the literature, we had to work through a phase of patterning the community mental health workers' curriculum after diploma-professionals. We started by presenting a miniature "pro-

* There are now a total of twenty-six nondegree treating persons in the community mental health program.

fessional curriculum" with more classroom work than learning by application.

It soon became apparent that there were many serious unsolved conflicts between the community mental health workers and the degree-professionals. Although, in this first group, all of the community mental health workers were black, conflicts existed with both black and white professionals. We found these conflicts to be a positive focal point of training because they led us into the areas of group experience, group dynamics, and group process. This phase was later very helpful in black-white confrontations and dialogue groups conducted by the team.

In the beginning, the professional wanted the structure he "made it in" and became angry when he couldn't impose it on his students. Some time had to be spent in showing him how he was attacking the community mental health worker both verbally and nonverbally in trying to force him into his mold.

The newly hired community mental health worker also viewed the situation around the supervisor-supervisee relationship with suspiciousness and distrust. Closed doors were thought of as a place for the professional to decide what "to do" with the nonprofessional. The jargon of the various disciplines was viewed with suspicion and revived earlier memories of home when experiences with professionals were viewed as control measures around the welfare check, public health inspection, and the like.

Content also proved to be important throughout the early and continuing training experience but the method of its presentation changed radically. Many community mental health workers had "oral" needs to satisfy and many gratifications were required for self-realization and status. Only by a recognition of these needs, a willingness to persevere, and an ability to understand on the part of the leaders and teachers were many of the workers able to complete their training and become effective community workers.

The curriculum included seminars in the usual mental health subjects, interview techniques, information regarding available services in the community, the community mental health center and the parent institution, material regarding the "community" and community organization, how to be a "helping person," and other ego-enhancing techniques were among the subjects taught.

Teaching methods were most successful where group process was carefully considered. Two anthropologists were involved in discussions of ethnics including the composition of the Hill and the community aspects of the team approach. One anthropologist was an expert in group dynamics and group process. A visiting professor in social psychiatry and an expert in group methods spent many hours with the Hill Team over a two-year period. Family dynamics and transactions were an integral part of the program. Since many aspects of their work involved the law, a forensic psychiatrist served as teacher and consultant. Continued discussions in psychodynamics with the two psychiatrists who, at different times, served as team leaders, were of major help in understanding behavior, both normal and pathological.

TRAINING FOR WHAT?

In outlining the center's values and goals, it had been decided that we should provide both direct care and work in prevention. We have felt for a long time that community mental health workers did not receive full credit for their work performed since most credit is given for those persons treated when they are subject to statistical analysis or counting. These persons are in the "fee for service" category and, hence, fairly complete records are kept. Although we have not necessarily improved the records, we have delineated several types of services that we feel the team accomplishes and are in the process of trying to develop records to account for time spent in each of these activities.

The types of service our teams are involved in are direct patient care, tandem direct patient care, and indirect patient care. Type A includes individual technical, clinical, educational, and health facility operational services. Type B encompasses community organization development activity, the facilitation of new supports and improvements within the formal community.

A short statement about each will illustrate the function of the community mental health workers as they interrelate with the diploma-professionals.

Direct Patient Care All of the residents of the Hill subcatchment area who seek help are referred to the Hill Team for direct care. The team members are on call for emergencies and for persons who come to the walk-in clinic. This essentially mixes the degree-professional and the community mental health workers. The workers use individual and group methods, home visiting and family care. When needed, psychiatric consultation is always available either through the team psychiatrist or through one from another unit of the community mental health center.

If a patient enters the inpatient unit or the day hospital, the community mental health worker continues his relationship in order to provide continuity of care. Should a patient enter these units through another part of the system, the community mental health worker is assigned at the time of admission in order to plan and prepare for aftercare. This system has made the community mental health worker an important part of the continuity of care system for persons listed or registered as patients.

Tandem Direct Patient Care We have realized that team members spend a great deal of time and energy with unlisted or unregistered individuals, perhaps potential patients living in the community who are in need of some support but who would not be labeled "patient" at that time. This includes regular or intermittent advice, counseling and supervision to this person with a "health" problem of either long or short duration, and to those persons immediately affected by the difficulties experienced by this individual (friends, relatives, or neighbors). It also includes time spent in consultation and advisory capacity with other team members seeing clients of this type. Much of this type service takes place in the community at the curbstone, on the street corner, in the bar, at a church, in the home, but always within the social network of the client.

Indirect Patient Care Although some consultation and education service activity would be classified under Tandem Direct Care, the vast majority would be listed here under Type A where consultative relationships exist with individuals or groups of caregivers within already established health or mental health related facilities including parent groups, teachers, police, management, and vocational counseling organizations. It is felt that consultation of this type is a form of indirect patient care because it leads to more effective use of available and existing caregiving resources.

Type B of Indirect Patient Care we call "Community Organization Development and Health Facility Care Improvement." This may well be the most difficult to defend as patient care since it involves organizational change and social action. It, at times, seems removed from patient care of any type. We feel, however, that the consultative activities with formal and informal social action and service groups in the community, in time, will result in an increase in the impact of services or a decrease in factors in the community which interfere with proper delivery of services. It is also hoped that the result of working with emerging or already existing civic associations or organizations which are engaged in an effort to rethink and redirect their common interests will result in improvement of the quality of life in the community.

An example of the community mental health workers' role in the area of indirect patient care has been an attempt to deal with white racism through the use of encounter or black-white confrontation groups. How much change has taken place is difficult to evaluate, but we feel that there has been acceptance of this technique. Groups have been held for many organizations including public health nurses, rookie policemen, emergency room and outpatient clinic personnel. The chancellor of the university has invited the community mental health workers to work with the vice-chancellors, deans, and the department heads of the university; the secretary of public welfare held a two-day program around race relations for central (Harrisburg) office employees with the team providing the black-white confrontation which was the central core of the conference. Following this meeting, a relationship to train trainees in encounter group techniques for the Department of Public Welfare was established.

The community mental health workers are also involved in school projects and work with a community group known as the Crusaders who are attached to the school. This is an organization of young adults with school children and other interested young adults who supplement the regular school schedule by supplying volunteers for conducting evening classes for tutoring, small group experience, and recreational activities.

One community mental health worker has been instrumental in the planning of a therapeutic community program for drug addicts of the Hill.

Mothers' groups and other community organizations have been the result of community development efforts.

Our Hill Team started in late 1967; and in the spring of 1968, following the assassination of Martin Luther King, Jr., the Hill was aflame. The response of our workers was immediate and excellent. Their knowledge of the conventional and unconventional matrices of the community proved very valuable in organizing for patient and community care. Many crises, both individual and community, were resolved with the aid of the team. Community agencies were coordinated for food and clothing delivery. Housing was arranged. Patients were transported in and out of the National Guard cordon. The community was in an uproar, fear was rampant and reprisal expected. When it was announced over the radio that refugee beds were available at local state hospitals, these fears mounted. Several of our workers appeared on TV or spoke over the radio to reassure the community and also to talk about shame and guilt, particularly in relation to the older residents of the Hill. Although some did not see this as a mental health team function, it seemed vital to most of us at this time and also in retrospect.

Educational activities have included classes in black history for the total staff, encounter and confrontation groups, and a unique seminar in the Hill district where the community mental health workers present cases for discussion. These seminars are attended by many professionals from organizations serving the Hill area and by nondegree individuals from other health and mental health facilities, and by medical students and residents in psychiatry as well as staff psychiatrists.

PROBLEMS

There have been and are still problems as they relate to the utilization of nondegree individuals in the program. Many of the problems are related to the fact that in this university and medical school setting, nondegree workers have never before been asked to assume the responsibilities we have required of them. Our study of attitudes among the institute's personnel, both in and out of the community mental health center, reflects some of these.

Answers regarding composition of the team tended to reflect inadequate communication and, in general, this lack was blamed on the team. The function of the rationale behind the formation of the team elicited responses that suggested a fairly good grasp such as: "to increase communications between those in the community who need help, and those who can give it"; "to insure that as many in a community who need help, get it"; and "deal with mental health problems on the Hill—there are many there."

Few respondents, however, saw anything beyond direct patient care as a function of the team.

A criticism constantly voiced was:

"We don't know what the goals of the Hill Team are. Their entire operation seems to be so unstructured. In any case, they never attempt to tell us what they are up to."

Additional criticisms revolved around personal feelings such as:

"Their way of dress was upsetting at first."

"Their familiarity with some of the staff was unforgivable."

"Some of my friends were quite upset at their behavior."

"Some, not all, now, seem to be rowdy characters."

These criticisms came early in the career of the Hill Team and attitudes two years later were different and generally based on the positive aspects of their work, although individual members are still subject to criticism. Scapegoating was not uncommon and the team rather than the community mental health center or the administration was blamed for bringing addicts, prostitutes, "dirty people," and "people who should be in jail" into the hospital.

It appeared that lower echelon staff were more threatened, more jealous, and, in general, more critical in a negative way than team leaders, degree-professionals, and administrators.

Some behavior of individuals brought criticism from nearly everyone. Early in the formative period political activity and social activism, such as supporting a school boycott and using the team's and Western Psychiatric Institute and Clinic's name as supporting agents, brought criticism from team members as well as other staff.

Many statements about poor records and lack of accountability are justified and we are working to correct these deficiencies. Many criticisms are, however, the reaction of people to change, the new institution building, and the deep rooted problems in relation to racism.

It appears that many persons in the institute are grappling with the problems of institutional racism and many deal better with their own emotions and feelings. It appears that as an institute we are more relevant and more a part of our community than ever before. A good share of the credit must go to the Hill Team regardless of how one views individual members.

CONCLUSION

The characteristics of a group of community mental health workers both with and without degrees and their involvement with a segment of a catchment area have been described. It is our opinion that without this group of workers and the nondegree workers, in particular, we would have been unable to deliver services to this area and establish relationships as they now exist. There has been a positive influence on the staff of the institute as well as of the mental health center with reference to looking at ourselves in relation to a community of black citizens.

48 *Shirley R. Reff,* PH.D.

Income Sources for Community
Mental Health Centers

INTRODUCTION

Mental health problems are still of great magnitude. While there are still 314 public mental hospitals in the United States, the number of resident patients has been decreasing each year since 1955 when it reached a ten-year peak of 559,000.

Since that time, the patient census has dropped to fewer than 366,815 patients at the close of 1969, according to provisional statistics from the Office of Biometry, NIMH. This is half the number of patients who would have required hospitalization if the spiralling trend prior to 1955 had not been reversed. Because the trend, however, has been reversed, it was estimated that it was unnecessary for the states to appropriate the $4.5 billion for the care of the mentally ill in state mental hospitals.[1] The downward trend is now accelerating and NIMH estimates that the total resident patient population will drop to 186,000 by 1973, generating even larger sums—money that would have been required for capital investment and patient care—to be used in other ways.

Parallel to changes in the state hospital is the impact of the community mental health center movement. There is a reason to believe that the community mental health centers now in operation are contributing to the drop in numbers of hospitalized patients. In 1969, the NIMH began a nationwide evaluation of the progress to date of these new community service programs. Data, however, already available from selected areas where centers went into operation relatively early indicate that reduction in hospital population in some areas can definitely be attributed, at least in part, to the existence of community mental health center services.

For example, by June 30, 1968, almost eighty-four percent of the population of Kentucky resided in areas covered by federally-funded community mental health centers. There had been a continual steady drop in the number of patient residents in Kentucky mental hospitals from 1963 to 1966. From July 1966 to June 1967, there was an additional drop of 8 percent, more than in any of the preceding one-year intervals. Mental health personnel in Kentucky reported that this change was a definite reflection of the impact of community mental health centers and noted that the number of patients under care in community centers rose during the same period of time from 2,681 in 1966 to 3,580 in 1967.

While community mental health centers are being developed with the impetus of federal support, new sources of financing will be required as the federal share decreases. These sources can be both public and private.

OTHER FEDERAL SOURCES OF INCOME

Within the last decade there has been other national legislation passed relevant to the community mental health center program. The centers could turn to some of these programs as potential sources of monies for specific and defined aspects of their services programs and construction. Among these are the following:

1. *Matching monies.*

a. *Appalachian Regional Development.* Program provides grants for special programs, including construction and equipment in the Appalachian states.

b. *Model Cities and Metropolitan Development.* Federal money committed to Model Cities projects may be used as matching money to other federally-funded projects including community mental health centers.

2. *Service programs.*

Community action programs developed since 1968 provide money for program development, project administration, research, and pilot programs in areas where urgent mobilization of community resources is required to combat health and mental health problems.

3. *Construction monies.*

The Health Research Facilities Construction (DHEW) program provides federal grants for the construction and equipment of facilities for research and research training in health fields.

4. *Manpower and Training Programs.*

a. DHEW provides manpower and training grants for mental health personnel and allied health professionals.

b. DHEW provides, through grants and contracts, for the development of the Work Incentive Program.

c. The Department of Labor provides manpower and training for special population groups such as the unemployed and the underemployed.

408

5. Purchase of care for a patient population for which a federal agency has special legislative responsibility for medical care.

   a. *Indian Health Program (DHEW)*. Medical care is provided through contract facilities.

   b. *Veterans Administration Program (VA)*. Outpatient services may be contracted for by Veterans Administration facilities for service-connected illness.

6. *Federal health insurance programs.*

   a. Medicare will be discussed in detail later in this chapter.

   b. *Federal Employee Health Benefits Program.* There are 36 health plans for civilian federal employees and their dependents (7.5 million people) which provide some coverage for mental health services.

   c. *CHAMPUS* (Civilian Health and Medical Program for Uniformed Services). The military will reimburse community mental health centers (or other health facilities) for direct patient fees charged when such services are authorized by the military.

7. *NIMH Research and Training Grants* as well as research and training grants from other federal agencies.

8. *Medical Assistance Program (Medicaid)*. This federal-state partnership which varies from state to state is another potential source of funds that will be discussed in greater detail later in this chapter.

STATE SOURCES OF INCOME

One of the most important developments in mental health programs in the last decade was the passage of state "Community Mental Health Services Acts" which provided for state grants-in-aid.* Thirty-five states had such laws as of January 1971.†

Historically, it appears that the legislative intent of state acts passed before the 1963 federal legislation was a commitment by the state for the support of psychiatric services; whereas, the intent of state acts passed after 1963 was to provide states with a tool for matching federal

* The federal grants-in-aid were introduced in this country in 1787 with an ordinance which provided sections of land to assist states and localities in establishing and operating public schools. The state grants-in-aid suggest a partnership of the state and local government for the purpose of inducing the localities to establish or improve services which are considered to be in the state's interest and which otherwise may not receive sufficient attention.

† State Community Mental Health Services Acts are called Mental Health Services Acts regardless of the title. If the act contains the following elements: (1) continuing legislative authority; (2) a designated administrative structure defining areas of state and local responsibility; (3) authorization of state financial assistance; (4) mental health services designated as eligible for state financial support; (5) authority for expenditures in connection with providing mental health services designated as eligible for state reimbursement; and (6) authority for a local mental health services advisory board, it is considered a mental health services act.

money with state and local funds. The later state acts pledged state support to the community mental health centers program rather than to all mental health services.

New York, for example, which passed a Services Act in 1954, a decade before the federal legislation, did not show a commitment specifically to community mental health services, but a commitment to all mental health services. Estimates showed that community psychiatric services were available for only 19 percent of the population. Since New York's legislative commitment provided support for all mental health services, the centers formed only a small part of the facilities that could compete for mental health funds.

Where states passed Services Acts after the federal centers legislation, these laws generally accepted a continuing responsibility to pay for part of the cost of locally-administered community mental health programs. In Kentucky, for example, the legislation fostered rapid expansion and development of local mental health services. Since the passage of the Kentucky Act in 1964, estimates showed that community mental health services are available to almost 84 percent of the population.

Mississippi is an example of a state that does not have a Community Mental Health Services Act. This requires the introduction of special bills for the support of the centers' program and the appropriations for their support. This type of legislation places the centers in a disadvantaged position for both current and long-range planning for the development of services. When the state budget is reviewed, the centers program competes for funds with all other individual programs, mental health or otherwise. Without a Services Act, a state does not have a continuing commitment to the community mental health centers program.

Most state acts are specific concerning the kinds of community mental health services that are eligible for state support. For example, California and Pennsylvania authorize support for a full range of comprehensive community mental health services as defined in regulations relating to the federal Community Mental Health Centers Act. Louisiana authorizes support for all of the five services considered essential for participation in the federal program, but specifies by name which local centers will be state-supported.

In other state laws, provisions were written very generally without defining specified services or citing only certain services. Of special interest is that few states include emergency or partial hospitalization services and only three include inpatient services. This definition of services in state mental health laws is merely an authorization for state support,

410

with the exception of Pennsylvania and California which mandated their communities to provide services.

Examples of other potential state money that community mental health centers can use for operating support for specific mental health programs include:

1. The State Department of Education in California provides money for a preschool development program for doubly disadvantaged children.

2. Money is available from state departments of welfare for payment for services provided to indigent patients.

3. Some state departments of vocational rehabilitation reimburse community mental health centers for patients receiving rehabilitation services.

4. Some state budgets provide for research and training grants in mental health.

5. Some state budgets specify line items for community mental health services.

LOCAL FUNDS

Bond issues have been used as a source of local funds for mental health. Not all bond issues are for the same purpose. Some provide local funds for center operation and can (if approved by local taxpayers in referendum) be used for construction. In Kansas, local governments are primarily responsible for the operation and financing of mental health centers.

There are many local sources of income that have been identified as having contributed toward the operation of a community mental health center. The Community Chest and United Fund, endowments, bequests, and other fund-raising campaigns can make visible inroads in the quest for local support.

THIRD PARTY PAYMENTS

In the early years of the development of health insurance plans, little consideration appeared to have been given to the coverage of mental illness even though these plans were the major means of financing health services.

For the population under 65, what they do for a living, where they work, or whether they are self-employed or underemployed will affect their mental health benefits and those of their families.

Insurance is essentially a fee for a service which is rendered by a physician or allied professional. Programs in voluntary general hospitals have a greater chance of being covered if they are related to fee for service. Day and outpatient care are two services that are not covered to the fullest because of the fee-for-service provision.

The financial status of the community mental health centers program could benefit from prepayment plans. Centers emphasize early, intensive, short-term treatment on an outpatient basis, when possible, or through partial hospitalization (day and night care). Where short-term, full-time hospitalization is necessary, it is also provided. At present, outpatient care and partial hospitalization are the services covered least by prepayment and other health insurance plans. Since almost all psychiatric care was provided in mental hospitals until the last twenty years, none of the early health insurance plans contemplated outpatient coverage of any kind and the issue was never raised. Later, as psychiatric units appeared in general hospitals and outpatient treatment became more available, insurers were apparently subject to the same fears and hesitations evidenced by the general public in regard to the treatment of mental illness.

President Kennedy, in his Special Message to Congress in 1963, recognized that an expansion of insurance coverage would be needed to insure the success of the centers program. "The success of the pattern of local and private financing will depend in large part upon the development of appropriate arrangements for health insurance, particularly in the private sector of our economy. . . . I have directed the Secretary of Health, Education, and Welfare to explore steps for encouraging and stimulating the expansion of private voluntary health insurance to include mental health care."[2]

Since the Kennedy message, there has been a steady upward trend in the coverage of mental illness by voluntary, prepaid, and union insurance programs with wide variability in the type and extent of services covered. Most voluntary, union, and prepaid plans, however, do not cover services provided in public mental health hospitals.

There is great variability in the mental health benefits provided by private carriers. At the end of 1968, 26 percent of Blue Cross plans included some coverage for mental illness in their benefit packages.[3] Prepaid independent health insurance plans provided mental health benefits for almost one million participants. The largest of these, the Health

Insurance Plan of Greater New York, limits coverage for the services of psychiatrists to diagnosis and does not cover treatment. More than three and one-half million beneficiaries are covered by union plans. These plans either contract with mental health facilities for services or provide services in union-operated facilities. These plans have been expanding rapidly both in the scope of services provided and the number of beneficiaries covered. More than one and one-half million beneficiaries receive some coverage for mental illness in employer plans. Approximately 27 percent of the total number of aged persons covered under Medicare's hospital benefits were covered by Blue Cross under complementary contracts,° and 22 percent were covered by Blue Shield for complementary benefits. Thus, new sources of financing mental health services are appearing in some insurance plans.

The subjectivity of mental illness has been one of the rationalizations used over the years to explain the absence or limited extent of insurance coverage, especially for outpatient treatment. The lack of precision in the definitions of psychiatric conditions and the lack of agreement as to appropriate therapy have been cited as justifications for a "go-slow" approach.

The claim has also been made that adequate actuarial data to permit sound financing are unavailable. This reason hardly pertains now since substantial data indicating the feasibility of comprehensive benefits are now available from a number of pioneering programs.[4]

Another major rationale for limited benefits in the mental health field was that there is a lack of demand for such benefits. The now famous United Auto Worker Program has indicated otherwise.[5] This collectively-bargained program forced reversal of several long-standing contentions by insurance carriers and is an example of what can be accomplished through labor leadership.

MEDICARE

Title XVIII, or Medicare, established a national program of health insurance for persons over 65.[6] American citizens over the age of 65 are eligible for this insurance. It is provided in two parts—Hospital Insurance, and Supplementary Medical Insurance which includes payment of physicians' fees. The benefit structure is determined by legislation. It is

° A contract held in conjunction with another one. The complementary contract pays additional benefits after the primary contract.

not intended to cover all medical costs, but certain high cost items and care during acute phases of illness.

The Hospital Insurance Plan provides psychiatric benefits payments for hospital expenses up to ninety days of hospitalization during a spell of illness. There are no special limitations on inpatient services in the general hospital, but there is a 190-day lifetime limitation for care in a psychiatric hospital. Limited outpatient diagnostic services are also available under the Hospital Insurance Plan.

The Supplementary Medical Insurance pays for doctor bills and for additional home health agency services. Maximum payment in a calendar year is limited to $250 for out-of-hospital psychiatric treatment. Patients pay a $50 deductible and 20 percent of the reasonable charges for covered services.

By July 1, 1968, 6,406 general hospitals were certified for participation in the Medicare program. About 800 of these provided psychiatric services. A total of 1,400 home health agencies and 4,507 extended care facilities have been certified. Presently, the ratio of mental health services to other services provided by these facilities is not known. A total of 341 psychiatric hospitals have been certified as providers of service.

Medicare has developed no special conditions for the participation of outpatient psychiatric services. If an outpatient clinic is a part of a general hospital, it is considered an outpatient unit of that hospital and comes under the general outpatient hospital standards.

Amounts paid for psychiatric services under Medicare are difficult to determine although some estimates may become available as soon as the results of a study on financing of the care of the mentally ill aged requested by the Senate Finance Committee are available.

MEDICAID

Title XIX of the Social Security Amendments of 1965 (Medicaid) is a partnership between the federal and state governments in which they participate in a program for medical services to the poor. The rate of federal participation is determined by a formula established by the DHEW. In order to be eligible for Title XIX funds, states must adopt payments to the categorically needy who include dependent children, families of dependent children, the blind, those over 65, and the totally and permanently disabled. States that have adopted Title XIX have the discretion of providing for the medically needy. Each state establishes its own criteria of income eligibility for the medically needy.

414

The federal law is broad concerning the extent of psychiatric benefits included within the Title XIX plan. It excludes, however, federal participation in payment for care of patients under 65 in psychiatric hospitals.

Medicaid reimbursements are becoming an identifiable and important source of funds for community mental health centers and, together with other third-party payments, account for 6 percent of the expected operating income of centers.

SUMMARY

This section highlights the major potential sources of income available to centers except the most obvious one, out-of-pocket fees. It should also be noted that only a few community mental health centers report income for providing consultation and education to the community. The costs of providing these services are usually absorbed in the overall budget. Increasingly, however, centers are establishing fees for certain consultation services which are either a fixed sum provided through a contract covering a defined period of time or a fee for service for a specific consultation.

NOTES

1. Stanley F. Yolles, "Mental Health Services in Action," *A.F.L.-C.I.O. Federationist,* 76(March 1969): 11.

2. John F. Kennedy, "Bold New Approach," *Vital Speeches,* 27(February 5, 1963): 62.

3. NIMH Special Report FY 1970—Budget Hearings.

4. Raymond Fink, "Financing Outpatient Medical Health Care," paper delivered at the Conference on Mental Health Services and the General Hospital, July 15, 1969, Pocono Manor, Pa.; Melvin A. Glasser, and Thomas Duggan, "Prepaid Psychiatric Care Experience with U.A.W. Members," paper delivered at APA, May 6, 1969, p. 22.

5. Melvin A. Glasser, "Problems and Prospects for Mental Health Coverage through Collective Bargaining Agreements," *American Journal of Orthopsychiatry,* 36, 1(January 1966): 119–124.

6. Title XVIII, Social Security Amendments 1965.

REFERENCES

Barr, S. "A Professional Takes a Second Look." *American Child* 49(Winter 1967): 14–17.

Christmas, J. J. "Group Methods in Training and Practice: Non-professional Mental

Health Personnel in a Deprived Community." *American Journal of Orthopsychiatry* 36(April 1966): 410–419.

Cohen, W. J. "What Every Social Worker Should Know About Political Action." *Social Work* 11(July 1966).

Day, M., and Robinson, A. M. "Training Aides Through Group Technique." *Nursing Outlook* 2(June 1954): 308–310.

Gordon, J. E. "Project Cause, the Federal Anti-Poverty Program and Some Implications of Subprofessional Training." *American Psychologist* 20(May 1965): 334–343.

Grosser, C. F. "Community Development Programs Serving the Urban Poor." *Journal of Social Work* 3(July 1965): 15–21.

Grosser, C., Henry, W. E., and Kelly, J., eds. *Non-professionals in the Human Services*. San Francisco: Jossey Bass Inc., 1969.

Hallowitz, E., and Riessman, F. "The Role of the Indigenous Non-professional in a Community Mental Health Neighborhood Service Center Program." *American Journal of Orthopsychiatry* 37(July 1967): 766–778.

Institute for Youth Studies. *Training Non-professional Workers for Human Services, A Manual of Organization and Process*. Howard University, May 1966.

Jacobson, S. L., Melvin, R., and Kaplan, S. R. "Training Non-professional Workers." In *The Practice of Community Mental Health*. Edited by H. Grunebaum. Boston: Little Brown and Company, 1970.

Kaplan, S., Levin, Z., Meltzer, B., and Roman, M. "The Role of the Non-professional Worker." In *The Practice of Community Mental Health*. Edited by H. Grunebaum. Boston: Little Brown and Company, 1970.

Lee, A. N. "The Training of Non-Professional Personnel." *Nursing Outlook* 6(April 1958): 222–225.

Levinson, P., and Schiller, J. "Role Analysis of the Indigenous Non-professional." *Social Work* 11(July 1966): 95–101.

MacLennan, B. W., Klein, W., Pearl, A., and Fishman, J. "Training for New Careers." *Community Mental Health Journal* 2(Summer 1966): 135–141.

Palmbaum, P. J. "Apprenticeship Revisited." *Archives of General Psychiatry* 13(October 1965): 304–309.

Pearl, A., and Riessman, F. *New Careers for the Poor; The Non-professional in Human Service*. New York: Free Press, 1965.

Riessman, F. "The 'Helper' Therapy Principle." *Social Work* 10(April 1965): 27–32.

INDEX

academic psychiatry, community mental health centers and, 94–99

Action for Mental Health, 7, 231

Adams County Mental Health Center, 156–161

administration, 80–83, 90; funding and, 86

administrator, role of, 388–396

adolescents, programs for, 15, 101, 332–336, 365–366; consultation, 281; day treatment, 188–189; inpatient, 150. *See also* children, programs for

advisory boards, community, 27, 29–31, 52, 75–77

affiliation contracts, 116–124; consideration for, 118–119; mutual obligations, 119–123; omissions in, 121–124

aftercare, 82, 109, 140, 164, 217, 364, 379

after-school therapy groups, 249

Albert Einstein College of Medicine, 194

Albuquerque Concentrated Employment Program's New Careers Program, 349–356

Alcoholics Anonymous, 202–206, 328, 340

alcoholism programs, 15, 35, 40, 116; for American Indians, 340; emergency, 228–229; inpatient, 150; ministers and, 202; partial hospitalization, 178, 202–207; volunteer, 328

Amarillo Crisis Intervention Center, 234–240

ambulatory services, 40, 46

American Indian Committee, 340

American Indian mental health workers, 337–343

American Medical Association, 128

Appalachian Regional Development Program, 408

Arapahoe Mental Health Center, 247

armed forces, mental illness in, 5, 6, 8

art therapy, 196, 209, 314

attorneys, release of information to, 128

automated clinical information system, 145

Bahn, A., 33

behavior modification, 180, 185–187, 367; children's programs, 264–270, 299–303, 350; in consultation-education element of service, 263–270; economics of, 265; ministers and, 264; parents and, 264–267, 286; personality theory and, 265, 268; prevention and, 264, 265; schools and, 266–270; simplicity of, 264, 265; teachers and, 264–270; volunteers and, 266

Beigel, Allan, 33

Bernalillo County Mental Health Center, 349–356

Bierer, Joshua, 378, 385

Bi-State Mental Health Foundation, 202–206

"bleeding heart" social worker, 261

Blue Cross plans, 412, 413

Blue Shield, 413

Borislow, Bernard, 112

Bradley, C., 294

breakthrough experience, 152

Bronx Municipal Hospital Center, 195–199

Broom, Leonard, 374

Bureau of Indian Affairs, 167

Carlson, J., 384

Carlson, Robert, 328

Carter, Carolyn, 399*n.*

catchment area(s), 9–10, 13, 16, 36–39, 378, 380, 382–384; children's programs and, 277–283; functional, 21; mental health agencies and, 27–32; planning and, 20–32; schools and, 282–283

Caucasian Alcoholics Anonymous Committee, 340

417

CHAMPUS, 409
chemotherapy, 294, 302–303
child psychiatrists, 247, 248, 288, 292; training of, 97–98
children, programs for, 15, 35, 36, 101, 116; after-school therapy, 249; behavior modification, 264–270, 299–303, 350; catchment areas and, 277–283; clinical, 106; consultation, 247–251, 275; day treatment, 188–189, 275, 277, 279, 280, 283–287; emergency, 275, 276; group therapy, 285; hyperactive children, 290–298; inpatient, 150; occupational therapy, 287, 289; partial hospitalization, 299–303; problems in, 273–274; recreational therapy, 188, 285–289; residential treatment, 275–279, 283–287; school, 283–290, 299–303; specialized, 150, 273–303, 386; therapeutic day school, 299–303
Children's Re-Education Center (Greenville, S. C.), 283–287
chlorpromazine, 296
clergymen (see ministers)
Cleveland, Harlan, 396
clinical information system, 145–146
clinical psychologists, 205, 247, 248, 285, 357
clinical research, 21
college students, use of as employees in a center, 332–336
communities, corporate, 383; functional, 376; of patients, 378–380
Community Action programs, 408
community advisory boards, 27, 29–31, 52, 75–77
community, broader, 380; concept of, 374–387; creation of by staff, 378; definitions of, 374–378; social organizations and, 375–377; therapeutic, 158, 195, 315–316, 350, 378, 379; tribal aspects of, 378–380
Community Chest, 411
community mental health center(s), academic psychiatry and, 94–99; administration of, 80–83, 86, 90; comprehensive, 20–21, 99–100, 163, 278, 280; critical issues for, 373–416; evaluation of, emphasis on, 32; federal program for, 7–16, 73–74, 115–116 (see also Community Mental Health Centers Act); function of, 53; funding (see income sources); general hospitals and, 89–94, 99–102, 175, 179–190, 363–369; information system, 142–148; legal responsibility of, 122–123; multiagency, 72–88, 116, 120; organization of, 71–80; in poverty areas, 13–15, 29; records of (see records); rural, 54–59, 320–332; services (see community mental health services); staffing (see staffing); state hospitals and, 116–117, 135–141, 155–159, 174; unitized, 379
Community Mental Health Center of Escambia County, Inc., 364
Community Mental Health Centers Act (1963), 3, 7, 11–13, 16, 35, 60, 177, 202, 240, 275, 278, 410; amendments to, 13–15, 20; basic concepts embodied in, 8–11
community mental health services, 8–11; comprehensiveness of, 8–10, 32, 174, 385; coordination of, 384–385; duplication of, 385; fragmentation of, 385; interchangeability of, 174; multiple, 8, 149, 174; planning for (see planning); quality and quantitative, 82
Community Mental Health Services Acts, state, 409–411
community psychiatry, 94–95, 379–380
comprehensiveness of services, 8–10, 32, 174, 385
concretistic thinking, 186–187
confidentiality, 116, 120–121, 124–135; breach of, justification for, 130–131; within center, 132–134; group therapy and, 133–134; legal liability and, 131–132; nonprofessionals and, 132, 133. See also records
Conners, C. K., 294
Conrad House, 87
construction, federal support for, 11–13, 23, 99, 116, 307, 408
consultation programs, 9–11, 73, 106, 165, 170, 233, 245–273, 383; for adolescents, 281; avail-

ability of, 246; behavior modification and, 263–270; for children, 247–251, 275; emergency, 225; fees for, 415; financial considerations in, 246; in general hospital, 368; in nursery schools, 275; for police, 251–262; prevention and, 245, 385; for schools, 247–251; social action and, 246; staffing for, 245–246; training for, 364
continuity of care, 8, 10, 14, 24, 43, 45, 96, 100, 141, 179, 277, 303, 308–309, 385; provisions for, 115–148
Convalescent Hospital for Children (Rochester, N.Y.), 36, 37, 274–281
corporate communities, 383
county hospitals, 23, 25–26
credit bureaus, release of information to, 128
crisis intervention, 81, 82, 87, 139–140, 223–225, 350, 364, 379; police and, 238, 259–262; suicide prevention, 227, 236, 238; volunteers and, 234–240
cross-commitment, political process of, 384
cultural revolution, 378
custody cases, 126n., 127, 128

Dalley, C. W., 163
D'Amico, Robert, 67
dance therapy, 196, 314
Dawson, Michael E., 294
Dayton State Hospital, 183
day-treatment programs, 81, 122, 177–190; for adolescents, 188–189; approaches and activities, 185–188; challenges in, 180–181; for children, 188–189, 275, 277, 279, 280, 283–287; emergency, 226; role of, 189–190; staffing for, 185; vocational rehabilitation, 194–201. See also partial hospitalization programs
decentralized outpatient services, in rural area, 216–220; in urban area, 210–216
defamation, breach of confidentiality and, 131–132
delinquency prevention, 81
detoxification center, 150

Deutsch, Albert, 6
dextroamphetamine, 294, 295
diagnosis, 10, 21, 24, 178, 299
displacement, concepts involved in, 256–257
divorce cases, 126n., 128
Dix, Dorothea, 3–4, 6
Drucker, P., 83
drug-abuse programs, 15, 85–86, 100, 400, 404; emergency, 229, 238–239; inpatient, 150; partial hospitalization, 178; volunteers in, 238–239, 318

East Mississippi State Hospital, 231, 232
educational enrichment, 350, 351
educational psychologists, 247
education programs, 9–11, 73, 94–95, 106, 138, 170, 229, 233, 245–273; availability of, 246; behavior modification and, 263–270; centralized, 366–367; financial considerations in, 246; in general hospitals, 365–369; prevention and, 245, 385; social action and, 246; staffing for, 245–246; training for, 364. See also consultation programs
ego development, 96
Eisenberg, L., 294
electrocardiography, 92
electroencephalography, 92
emergency service(s), 9–10; for alcoholics, 228–229; ambulatory, 40, 46; back-up, 225, 227, 228, 237; boarded patients and, 240–244; for children, 275, 276; consultation, 225; crisis intervention (see crisis intervention); day, 226; drug-abuse, 229, 238–239; inpatient, in rural area, 169–175; ministers and, 231–234; new approaches to, 223–244; night, weekend, and holiday, 226–227, 233, 237–238; nurse as director of, 224–230; planning for, 45–46; problems in initiation of, 229–230; staffing for, 226–227; telephone, 170, 224, 227, 233–235, 237–238; training program for, 227–229; twenty-four-hour, 73, 81, 87, 170, 224, 233–235, 379;

emergency service(s) *(cont.)*
  volunteers and, 224, 232, 234–
  240; walk-in, 46, 81, 87, 224, 233,
  350–351, 379
emotional rehabilitation, 282
environmental modification, 264, 266
epidemiology, planning and, 25, 32–
  48
Etemad, Bijan, 112
evaluation programs, 10, 21, 47, 106,
  110–111
expected patient load, determination
  of, 39, 40

family counseling, 122
family service agencies, 260, 261
family therapy, 379
Federal Employee Health Benefits
  Program, 409
federal fair employment practice requirements, 121
federal support, 3, 11–16, 20–21,
  84, 163, 407–409; for construction, 11–13, 23, 99, 116,
  307, 408; for general hospitals,
  11; for staffing, 13–16, 23, 73–
  74, 89–90, 116–119, 141
fees, patient, 85–86, 415
field workers, 171
First Training Record in Suicidology,
  236
flattened affect, 186–187
Fleckenstein, Robert, 68
Fort Logan Mental Health Center,
  156–161
foster homes, 167, 193
"Fourth Psychiatric Revolution, The,"
  155
Frazier, T., 34
functional catchment area. 21
functional communities, 376
funding, 83–88; administration and,
  86. *See also* income sources
"Future of the Public Mental Hospital, The," 155–156

Gardner, E. A., 33, 35
Gemeinschaft, 374
general hospitals, 7, 23, 36; community mental health centers and,
  89–94, 99–102, 175, 179–
  190, 363–369; consultation in,

368; education in, 365–369;
  federal support for construction of,
  11; partial hospitalization and,
  179–190
general practitioners, 46, 50, 119,
  121, 171, 291
geriatrics programs, 116, 140
GLOW Fund Agencies, 232
Goodwill Industries, 188
Gorman, Mike, 6
Gray, Lord, 390
Greater Little Rock Community
  Mental Health Center, 300
group therapy, 46, 209, 309, 312–
  316; for children, 285; confidentiality and, 133–134; geriatric, 140;
  parent, 303; volunteers and, 330
guidance counselors, school, 268–269
Guy, William, 325

Hahnemann Community Mental
  Health Center, 96–98
Hahnemann Medical College and
  Hospital, 96–98
halfway houses, 73, 85, 87, 203–206
Haynes, M. A., 78
Health, Education, and Welfare, De-
  partment of, 142, 408, 409, 412,
  414
Health Insurance Plan of Greater
  New York, 412–413
health insurance plans, 384, 409, 412;
  Blue Cross, 412, 413; Blue Shield,
  413; Medicaid, 74, 85, 384, 409,
  414–415; Medicare, 85, 384,
  413–414; union, 384, 412, 413
Hennepin County General Hospital
  Community Mental Health Center, 307–308
here-and-now encounters, 152
heroin addiction, 85
Hill-Burton program, 11
Hill-Harris program, 11
Hill Team, 398–406; composition
  and recruitment, 399–400; education and training, 400–402;
  problems of, 405–406; services
  provided by, 402–405
Hoffmann, Heinrich, 290
home visits, 82, 133, 187, 350; volunteers and, 319
hospital commitment law, state, 122
hospitalization, emphasis on alterna-

tives to, 82, 167, 189, 225–226, 230; partial (*see* partial hospitalization programs); planning for, 43–45

hospitals, county, 23, 25–26; partial, legal status of, 178; reports to, 127; Veterans Administration, 35, 40, 43, 167, 180, 184. *See also* general hospitals; state mental hospitals

hyperactive children, development of evaluation and treatment clinic for, 290–298

implementation, planning and, 34–35, 47, 53–54

income sources, 83–88, 407–415; county, 179; federal (*see* federal support); foundations, 85; local, 411; multiple, 84–85; patient fees, 85–86, 415; philanthropic, 85; state, 74, 171, 179, 409–411; third-party payments (*see* health insurance plans)

Indian Health Program, 409

indigenous nonprofessionals, 133, 349, 398; American Indian, 337–343

information system, 142–148; automated, 145; clinical, 145–146

Ingleside, 332–336

initiation and development grants, 15, 20

inpatient services, 8–10, 73, 81, 149–175; for adolescents, 150; for alcoholics, 150; for children, 150; drug-abuse, 150; emergency, in rural area, 169–175; partial care, organization of, 150–155; specialized, 150; state hospitals and, 155–169

Institute of Living, 144

institutional neurosis, 96

institutional racism, 406

internists, 46

interstate transfers, 12

invasion of privacy, breach of confidentiality and, 131–132

jails, confinement of mentally ill in, 3

Jefferson Community Mental Health Center, 139–141

Jefferson County Mental Health Center, 287

Jefferson Medical College, 135–141

jobs, 76, 81, 195

Joint Commission on Mental Health of Children, 270, 273

Joint Commission on Mental Illness and Mental Health, 7, 231

Jones, Maxwell, 378, 380

Juvenile Courts, 167–168

juvenile probation, 167

Kennedy, John F., 7, 11, 412

King, Martin Luther, Jr., 404

Klein, Donald C., 374

Kramer, M., 33

Krasner, Leonard, 166

Lanterman-Petris-Short Act, 74*n.*

Levenson, Alan I.; 33, 155–156

liaison workers, 52, 227, 281; agency-community, 28; teacher-counselor, 284–286

libel, breach of confidentiality and, 131–132

Lindeman, Eduard C., 374

Listening Post, 231–234

Los Angeles Suicide Prevention Center, 236, 238

McCracken, Jean, 332

malpractice, legal responsibility for, 122–123

Managerial Behaviour, 392

manpower problem, innovative approaches to, 305–346

manpower and training programs, federal, 408–409

Marin General Hospital, 150–155

Marion County General Hospital, Community Mental Health Center at, 99–102

"Maximizing Therapeutic Inefficiency," 378–379

Meadowbrook Community Mental Health Center, 89–94

Meadowlark project, 287–290

Medicaid, 74, 85, 384, 409, 414–415

medical model, 384

medical records (*see* records)

Medicare, 85, 384, 413–414

mental health agencies, 21–26; catchment areas and, 27–32

mental health assistant, 109; training of, 356–363

Mental Health Association of Southeastern Pennsylvania, 103–107, 112

mental health care statistics, planning and, 32–48

mental health nurse coordinator, 365–368

mental health services, community (*see* community mental health services); county, 153; federal interest in, 3–8; federally sponsored approach to, 8–11; local, 3, 8, 381, 382; state, 3–4, 8, 11–13, 15, 381 (*see also* state mental hospitals); during World War II, 5, 6, 8

Mental Health Study Act, 7

mental illness, in armed forces, 5, 6, 8; "bold new approach" to, 7, 17; change in public attitude toward, 5–6; prevention of (*see* prevention)

mental retardation programs, 116, 135, 169–175. *See also* Philadelphia Forum of Mental Health / Mental Retardation Centers

Meridian Counseling Foundation, 232

Mering, Otto von, 399*n*.

Meschke, Herbert, 325

methylphenidate, 294, 295

Metropolitan Community Mental Health Center (Minneapolis), 307–316

Michigan State University, 228

Mikulich, Walter H., 112

military, mental illness in, 5, 6, 8

ministers, 11; and alcoholism programs, 202; behavior modification and, 264; Listening Post manned by, 231–234; training program for, 98

Minneapolis Clinic of Psychiatry and Neurology, 310

Model Cities program, 100–102, 355, 408

Monroe County Psychiatric Case Register, 35–48

Multicounty Mental Health Center, 263

music therapy, 196, 209, 314, 317

Narcotic Addiction Rehabilitation Act, 86

narcotics hospitals, 4

narcotics programs (*see* drug-abuse programs)

National Council of Community Mental Health Centers, 108

National Institute of Mental Health, 4, 16, 60, 66, 97–98, 105, 106, 142, 170, 216, 236, 274; grants, 84, 85, 89, 169, 171, 307, 409

National Mental Health Act, 4, 5

negligence, legal responsibility for, 122–123

neighborhood health centers, 46, 210

New Careers Program, 349–356

Nisbet, Robert A., 375, 377, 378

nondegree workers, 397–406. *See also* Hill Team

nonprofessionals, 247–248, 306–307; American Indian, 337–343; confidentiality and, 132, 133; indigenous, 133, 337–343, 349, 398; problem of utilization of, 348; training of, 348

North, C. C., 374

North Central Mental Health and Retardation Center, 321–331; planning for, 323–324; use of volunteers in programs, 324–330

North Dakota, rural mental health centers in, 320–332

Northern Wyoming Mental Health Center, 191–194

Northwest San Antonio Community Mental Health Center, 356–357

nurse(s), 100, 164, 303, 360; emergency service under direction of, 224–230; role of, 364–365; training of, 363–369

nursery schools, consultation and prevention in, 275

nursing homes, 188, 191, 192, 327

occupational therapy, 90, 92, 185, 309; for children, 287, 289

O'Connor, J. F., 96

Office of Economic Opportunity, 50–51

Ogden Mental Health Clinic, 164

organization, 71–80

Osterweil, J., 33

Our Lady of the Lake College, 359, 362
outpatient services, 8–10, 73, 81; decentralized, 210–220; delivery systems for, 209–222; increased demand for, 210; planning for, 45–46; in rural area, 216–220; in urban area, 210–216
Ozarin, L. D., 155–156

Panaccio, Robert C., 112
Panhandle Mental Health Center, 337–341
parent group therapy, 303
parents, behavior modification and, 264–267, 286; and hyperactive children, 291–295
Parsons, Talcott, 377
partial care services, inpatient: organizing for, 150–155; volunteers and, 318–319
partial hospitalization programs, 9–10, 43, 73, 165, 177–207; for alcoholics, 178, 202–207; for children, 299–303; drug-abuse, 178; general hospital and, 179–190; in rural areas, 178, 190–194; vocational rehabilitation, 194–201. See also day-treatment programs
partial hospitals, legal status of, 178
patient fees, 85–86, 415
patients, communities of, 378–380; legal rights of, 131–132; rights of, 121–122; transfer of, 115–116, 120, 141
Peace Corps, 58
pediatricians, 285, 291, 292
pediatric neurologists, 292
Pensacola Junior College, 367
personality theory, behavior modification and, 265, 268
pharmacotherapy, 294
Philadelphia Association for Retarded Children, 104
Philadelphia Forum of Mental Health/ Mental Retardation Centers, 103–113; activities of, 107–111; component parts, 105–107; conception and birth of, 104; current projects, 111–112
Philadelphia State Hospital, 104, 109, 110, 135–141
physical health services, 81

physicians, reports to, 127, 129
Pierce, Franklin, 4
planning, 19–69; agency-catchment area relationships, 27–32; catchment area concept and, 20–32; for emergency services, 45–46; epidemiology and, 25, 32–48; for expected patient load, 39, 40; for hospitalization, 43–45; implementation and, 34–35, 47, 53–54; importance of, 20; involvement of local residents in, 19–20, 54–59; mental health care statistics and, 32–48; in Monroe County (New York), 32–48; for outpatient services, 45–46; rational, 34, 390; of rural mental health center, 54–59; in urban ghetto, 48–54. See also Ventura County Mental Health Center
play group therapy, 302
Pogue, Frank G., 399n.
police, consultation with, 251–262; and crisis intervention, 238, 259–262; house calls with, 59; problems of, 252–254; release of information to, 128
police escorts, 226–227
polio, 275
Pomp, H. C., 34
postdischarge services, 10
poverty areas, mental health centers in, 13–15, 29
poverty programs, government, 50–51
Prairie View Mental Health Center, 55–59
preadmission services, 10
prevention, behavior modification and, 264, 265; commitment to, 9–11, 24, 29, 135, 275; consultation programs and, 245, 385; education programs and, 245, 385; in nursery schools, 275; primary, 10–11, 264, 265; secondary, 11; tertiary, 11
primary prevention, 10–11, 264, 265
private psychiatrists, 164, 323; as staff team leaders, 307–316
privileged communications statutes, 129–131
probation officers, 11
psychiatric mobile team, 216–219

psychiatric records (*see* records)
psychodrama groups, 314
psychopharmacology, 227, 228
psychotropic drugs, 192, 228, 229
public health services, 381–383
purchasing procedures, 91

quality services, 82
quantitative services, 82
Quest for Community, The, 375

racism, 49; institutional, 406
rational planning, 34, 390
Reality House West, 85
reality testing, 180
records, access to, 133–134; author-
    ization to release information in,
    125–130; confidentiality of (*see*
    confidentiality); court orders to
    produce, 129–130; storage of,
    120, 144; transfer of, 115–116,
    120, 141, 364
recreational therapy, 90, 181, 191,
    192, 209, 309; for children, 188,
    285–289
Red Feather, 85
rehabilitation, 10, 11, 26, 109; com-
    prehensive program, 199–200;
    emotional, 282; residential, 198,
    199; social, 197–201; vocational
    (*see* vocational rehabilitation ser-
    vices)
reinforcement theory, 166, 186
research, 10, 94–95, 106, 110–111,
    142, 165; access to records for,
    134; clinical, 21
research psychologist, 247
residential rehabilitation, 198, 199
residential-treatment program, chil-
    dren's, 275–279, 283–287
resocialization activities, 178; volun-
    teers and, 316–320
Rio Grande State Center for Mental
    Health and Mental Retardation,
    169–175
Roberts, Alfred S., Jr., 112
Rochester Mental Health Center, 36–
    45, 241
Rockland State Hospital, 144
roentgenology, 92
Ross, Murray, 376
Rueveni, U., 379

rural mental health center(s), com-
    munity involvement in planning of,
    54–59; in North Dakota, 320–
    332; volunteers in, 324–330
rural mental health services, decen-
    tralized outpatient, 216–220; de-
    livery and development of, 320–
    332; emergency inpatient, 169–
    175; partial hospitalization, 178,
    190–194; volunteers and, 324–
    330

St. Barnabas Hospital (Minneapolis),
    307, 308
St. Elizabeth's Hospital (District of
    Columbia), 3
St. Lawrence Community Mental
    Health Center Emergency Ser-
    vice, 224–230
San Antonio State Hospital, 359–
    360
San Francisco Westside Community
    Mental Health Center, Inc., 72–
    88; administration, 80–83; back-
    ground, 73–75; funding, 83–
    88; policy, 75–80
San Mateo Police Department, 254,
    262
Sata, L. S., 33
"satellite" centers, 170–175
Satterfield, James H., 294
Sayles, Leonard, 392, 396
schizophrenics, 21, 43, 166, 192
school authorities, release of infor-
    mation to, 127
school programs, children's, 283–
    290; therapeutic day school, 299–
    303
schools, behavior modification and,
    266–270; catchment areas and,
    282–283; consultation programs
    for, 247–251; guidance coun-
    selors in, 268–269
secondary prevention, 11
Selznick, Philip, 374
Short-Doyle Act, 74n., 85
Simon, Stanford H., 378–379
Sisters of Charity of the Incarnate
    Word, 210
slander, breach of confidentiality and,
    131–132
Sloane, R. Bruce, 113

social action, 77; consultation-education programs and, 246
social breakdown syndrome, 96
social isolation, 316
socialized medicine, 49
social organizations, community and, 375–377
social rehabilitation, 197–201
social revolution, 378
social service agencies, 73, 85, 154
social workers, 100, 109, 153, 164, 166, 171, 180, 199, 216, 217, 225, 247, 248, 288, 302; "bleeding heart," 261
Sound View—Throgs Neck Community Mental Health Center, 194, 198–199
specialized services, 386; for children, 150, 273–303, 386 (see also children, programs for); inpatient, 150
Speck, R. V., 379
staff, creation of community by, 378; development of (see staff development); transfer of, 115–116, 120, 153
staff development, 347–369; New Careers Program, 349–356. See also training programs
staffing, for consultation programs, 245–246; for day-treatment program, 185; for education programs, 245–246; emergency service, 226–227; federal support for, 13–16, 23, 73–74, 89–90, 116–119, 141; for inpatient/partial care services, 151–152; NIMH grants for, 84, 85, 89, 169, 171
staff team leaders, private psychiatrists as, 307–316
Starr, R., 384
state mental hospitals, 4–8, 23, 25–27; appropriations for, 407; community mental health centers and, 116–117, 135–141, 155–169, 174; decentralization units of, 378, 379; drop in total population of, 407; inpatient services and, 155–169; unitized, 379
Stein, M. R., 377
Stern, Daniel, 399n.
stimulant drugs, hyperactive children and, 294–295
storefront centers, 210

strangerhood situations, 397
Strong Memorial Hospital (Rochester, N. Y.), 240–241, 275, 276
students, use of as employees in a center, 332–336
suicide prevention, 227, 236, 238
Suicide Prevention Around the Clock, 238
Swedish Hospital (Minneapolis), 307, 308
sympathomimetic amines, 294

Taber, Robert C., 112
teacher-counselor liaison workers, 284–286
teachers, 11; behavior modification and, 264–270; and hyperactive children, 291–295
Techniques in Crisis Intervention: A Training Manual, 236
telephone inquiries, confidentiality and, 126–127
telephone service, emergency, 170, 224, 227, 233–235, 237–238
tertiary prevention, 11
therapeutic community, 158, 195, 315–316, 350, 378, 379
therapeutic day school, 299–303
thioridizine, 296
Tönnies, Ferdinand, 374
training programs, 10, 81, 138; child psychiatry, 97–98; consultation-education, 364; emergency service, 227–229; emphasis on, 347; federal, 408–409; for mental health assistant, 356–363; for ministers, 98; New Careers, 349–356; for nondegree workers, 400–402; for nonprofessionals, 348; for nurses, 363–369; prevocational, 92; professional, 347; for volunteers, 236–237, 319–320, 330
tranquilizers, hyperactive children and, 296
transfer, of patients, 115–116, 120, 141; of records, 115–116, 120, 141, 364; of staff, 115–116, 120, 153; of therapist, 120
Trinity University, 361
twenty-four-hour emergency service, 73, 81, 87, 170, 224, 233–235, 379

Ullmann, Leonard P., 166
Uniform Narcotics Drug Act, 131
United Auto Workers Program, 384, 413
United Crusade, 85
United Fund, 85, 232, 411
University of Colorado Medical Center, 157–158
University of Rochester Medical Center, 240–242, 275, 276, 280
University of Rochester Mental Health Center, 36, 37, 46, 240–241, 276, 281
University of Texas Medical School, 357
urban area, decentralized outpatient services in, 210–216
urban ghetto, planning mental health services in, 48–54
Utah State Hospital, 163–169

Varah, Chad, 235
venereal disease, confidentiality and, 131–132
Ventura County Mental Health Center, 59–69; architectural planning, 61–65; bids and construction, 65–67; interior designer, 67; landscape architect, 68; preparatory stages, 60–61
Veterans Administration hospitals, 35, 40, 43, 167, 180, 184
Veterans Administration Program, 409
VISTA, 338
vocational rehabilitation services, 120, 122, 140, 178; American Indians and, 341; in day hospital, 194–198; partial hospitalization, 194–201
volunteers, 58, 191, 306, 323–324; in alcoholism programs, 328; in Amarillo Crisis Intervention Center, 234–240; and behavior modification, 266; in drug-abuse programs, 238–239, 318; in emergency services, 224, 232, 234–240; and group therapy, 330; home visits made by, 319; in partial care services, 318–319; resocialization and, 316–320; in rural programs, 324–330; training of, 236–237, 319–320, 330; VISTA, 338
voter registration, American Indians and, 340–341

Walden House, 85
walk-in services, 46, 81, 87, 224, 233, 350–351, 379
Warren, Roland, 376–377
Weber County Comprehensive Mental Health Center, 163–169
Weed, Lawrence L., 145
Weems Community Mental Health Center, 231
welfare agencies, release of information to, 127
welfare workers, 11, 379
Western Interstate Commission for Higher Education, 146
Whittington, H. G., 117, 383
Woloshin, A. A., 34
World War II, mental health services during, 5, 6, 8

yoga, 317
Yolles, Stanley, 162